SKY

SKY

Memoirs

Blaise Cendrars

Translated by Nina Rootes
Introduction by Marjorie Perloff

Paragon House
New York

First American edition, 1992

Published in the United States by

Paragon House
90 Fifth Avenue
New York, N.Y. 10011

Copyright © 1992 by Paragon House

Originally published in French under the title *Le
Lotissement du ciel*. Copyright © 1949 by Éditions Denoel

Manufactured in the United States.
10 9 8 7 6 5 4 3 2 1

Library of Congress Cataloging-in-Publishing data

Cendrars, Blaise, 1887–1961.
[Lotissement du ciel. English]
Sky: Memoirs Blaise Cendrars: translated by Nina Rootes.
1st American ed.
p. cm.—(European sources)
Translation of: Le lotissement du ciel.
ISBN 1-55778-319-5
1. Cendrars, Blaise, 1887–1961—Biography. 2. Authors,
Swiss—20th century—Biography. 3. Adventure and
adventurers—Biography. I. Title. II. Series.
PQ2605. E55Z46913 1991
841'.912—dc20
[B]

90-22862
CIP

Translator's Acknowledgments

I am greatly indebted to Monsignor McCoy of the Beda College in Rome for his patient and erudite responses to my endless questions about saints and sainthood and other ecclesiastical matters. My gratitude must also be expressed to the Venerable English College in the same city, for allowing me access to its splendid library. My thanks, in particular, its librarian, Steven Shield.

I would also like to thank Mrs. Joyce Pope, former enquiries officer at the Natural History Museum in London, who was kind enough to answer a whole list of questions concerning South American fauna in her own private time.

Last, but not least, I must thank Monsieur Lucien Israel for helping me untangle some of the extremely knotty linguistic problems posed by Cendrars's bizarre and totally idiosyncratic style in parts of this book.

Nina Rootes

EUROPEAN SOURCES

LITERATURE

AMERICAN JOURNALS
Albert Camus

CELINE: A BIOGRAPHY
Frédéric Vitoux

DESTINY'S JOURNEY
Alfred Doblin

FRAGMENTS OF A JOURNAL
Eugene Ionesco

JOURNEY TO POLAND
Alfred Doblin

LETTERS TO GALA
Paul Eluard

LOOKING BACK
Lou Andreas-Salomé

ON NIETZSCHE
Georges Bataille

SKY: MEMOIRS
Blaise Cendrars

SOUVENIR PORTRAITS
Jean Cocteau

HISTORY

BERLIN UNDERGROUND: 1938–1945
Ruth Andreas-Friedrich

BATTLEGROUND BERLIN: 1945–1948
Ruth Andreas-Friedrich

I WAS A GERMAN
Ernst Toller

SERIES EDITORS
Russell Epprecht and Sylvere Lotringer

Contents

Other Books by Blaise Cendrars in English

The African Saga, translation by Margery Bianco of *Anthologie nègre,* New York, 1972.

The Astonished Man, translation by Nina Rootes, of *L'Homme foudroyé,* New York, 1970.

The Confessions of Dan Yack, translated by Nina Rootes, London, 1990.

Dan Yack, translation by Nina Rootes of *Le Plan de L'Aiguille,* New York, 1987.

Gold, translated by Nina Rootes, New York, 1970.

Lice, translation by Nina Rootes of *La Main coupée,* London, 1973.

Moravagine, translated by Alan Brown, New York, 1990.

Planus, translation by Nina Rootes of *Bourlinguer,* London, 1972.

Selected Writings, edited by Walter Albert, introduction by Henry Miller, New York, 1962.

Shadow, translation by Marcia Brown of *La Féticheuse,* New York, 1982.

Biographical Note

Blaise Cendrars (1887–1961) was born in La Chaux-de-Fonds, in Switzerland. His father was an inventor, a restless fantasist who could never stay in one place. His mother was dreamy and ethereal. Blaise spent part of his childhood in Egypt and part in Naples, "in an immense garden, like a park, full of bushes and planted with trees of all the different indigenous species".* An English tutor, an out-and-out drunkard, took him camping in Sicily and taught him to drink.

At sixteen, he ran away from home. He wandered through Germany. There he met the merchant Rogovine and became his assistant, as he describes in *Sky*.

"At that time I was an adolescent... and I left with him, I left to accompany this traveler in jewelry, who was going to Harbin. We had two sleeping compartments and thirty-four chests of Pforzheim jewelry, tawdry rubbish 'Made in Germany.'"

For the crossing of Siberia, Rogovine fitted him out with new clothes and gave him a nickel revolver.

And it was from these adventures that the great poem "La Prose du Transsibérien" was born.

His life was made up of similar images:

In Peking, his job was to take care of the central heating in the Hôtel des Wagon-Lits; he stoked the furnace with back numbers of the *Mercure de France,* which he read avidly before burning them.

He became a whale-hunter because he had fallen in love with the

---

* From my own translation of *Bourlinguer,* English title *Planus* Peter Owen, London: Peter Owen, 1972. (Trans.)

vii

daughter of the Norwegian "King of the Whales," a girl he describes as a "Nordic of the dark type." The whales inspired *Le Plan de l'Aiguille,* the first of the two books about Dan Yack.*

In Paris, he spent days and days in the Bibliothéque Mazarine copying out, by hand, romantic tales of chivalry. He was "working for Guillaume Apollinaire, who was working for Pierre-Paul Plan, who was working for the publisher, Payot." Cendrars was paid 100 francs for each incunabulum he copied.

He kept bees, invented watercress salt, and had a love affair with the daughter of a deep-sea diver who initiated him into the art of diving.

He appeared as a juggler in an English circus where his friend was an obscure clown by the name of Charlie Chaplin.

He traveled the roads with the gypsies, in a caravan. And, later, in an extraordinary Alfa-Romeo whose coachwork was designed by Braque, he drove down the Route Nationale No. 10, which, according to Cendrars, "goes much further than Biarritz, through Spain, Portugal, and across the ocean as far as Tierra del Fuego." In Brazil, he befriended Manolo Seca, pump attendant of the most remote gas station in the world.

In Chicago, he knew Al Capone, helped film *La Roue* directed by Abel Gance, published Casanova, and invented an air screw for the Borel tri-plane, the first large aircraft. In *Moravagine,* written in 1926, he predicted the atom bomb.

But, above all, he invented modern poetry.

It was in April 1912. All day long, he had been roaming the streets of New York. He was hungry. He was hallucinating. He passed by a church. A poster announced: *"The Creation* by Haydn." The snow was falling. That night, in his room, with a morsel of bread in front of him, he wrote "Pâques à New York" (Easter in New York).

There is still considerable argument as to whether "Pâques à New York" influenced Apollinaire, or the two poets invented this new "voice" at the same moment.

In 1914, Cendrars married a Polish woman, Fela Potzanska, who gave him three children. He joined the Foreign Legion and came back from the war minus an amputated arm. His son Rémy was killed in a flying accident during the Second World War. His memory is evoked in the present work.

---

* *Le Plan de L'Aiguille* and *Les Confessions de Dan Yack,* translated by Nina Rootes into English as *Dan Yack* (1987) and *Confessions of Dan Yack* (1990) published by Peter Owen, London (Trans.)

Blaise Cendrars married again, his second wife being the actress Raymone.

His life, which had been incomparably rich and eventful, ended in sickness and poverty. There was in him a unique mixture of the adventurer and the bookworm. He had read everything. He claimed to have destroyed unpublished manuscripts, hidden others in banks in South America—he no longer remembered where—and to have composed poems solely for himself, which he did not bother to write down.

But even better than this legend, there remain to us the works of Cendrars, which will seduce future generations.

"Les Pâques à New York", "La Prose du Transsibérien," "Le Panama," "*Dix-neuf Poèmes élastiques, J'ai tué, L'Or, (Gold), Moravagine, Les Confessions de Dan Yack, L'Homme foudroyé (The Astonished Man), La Main coupée (Lice), Bourlinguer (Planus),* and the present book have brought us the social fantasy, the pathos of the man who seeks to find himself by traveling the world with no other baggage than his compassion for other men.

Introduction

Le Lotissement du ciel ("lotissement" means a parcelling out, but the publishers have wisely chosen the more indeterminate title Sky) is the final volume of a tetralogy begun during the dark days of World War II when Blaise Cendrars, having resigned from his position as war correspondent for the British army, went into hiding in Aix-en-Provence. Like its predecessors—*L'Homme foudroyé (The Astonished Man)*, *La Main coupée* (literally "the cut hand" but translated as *Lice)*, and *Bourlinguer* (literally "roughing it" but translated as *Planus)—Sky* is subtitled "Memoirs" but it is more properly understood in terms of the genre Cendrars had hit upon as early as 1913 when he published his great poem *Le Prose du Transsibérien et de la petite Jehanne de France*—namely *collage*. Prose poetry, travel writing, found text (the scholarly documents regarding the levitation of saints and others, from ancient times to the present), reportage, detective stories, personal memoirs, fairy tales—fragments of all these are pasted together to create the complex space which is Cendrars's text.

But this is not to say that the structure of *Sky* is in any way random. Consider its frontispiece:

INJUSTICE
From her window in the Palais-Royal, Colette was contemplating the pigeons and doves cavorting in the sun.
Perhaps the greatest injustice that exists in all creation, she said, "is that certain creatures possess wings...."

There is something comical about this pronouncement, the grande dame looking *down* on the pigeons whose *upward* flight she claims to envy. Which one of us, after all, really wants to be a bird?

Indeed, the idea of flight—escape, ambivalence, the longing to get outside oneself—is regarded by Cendrars with an acute ambivalence. One
wants to fly away, to leave the ground and be suspended in air as is the case
with the many saints studied in the first part of *Sky* called "The New
Patron Saint of Aviation"; one wants, as does the narrator of "The Sidereal
Eiffel Tower," to penetrate the heart of darkness of the Amazon jungle. But
such "levitations," however appealing they seem to the poet at times of
special stress and anxiety, are finally less challenging than the ordinary
events of everyday life, or should I say everyday death, *Sky* being first and
foremost a *death* book, specifically the death associated with twentieth-cen-
tury warfare.

Cendrars may well have been the only European poet who was at the
front in both of the World Wars. In the first, he lost his right arm, an
amputation that was to haunt the rest of his writings but which had been
oddly anticipated in his own *Le Prose du Transsibérien,* with its hallucinatory
imagery of mutilated body parts:

> In the pesthouses I saw gaping wounds bleeding full blast
> And amputated limbs danced about or too flight into the raucous air...

Yet despite what the First World War had done to him, in 1940 at the
time of the "phoney war," the fifty-three-year-old writer signed on as war
correspondent for British headquarters in Paris, working closely behind the
front lines. One of the French aviators who was killed in the early months
of the war was his own son Rémy. And that story, like the story of *La Main
coupée,* is alluded to in a series of episodic fragments in *Sky.*

Was Cendrars merely courting danger? Or was it that, like the young
Ludwig Wittgenstein, who fought on the opposite side in World War I, he
regarded the sheer condition of war as one that had to be undergone.
Escape—levitation in theory, the flight to Brazil or to other "exotic"
realms, in practice—was a peacetime luxury. In war, engagement was
required, at least mentally if not physically, even though Cendrars was
always torn between such engagement and the deepest of cynicisms about
the whole patriotic-military adventure, indeed about life in general. At the
heart of *Sky* is the *black hole,* the narrator, driving from São Paulo to the
valley of the Morro Azul, discovers in the night sky:

> In these latitudes, the Southern Cross is the mistress of the hemi-
> sphere. The coal-sack is situated immediately below and slightly to the
> left of the hypothetical point where the two arms of the cross of the

symbolic southern constellation meet. In fact, there is a black pocket there. It is such a hypnotic gulf, and of such an intense black, that it seems to recede, to detach itself, throwing into relief all the stars in fission that flare for a moment in the foreground and, the more you gaze at this hole, the hollower it seems to become.... It looks as if it has been polished with a velvet cloth, it shrinks and swells…so that, in the long run, all the stars in the sky are reduced to nothing more than smoking candle ends melting into this intense blackness which absorbs them like blotting paper.

Such is the abyss, the abyss of the sky…this stain, this damp mildew… A living sponge. The sky is a blackboard. Not a single algebraic formula, written in frost-rimed chalk, nor star dust in suspension, not the faintest sparkle remains on its surface. All is effaced.

I have seen this sponge, seen it with my own two eyes. It is an enigma.

The natives of the Morro Azul call this black hole "the Devil," but— and this is the point—we don't need to go to the mountains of the Amazon to find the "coal sack." In Chapter 6 of "The Sidereal Eiffel Tower," Cendrars relates it to the "coal scuttles" of World War I "as the French troops, the *poilus,* nicknamed those homely projectiles, the huge aerial torpedoes surmounted by a ululating copper rod that the *Minenwerfer* rained down on us." More important, the "coal sack" reappears as the night sky seen through the "loop-hole cut through an armored plate, a slit, a Judashole, through which I could take a look at the world beyond or fire a rifle at the enemy or lob a grenade over the top like a child who kicks a big stone into a ravine and listens excitedly as it bounces down and down until it reaches the bottom, so as to judge the depth of the gulf." "Nothing on earth," Cendrars recalls "was as black as the darkness of night at the front."

No wonder the "coal sack" comes to have such familiarity to the poet. The black hole is perhaps the central reality of *Sky,* the opening chapter providing a frame narrative that immediately sounds the death note. Yet— and this is the irony—this chapter, like so much of Cendrars's memoir, is characterized less by night thoughts than by exuberance and fantasy. An account of a sea voyage from Rio to Cherbourg, it begins with the poet's reluctant refusal to bring a *bandeira,* a giant anteater, which an old black man on the shore wants to sell him, on board. But he does bring on the eighteen-day voyage "67 marmosets, the wistiti with bleached manes, a race that is on its way to extinction and can only be found on one island, behind Paqueta, at the far end of the Gulf of Guanabarà. They are fragile little princes, and I was feeding them on the local bananas, rice and the white meat of chickens." And as if this weren't enough, he also brings 250 of the tropical birds called "seven-colors," birds that have never been known to survive the Atlantic crossing.

Colette, we recall, thought it was the "greatest injustice" that "certain creatures contain wings." But immediately, Cendrars presents us with creatures whose wings do them precious little good: "By the time we reached Lisbon, I had only seven birds left. At Cherbourg, three. Two died in the train from Cherbourg to Paris, in spite of the hot-water bottle Gasperl had ingeniously tucked into their cage." The "dear little girl" the narrator is going to visit in Les Batignolles thus gets to see only one solitary "seven-colors" perform tricks on her kitchen table before it dies in the early morning. As for the marmosets, they had to be put to sleep on board ship. Flight and death, the two seeming antitheses, thus come together, even as the *Gelria,* the Dutch steamship on which the poet returns to Cherbourg, is described as a "real steamship," one of "those old 'hen-coops'" no longer in existence, having been "sent to the bottom during World Wars I and II." This is the only war reference in what is otherwise exotic travel narrative; Cendrars clearly puts it in to prepare us for what comes later, even as the journey itself takes place in an unspecified moment of peace (in fact, the reference is to one of the three long visits he made to Brazil between 1924–1928). But what is strangest about this "bird chapter," is that it ends with the following *"postscript for sensitive souls":*

> When my mother died, in 1907, they found amongst her trunks and hat-boxes some feathers, aigrettes, quills, panaches, bird-of-paradise tails, cockades from a black cock, like a Bersagliere's plumes, others from a white cockerel, like the ones the military cadets at St. Cyr wear on their *shakos,* a tuft of capercailzie feathers, some humming birds skewered on a brooch, toques and muffs of lophophorus, the crest of a hoopoe, swansdown, ostrich feathers, pheasants' tails, feathers from doves and seagulls, Bengalis, pigeons' throats and even a tender partridge. They were worth several hundred thousand francs. Everything smelled of camphor but, one day, they will all come back into fashion and, once again, sensitive souls will be wearing them.

I cite this passage at some length because it is so characteristic of Cendrars's style. The extravagantly long catalogue, whose effect depends upon intensification and hyperbole, is followed, as is so often the case, by flat, matter-of-fact assertion ("Everything smelled of camphor"), this giving way, in its turn, to an apocalyptic note. The effect is that of a lyric poem: A series of noun-phrases in apposition present us with the gradual transformation of birds into mere feathers, the "humming birds skewered on a brooch" testifying to the actual uses to which those birds we envy are actually put. True, on Judgment Day, they will re-emerge, "perched at a rakish angle on a ridiculous Parisian hat worn by an elderly old-fashioned angel." But Cendrars himself takes nothing on faith, not even the love between mother and son. Having juxtaposed his mother's death to that of the birds, he finds himself in a condition not unlike that of Beckett's Unnamable:

> Personally, since I have no faith, I will not be there to see the parousia. Nor will I be on the side of the sensitive souls. I chose my corner a long time ago, not in the graveyard of the Church, but in an ideal spot on a steamer's course where a suicide can easily dive overboard and plunge in amongst the sargasso weed that floats there in the great indigo vat. This is situated at: *latitude zero, 1, 2, or 3-tenths South, by 1, 2, or 3-dozen degrees West, due West, let us say from 13 to 33....*

It is within this context that we must understand the long (roughly a third of the book) section called "The New Patron of Aviation." For the contemporary reader, this compendium of saints' lives—the stories told all having to do with levitation, and much of it quite simply lifted from other sources, especially Olivier Leroy's 1928 study *La Lévitation,* upon which Cendrars relies heavily, along with such works as Domenico Bernino's *Vie de saint Joseph de Copertino, de l'ordre des Frères Mineurs* (1856) and Emile Baumann's *Mon frère le Dominicain* (1927)—may at first seem somewhat off-putting. Do we really need the life history of the young cobbler's son Joseph Desa, who was considered hopelessly stupid and inept until he demonstrated the ability to remain suspended in air? Do we need a scholarly disquisition on the meaning of the word *levitation* and its relationship to "ecstatic ascension, ecstatic elevation, corporeal ravishment, or the fire of divine love" (p. 89)? And what about the lengthy account of levitating saints and prophets, beginning with Enoch and Elijah in the bible and culminating in the legends of our own time?

Here the understanding of the book's genre is essential. If we read *Sky* as the poet's "memoirs," however fictionalized, as the story of what he experienced where and when, the documentary sections pasted into the narrative are sure to seem irritating. But if we look more closely at the juxtapositions of this material with its "contemporary" counterparts—the meeting of Blaise with his son Rémy at Rheims and the dinner with the British general and Rémy's absurd girlfriend, the prewar exploits of the Dada poet Arthur Cravan, who was terrified of the war itself, the visit to Dr. Oswaldo Padroso in the Morro Azul, and so on—a certain logic emerges. In the chapter called "Flying Backwards," Cendrars recalls his "agonizing years of silence," following the battle of Stalingrad in 1940. Hiding from the Gestapo in Aix-en-Provence, he began to frequent the library in La Méjanes, and it is in that library that he began to investigate the life of St. Joseph of Cupertino more fully. It was as if immersion in the life of the patron saint of aviators could compensate for the death of his own young aviator Rémy. By 1943, Cendrars was able to write again, the two "levitations" somehow merging in his mind.

The saints' lives, in other words, are not recounted for their own sake but to dramatize the state of mind of the narrator who retells them. To contemplate miracles of levitation achieved by men and women in past centuries becomes a way of coming to terms with what would otherwise be impossible to accept:

> I must admit that, just as, after 1943, when an informer for the Gestapo came to lodge next door to me in Aix-en-Provence, taking a room on the same floor as my furnished apartment, I used to put my radio in my bed, turn it very low and smother it under seven blankets of St. Joseph of Copertino... came to weave a blanket of dreams between St. Joseph of Copertino and myself. (p.... 40.)

But *flight,* as we have already seen in the case of the exotic jungle birds, is a two-edged metaphor. The "miraculous" and unwilled levitation of Joseph of Copertino must be read, not only against the tragic flight of Rémy, but against those other flights, beginning with the fall of France on May 10, 1940, when, as Cendrars puts it, "surrealism had been stalking the land, not the work of those absurd poets who claim so much and who are, at best, sub-realists, since they extol the sub-conscious, but the conscious work of Christ, the only true poet of the surreal. He has never written a line. He acts. And everyone interprets it in his own way" (p. 67).

Cendrars's own "interpretation" is to downplay the question of Christ's divinity (as he says in the passage cited above, "I have no faith"), and to foreground the emblematic character of His suffering. Consider the brilliant account of the "Armageddon-like scene" of the flight from Paris in the wake of the arrival of the Germans, marked by "Fire, flames, smoke. Bombs feeding the fires. Bridges, railway lines and locks blown up":

I am confused about dates. It is not possible that so many things, so many misfortunes, so many acts of cowardice—panic, lost battles, deaths, the sick abandoned in a burning hospital, orphans straying, lunatics let loose, cows mooing in pain because nobody had come to milk them, petrol pissing out of the pump in front of a gas-station because the owner had fled in such haste that he had forgotten to turn it off, wanting to know more.... No, it is not possible that so many events could have happened in such a short time. It was hysteria. The sun had stopped in the heavens (pp. 67–68).

Such "flights" are marked by terrible pathos. Others, like the "flight" of the Dada poets to Zurich in World War I proclaiming that "art has no country!," or Robert Delaunay's comparable flight to Madrid where he sat out the war, are judged cowardly by Cendrars, the most prominent case being that of Arthur Cravan, the "handsome Arthur," nephew of Oscar Wilde, prizefighter, poet, notorious womanizer and drinker, who was so afraid of having "his pretty face spoiled," that when the United States entered the war, "he slipped over into Canada, since that happened to be the nearest frontier and he could reach it in a single night." The "handsome Arthur" finally made his way to Mexico where he vanished.

Finally, there is the flight of Dr. Oswaldo Padroso, so vividly described in "The Sidereal Eiffel Tower." A friend in São Paulo tells Cendrars about the mysterious Padroso, who inhabits an ancient *fazenda* in the mysterious valley of the Blue Mountain called *Morro Azul*. Padroso's retreat into the wilderness evidently has something to do with an unknown woman with whom he is in love. Cendrars sets out on the journey into the valley, the description of the treacherous ravine, fraught with myth and legend, being one of the great set pieces in *Sky*. But when he finally reaches the strange plantation and dines with Dr. Padroso, he learns to his dismay that the object of the Doctor's love is none other than Sarah Bernhardt, the "divine Sarah," who had visited São Paulo exactly once in 1909 and whom the Doctor had kissed a single time. Obsessed by the memory of Sarah, the Doctor retreats into the wilderness, neglects the plantation and its natives, and spends his days and nights in idle fantasies. A fanatic Francophile, he has made a "discovery" which he takes to be his claim to fame: He has found in the sky a "constellation" that closely resembles the Eiffel Tower in its configuration. For years, he has been trying to alert the authorities in Paris to this discovery, but his quest has been in vain.

Padroso's flight thus becomes the emblem of futility, of self-deception. *Sky* ends with a "Postscript for the pessimist I am," which is an account of August 1, 1944, the day when Aix-en-Provence was liberated by the invading American army. In the course of the endless toasts and celebrations, Cendrars turns to a Brazilian colleague and asks him what has become of Senhor Oswaldo Padroso:

> Dr. Oswaldo of the Morro Azul? Who *doesn't* know him in São Paulo!" exclaimed my Brazilian colleague with a laugh. "Just imagine, he's left the fazenda and gone to live in the capital!" You didn't know? And what's more, he's married!.... Well, what can you expect... after the defeat of France in June 1940, and Pétain's Armistice, Dr. Padroso lost faith, he no longer believed in anything....

Cendrars is "delighted with this prosaic end which, for my friend, marked the end of a long hypnotic trance," but he also sees it as a kind of abdication—a humiliation for Poetry." And there is the paradox that this book has explored so stringently. *Flight*—and Cendrars is surely thinking of his own flights, beginning with the escape from his family home as an adolescent boy—easily turns into escapism, the "hypnotic trance" of the self-indulgent. And yet "levitation" is also the marker of our most persistent aspirations.

Sky refuses to sentimentalize this situation. The book reaches no point of resolution; it provides no answers. Perhaps this is why Cendrars's late prose has been relatively neglected, why *Sky* has not been translated into English until now. But today, when the literature of the world wars is being reassessed, *Lotissement du ciel* emerges as one of the most poignant studies of brinkmanship, of living on the edge—and somehow even enjoying it.

Marjorie Perloff

INJUSTICE

From her window in the Palais-Royal,
Colette was contemplating the pigeons and
the doves cavorting in the sun.
"Perhaps the greatest injustice that
exists in all creation," she said, "is
that certain creatures possess wings…"

Aux Écoutes, June 1948

To the Madwoman of Saint-Sulpice

THE LAST JUDGMENT

"Only birds, children and saints
are interesting."

Declaration by O.W. Milosz
to Armand Godoy

They were weighing anchor.

"*Godverdam,* if you bring that filthy beast on board, I'll have to..."

The Purser was swearing at me through his megaphone. The "filthy beast," as he called him, was a magnificent ant bear, a *bandeira,* a huge anteater over six feet tall, and more than once the pair of us had only just missed falling into the water as I tried to make friends with him and exchange a few hugs. Already the harbor tugs were swinging the ship's bows around to face the open sea, I was wobbling perilously on the bottom step of the gangway, and the giant beast, with his absurd banner-like tail and his long, even more absurd snout like an inverted funnel, was standing in the stern of the pirogue belonging to his master, an old Negro with only one eye, who was having a lot of trouble keeping his boat steady now that the ship's propellers were churning up the seething, muddy waters, creating the start of the wake, the long trail of foam that would stretch from Pernambuco to Cherbourg, a crossing that would take eighteen days.

I looked up.

Perpendicularly above me, the Purser was bawling threats and insults into his megaphone, swear words that I could not hear above the hissing of the steam escaping from the windlasses and the third blast of the siren as it shrieked its emotional farewell. Everything was in motion, swinging around, foaming, and all along the rail, to the left and right of the Purser, the heads of the passengers were caught in an oblique ray of sunlight sneaking through the gaps in the canvas awnings stretched over the deck, and then, from behind, they were surreptitiously decapitated and turned upside down, all together, their faces congested, as the high white hull of the steamer listed; the brass portholes flashed and were extinguished again, like spotlights in a theater, the gangway I was clinging to was suddenly hoisted up, and the ant bear watched my ascent, holding out his inordinately long front paws, with their long inverted claws, as the pirogue disappeared under the gangway, almost colliding with it, and the old Negro shouted to me:

"Take him, *senhor.* Give me 300,000 *reis.* It's a gift, I won't make a cent on the deal. *Bicho tão bonito!* Such a well-trained animal!"

But it was too late. We were already making for the open sea. The pirogue was left far behind, bobbing about in our wake. The Negro, reluctant to part with the animal, had gone on haggling too long. The folded gangway reached the level of the rail and a laughing sailor put out his hand and hauled me aboard.

"Now, isn't that just like you, Monsieur Cendrars," said the Purser, "you could have broken your neck or fallen into the water. The Captain is sure to bawl me out. But, God be praised! You didn't bring that filthy beast on board!"

The Purser was right. Short of getting the entire crew to search the Provision Rooms for ants during the crossing, how would I have managed to feed that extravagant creature of the virgin forest, who eats nothing but ants and their eggs? In the forest, this edentate mammal, who walks awkwardly on the backs of his paws, with his claws sticking up in the air, burrows his long, funnel-shaped head into an anthill, thrusting it right in up to his ears, waves his tail like a flag—which is a sign that he's enjoying himself—unwinds God knows how many meters and meters of sticky, threadlike tongue, dribbles his sugary saliva, which the ants consider a delicacy, and then, when his tongue is covered in hundreds and thousands of seething ants, who are now trapped, this curious animal must surely press his navel with one claw to activate the secret spring that reels in his tongue at an amazing speed. One often comes across this animal sitting on his behind at the foot of a termite's nest, which he has already perforated in all directions, swallowing and blinking his eyes with an air of satisfaction. The giant anteater is a great lazybones and totally harmless, but you must not fall into his arms because his embrace, which is simply a reflex action, is fatal, he does not know his own prodigious strength, and his long claws, turned back and useless, are as sharp as cutlasses. He is an elegaic creature. He is easily tamed. I have come across them in several *fazendas.* Some of these solitary nomads measure three meters from the tips of their muzzles to the tips of their tails. Their hair is long and flowing, and, like the Cashmere goat's, it is brownish gray mixed with darker curls. But I have never seen such a fine specimen as that *tamandua* I just missed buying in Pernambuco. I will regret him all my life, for having such an extravagant animal as a pal opens your eyes to the mysteries of creation and allows you to touch, just with your fingertips, the absurdity of all the long history of the evolution of living beings. To have a pal who holds you dear to his heart, and a stimulating traveling companion like that, keeps you laughing from morn till night. He is, perhaps, God. His habits and his thinking are obscure, and his ways are incomprehensible. No one has ever been able to tell me what kind of dung he produces, and whether he makes "treddles" like a goat. Be that as it may, ants eat their own dung.

2

The *Gelria* was a real steamship, built to navigate like those old ships you used to see in vast numbers, ploughing the seven seas, before the era of transatlantic luxury liners, competition between shipping lines, international rivalry, fashionable, publicity-seeking cruises, snobbery, and tourism, and before the intrusion of modern decorative art into the construction of ships made such startling changes in the furnishings and fittings, all of which were doomed to burn. Never again will we see the like of those old "hen-coops," riding high in the water, for all those good old valiant ships were sent to the bottom during World Wars I and II. The *Gelria* was a Dutch ship, and I had my routine on board and everyone knew me because this was the fifth or sixth time I had made the return crossing aboard her. I had deliberately waited till she sailed down the Brazilian coast so that I could embark all my animals, for only on a Dutch ship do they know how to take care of animals, and during the crossing Gasperl, the ship's carpenter, with whom, in accordance with ancient seafaring tradition, all the animals on board were lodged, took care of my little charges and built them crates and cages that were practical, comfortable, and easy to handle; they were virtually cabinet quality for he put so much love and good taste into them, as well as his intuitive sense of the needs, habits, and characters of the animals. Moreover, with a great deal of ingenuity, he arranged hiding places, false bottoms, secret drawers, and compartments in the crates and cages, so as to outwit the Customs when we arrived and smuggle in the bottles of white rum and the boxes of good cigars that I was bringing back for my friends. I was also taking my animals to friends in Paris, and not trading in them, as that idiot Serrhuis (the Purser who had made me miss my chance of buying that splendid anteater in Pernambuco) imagined. I was bringing the marmosets for the dancers in Rolf de Maré's Swedish Ballet and the birds for a little girl whom I loved more than all the world, and for whom I always brought back one of the living wonders of Brazil.

But this time I had really overdone it, and the Purser was absolutely within his rights to throw a fit and threaten to withdraw all the privileges I enjoyed on board. In Rio, I had embarked 67 marmosets, the ones with bleached manes, a race that is on its way to extinction and can only be found on one island, behind Paqueta, at the far end of the Gulf of Guanabarà. They are fragile little princes, and I was feeding them on local bananas, rice, and the white meat of chickens. I had installed them in my cabin to save them from the promiscuity of the other animals, who were all housed with the carpenter, and, in Bahia, I had taken over a large luxury cabin, just opposite mine, which happened to be empty, so as to keep my 250 seven-colors out of draughts. These are tropical birds, and not one has ever been able to survive the Atlantic crossing, which is why I had carried off every seven-colors I could lay hands on, buying them from the bird-sellers in Bahia and telling myself that, out of 250 birds, I would surely be able to keep one living specimen to show to the little girl I loved so much. They cost me a small fortune, and it was his respect for the money I spent ("stupidly for stupid beasts," as he said) rather than any of my arguments, that finally persuaded the Purser to allow me to take over the large vacant cabin, invoicing me, nevertheless, for "One parrot," that is, one pound sterling, which was the price for the board and lodging of one parrot on board. The carpenter had numbers and numbers of these insupportable chatterboxes in his keeping, the little gray-blue ones with red "braiding," who are the sharpest-witted, and most villainous, of all the parrots in Brazil.

One evening, when we were strolling up and down the deck together I said to the Purser:

"What were all those threats you were making when I was busy haggling with that old Negro from Pernambuco? I couldn't hear what you were saying, in spite of that raucous megaphone."

"I was threatening to count every one of your little monkeys and your birds and charge them as 'one parrot' each. That would have put my accounts in order for the ship's owners, and I would have cured you of your mania, your ridiculous love of animals, your curiosity."

"Do you think so, Purser? That anteater went straight to my heart and I'll mourn him for the rest of my life. Come on, let's go and have a drink and a smoke."

We settled ourselves in the bar.

After an hour's silence, Serrhuis, who was hardly a chatty type, said to me

"I don't know how you do it, Monsieur Cendrars, but one can't refuse you anything."

"Why do you say that, Purser?"

"Because of your monkeys, and because of your birds."

"Have you got a guilty conscience?"

"It's most irregular, you know. One shouldn't put animals in a luxury-class cabin."

"You know perfectly well there aren't any inspectors on board and that I'm disembarking at Cherbourg."

"Thank God!"

Serrhuis was getting cold feet, afraid the Assistant Purser would report him, and I, too, had my worries. My marmosets were growing melancholy and every morning I was throwing dead birds overboard.

Would the little girl in Les Batignolles see a single one of my seven-colors alive?

"Bartender, same again!"

Serrhuis relit his pipe and wrapped himself up in smoke and silence.

He was meditating.

A phonograph was playing blues.

Passengers were dancing among the tables.

I could not take a dead, or even a stuffed, bird to a dear little girl.

"Bartender same again!"

I was encouraging the Purser to indulge in his vice so as to drown his bookkeeping scruples.

"Skal!"

"Skol!"

He made me laugh, but not as much as the anteater would have done. Neither the night nor the ship were moving fast enough for me. I was eager to arrive, to give pleasure to a little girl. Oh, the wonders of the world!

"Bartender..."

3

The seven-colors is a tropical bird with a tail like a blackbird's, and he has the same impudent eye, but, whereas our own blackbird is a dashing rascal, glossy and tightly corseted, the seven-colors is perpetually startled, an animated ball of ruffled feathers; he flutters in all directions, like the tuft of feathers on the shuttlecock that flies tirelessly to and fro in a game of badminton. He is a bewildered, passive bird.

They say that, with the exception of two species—the sacred python of India and the horned viper of Formosa—Brazil contains every species of snake in the world, as well as some of her own, which is why this fiery land, this hell of virgin forest, is known as the Snakes' Paradise. Well, then! Just imagine this: with the exception of two kinds of feather—those of the peacock and the lyrebird—the seven-colors carries a pair of all the distinctive feathers that are the pride and the coquetry of all the other birds in the world set into his black jerkin, and that is why the natives have nicknamed him the "seven-colors," meaning that he is a rainbow, a creature that lives off the light, a dewdrop, a sprite, a breath, a quiver, and they say that he brings good fortune, which is why they keep so many in cages. You see them outside every hut.

When you startle a flight of seven-colors in a solitary clearing in the virgin forest, where these birds disport themselves in flocks of thousands, it is a dazzling sight, and it leaves an unforgettably moving impression on you when you see this cloud of wings, feathers, and multi-colored down sparkling, flashing, and reflecting like mica in the sunlight, as if a million precious gems were dissolving in the overheated atmosphere, palpitating in the somber depths of the forest. It is a marvelous experience. And 25 years later, when I saw the first color film of the explosion on Bikini and the prodigious formation of its mushroom clouds, this terrifying phenomenon reminded me of the flight of the seven-colors in brilliant tropical sunlight, in the magic circle of the clearing in the depths of the virgin forest, for this, too, was like an image and a symbol of the disintegration of matter.

Once things reach a certain grandiose scale, everything is fairy tale to the man who feels himself to be cut off from nature, and neither perfumes, nor colors, nor sounds can reach him anymore.

I was determined to bring back a live specimen of these spectacular birds, not so much because I wanted my little girl to admire the extraordinary display of his feathers, but rather because she lived in Les Batignolles, where, all day long, she could hear the whistles of the trains as they were swallowed up in the nearby tunnel, and I wanted her to hear his cry, his living voice. I say his cry, his voice, and I dare not say his song, for how can you define the warbling of the seven-colors as song? Once you have heard it, you think of the bird as if he were some delightful toy from the bazaar. And you don't have to wind him up to make him go. When he is anxious to perform his vocal fireworks, the seven-colors throws himself on the ground, wallows in the dust, is afflicted with Saint Vitus' Dance, does two or three pirouettes, beats his semi-rigid wings, tips back his head, and, with his throat swelling and throbbing from the effort, emits a snort, a gargle, a whistle like a choked valve when it's letting off steam, and then suddenly lets out the strident whistle of a train traveling at full speed, a whistle that is eventually throttled, to the accompaniment of chest notes, as the ecstasy of the seven-colors reaches its climax, and this varies according to the power and endurance of the vocal cords and the talent of the individual: It may be a long cascade of chuckles, or a tearing rattle, or a series of sobs. It is the funniest thing in the world. Afterward, the enraptured bird comes back to his senses, shakes himself, and flies off, but as long as he is in his trance you can easily catch him. Every native kid has one as a pet. They hang them up in rush cages outside the doors of their huts. And when the bird sings, the kids laugh. The bird lets out his cry several times a day, more out of some secret affectation than as a matter of ritual. He is a talisman, a toy, a lucky charm. And God knows one needs them in the forest, where even the fall of a leaf is ominous.

Personally, the thing I find most striking about birds is their eyes, with their other-worldly, beyond-the-grave look, for where is the cemetery of the birds? Have you never been struck by that impersonal look, that look of Eternity, when the Bird, instead of focusing directly on you, seems to pierce you through and through with his gaze, as if you were transparent, as if he could see your soul, your shadow behind you, as if he were communing with your doppelgänger, preparing himself for the mystical union, preparing to fly into immortality or to peck out the eyes of your guardian angel and eat them? There is no creature who is so alien to this world as the bird, for where is the graveyard, the ossuary of the birds? They are fragile, and they die in their millions every day, and yet you never find a bleached skeleton and very rarely a bloody corpse. For a long time, it was believed that birds perished at sea and that whole flocks of them disappeared into the oceans, but this is a false belief, no sailor has ever reported sighting flocks of migratory birds, so numerous that they blackened the sky, committing suicide *en masse* on the high seas; on the contrary, nowadays it is known for certain that even hummingbirds fly over the oceans, and that clouds of these tiny birds emigrate periodically from the confines of Canada and the Rocky Mountains as far as the northern limits of the southern hemisphere, on the borders of Colombia and Venezuela, undaunted by the fearful tornadoes in the Caribbean and the furious squalls of wind from the Gulf of Mexico.

The eye of a bird. Its lucidity is straight out of hell. What is it looking at? It bears the mark of metempsychosis, and how hallucinating it would be if women had the eyes of birds!

That is what I was trying to explain to a couple of bright sparks, two shipmates of mine called Fontaine de l'Albley and Babot du Lac, a pair of illicit financiers who had dreamed of making their fortunes through some ingenious swindle but were now on their way back to Belgium, flat broke. To take their minds off high finance, I had been dragging them around Bahia, one of our ports of call, touring all the bird-catchers, but the iced *pinga* and the heat had proved too much for us. The three of us had come back on board, very much the worse for wear, escorted by the black porters who set down the little wicker cages, containing the 250 seven-colors I had just bought, at the foot of the *Gelria's* gangway.

"It was Hudson, the English naturalist from the River Plate, who first had this idea," I explained to them as I hung up the cages. "After praising the women of Bahia as the most beautiful in the world, he takes it into his head to suggest, without a trace of humor: 'Wouldn't these negresses, with their nut-brown eyes, be absolutely irresistible if they had the eyes of an eagle or a sparrow hawk? It would be the crowning glory of these goddess-like creatures.'"

And I seized on this at once and took it a stage further, exaggerating in my usual fashion: "That beady eye. Can't you just see Greta Garbo with the eyes of a tawny owl, or an eagle owl, or the daughter of the London Rothschild with the eyes of a vulture? And how about Parisian women—imagine them with the motionless eyes of a linnet, a warbler, or a tit, wouldn't that make them divine? And the greedy eye of the domestic goose would be the finishing touch to the august physiognomy of Nietzsche's sister, the eternal Elisabeth! Even statues would take on an amusing look if you put the eyes of gratified birds into their empty eye sockets. Imagine Minerva with the devouring eyes of an owl, Venus with the red, lidless eye of the cormorant, Eve with the carbuncle eye of the serpent-eater, flashing in anger as it confronts a snake, Leda and her swan, both with the same white, treacherous, spell-binding, cold eye, streaked with malice, and, on the street corner, the whores with the astonished eye of the jay!"

Having hung up the native cages in the large luxurious cabin (under vehement protest from the Purser, who had turned up at last and was pulling a face—and what a face!—at the sight of this invasion), and with my seven-colors safely protected from draughts, the three of us, the three drunks from Bahia, went to the bar of the *Gelria* for a pick-me-up, a tropical blue with ginger.

I was worried. My little monkeys were unhappy and every morning I was throwing dead birds overboard.

We had put in at Las Palmas in the Canaries. There was nothing I could do for my birds. Seven-colors do not survive the Atlantic crossing and I had already lost more than half of them. And the marmosets were growing sadder because the fresh bananas I had bought for them in the Canaries did not suit them, and these blond sons of Capricorn must have discovered the taste of northern beet in these bananas from Las Palmas, or worse, the taste of turnip. Gasperl, the carpenter, advised me to add some small chilis from their native land to their rice, to stimulate their appetites, to stuff them with jam, to have no scruples about getting them drunk so as to cheer them up, and to administer some *caninha,* the brandy made from cane sugar, in case of colds. It was September, the cold season was approaching, and I preferred to dose my pets with tablets containing peptone, to fortify them in advance against the rigors of the Parisian climate.

The most cheerful place on board was the carpenter's locker, on the lower deck, a little astern of the mainmast, where the carpenter's sweetheart, "Daddy's Girl" as he called her, acted as hostess to her master's lodgers, whom she kept among the wood shavings. She was a lissome, monkey-faced girl from Sumatra, with blue-black skin. The old man petted her, spoiled her, tarted her up, and adorned her with rings, earrings and necklaces of glass beads. She was not in the least jealous, but she did not like the parrots crowded into the Provision Room, so she was always playing tricks on them, and when she plucked a tail feather from the most magnificent of them all, there ensued a squawking and a hullabaloo fit for Noah's Ark, for there were all sorts of other creatures in the room besides the parrots shrieking high up, near the ceiling: there were monkeys, who got tangled up in their leashes, white squirrels and palm rats on their perches, valuable little snakes and horrible batrachians in big jars, indefatigable tortoises of all sizes, roly-polying all over the floor, not to mention a multitude of pitter-pattering mice and guinea pigs and armadilloes curled up into balls. In one corner lived a dwarf nanny goat from Tenerife who, with her swollen udders, served as wet nurse to the young of sick animals. Gasperl had a wooden leg, he was an old sailor from the days of sailing ships, and I loved to smoke a few pipes, drink gin, and sit in front of his door late into the night, listening to him tell stories about his animals, while the monkey-faced girl cuddled up against his chest and finally went to sleep, with one arm under his sweater; sometimes other members of the crew, and some of the steerage passengers, came to join us.

By the time we reached Lisbon, I had only seven birds left. At Cherbourg, three. Two died in the train from Cherbourg to Paris, in spite of the hot-water bottle Gasperl had ingeniously tucked into their cage, but

21

the little girl who lived in Les Batignolles was able to see, hear, and admire a living seven-colors who was performing his tricks on the kitchen table (before dying in the early hours of the following morning) under the crude light of a naked light bulb and in front of the gas fire that was warming the room.

My dear little girl, do you remember that bird?

Postscript for sensitive souls—When my mother died, in 1907, they found among her trunks and hatboxes some feathers, tufts, quills, plumes, bird-of-paradise tails, cockades from a black cock, like a *bersagliere's* plumes, others from a white cockerel, like the ones the military cadets at St. Cyr wear oh their *shakos*, a tuft of capercailzie feathers, some hummingbirds skewered on a brooch, toques and muffs from Himalayan pheasants, the crest of a hoopoe, swansdown, ostrich feathers, pheasants' tails, feathers from doves and seagulls, Bengalis, pigeons' throats and even a tender partridge. They were worth several hundred thousand francs. Everything smelled of camphor but, one day, they will all come back into fashion and, once again, sensitive souls will be wearing them. But among all these motley trimmings, there was not one to equal the plumage of the seven-colors, and, on Judgment Day, my dear little girl will once more clap her hands and burst out laughing when she recognizes her tropical bird, and the cohorts of little black angels—all those innocents who died of yellow fever behind the lagoons and in the *paranas*—will clap their hands with her when they see the bird of their childhood reawaken, perched at a rakish angle on a ridiculous Parisian hat worn by an elderly, old-fashioned angel.

Personally, since I have no faith, I will not be there to see the Second Coming. But nor will I be on the side of the sensitive souls. I chose my corner a long time ago, not in the graveyard of the Church, but in an ideal spot on a steamer's course, where a suicide can easily dive overboard and plunge in among the sargasso weed that floats there in the great indigo vat. This is situated at: *latitude zero, 1, 2, or 3-tenths South, by 1, 2, or 3-dozen degrees West, due West, let us say from 13 to 33...*

I hope they will let me choose this spot in peace.

I will not ask for any fanfares.

At the most, a big sperm whale to swallow me.

To an Out-of-work Baker's girl

THE NEW PATRON SAINT OF AVIATION*

"…make my mind lively and alert,
keep timidity from my heart, and
darkness from my soul…"

Saint Joseph of Copertino's prayer

---

* With reference to the standard work: La Lévitation, by Olivier Leroy, *Professeur agrégé de l'Université* (1 vol. in octavo Les Éditions du Cerf, Juvisy, 1928).

N.B. The numbers in the text refer to notes, which will be found at the end of each section.

I

FLYING BACKWARDS

"I have found a man after God's heart
and after my own."

St. Teresa of Avila

1

He cried out and flew away...

He hovered in front of the altar, not like a bird who gazes into a mirror and knocks his head against his own image, but in ecstasy before the face of God.

2

Domenico Bernino, at one time the Bishop of Osimo, was the son of the famous Bernini, known as the Cavalier Bernini, the painter, sculptor, and architect whom Louis XIV summoned to France, where he created the great masterpiece of Baroque sculpture, his prodigious equestrian statue of the Sun King. For some unknown reason—probably because the King had an aversion to anything that seemed to overturn the rules of classical art—this monument was relegated to the end of the ornamental lake known as the *pièce d'eau des Suisses,* in an inaccessible corner of the park of Versailles, and there it has been left to deteriorate from the eroding effects of the spray that splashes up from the muddy pool, and the parasitic mosses that are cracking the stone. (You can see this statue quite clearly, from the right-hand side of the train, when pulling out of the Gare des Chantiers in the direction of Saint-Cyr.) This Domenico Bernino, then, was Saint Joseph of Copertino's biographer. He writes:[1]

"One Christmas Eve, while listening to the shepherds playing their bagpipes in celebration of the Nativity, Joseph began to prance about in an access of ecstatic jubilation, then, rising from the ground with a cry, he flew through the air until he reached the High Altar, a distance of about twenty-five meters." (Taken from the Bollandists' *Acta Sanctorum,* Vol. V, September, p. 1021 AB.)

And, further down, Bernino quotes from the deposition of one of the shepherds as recorded at the process of canonization (Folio 65, No. 12, B, para. 77): "My job as a shepherd was to guard the flocks near La Grotella. On Christmas Eve, Brother Joseph came to seek us out, me and the other shepherds on the plain, and said: 'Wouldn't you like to come and play your bagpipes, this evening, in the church of La Grotella, to mark your joy at the birth of Jesus Christ?' At this invitation, we gathered together in great numbers, the shepherds and me, and we took our bagpipes and our fifes. Brother Joseph came to meet us with a joyful air. We entered the church all together, with him at the head and us behind, at about ten or eleven in the evening, and there, in the nave, we played on a multitude of bagpipes and fifes. Then we noticed that Brother Joseph was so filled with joy that he was beginning to dance to the sound of our music. But all of a sudden, he sighed, then let out a great cry. At the same time, he rose into the air and, from the middle of the church, flew like a bird to the High Altar, where he kissed the tabernacle. Now, from the middle of the church to the High Altar, the distance must be at least 50 cannes.[2] But the most wonderful part of it is that the altar was covered in lighted candles, yet Brother Joseph came to rest among them without knocking over a single candle or candlestick. He stayed like that, kneeling on the altar, clasping the tabernacle in his arms, for about a quarter of an hour, then he came down without any assistance, and without upsetting anything. He moved away from us, his eyes and his cheeks bathed in tears, and he said to us: 'My brothers, it is enough, may the love of God go with you!' We were all terrified..." (Bernino, p. 68).

3

"Giuseppe [Joseph] Desa was born in Copertino, on the 17th of June 1603, to a poor family. He learned the trade of shoemaking and then, at the age of seventeen, entered the order of the Capuchin Friars in Martina as a lay brother. After spending eight months there as novice, he was sent away because of his incapacity both physical and intellectual. He then managed to gain acceptance by the Friars Minor at the convent in La Grotella, near Copertino (south of Apulia), where he made confession as a lay brother. In spite of his ignorance, his exceptional goodwill earned him a place among the religious of the choir, and he was ordained as a priest in 1628. His popularity as a thaumaturge, or miraculous healer, brought him under suspicion and he was summoned to appear before the Inquisitors of Naples, who ordered him to retire to the monastery in Assisi. He was later transferred to the Capuchins at Pietrarubbia, then to Fossombrone (Duchy of Urbino), from where he was sent to the Friars Minor at Osimo (the Marches). It was there that he died, on the 18th of September 1663, aged sixty years."[3]

4

It was during the "phony war." I was in Paris. It was the last day of my leave before returning "to the front," so, to take my mind off it, I was browsing through some books and making notes.

A knock at the door.

"Come in!"

It was my son, the fighter pilot.

"Is it really you, Rémy? Everything OK?"

"Are you on leave?"

"If you can call it that. Just twenty-four hours off."

"Lucky you didn't miss me. I'm leaving tonight, you know."

"Me, too."

"Come here and let me give you a hug. Where are you? What are you doing? Is it hell? I thought you were in eastern France. You know, I get bored in Arras, so I often go and visit the Maginot Line, and, once I get to Rheims, I ask every French squadron I come across whether it's the one you're in. But I've never had the luck to run across you, nor your brother. His regiment must be somewhere in the Vosges. Have you heard anything from Odilon?"

"Odi is at the front in the Alps, I heard from him recently. He's enjoying himself, doing winter sports. As for me, I've been drafted to the night defense of Paris, so you won't be able to meet me in Rheims anymore."

"Pretty grim, huh?"

"Yeah, not much fun. We patrol at a height of eight to ten thousand meters. After a while, the oxygen mask becomes a pain in the ass."

"Poor old fellow!"

"And you, Blaise, are you happy?"

"I'm all right. I get on very well with the English. They're good chaps. We drink together. I'm always dashing about all over the place, and I'm always hoping to run into you or your brother. You must admit, that would really be something, eh? And what a great subject for a Christmas calendar—father and son meeting at the front, the old guy and the youngster, the amputee and the hero, the father wearing an English uniform and hugging a young French pilot or an elegant staff sergeant in the Alpine Infantry! The Entente Cordiale, eh? France and England forever!"

"You're kidding me, Blaise. Anyway, I hope I'm not disturbing you. Were you writing something?"

"Oh, nothing! Just browsing. By the way, tell me, Rémy, who is your patron saint of aviation nowadays?"

"Our patron saint? I don't know, Blaise. In our squadron, we have a Sioux's head as our emblem."

"But that's not what I'm asking you, dear boy. The Sioux's head is an insignia, the insignia of the Lafayette Escadrille. It's the distinguishing mark of a group. Originally, when the Lafayette Escadrille was formed in the First World War, it was, at most, a sentimental emblem for the American pilots who had come to France to enlist, like my friend Joseph W. Stilwell, who is now a general in the Chinese Air Force.[4] It was a totem, a kind of talisman, a mascot if you like, or a good-luck charm. The Sioux's head isn't a patron saint."

"What do you mean by a patron saint, Blaise?"

"A patron saint? Why, a saint who protects you, dear fellow. Someone to whom you can address your prayers. A personification of the guardian angel. You can choose anyone from the long list of male and female saints of the Catholic Church, which, whatever you may think, is among the most active and the most modern…"

I saw my son smile surreptitiously.

"So, nowadays, you don't have a patron saint of aviation?"

I pressed the point.

"Not as far as I know," Rémy replied. He'd got his pilot's license, in 1936, at Bourges, that is to say, during the most catastrophic period of French aviation, when the schools for pilots lacked not only planes and fuel but also discipline and, above all, faith. A whole series of ancient crates and kites had been assigned to the student pilots on account of their poor maneuverability, including—although they only used them two days out of three, to cut down the risks—the infamous Bloch 210, known as the "flying coffin."

"A lot of our guys," Rémy continued, "have a Saint Christopher's medal screwed into their instrument panels. But that's just bunk, OK for Sunday drivers, maybe. They're overdoing it, putting them in their kites. Can you imagine, Blaise, what it's like to be on board a Curtiss, doing five hundred kilometers an hour? I can assure you, it's very different from driving along a macadam road in your little run-about, with momma's dear little pooch sitting at your side!"

"So, you don't carry anything in your cockpit, not a medal, not a lucky charm, not even your penpal's silk stocking? You must have a wartime sweetheart who writes to you, huh?"

"A silk stocking for a crash helmet, oh boy, that's a laugh! But, Blaise, the girls don't wear them anymore, they go bare-legged."

"And your wartime girlfriend?"

"That's old-fashioned."

"But you must have a girl?"

"Yes. Just for my leave. Twenty-four hours. Picked her up at the movies."

"Well, then, what are you waiting for? Bring her here! Wait, I'll give you the cab fare, go and get her, we can have lunch together."

"Oh, she wouldn't like that!"

"Why not? Do I know her?"

"No. She works for a baker, delivering the bread, but she's out of work right now, she wouldn't dare..."

"What the hell does that matter! I bet she's pretty. Tell her I'll have an English general at my table, and that old Mother Lampen, who runs the restaurant, will make us a splendid *fricassée*. In my day, the medal of Notre-Dame de Lorette was very popular among pilots, is that passé now, too?"

"No, not at all, but I think it's only the mama's boys in our squadron who carry those."

"And animal mascots? I knew an English pilot who carried a panda in his cockpit."

"No, all we've got is a big dog somebody brought from a farm, and we use him as a punching bag every morning. Ah, he's a good old brute and we have a lot of fun with him!"

"Great, you could use him as a tennis ball, too. But I see that you don't have a patron saint of aviation, so I'm going to provide you with one. Tell me, Rémy, do you want to get rich after the war?"

"Of course, old man, that's all I want. But how?"

"All you have to do is make one of the great saints fashionable and launch the new patron saint of aviation."

"And you've got one, Blaise?"

"Yes, dear boy, and an ace, a pioneer, a record-breaking champion who flew without wings and without an engine, and even managed to fly backwards! And that's a record that's never been beaten since, in spite of all the progress in aviation. You see, he's a very modern saint..."

"And he is...?"

"Saint Joseph of Copertino."

"Oh, shit! The patron saint of exams!"

"The man himself. But he's not been properly appreciated. His place is not among students, he'd be much happier among aviators. You'll see, one day I'll write his history for you. He's the champion of levitation. As I told you, he's an ace. But it's time to go. Hurry up! Run and fetch your sweetheart. Lunch is on me."

5

The kids had not turned up. I was pacing up and down outside my house on the Avenue Montaigne, arm in arm with General Winter, explaining to him that I was waiting for my son who had gone to fetch his girlfriend, who was sure to be quite a character, and that I hadn't seen my son for five months, that is, not since the beginning of the war, and that he had to rejoin his squadron that very evening, like me, for I had to return to Arras. I also told him that, at his own request, I had arranged for my youngster to be transferred from the bombardiers to the fighter squadron, thanks to the personal intervention of President Lebrun. Meanwhile, Mme. Lampen was worrying about the lunch, which was already cooking, and she kept coming to the door to see whether we had made up our minds to sit down to table yet, and some of the locals from my *quartier,* failing to recognize me in my British uniform, were turning around for another look, and probably taking me for a second English general.

General Winter had been through all the British Empire's campaigns during the last fifty years, including the campaign in France in 1914–18. On the declaration of war in September 1939, he had reenlisted, but, because of his great age, he had been appointed courier to the King, not to save him from the risks, but to spare him, as far as possible, from the exertions of a campaign that was expected to be extremely tough for the British Expeditionary Forces. He was a distinguished old gentleman, intelligent and well read, and his conversation covered an amazingly wide range of topics, illustrated and documented by things he had seen in the four corners of the world; he was a free spirit, without prejudices, delightful company, courteous in an almost oriental fashion, and this old gentleman had taken a great liking to me, questioning me, making me talk, taking notes, and asking my permission to write my biography one day.

And that was what astonished me most in my dealings with the British officers at General Headquarters in Arras: this mania they all had for taking notes, recording the most minute items, and keeping detailed and circumstantial secret diaries. It was probably a habit they had acquired at university in England, where debates, meetings, reports, and clashes of conflicting opinion are daily events. This practice gives great flexibility to the critical mind and sharpens one's powers of observation, and, through its constant exercise, accustoms one to take account of realities. Rémy de Gourmont remarked that only the English know how to write a biography giving the weight, the measurements, the bodily temperature, and all the physical details of a life, no matter how spiritual it may be, and all this without resorting to anthropometry or tracing documents, but simply as if perceived in a vision. I have always claimed that the English are the greatest dreamers in the world, and that they would never have succeeded in, for example, building their Empire, achieving this concrete reality in time and space, without a profound indulgence in dreaming, the daydreaming of an entire nation. And the living word of Churchill—in contrast to the mealymouthed democratic abstractions of Roosevelt, the marvelous silence or the holy wrath of Stalin, the recriminations, complaints, accusations, threats, whinings, *mea culpas,* and all the posturings of masochistic madness of Hitler, the bark and bluster of Mussolini, the mongrel yelps or the crocodile tears of Reynaud or de Gaulle—the living, prophetic word of Churchill during the Second World War, announcing: "blood, toil, tears and sweat," gave renewed life and hope to the millions of listeners tuned in to the BBC, because this dreamer, whose humor, and conviction shook the Jerries to the core, derived his ideas from reality, tragic and desperate though it was, and this prophet, with his profound good sense, his cynicism, his way of calling things by their name without sentimentality and without letting himself be led astray by preconceived theories or gulled by received ideas, spoke from day to day as a good fighter, without ever losing sight of the Earth, and the destiny of Man, and herein lies the key to the English dream.

I do not know what became of General Winter's secret notebooks, or what they contained, but probably they were destroyed by the explosion of the bomb that killed him, during the first air raid on Arras, on May 7, 1940. Toward ten in the evening, the old gentleman, who was in the habit of staying in the mess with us until midnight to drink a final whiskey, excused himself, got up and went to bed, feeling ill-at-ease. A few seconds later—although no Alert had been sounded—a German bomb blew up the Hôtel de l'Univers. The mess, which was across the road in an annex, was untouched. The bomb had gone off on the mezzanine floor, right in the General's room.

"The old man died in bed, as all generals do," remarked a Canadian major.

Amid the wreckage, I found my radio, and it was still going. It had come crashing down with the rest of the fourth floor. I never found out who had turned it on.

There were some thirty dead, including the prettiest waitress in the hotel and the children of the owner.

Beneath the debris, all the General Staff's red tape was burning.

The German bombers had excavated a new avenue through the town, an avenue that cut perpendicularly across the main street of Arras.

6

A taxi had just pulled up at the curb, and before it had even stopped, my son leaped out, smiling, alert, brisk, and doing his utmost to extricate his girlfriend from this absurd aerodynamic vehicle. Rémy, who was a good-looking kid, was bare-headed. If it had not been for his uniform, and the heavy leather jacket he was bundled up in (there was a badge in the shape of a dog dangling by a cord from one lapel), you would have guessed him to be seventeen. General Winter and I were some six feet away, watching the scene. A pair of long bare legs emerged from the cab, with the skirts tucked up to mid-thigh, there was a resounding burst of laughter and then a tall girl stepped out and shook herself like a wet dog. She had on a hat of tarred canvas, like the ones worn by old-time sailors.

My God! Where had this great big *gamine* unearthed such a hat in Paris? But I did not have time to think of the answer, for the girl was already hanging around General Winter's neck, having mistaken him for the father of her darling pilot, and, chattering non-stop, she was dragging him into old Mother Lampen's restaurant.

The girl was impossible—a great, vulgar, strapping wench, and she was wearing the most miserable little dress, but she was as beautiful as an angel; she had youth and vivacity and she was the most ravishing daughter of the people I have ever had the good luck to meet. And she was dirty, but really dirty, as dirty as she was greedy, which is saying a good deal, for no sooner were we at table than she began dipping into all the dishes, guzzling away like someone who does not get the chance to eat every day, who is still a kid, but avid, for she has all Paris to conquer yet, and she has just worn herself out during a whole night of love in the arms of her young lover.

"Ah! Your son, M'sieu," she said to General Winter between two mouthfuls. "How kind he is. I'm just crazy about him!"

Rémy was amused at the girl's mistake, but he was full of little attentions, fussing over his mistress-of-the-moment, refilling her plate and her glass, urging her to eat and drink, whispering into her ear: "Don't be shy, Dad's paying, give yourself a treat..." and we, the old general and I, were enchanted, this girl was so beautiful to look at with her teeth, her fingers, her jaws constantly working, her stomach dilating, her sighs of contentment, her appetite like a young animal's, her total lack of embarrassment at her bad manners, her fire, her ardor, and for once I will not even mention the food, although old Mother Lampen's cooking—her ham in Madeira, her *poulet cocotte,* her cheese soufflé—was famous and she had really surpassed herself that day. Nor will I say anything about the Montrachet that I had bottled myself, in the days when old Lampen was still alive, in 1927, a vintage year.

To see this little tart eat was a spectacle, but to study her dirt was a rare treat, it was as entertaining for me as deciphering a palimpsest would be for a scholar of ancient documents. I am not referring to her red hands, her nails in mourning, nor to her uncombed hair that hung down in two tufts, two frowzy lumps, from under her astounding hat. She had at least two weeks's makeup on her mug, which made a curious color-foundation, and beneath this, the furrows of dirt running down from behind her ears and in the folds of her neck blurred her features and made it hard to decipher them and reestablish the natural harmony and the graceful proportions. She was like a portrait by Picasso. Worse. And what's more, probably in her joy at being invited, and in her haste to sit down to table, she had plastered rouge on her cheeks and blue eyeshadow under her eyes, and these colors made two contrasting circles; her lips were like parallel bars hardened and encrusted with stale lipstick, and in spite of all that, her pert manner was so vivacious, her eyes so full of laughter, her smile so luminous, her teeth so dazzling, her laugh so infectious when it gurgled up from her throat, that this dirt and this grotesque makeup, like a gilded and over-ornate frame encircling a fragile hand mirror, this dirt and the layers and layers of makeup threw her soul into relief, showing it up as a twittering of birds, a pure heart, a naive sauciness and insouciance, and there was not the shadow of an ulterior motive or vice or studied affectation.

She was Nature herself.

"Mademoiselle may I do something for you?" I asked her at the end of the meal, while she was gleefully dunking a marzipan cake into a *crème au chocolat* and smearing it all over her cheeks like a baby. "Rémy tells me you're out of work..."

"That's right, M'sieu, there ain't no more work for me. I used to work in the bakery on the Rue Jacob."

"Oh, is that bakery closed now?"

"No, M'sieu, but I ain't got no more customers. They've all went. And the boss don't want me no more. It's the war."

"Let's see, I know that bakery on the Rue Jacob. They had lots of customers there at one time, Americans and..."

"Yeah, that gang are gone, cause of the war. Just my luck. I used to make hundreds of francs in tips. They weren't a stuck-up lot, all them artists. But I didn't drink, I spent the money on goin' to the movies, instead. That's where I met Rémy."

"Well, then, you must have delivered bread to some of my friends. Do you know Gertrude Stein?"

"No kiddin', you know 'er, M'sieu? You're talkin' about a funny customer there! She used to make me stop and talk, and she asked me this, that, and the other, wanted to know everythin'. She'd've made me late on my rounds, so I went to 'er last of all. But she was my best customer."

"And Miss Sylvia, Hôtel de la Grille?"

"Mme. Sylvia, she was a tart. Three cakes a day and lots of hot croissants and millefeuilles."

"And Mme. Bruce, the painter's wife, on the Rue Furstenberg?"

"Ugh, don't make me laugh, M'sieu! I can see you know 'em all. How funny she was, that dumpy little woman, always grumblin' and grousin' at you and sayin' she didn't get no service. For her, it was long loaves and bread sticks. She said they was never well-done enough, she had to have 'em crusty. But she was a good soul. One day, she give me a lovely dress with a train, but I've never been able to wear it. Too big, I was drownded in it. So I chucked it out, cause I wasn't goin' to give a lovely dress like that to any of my pals."

"And The Kid, on the Rue Jacques-Callot?"

"Ow, Miss Kid! That one! She always wanted me to dance in her studio and, to annoy her cleaning lady, I did an act for her, cause I knows how to walk on my hands, M'sieu. After that, when I rang the bell, I used to hand in the bread with my head hangin' down, and the old char used to go mad and insult me."

"And you don't know anything else, you don't have a trade?"

"No, M'sieu, I'm a baker's girl. And now all them ladies have gone back to America, the boss don't need me no more. I'm out of work. Oh, this war!"

"Listen, Mademoiselle, next time I come back on leave, I'll introduce you to a friend of mine. He's a *couturier,* and he'll make you into a model."

"Wassat? An' what'll I have to do?"

"They will teach you to wash your face and to do your hair nicely, they will dress you in the most beautiful gowns in Paris, and all you'll have to do is saunter around the salons, not on your hands, of course, but like a great lady, with fine manners, full of airs and graces. You must have seen them at the movies."

"And d'you think they'd have me, M'sieu?"

"Why not, Mademoiselle? You are beautiful."

"Ooh, that'd be heaven! Ooh, you're a good sport, you are!"

7

The four of us were riding in a cab. I had to drop General Winter at the British Embassy where I myself had to go to get a copy of the latest communiqué from the Air Ministry. It would only take me a moment. On the Rue du Faubourg-Saint-Honoré, I told the driver to wait for me at the corner of the Rue d'Anjou, and I told the kids to behave themselves.

"I'll be back in a minute, Rémy. Then we'll go and find a medal of Saint Joseph of Copertino for you. Surely to God I'll be able to get one somewhere."

The kids, sitting facing one another, were as good as gold, the girl, surfeited and happy, with her hat squashed against the back of the seat; my son, who had left off his leather jacket, so that I could see the pilot's rosette on his chest as well as the insignia of the Sioux's head, sitting bolt upright on the jump seat. His features were drawn and there was faraway look in his eyes. I was struck by both the somberness of that look and his resemblance to his mother. Poor fellow! A tough job.

"OK?" I said to him.

"OK," he answered.

General Winter was waiting for me in the porch of the embassy. When I rejoined him, he took me by the arm and guided me across the main courtyard. As we were climbing the narrow staircase that led to the Air Attaché's suite, he said: "*That fille française* is most amusing."

And he pushed open the door of the office.

Once again, there was nothing in the communiqué.

"What a phony war!" I murmured. "It's disappointing."

"No," he said, "it's worrying, extremely so..."

Before we parted at the foot of the stairs, he said, "You're going back to Arras tonight. Well then, take this." And General Winter opened his briefcase and extracted a small package wrapped in tissue paper and pressed it into my hand.

"Oh, it's nothing much! Just a *pagal*. It's for *la fille française*. Tell her it's in memory of a young native girl, a girl who died. I've been carrying it around with me for over forty years. I wanted to make a present of it, but never found the right person. So, you're off back to Arras? See you soon, Cendrars, my friend. That was an excellent lunch. Excuse me now, I must go and see our ambassador."

"To Saint-Sulpice!" I said to the driver. "And hurry..."

Inside the cab, the kids were laughing. Rémy had explained to his baker's girl the gaffe she had made, mistaking General Winter for his father, and she guffawed, "But what's it matter, Rémy? Ha, ha, ha! The old turkey! He looked at you so lovin'-like I thought he was your Dad... I bet he ain't got a son like you!"

"The old turkey, Mademoiselle, begs you to accept this little gift. He asked me to give it to you," I said to the baker's girl, handing her General Winter's little package.

"Whatever is it?" asked the girl in surprise as she unwrapped the crackling, crumpled tissue paper.

"Oooooh, such a bee-you-tiful bracelet!" she cried, slipping the *pagal* on to her arm.

"It's an anklet," I explained to her. "To be worn on the ankle. It's a kind of bell. It's hollow, and inside it there are some little gold nuggets that tinkle when you walk, little slivers of gold."

"Oooooh," said the girl, "d'you think it's made of gold?"

"Well, of course it is. It's the most personal ornament worn by Hindu women. Some of them contain two or three small diamonds that tinkle, very softly."

And I recited:

> He had seen the bayadere for an instant only,
> When she called him,
> Richer was the silver in her voice
> Than in the hollow pagals
> That made a moonlight about her ankles!
>
> O ye Çramanas, women are not to be looked upon!
> (Lafcadio Hearn)*

"Ow!" cried the baker's girl.

She put the *pagal* on her ankle, shook her dirty feet, made the anklet tinkle, burst out laughing, and clapped her hands. And suddenly she started beating the glass panel behind the driver with both fists,

"Driver! Driver!" she shouted. "Go back to the British Embassy! And make it snappy! I gotta give the General a kiss!"

"Driver!" I shouted even louder. "Keep going. To Saint-Sulpice! And make it snappy!"

And to the young girl I said; "My dear, you are crazy. The General sent you this in memory of a young Indian girl, a girl who died more than forty years ago."

The baker's girl took the anklet off her playful ankle, put it away in her handbag, and, without a word, began to cry.

Big tears made furrows through her plastered makeup.

And Remy laughed at her because these tears made her mascara run. The girl wiped them away with a corner of her handkerchief, wiping off her false eyelashes at the same time, then she bit her lips, made faces into the little mirror in her handbag, fluttered her eyelashes because the mascara was stinging her eyes, and finished up by laughing again and putting

---

*I am greatly indebted to Ms. Sylvia V. Metzinger, the Rare Books Librarian at Tulane University, for tracing the source of these lines in a brilliant piece of literary detective work. They come from "The Tradition of the Teaplant", included in Lafcadio Hearn's volume *Some Chinese Ghosts*. They do not, however, constitute a poem in themselves; it would appear that Cendrars lifted odd lines from various parts of the work and put them together to compose this poem, although, of course, his version was in French. According to the glossary at the end of this work, a Çramana is "An ascetic; one who has subdued his senses." (Trans.)

the *pagal* on one arm, then the other, on her ankle, the other ankle, shaking it, shaking it again, and making it tinkle close to her ear.

"And to think it's all made of gold," she said proudly, "and that it's mine!"

Meanwhile, the cab was carrying us across Paris. I dragged Rémy into all the shops that sold devotional objects. My son was amused by it all. But nowhere could I unearth a medal of Saint Joseph of Copertino, neither at Saint-Sulpice nor on the stalls around Notre-Dame des Victoires. Finally, we discovered a statuette of the saint in the chapel of the Orphelins d'Auteuil, and even his statue—but it was a wretched, ridiculous figure— at Saint-Jacques-du-Haut-Pas, his parish in the Latin Quarter.

But there was nothing for sale, not even a novena.

"It doesn't matter a damn, Rémy, I'll still write his history for you and, with a little publicity, you'll still make your fortune. It's up to you to launch the campaign after the war. *Au revoir*, Rémy, and good luck!"

"Good-bye, Blaise."

We were standing in front of the Gare de l'Est, my son was going back to his squadron, and I, I was in a hurry to get to the Gare du Nord in time to catch the train back to the British GHQ, where I was attached as a war correspondent, representing half-a-dozen French newspapers.

Back at Arras, I learned that I was to leave that same night for a big assignment in England, where I was to cover the munitions factories.

Before embarking, I sent my son a postcard, bawling him out:

> Pilot-Sergeant RÉMY,
> Squadron 1/16,
> Postal Sector 897,
> Somewhere in France.   21.2.1940

> My dear old fellow,

> When you are lucky enough to take out a girl as pretty as your baker's girl, hell! The least you can do is pay for her to have a bath and buy her a few rags to put on her back! And if your airman's pay isn't enough, just ask your father for the dough. That's what he's there for. And that's the way it should be.

> With my love,

> Blaise

In the cab taking us from the Gare de l'Est to the Gare du Nord, the Baker's girl, whose address I had noted down so as to recommend her to my friend the couturier asked me:

"D'you think, M'sieu, that it might be the old general's daughter who's dead?"

"What daughter?"

"Well, the one whose ankle bracelet he give me. Probably it was his little girl, don't you think?"

"Why?"

"Cause it's so small."

"She must have had slim ankles. Like Cinderella."

"What? Was she called Cinderella?"

"No, you big ninny. She was a dancer."

"Ow! Cinderella was a dancer?"

And so on. She was dumb. But what a beautiful girl!

Black eyes...

8

I know quite well the kind of criticism I will draw down on my head by writing the life of Saint Joseph of Copertino, I, who have neither the faith nor qualifications for the job.

When it comes to hagiography, scholars and experts are willing to accept as true (or capable of becoming true after they have pored over them) only the *ancient Lives of the Saints,* and it is a fact that, contrary to current opinion, the accounts of the exemplary lives of the more credible saints *which were written by their contemporaries* are rarer, shorter, and stick more closely to the facts, whereas the legendary "Lives," written long after the lifetime of the holy person, are full of *longueurs,* errors, interpolations, mistaken identities and data, romance, dissertations, inventions and propaganda, in short, of fiction, to such an extent that one can safely assert that the introduction of the marvelous into the life of a saint is an infallible sign of untruth, Byzantinism, or Romanticism.

Let me hasten to add that I am not revealing any new facts or uncovering any new documents in my account. Due to the circumstances and the conditions under which this study was made and my tale written, while I was moving about from pillar to post during the "phony war," in France and England, and later, during the retreat, the exodus, and the Occupation, I did not have access to the sources, nor was I able to haunt the libraries and study the archives (nor did I have any wish to do so!); my documentation is made up of bits and pieces gathered along the way, from chance encounters, conversations, and browsing in old books, and I have not done any systematic research. I have simply used whatever fell into my hands during the long war, and my various moves and peregrinations, which means that, principally, all my quotations are drawn from the standard work by Olivier Leroy, *La Lévitation,* a work I have already mentioned and, for certain small details, from third- and fourth-rate works of popularization, and if, in spite of everything, I have written this story, it is not to try my hand at a genre that has produced some succinct masterpieces, nor as an exercise in writing, or in Holy Scripture, nor in imitation of anybody, nor out of simplicity, but *primo:* because I promised Rémy I would do it— Rémy, who will not be launching the new Patron Saint of Aviation because the Americans have beaten him to it, and because, meanwhile, my son has been killed in a flying accident; *secundo:* because, although he has been canonized, Joseph Desa, a native of Copertino (Apulia), is a droll personality who fascinates me, and *tertio:* because levitation is the art of instantaneous travel, and I would very much like to know how to do it since I have seen natives in the great virgin forests of the Amazon indulge in it by taking *ibadou.* And besides, as I said to Rémy, St. Joseph of Copertino is a pioneer, a precursor, a champion, and an aviation ace, since, to this very day, he is still the only one to succeed in flying backwards, *retrorsum volantem,* as the Bollandists put it.

But I must admit that, just as, after 1943, when an informer for the Gestapo came to lodge next door to me in Aix-en-Provence, taking a room on the same floor as my furnished apartment, I used to put my radio in my bed, turn it very low, and smother it under seven blankets when I wanted to tune in to London or Moscow, so, in the same way, the flights of Saint Joseph of Copertino (at that time, I was studying their characteristics in the Bollandists' *Acta Sanctorum* in the library at La Méjanes during the daytime, and often following them in my thoughts at night before falling asleep) came to weave a blanket of dreams between my disturbing neighbor and myself—otherwise, I might have heard him laughing and indulging in solitary drinking bouts—and create visions for me, such as one of Saint Joseph of Copertino flying in the church at Assisi one Sunday morning when it was full to bursting with the faithful and the curious, as well as with a noble congregation of the learned and the worldly, who had come to see for themselves the aeronautic feats of the holy-man-of-the-people, and to report on them and spread the word abroad, for at that time ecclesiastical society was riddled with a kind of snobbery and took sides for and against the flying monk, and it was the disembodied presence of Saint Joseph of Copertino who, hovering in a kneeling position before the tabernacle, dropped one of his sandals, creating such a scandal that his superiors forbade him to appear in public, and who, in some way, padded my door and windows, as if he had covered them with his homespun cassock to keep out the infiltrations of debauchery that came from my disgusting neighbor. This man was a murderer who had killed a coachman, right in front of the house, with a single blow of his fist. He was an Alsatian, and he was dying of shame and male aggression in his breeches, his white stockings, his pigskin gloves, his glistening, greasy skin, his burly shoulders, his bogus air of respectability that was belied by a green Tyrolean hat and an all-too-familiar little clipped mustache, like a circumflex accent above his cigar (and to think nobody shot the bastard, and he lived off the fat of the land in Aix!). I shuddered with repulsion whenever I met him on the stairs, and the skunk used to hum when he was alone in his room, the sound percolating through to me like a subtle infection. I have just said that Saint Joseph of Copertino was a droll character. Another day, he flew from his place in the refectory, brandishing a sea urchin!

I am writing all this in good faith, to excuse the disjointedness of my account.

9

His co-disciples had nicknamed him the Gaper, because his mouth was always hanging open!

Up until his death, at the age of sixty, Joseph of Copertino was constantly being reprimanded.

At home, his father, who was a cobbler, tried to teach the boy his trade, but had to scold him repeatedly for his absent-mindedness at work. Since Joseph was the eldest of twelve children, a good-for-nothing and a bad example to his brothers on account of his perpetual wool-gathering, the father was at his wits' end as to what to do with him; they could not keep him and feed him if he did not work, for it was a poor household and the cobbler's trade brought in only a pittance, so, throughout the long winter evenings, Felice Desa, Joseph's father, sat before the hearth and discussed the matter with his wife, Francesca Panara, two of whose brothers were monks with the Friars Minor. At last, they decided to send Joseph to the monastery and try to get him educated.

Early one Sunday morning, therefore, the cobbler closed his little workshop and, leaving his brood in the care of a neighbor, set out with his wife to present Joseph to Uncle Anselmo after Mass. This uncle, who was also one of the mother's brothers, was the parish priest of Copertino. All along the way, the cobbler was berating his son:

"Walk ahead of us, you big dawdler. Can't you see you're getting on our nerves, always lagging behind? We're ashamed of you. Come on, get going, walk in front! Hup two!"

And very docilely, without a word, Joseph took the lead. He was a sturdy, well-built boy. He was not yet fifteen, but looked eighteen, and already had the shadow of a mustache and downy hairs on his chin and cheeks. His mother sighed with relief to see him stepping out smartly ahead of them. But soon the father started grumbling again because—although nobody quite knew how it had happened—Joseph was again dawdling behind them, and daydreaming instead of hurrying along on the heels of his parents.

It was a beautiful spring morning. The sky was translucent. The chimes of the churchbells were wafted on the pure air.

"Come on, giddy-up, you big donkey, walk in front!" shouted the father.

Humble and docile, the taciturn, incomprehensible boy once again began to trot along in front of his parents, twisting his ankles on the roughly-laid cobbles of the tortuous little roads that ran from the distant hamlet toward the cathedral, whose pierced towers rose above the rooftops and the jumble of terraces at the summit of the old town; but his eyes were fixed on heaven, his mouth agape, he kept stopping, and starting, silently, obstinately, zigzagging like the donkey who turns the mill or staggers beneath his burden, and slips backward, on the steep hill and gets beaten for his pains. Everyone has seen these little donkeys in Italy, skinny creatures who walk as if they had sprained their ankles, half-smothered beneath their load, their backs rubbed raw, the sores on their haunches kept constantly open by their master's crooked stick and the swarms of blue-bottles; they hang their heads down lamentably, their heads with those atrophied wings, the angelic ears of the ass, one of which is often broken and the other ocellated with a cyst. This little creature is the very image of humility and resignation, but have you ever put your arms around one of these donkeys' muzzles? Their gaze is unfathomable. Under their frizzy skulls, great philosophical thoughts are churning, as well as plenty of lively humor, a repressed wildness, and something strangely fraternal, which makes them wink their eyes and smile.

> ORISON: *Prayers that we may go to Heaven with the asses.*
> *...O Lord...*
>
> (Francis Jammes)

10

So Uncle Anselmo presented Joseph to the Friars Minor, but they refused to accept him, largely at the instigation of two other uncles, eminent members of this order, who judged the boy to be incapable of studying anything and would in no way yield to the arguments of the good parish priest who appealed to their family sentiments and pointed out that, with each new birth, their brother-in-law, the poor shoemaker, was crushed by yet another burden.

Undaunted by this first setback, the priest of Copertino persuaded the Capuchins of Martina to take in his nephew as a lay brother, but, at the end of eight months' novitiate, they dismissed Joseph and sent him back to his parents on account of his notorious clumsiness, his absent-mindedness, and his incapacity for manual labor.

One can imagine the father's fury, and how he grumbled when he saw his overgrown booby of a son (Joseph was going on seventeen by now) return to his place in the wretched little cobbler's workship, a boy who was hopelessly inept at the shoemaker's trade and often so distracted that, when he hammered the sole on to a shoe, he would hit his fingers, or let the hammer slip from his hand, without even noticing, and there he would sit, nailed to his stool, his eyes turned up to heaven, his mouth gaping, like the village idiot. The father shrugged his shoulders, weary of scolding the boy, and turned back to his cobbler's last:

"If only you could run errands for me, it would be something," he complained, "but you're useless, you forget everything."

The parish priest of Copertino, moved by the mother's tears and lamentations, and by compassion for this pious, docile boy, whom he did not want to see driven to despair, finally won over the other two uncles and, this time with their support, persuaded the Friars Minor to accept Joseph as an oblate. He was given the special task of caring for the convent mule, and the humble stable boy—of whom it was later said, *"He spent half his life in the air"*—did his utmost to carry out the simple tasks he was given at the Convent of La Grotticella.

Joseph was a model of obedience.

Years and years later, when "Obedience" proved to be the only word that had the power to bring him out of his frequent trances and ecstatic levitations, he was in the habit of saying: "Obedience is the knife that cuts off the will of man... 'Obey!'... At this word, God closes the curtain..."

11

"From his earliest childhood," state the acts of his process for canonization, "he showed such signs of sanctity that it was only his youth that prevented his already being venerated as a perfect being."

But at the Convent of La Grotticella, the humble servant-monk, who was not destined for holy orders, was always being reproached, growled at, bullied, and treated like a donkey and a dolt, because never before had the monks seen such a simpleton.

"Sir, do you remember Brother Jean, whom Jacques de Voragine talks about?" a certain Irish padre, chaplain to the Welsh Fusiliers, asked me one evening when we were standing under the eaves of a barn, sheltering from the rain, and the pair of us were dying of boredom. We were on night maneuvers near Carvin (Pas-de-Calais); the First Brigade was moving in convoy with headlights full on, and we were expecting to see German planes swoop down at any moment on this long serpent of fire wriggling across the plain.

"It's a simple exercise," the Brigadier had said when he heard our gasp of astonishment at this rash spectacle and the comments we could not help making. He had been sheltering with us under the overhanging roof.

The Staff Captain had gone one better:

"An exercise and an inspection," he had said. "All parts of our vehicles must function well. Including the headlights."

"Yes, but there's a war on!" I had said.

"And what a phony war!" the Irish chaplain had added. "A very phony war indeed."

"I have given my precise orders," retorted the Brigadier-Major, fuming, as he strode off into the rain, followed by his little Staff Officer, to go and sit in the command car.

We could hear the radio crackling.

The chaplain and I had been discussing aviation, and I had mentioned the name of Joseph of Copertino, so we had started talking about the saint, each of us puffing away at his pipe. They were racing the engines and the continual changing of gears set our teeth on edge. Wherever we looked, it was nothing but vehicles bumping into one another, bouncing, floundering, bogging down, even the caterpillar treads were slithering about and the men were paddling in the wet mud. We could hear them cursing and swearing, exasperated by this infamous mud of Flanders, which, so many times in history, had proved fatal to the success of English armies: "Bloody hell! Damn and blast it!"

"Don't you remember Brother Jean in *La Légende Dorée?*" the Father asked me. "He was a gardener-monk, and the laughingstock of his community. Out of all the prayers, the only thing he ever learned to recite by heart were the first two words of the *Ave Maria*. And he recited them incessantly. After his death, they saw a lily growing out of his tomb, and imprinted on the calyx were the words that Brother Jean had been in the habit of repeating endlessly and under all circumstances: *Ave Maria!* The Superior gave orders to exhume the body. And then the whole convent saw that this miraculous lily had its roots under Brother Jean's tongue and was blossoming out of his mouth. So they all understood, then, that the gardener they had so despised for his simplicity was a saint, the saint of pure humility."

And the Irish chaplain went on with some rancor:

"I don't know what old book I read it in, but your Joseph of Copertino was even denser than the gardener-monk. It seems that, out of all the prayers recited at office, Brother Joseph only managed to grasp one word, the word *Amen!* And as for the science and the theology they tried to teach him at the convent, he retained nothing, absolutely nothing of all that. Ach, what a dope! and to think they've made this scatterbrain the patron saint of candidates for the priesthood and people taking university degrees, yes, they've actually recommended that students address their prayers to him, to intercede for them in their exams! You would have had to be an angel straight from heaven not to lose patience and despair of such a pupil—stubborn, backward, taciturn, absent-minded, never saying a word in answer to all their reproaches, a lad who, when they questioned him in class, replied triumphantly: *Amen!* then sat there with his mouth open, no matter how perseveringly, how gently, how caringly they tried to rouse his attention. He must have been a bad example to his fellow pupils, and such strange behavior on the part of an ungrateful boy, who had only been taken in out of charity, must have been a stumbling block to his teachers, since it must often have caused them to fall into the sin of anger, so it's only natural they should have turned away from him, little by little, relegating him to the kitchens and then, as he broke far too much crockery, being clumsy as well as lazy, to the pigsty..."

"I beg your pardon, Father," I interrupted him, "but I believe he was sent to the stables, to take care of the convent mule."

"If you like," replied the Irishman, "well then, they sent him to the stables, where he had time to stand gaping all day long and give himself up to his tiresome, incomprehensible stupidity."

"Perhaps he conversed with God?"

"Oh, do you think so? I used to teach in a college in England, and I distrust these silent types. They're generally the crafty ones."

"Forgive me once more, Father, Jospeh may have been a donkey, but he wasn't wicked," I said.

"And that was the worst fate that could have befallen him!" the chaplain of the Welsh Fusiliers retorted. "In fact, there was no ill will in him, no passion, no trace of morbid pleasures. He was as healthy and robust as on the day he entered the convent. And that was the worst possible thing— since *he* wasn't interested in anything, nobody took any interest in *him* anymore. There was no longer anything to reproach him for, except his woolly-mindedness. They'd had enough of his clumsiness, so they turned him into a groom or a swineherd. And little by little they forgot him. Can you imagine, Sir, what that would mean? To be forgotten in a convent? It's like, well, it's like a sentry forgotten in the depths of the night... Just imagine what it would be like if a man were forgotten tonight... all alone, at the far end of this plain... lost in solitude and the rain."

"I think you're exaggerating, Father. He was admitted to the choir. Certain of the friars at the convent had noticed him. They spoke of him with considerable respect. They had guessed that Joseph had been specially marked out by Our Lord. In their writings, they speak of his constant union with God, his active charity, his mortifications, and, at the process for his canonization, others bore witness for him, saying they had learned more from their conversations with this bumpkin than from the most venerated theological works. Besides, this poor boy never lacked for powerful protectors, the Bishop of Nardo, the Bishop of Castro, the Pope himself, Urban VIII, Benedict XIV, Clement XIII who canonized him."

"Oh, that's what people always claim after the event, and besides, it's quite possible that, in the end, everyone was impressed by the extravagant tales told about this madman. But do you believe in that, in levitation? It's nonsense. Humbug. If I'd been his teacher at school, I'd have tanned his backside for him, as we do at home in Ireland."

"And who told you, Father that God didn't do just that?"

The Father looked at me, dumfounded. He took his pipe out of his mouth: "Are you turning this into a joke?" he said.

"No," I said. "He did it to teach him to fly. One hefty kick and you fly away, you're launched."

At this point, we separated. The night maneuvers were over. The Jerry planes had not appeared. We had been damned lucky! Everyone went back to his distant billet. But, in the little Morris that was taking me back, I carried on the conversation with the Irishman in my mind, and I thought of Roland Garros's journal, and of those emotional disturbances, that strange longing to fly, to fly away, that a great many youngsters experience during puberty, and about which Garros speaks at some length. I myself, at the age of fifteen, often experienced these flights in dreams, and they were deeply satisfying.

What is it these boys dream of? Roland relates how they would throw themselves out of windows in sensuous delight and go and peer in at other people's windows, especially the skylights and the *oeils-de-boeuf* in the attics where the maids slept. Rarely did they stray far from their parents' rooftops—the cases he describes were in Nice—although sometimes they would risk a flight above the town, but, when this occurred, they were seized with such terror that they hurriedly returned, waking up with a start. As for me, I made my flight over the basin of the port in Neuchâtel, Switzerland, where my father had had the bizarre idea of sending me to the Commercial School (in 1902) and from which I escaped to make my way to China (in 1904), and I soared, I looped the loop, I indulged in delightful and somewhat vertiginous evolutions, plunging down to sea level or rising very high in the air, as high as the tips of the poplars that line the quay to the left of the basin, in front of the western facade of the Musée de Pury, and this windowless facade, with its heavy masonry, attracted me so strongly and made me so dizzy that I was just about to crash into it head-first when I woke up, and for a moment I stayed there, unable to return to my bed, totally bewildered and amazed.

Garros's journal is the most extraordinary document, and the most pic-turesque and vivid account you could ever wish to read of the early days of aviation in France and throughout the world; a hundred or so pages are devoted to the displays Garros was obliged to give with a circus in the United States to earn some money, since his family had cut off his allowance in the hopes of bringing him to heel, and he sketches a hundred pen portraits of eccentric characters who had suddenly been smitten with a passion for flying and who wanted to be pilots: cowboys, financiers, mechanics, drunks, women, all more or less nut cases who wanted to undergo at least the baptism of the air, and who dragged him into all sorts of wild adventures, generally ending up in bars where they drank dazzling cocktails (an innovation!); Garros gives a spectacular list of them. He also describes the training of an elite pilot who emerged safe and sound from the thousand and one risks, and the innumerable crashes endured by a daredevil.

This journal has never been published. Garros had five copies typed out and sent them personally to five of his friends, mostly his former companions-in-adventure in New Orleans, Mexico, and Havana, on the express condition that they would never publish it or report its existence to the press. In spite of this, I had managed to get hold of one of the copies, but it disappeared, along with all my other papers, when my country house in the region of Seine-et-Oise was burgled, in June 1940. My copy was a 286-page manuscript in the small format known as "large post," carefully typed on both sides of the Dutch paper—the sort of thing a society woman or a courtesan would write her letters on: there were no paragraphs, no spacing, and practically no margins, the whole thing had been typed consistently, in a block, solid as concrete, without a mistake, without an erasure. I have never seen anything like it. A perfect piece of work. To explain who I got it from, and how it came into my hands, would take a whole novel. Perhaps I will write it one day, but it is extremely unlikely. Ah! If Adalbert had known about it, what would that madman have made of it! And there is that amusing page, written so calmly and with such self-mastery, where Roland relates how he lay in the shade beneath the wing of his airplane, smoking a cigarette, contemplating the sea, smiling with pleasure and enjoying his triumph all by himself, before climbing back on board and taking off for Tunis, to be checked in and timed by the officials there, and to announce to them, by his presence, that he had just flown across the Mediterranean. The first man to do it!

12

The years passed.

In June of 1625, a provincial community, the Minor Conventuals of Osimo (the Marches of Ancona), decided to admit Joseph into their order as a cleric. He was overjoyed at being invested with the holy habit and made a fervent novitiate, which brought him to the solemn profession.

The account given by the Capuchin Minor Conventual Friars explains how it was that, through the miraculous aid of God himself, this poor little lay-brother from the Convent of La Grotticella, who could barely read, still less write, was enabled to sail victoriously through what were, for him, the extremely dangerous waters of the examinations, and how and why this poor little brother of the seraphic order—who was, nevertheless, the greatest ecstatic in history—became the protector and patron saint of examination candidates, a role that both the Irish Father and my son Rémy, the aviator, seemed reluctant to grant him:

"The Bishop of Nardo, who admired his virtues, had conferred minor orders and the office of sub-deacon on him, without difficulty. But it was pointed out to Joseph that, in order to be raised to a Deacon, he would have to undergo an examination. Brother Joseph appeared with all the self-confidence of a consummate scholar of the Holy Scriptures. This was not presumption, but filial faith in the Virgin Mother—he had placed his hopes of success in her hands. The Bishop opened the New Testament. As if the Virgin Mary were guiding his hand, he stopped at the Gospel text: *Beatus venter qui te portavit,* on which Joseph meditated constantly, for he adored the Madonna in her maternal aspect. Inwardly thanking his divine protectress, the young cleric read this passage to the glory of the Virgin Mother and then commented on it, piously and knowledgeably. He was congratulated and made a Deacon.

"He still had to pass the most formidable examination, which precedes admission to the priesthood. In the company of several of his brother monks, Joseph appeared before the president of the examinations, the Bishop of Castro, who was renowned amongst the ordinands for his great severity. The first candidates, the elite of the group, answered with faultless learning and skill. The prelate adjudged that it was unnecessary to question the others and admitted them all, including Brother Joseph.

"The hand of God was in it...."[5]

13

Joseph of Copertino was ordained a priest in 1628 at the age of twenty-five.

But I know another version of these famous examinations, which made him so well-known in the world of students. I *could* say, echoing the chaplain of the Welsh Fusiliers, that I no longer remember in which old book I read this, but, in fact, I can state quite definitely that it was in a voluminous and anonymous old tome I picked up in the library in the basement of a fort on the Maginot Line—at least, it said "Library" on a handwritten notice on the door, but when I pushed it open, I found myself in a little cubbyhole where they stored the bundles of out-of-date newspapers and the tattered old books that nobody read, and which the patriotic leagues behind the lines collected indefatigably, appealing to the goodwill of the French nation to give away their collections of old newspapers and magazines that were cluttering up attics and cupboards, and all these unreadable papers, which had escaped the teeth of the rats, the burrowing of worms and the rusty stains of time, and which were meant, in theory, to enlighten the minds and occupy the enforced leisure of men buried alive in the depths of the impregnable concrete line, arrived by the truckload, and the soldiers had to hump all this confounded wastepaper, which was mounting up to the ceiling, and how they swore and blasphemed, furious at this back-breaking fatigue that had fallen to their lot, and never once have I seen a man pick up any of these blessed books and cast so much as a distracted glance at it. God knows what kind of novelty it would have taken to arouse their interest, but it would have had to be something ultra-modern, to match the setting, something in keeping with their ultra-modern armaments and the desperate boredom that was getting the better of them all, every one of these bronzed guys who, like film stars on the fashionable beaches, tanned themselves every day, artificially, with ultra-violet or infrared rays, which the sawbones of the fortress doled out to each of them in turn, just a quarter of an hour every morning, out of professional snobbery and to keep himself amused.

Here is the other version of Joseph of Copertino's examinations:

I do not know why the anonymous author, an Italian, sets the scene at the famous university of Bologna:

The time having come for the theological candidates to make the journey to Bologna, present themselves to the examiners, and take their doctorates, everyone at the convent was rejoicing, except Brother Joseph, who was unconcerned.

On the great day of the departure, the excited candidates piled into a mule-drawn cart, and it started off at a gallop under a hail of whip lashes and with a great ringing of bells.

Only Joseph was left behind.

The Father Superior sent for him to tell him that, now his classmates had left, they could no longer keep him at the seminary and there was nothing to be done but send him home to his father.

"My poor Joseph, you cannot present yourself as a candidate for the examinations. The fact is, you have wasted your time here. I am deeply grieved for your poor father. You will once again be a burden to him," said the Superior as he bade him good-bye.

Brother Joseph kissed the Father's hand and, as was his custom, went off without a word.

"Strange boy! Is he ungrateful?" The Superior asked himself as he looked out through the leaded panes of the window and watched Joseph cross the deserted courtyard and slip out quickly between the two halves of the main gate just as they were closing. They banged shut behind him.

"He left by the main gate. Can he be proud?" mused the Father Superior.

Twenty years later, when he was summoned to Naples, where the Holy Office was inquiring into the innumerable, allegedly miraculous cures that public rumor attributed to this thaumaturge, the tribunal severely admonished him to tell the whole truth, omitting not the smallest detail of his life, and Joseph, under pressure from their questions and a formal order from the judge delegated by the Inquisition, obediently and very humbly admitted that, on that morning, after being turned out of the convent on account of his ignorance and incorrigible stupidity, he went away heartbroken and full of unshed tears, and that he felt such a sense of shame that he did not know how to face his poor parents. But, hardly had he taken three paces on his road, when *he felt himself lifted up,* and this sensation was so intoxicating that he lost all sense of his real surroundings, and he could not say how it came about, but, instead of going home to his good parents, as ordered by the Father Superior, his steps were directed to the lecture hall of the university, and he arrived there just as they were announcing the names of the candidates from his class who had been accepted for examination. And so he, Joseph, the most unworthy and the most ignorant, presented himself before the examiner, *still impelled by this unknown force that had already carried him as far as Bologna,* and brazenly—but unable to stop himself, in spite of his awareness of the absurdity of his position—he asked to be interrogated in his turn, and to all the questions he replied confidently: *Amen!* at which, to his great confusion, instead of being crowned with the dunce's cap, they solemnly placed on his head the square bonnet of a

Doctor of Theology, and, thus adorned—again, he did not know how it happened—*he suddenly found himself transported to the home of his dear parents,* where he was welcomed with joyful demonstrations and tears of admiration, but this made him feel ashamed, especially before his mother. He also stated that, later, he hid himself, and later still, without his knowing how or why, wherever his steps led him, the people, followed him, and, no longer knowing where to hide his shame, in his confusion, *he flew away...*

14

According to the popular legend of his time, Saint Joseph of Copertino was a thaumaturge, a miraculous healer.

There were some crudely colored wood engravings illustrating the anonymous text of the old tome, which I lost on the evening of May 13, 1940, when orders were given for the baggage cluttering the British Expeditionary Forces' trucks to be burned, and for the GHQ to abandon Amiens at once, in the wee hours of the morning, and go to Paris-Plage— or at least, the Press Service was to be sent there—to await reembarkation. Time was pressing and the proud army was short of vehicles. And I couldn't carry all my books in my pockets, even though I had a great many of them, and big ones too, which the tailor had inserted into my uniform at my request, although I hate carrying things in my pockets, because, as a war correspondent, I was obliged to carry a notebook, a pen and, being lazy, my Petit Larousse, and, being a poet, a book on metaphysics, plus a camera! I no longer had a military car, so I went back to Paris by train (the last—and the bombs were falling!) to fetch my own car. Three days later, I rejoined the staff of the AASF (the Advanced Fighting Forces of the RAF), to which I had been accredited by the Air Attaché at the British Embassy in Paris, and it was while I was driving like a bat out of hell down a little road along the banks of the Aisne that, at long last, I had the lucky encounter I had so often wished for, and which was to prove so touching: I ran into Rémy and his crew. It was the evening of the 18th. In the early hours of the 19th, Rémy was to be shot down by flak and land behind enemy lines. How eventful were those tragic days, yet they were only just beginning then and were to rush headlong for another month before we were finally brought to our knees, once and for all! My memories of that time are still vivid and bleeding, and I cannot forget a single thing about that period, not even those seven images from another era, the illustrations to an old, tattered book (now reduced to ashes), a voluminous work of documentation, written in Italian, printed in Padua (probably around 1860), in large Épinal script, such a blessing for the weak eyes of old women, and for the illiterate. The seven images, old woodcuts, were put in for the distraction of idiots and to convert unbelievers, and the crude coloring for the amusement of little children:

FIRST IMAGE: Missing. It must have been a portrait of the saint. Bearded.

SECOND IMAGE: Brother Joseph setting out on the high road to Bologna. He is walking in such a weird manner that people are pointing at him. Peasants in the fields are laughing at him. Some are throwing stones.

THIRD IMAGE: The further he goes, the more conspicuous his unusual gait becomes. Women stare after him, follow in his footsteps. Brother Joseph appears to be gliding, and, when they see that *his feet are not touching the ground,* but move on without effort, his sandals leaving no trace, no footprint in the dust on the road, and that he walks miraculously, like Christ on the waters of Galilee, the women begin crying out that it is a miracle.

FOURTH IMAGE: (a whole series of little scenes in which the saint is rising higher and higher, soaring above the ever increasing crowd gathering in his wake): The women continue to follow him, reciting prayers and singing canticles; they are harvesters, shepherdesses, humble peasants leaving their fields and their cottages for the first time in their lives. And, as they pass through the villages, servants and housewives and wet nurses with their little charges join them. And the nearer they approach to the great city of Bologna, whose bell towers can be seen on the horizon, the more delirious the crowd hurrying on behind *Il santo* becomes. And in every hamlet through which the procession passes, craftsmen, shopkeepers, and villagers leave their workplaces and firesides to swell the crowd. As they go through the towns, the doors of the hospitals and the prisons fly open, the sick rise from their pallets and the prisoners are amazed to see the bars of their cells fall down. *"Il santo!... Il santo!..."*

FIFTH IMAGE: In the university lecture hall. Brother Joseph, perched like a bird on the extreme edge of the examiner's desk, where he is balancing precariously on his knees. With his hands clasped and his eyes turned up to Heaven, he is answering: *"Amen!"*

SIXTH IMAGE: Rome. Brother Joseph floating just beneath the vaulted ceiling of St. Peter's, to the utter stupefaction of the prelates who are standing around a personage labeled: URBAN VIII. (In fact, the general of his order sent him to Rome, and, in the presence of the Pope, Joseph fell into an ecstasy that lifted him off the ground. Urban VIII then declared that, if he outlived this saintly man, he would not fail to testify to this prodigious feat.)

SEVENTH IMAGE: Partly torn off. Portrait of another bearded man. The text says: "Raffaelle Palma, head gardener of the convent at Assisi. Joseph, begging him to repeat the words 'PULCHRA EST MARIA' with him, seizes hold of him, lifts him off the ground and begins to spin around with him in the void."

The other illustrations had been torn out.

15

History further records that, in Naples, when he entered the hall for audiences and presented himself before the Holy Office, who had summoned him on *suspicion of wizardry,* he felt so unworthy that he flung himself face-down at his judges' feet, but, to the amazement of all present, instead of groveling there, Joseph ascended gently into the air and did not stop until he was touching the ceiling of the hall, and there he stayed for half an hour. He was then brought down thanks to the kindly intervention of Father Silvestro Evangelista, his companion, who knew how to talk to him when he was in one of his bodily transports and bring him back to earth through the spirit of obedience. Father Silvestro called on Joseph by name, and he smiled and regained his senses.

Joseph of Copertino was severely censured for this untimely manifestation, which was taken to be a sin of pride, and for the other miracles and cures he had worked, all unwittingly, during the past twenty years. The Inquisition ordered him to retire to an isolated monastery. Urban VIII mitigated this sentence and sent him to the convent in Assisi, where he was enjoined to keep quiet and behave himself by the head gardener, Antonio of Saint Maura, who, considering Joseph a hypocrite, treated him with great coldness. Later on, he was transferred to the solitude of Pietrarubbia, then to the equally isolated Fossombrone (duchy of Urbino), but such was his popularity that hostelries and taverns soon sprang up all around the convent to lodge the curious who flocked to the place, so he was sent back to the Conventual Franciscans at his original convent in Osimo. And it was there that he died on September 18, 1663, at the age of sixty years.

The only clemency granted him, very late in the day, was permission for

Father Evangelista to accompany him everywhere, and without this man's devotion, life would have been impossible, for Joseph was so maladroit in everything he did.

16

But it was not the good Father Silvestro Evangelista, a daily witness to the aeronautical prowess of Joseph of Copertino, who was to give us the details and establish the records. Nor, moreover, was it the Bollandists, although, in their *Acta Sanctorum,* they were so conscientious and so meticulous in making their unprecedented revelations of the behavior that flows from inspiration by the Holy Spirit, for they were not in the least, no, not in the very least interested in these athletic exploits. To learn about them, you must read the heavy tome dedicated to levitation by Olivier Leroy, a university professor and author of several works on political economy. It was he who, with the honors list in his hand, established the figures concerning this form of flying without support, without wings, and without an engine. His book is not a panegyric, but a critical work that reviews all the manifestations of this phenomenon, from the most ancient times down to our own day, among civilized peoples as well as savages, and studies and analyzes the cases of saints of the Church of Rome as well as those of the most famous mediums and sorcerers, giving statistics on height and duration, and setting out comparative charts and synoptic graphs. Thanks to his scientific approach, the subject seems so new that it reads like a novel, the romance of the prehistory of modern aviation and, as with our own effort in the early part of this century, it starts off with tentative gropings and falls, little hops into the air and crashes, for the magicians and demiurges of antiquity and fable did not succeed in their first attempt to rise up and travel through the air, any more than did the Christian saints of the Middle Ages or, indeed, our contemporaries; the incontestable fact remains, however, that of all these conquerors of the pagan empyrean or the Christian heaven, the humble ignoramus Brother Joseph of Copertino holds the championship, not for duration (the Blessed Louis Morbioli of Mantua: three days), nor for height (Colette of Corbie: lost to sight, *oculis evanescens),* but for distance (on the 10th of July, 1657: thirty meters at a height of two and a half meters off the ground) and frequency (at Joseph's hearing for canonization, the role of Devil's Advocate was played by Prospero Lambertini, the future Pope Benedict XIV, who presented the most punctilious *animadversiones* to the Congregation of Rites, and reported seventy confirmed levitations in the environs of the town of Copertino alone! Not to mention the transports *(Raptus est!)* at the convent in Assisi, which were almost daily events and were observed over a period of fourteen years (1639–53). And besides, our poor Joseph is still the only one who has succeeded in *flying backwards!*

17

It was my friend Alexandre Rouhier, the manager of the Vega bookshop on the Boulevard Saint-Germain, the best-stocked bookshop in Paris for works on the occult, who had Olivier Leroy's standard work sent to me at the front. But in this masterly book, Leroy, who reviews all the manifestations of levitation, and even studies those among primitive races, does not mention a single case of posthumous levitation and seems to be totally ignorant of *ibadou.*

A case of post-mortem levitation was brought to my attention by my friend, Edouard Trouin, the owner of the hotel on the hill of the Sainte-Baume, but also the visionary architect who conceived the Cité de la Contemplation, which will one day be built facing the rocky cliff that forms the boundary of this noble and isolated spot from which Mary Magdalen launched herself several times a day and was carried right up to the seventh heaven by angels. It was the case of the Blessed James of Uzès, who flew, in his coffin, all the way from Metz to the ducal burial vault in his native town in Le Gard.

"Jesus, when he had cried again with a loud voice, yielded up the ghost.

"And, behold, the veil of the temple was rent in twain from the top to the bottom; and the earth did quake, and the rocks rent;

"And the graves were opened; and many bodies of the saints which slept arose,

"And came out of the graves AFTER HIS RESURRECTION, and went into the holy city, and appeared unto many." (Matt. 27: 50–53)

And here, it seems to me, we have a second example of posthumous levitation and, what's more, of collective levitation. And what about the Assumption, the carrying of the Holy Virgin up to Heaven? And the Ascension, the miraculous elevation of Jesus Christ? Although it is true that he was the Resurrected One, the living God. And his earthly life came to an end with a levitation:

"And it came to pass, while he blessed them, he was parted from them, and carried up into heaven." (Luke 26:51)

But even Alexandre Rouhier, who is not only a bookseller and a scholar

of the occult but also a Doctor of Chemistry and the author of a monograph, a model of its kind, on peyote, a little Mexican plant, vulgarly
known in Arizona as "dry whiskey," which has the power to induce wonderful visions, yes, even Alexandre Rouhier himself, this fount of knowledge, seems to be totally ignorant of *ibadou,* the plant that renders the
human body capable of rising into the air and moving about without visible support, and of traveling without the apparent action of any physical
force. All the Amazonians cultivate this plant in the secret little gardens
behind their huts, and, when they feel nostalgic, or desire to escape from
the grip of the virgin forest that holds them prisoner, they smoke it in
their short pipes; also, in moments of danger while fishing or hunting, or if
they are mortally jealous of their wives and want to return instantly to
their homes, they chew this weed like a wad of tobacco, it makes them sali-
vate, and they fly away, disappear into the air and land at home complete
with weapons and baggage, taking even their pirogues with them.

18

"In Amazonia, if a stranger happens to find his way into a clearing
belonging to *a man of the woods,* he must not tremble and, above all, he
must not turn his back, otherwise he will be pricked in the heel. He must
enter this ancient refuge of man in a candid manner, present himself openly, and remain calm.

"If he does this, he will be able to observe with his own eyes, and at
close quarters, *the man of nature* as he comes and goes in his lost clearing in
the unfathomable depths of the virgin forest, which is like an island amid
the oceans of chlorophyll.

"If you do not show too much astonishment, your arrival will not cause
alarm, and the Amazonian will carry on with his everyday tasks as if he
were unaware of your presence: he will lay his fire, handle his fencestakes
and his mallet, set his snares, play his reed pipe, tend his traps, and his
nets, throw his lasso or pull in his fishing lines, shoot his bow or blowpipe,
or go and crouch among his calabashes and half-calabashes, his earthen
pots, his utensils and his stone tools, his treasures scattered about on the
relatively clean floor of beaten earth, or squat in front of the oven where he
is heating manioc, or the grill he uses for smoking meat.

"If you are, by nature, a good man—but take care! the primitive creature you have surprised in his lair, even if he is already half-civilized, that
is, a *caboclo* or half-caste, has the gift of second sight and, like a pure-blood-

ed Indian, can read your thoughts—this man will not hesitate to go and stretch out in a hammock strung between two blackened posts beneath an awning, where he will take his siesta, or doze, with one eye open, his poisoned arrows or his *espingarda* (a nasty trader's rifle whose butt is a coilspring) within reach of his hand and guarded by a cascabel, his familiar black snake.

"But if you have succeeded in winning his trust, this 'savage' will even allow you to accompany him behind his hut, into a small secret enclosure he visits several times a day—being mistrustful—where he nourishes, watches over, and tends the plants he has appropriated and keeps hidden there, for he has learned how to domesticate these mysterious plants whose virtues and whose terrible pharmacopoeia he alone knows: sacred plants, demonic plants which he worships, but which he has had to steal at peril of his life from the savage woods, the stifling forest that besieges him, the jungle that is his unique, his mortal enemy, insidious, lethal, and eternal.

"Among these plants—lianas, bushes, ferns, thorns, tubers, palms, mosses, medicinal or poisonous fungi, which he waters with blood or forcefeeds with meat, diurnal and nocturnal plants, some of which bark like dogs at midnight, while others sing melodiously in the wind and still others have nervous breakdowns, like sensitive souls, when the weather is about to change, plants that tear, burn, scratch, cling, adhere, cut, bore, saw, stick like glue, distill perfumes in the night or nauseous stinks at the time of the full moon, plants sternutatory or soporific, and whose fruits, leaves, buds, roots, bark, pollen or seeds are poisons, febrifuge or stupefacient, and from which *the man of the woods* knows how to extract powders or tinctures or syrups, the marrow or the resin, alcohols or unguents, gum or crystals that enter into the composition, often in infinitesimal doses, of the elixirs or the tophus waters, divinatory drugs or love philters, health-giving meal or death-dealing concoctions that he uses lavishly but with careful deliberation—among these plants, then, there is one, the rarest and most magical of all (although it can be found in every secret garden, growing behind every native hut, and every Amazonian carries a little sachet of the dried leaves on him), and this is the most mysterious plant in the forests of Amazonia, for never has a white man succeeded in procuring a plant; because of the psychic disturbances it produces, European scholars, who know of it only by hearsay, have provisionally listed it among those poisons that are most damaging and dangerous to the intellect, those that, as they say, *act on the threshold of consciousness,* and yet every Amazonian smokes it tranquilly in his cutty pipe; it is the *ibadou,* the plant of levitation... a legendary plant thanks to which *the man of nature,* that prisoner of the forest, travels without being obliged, like us civilized creatures, to take ship or airplane."

19

I wrote the preceding chapter on my return from a journey to Amazonia and published it, together with some other articles and photographs, in the newspaper *Le Jour* in 1935. But what I did not write about, even then, was the story of my traveling companion, Captain X, adviser to the Brazilian Embassy in Paris and the only white man capable of giving a firsthand account of the effects of *ibadou,* since he himself levitated after swallowing a certain dose that the native owner of the pirogue he was in forced down his throat just as their fragile craft was about to sink. They had been caught in one of those furious hurricanes that transform the Amazon into a raging sea, falling on you with awful suddenness, and without any warning, when the weather is fine and the sky a cerulean blue. This is the devastating *pirrocca,* which cuts deep swathes in the surrounding forest, hurls down giant trees, makes the most powerful river in the world run backwards toward its source, lifts up huge columns of water, which fall in whirling tornadoes, and travels like a cyclone in abrupt leaps of undreamed-of ferocity. In the blinking of an eye, everything is wrecked. Lightning flashes unceasingly. The thunder rolls on like a tank. The panting firmament is streaked with yellow, and huge storm clouds charge across the sky. There is a smell of ozone, and the heat that comes out of all this turmoil suffocates you and sets you on fire. Electric sparks crackle at your nerve endings. Your eyes are dazzled. The diluvian rain that follows, marking the last phase of the phenomenon, slashes like the blade of a scythe, swinging now here, now there, mowing and reaping, ripping and tearing and razing everything to the ground as it sweeps on and overwhelms you, gashing your skin and drawing blood.

"Well then?" I asked my friend. "What happened to the men in your escort?"

"Drowned."

"Were there many of them?"

"A sergeant and six men."

"And were they in the big pirogue?"

"No, in three small boats, two men, with two native paddlers, in each."

"And you?"

"I was in the small leading pirogue with Jose-Antonho, the guide from Pau-Queimado, a *zambo*,[6] and his son Firminho, a kid of fifteen..."

"And then?"

"And then Jose-Antonho jumped on me, he nearly knocked me out with a blow from a paddle, right in the middle of my forehead, he pushed me over backwards, then held my head up as I lay in the bottom of the pirogue, which was shipping water and about to sink, and, as I opened my mouth to yell, he stuffed a handful of herbs into my mouth, choking me..."

"And did you fly away?"

"No, Senhor, I struggled. The last thing I remember was a sensation of water and icy cold... bitter water running into my mouth, a disgusting bitterness that made me spit and gulp, and a cold that froze my limbs, paralyzing me."

"And then?"

"Then I woke up. The women made me drink a hot broth, some Creole concoction. Jose-Antonho and Firminho were lying beside me. They were still asleep. The mother and grandmother were bustling about. I was sick. Fever..."

"So you weren't back at the camp?"

"No, I was in Jose-Antonho's hut, back at Pau-Queimado, the place he originally came from. It was 300 kilometers from the camp."

"What day was it?"

"The same day. Scarcely an hour had passed since the moment we were shipwrecked, which I had thought was my last..."

"And the pirogue?"

"It was moored to a landing stage."

The diplomatic adviser did not like to talk about this adventure. Nevertheless, I had sought him out in his own home to ask some questions. He was a trustworthy, calm, and level-headed man. He had been living in France for fifteen years and had rented Léon Bloy's villa in Bourg-la-Reine. He had the greatest admiration for this writer because he himself spent his nights writing novels, nostalgic novels in which he evoked, in a romantic language full of singularly complicated syntax and the richest and most precious vocabulary imaginable, the life and the past history of his lost country, for oh! how long they are, those nights when one is plagued by insomnia and bouts of malaria and haunted by the *Green Hell,* as the adviser called the virgin forests of Amazonia—and he had good reason to know them well, having explored them, suffered and battled in them, and barely escaped with his life. As a man of letters, he had acquired the habit of introspection, he was not deceived by words nor liable to be carried away by the sensational. I had every faith in his testimony, and that is why I had come to ask him some precise and particular questions in this peaceful suburban villa, just opposite the Lycée Lakanal, where I myself had been nursed in 1916, after my amputation. At that time, I had been a prey to so many nightmarish sensations, and my mind kept wandering, trying to follow, locate, identify, and pinpoint the surviving agony of that severed hand which still made itself felt, not at the end of my stump, nor in the elbow joint, nor in the center of consciousness, but as an aura, somewhere outside the body, a hand, hands that multiplied and unfolded and opened like a fan, the bony web of more or less crushed fingers, the ultra-sensitive nerve endings finally imprinting on my mind the image of Siva dancing and being rolled under a circular saw that cut off all his arms, one by one; then, I was Siva himself, the man deified. A bewildering sensation... hence Siva's smile...

We sat late around the table. We were drinking *cafesinhas*. I was smoking a black cigar my host had given me. Madame, his wife, throughout the entire recital of this adventure, had been touching wood and murmuring prayers. She disliked hearing her husband recount his exploits from the time when he had been Captain X, attached to Colonel Candido Rondon's peacemaking mission among the Muras Indians in 1921. Next door, in the drawing room, the adviser's daughter, accompanied by her younger sister, was tenderly singing the lovely Bahian song:

> *O, meu sabia!*
> *Deus canta...*
> *A mordinha d'ella!*
> *Non me faz lembra...*

Under these circumstances, what else could I ask the adviser? I could not keep pestering him. Nevertheless, I hazarded another question:

"Tell me, my friend, what were your sensations after swallowing this strong dose of *ibadou?*"

"I don't know. I was suffocating."

"But... don't you have any recollection at all of levitating, of being borne through the air?"

"None."

"No giddiness?"

The adviser did not reply.

"Tell me," I persisted, "what did Jose-Antonho have to say about it all? Did he think it quite natural?"

"Oh, my dear Cendrars, you know the people never speak about these things!" the adviser replied.

St. Joseph of Copertino never made any statement about his levitations, either, and we have every right to ask whether he knew, if he was even conscious of them? He never spoke of them and we know nothing of his personal impressions.

One of the mysteries of God.

20

Granges-les-Vieilles-Églises...

"And it shows great progress, that there, where once the women prayed, cows now ruminate..."

I had planned my route very carefully, so as to sneak away...

I, who for years had been seeking death, was driving like a maniac down the cross-country road that leads to Granges-les-Vieilles-Églises, endlessly repeating this phrase of Rémy de Gourmont's, which had popped into my head through an association of ideas: *"... and it shows great progress, that there, where once the women prayed, cows now ruminate..."*

Granges-les-Vieilles-Églises...

Since May, 10, 1940, surrealism had been stalking the land, not the work of those absurd poets who claim so much and who are, at best, subrealists, since they extol the subconscious, but the conscious work of Christ, the only true poet of the surreal. He has never written a line. He acts. And everyone interprets it in his own way. Logically.

If ever I had faith, it was on that day, when I must have been touched by divine grace.

The spirit bloweth where it listeth.

Fire, flames, smoke. Bombs feeding the fires. Bridges, railway lines, and locks blown up, and, on the roads, the great Allied armies, the soldiers with flowers stuck in their helmets as they marched along to the song of the vehicles' motors, soldiers who, that same evening, would be numbered among the dead, or among the survivors in the rout; ever since the early morning, they had been disrupted by the swarms of people fleeing in terror, and they had seen their giant columns cut by the long lines of American cars from Brussels and Amsterdam who were making a dash for it amid the cackling of high-class whores and the squealing of white-painted tires; it was an unreal, Armageddon-like scene, and overhead the sun shone relentlessly and the weather was set fair. A biblical vision, even if you discount the silent weeping of the little children lost in the turmoil, or that abandoned hearse, whose corpse, a very old woman, had tumbled out and was blocking an entire crossroads.

As Goya said: *"Yo lo vi,"* I saw it, with my own eyes.

I am confused about dates. It is not possible that so many things, so many events, so many misfortunes, so many acts of cowardice—panic, lost battles, deaths, the sick abandoned in a burning hospital, orphans straying, lunatics let loose, cows mooing in pain because nobody had come to milk them, petrol pissing out of the pump in front of a gas station because the owner had fled in such haste that he had forgotten to turn off the tap, or perhaps the lever on the pump had jammed itself on purpose, not wanting to know anymore—no, it is not possible that so many events could have happened in such a short time! It was hysteria. The sun had stopped in the heavens. (The weather forecast announced an anti-cyclone to last for forty days!) It is not possible! And that is why everything had gone off the rails, gears turned but failed to mesh, there was general breakdown, total disconnection.

No, on May 10th, men did not match up to events. God. The sky above was like a backside with gleaming buttocks and the sun was an inflamed anus. What could come out of it but shit? And men cried out in fear. But Jesus had said it:

"Do not ye yet understand, that whatsoever entereth in at the mouth goeth into the belly, and is cast out into the draught?

"But those things which proceed out of the mouth come forth from the heart; and they defile the man." (Matt. 15:17, 18)

It is not possible that the lesson had not been learned!

"Do not ye yet understand?..." asks Jesus, *"...out of the heart proceed evil thoughts..."* And Baudelaire declares: *"All is prayer. When a democrat shits, he says he is praying." (Mon coeur mis a nu.*[7])

And it was in perfect keeping with this that, in June 1940, Paul Reynaud, that patron saint of pretentious ignoramuses, came out of the Sacré-Coeur in Montmartre, where he had been paying an official visit with his pitiful government, and, dead to all sense of shame and with crocodile tears in his eyes, declared: *"I believe in miracles!"*

21

The war correspondents attached to the British GHQ crossed into Belgium on the evening of May 10th. Some of them pushed on as far as Louvain, where they saw the famous library burn down yet again. I traveled from Paris by train and joined them in Brussels on the night of May 11–12th. On the 13th, we were already in Lille. On the 14th, we evacuated Arras and quartered ourselves in Amiens, but during the night the order to burn our baggage arrived. Nobody knew where the GHQ had gone to. It was kept absolutely secret, and our little crew (we had been following in the wake of our censors on motorbikes) was disbanded; the Anglo-Saxon journalists were sent to Paris-Plage, where they embarked for home, and the French (André Maurois of *Candide,* J. H. Lefebvre of *Le Jour,* P. Ichac of *L'Illustration,* R. Lacoste from the Agence Havas, P. de Lacretelle of *Le Petit Parisien,* B. Franklin of *L'Intransigeant,* and I, who was representing *Paris-Soir* and half-a-dozen provincial newspapers, *La Petite Gironde, Le Petit Marseillais, La République orléanaise, Le Mémorial de Saint-Étienne, La Dépêche de Brest, La Dépêche algérienne, La Vigie marocaine* or *Le Phare,* I no longer remember exactly which, etc.[8]) were evacuated to Paris by train. On the 15th, I hurried to the British Embassy in Paris to seek a new assignment. The Air Attaché asked me if I would like to join the Air Force, but said it would take three days to get confirmation from London and obtain my pass and my marching orders from the War Office.

I took advantage of these three days to take Raymone and her aged mother to relatives in the Midi. I drove like a bat out of hell, choosing minor roads to avoid the congestion on the main highways, for the panic had now spread right down to the shores of the Mediterranean and was still further complicated by the movement of refugees away from the Italian frontier, and I made the return journey, against the tide this time, but still going like a rocket in my own car, on even narrower roads so as to avoid the thrust and counter-thrust of the battle and the chaos of the exodus on the main roads. I was going to Rheims, to join the General Staff of the Royal Air Force. I had carefully planned my route, via Granges-les-Vieilles-Églises, south of the river Aisne. It was the evening of May 18th. I wanted to get to Rheims before nightfall.

22

Granges-les-Vieilles-Églises..."*And it shows great progress, that there, where once the women prayed, cows now ruminate...*" A funny kind of progress. Poor France! I was crouched over the steering wheel. It was not so much the bumping of the vehicle as the jolting of my memory, and all the things that came into my mind, the sights I had seen during the battle, and the apocalyptic images of the fleeing refugees, that threatened to hurl me out of my seat, and when I let my thoughts linger over some horrific detail, I only just managed to avoid skidding off the road. I was driving like the devil, self-confident, sure of my reflexes and of the car's mechanical reliability, I was exhausted, harrowed, out of my skull, repeating over and over again that idiotic phrase of Rémy de Gourmont's, thinking of God and totally forgetting myself, evoking the Catholic saints who made this beautiful land of France that I had just crossed from one frontier to the other, there and back, and where, at each turn of the wheel, there was another village that bore the name of a saint and murmured his legend... tintinnabulating... I was falling asleep at the wheel, with my eyes open. I was dead tired... Bells... Will Rheims burn once more? The facade of the cathedral is still crumbling and the stones shattered in the last war have still not been repaired, apostles, saints, kings of France are flaking off... Church bells in the dusk... Granges-les-Vieilles-Églises... I was driving like a lunatic.

Granges-les-Vieilles-Églises is not, properly speaking, a village. It is a commune which, like so many others, is strung out in a dead straight line on either side of a road. Every hundred meters or so, sometimes on the left, sometimes on the right, there is a wretched looking farm or a broken-down fence, standing behind the row of heavily-laden telegraph poles. An ugly, stupid place. Night is falling. The cows moo, invisible, as if they were hidden inside the abandoned houses. Not a cat in sight. I put my foot down on the accelerator. Then, all of a sudden, I stamp on the brakes. My car skids to a shuddering halt. I reverse at top speed. I have had a shock. One of those fleeting impressions you catch out of the corner of your eye when you're driving fast. It's impossible. It can't be him...

Yes, it is. It's really him.

Rémy.

"What are you doing here, my boy?" I exclaim as I jump out of the car.

There they were, all three of them, Rémy and his crew, sitting around the one and only table on the threshold of a little café, drinking a bottle of lousy sparkling wine. Rémy introduced them to me. Among the three their ages did not add up to seventy-five. I hugged them all to my chest with my one arm, the little mechanic, the radio operator/machine gunner, and my son, the fighter pilot.

What were they doing here? Drinking to celebrate their first victory. The night before, Rémy had shot down a Dornier 17.

"But you know, M'sieu, it won't be officially confirmed," said the mechanic, "it crashed too far away, didn't it, Rémy?"

"Yes. But I certainly hit him. I kept right on his tail. He must have come down in Holland. I don't know how I got our kite home, we were out of gas. And it seems the Flight-Lieutenant can't confirm a hit."

"Never mind," said the gunner, "we're celebrating anyway. Cheers, old man!"

"Here's to you!"

"And to all of us!"

"Blaise, don't you want a glass?"

"I won't say no to that, Rémy. But what are you doing in this neck-of-the-woods, are you billeted here?"

"No, I'm on a special mission for GHQ. Tomorrow, at dawn, we're going on patrol to find out how far the German armored divisions have advanced toward Abbeville. And you, Blaise, what are you doing here?"

"I'm going to join the British Air Force."

"Hey, that's great, M'sieu!" exclaimed the mechanic, who was a Parisian.

"Oh, no, young fellow, I'm not a pilot. I'm a journalist. I'm not going into combat, I'm going to report on what's happening."

"Things are pretty bad, huh?" asked the radio operator, who came from Brittany.

"Very bad. And what do you see from up there?"

"Not much," Rémy replied. "The armored divisions are advancing in a vacuum. Without support. The infantry is three hundred kilometers behind them. That's a big gap. But there's flak everywhere. It's raining shit."

"Excuse me, young fellows," I said after a while. "I must be off. I'm in a hurry. I'd like to reach Rheims before it gets dark."

And once again I hugged them to my chest. I gave Rémy all the money I had on me.

"Buy some champagne," I whispered into his ear, "Get something decent, not this horse-piss…"

And I took off.

Those brave boys!

But I had not gone three hundred meters before I slammed on the brakes and backed up.

Opposite the little café, I called out to Rémy:

"Listen, don't fool around, the situation's serious. And, by the way, I've started writing the life of St. Joseph of Copertino for you. D'you remember? I've been browsing through a lot of old books and I've already written quite a packet for you. Good luck!"

"*Au revoir, Blaise!*" Rémy shouted after me.

But I was already roaring off.

This was the evening of the 18th. The following morning, at dawn on the 19th, Rémy and his radio-operator-gunner were shot down and fell behind the German lines. They were taken to Germany as prisoners-of-war. I only learned the details eighteen months later, when the two lads, by dint of a great deal of cunning and resourcefulness, managed to get themselves officially released from Stalag XVII, at Kaisersteinbrück, near the Hungarian frontier, and the pair of them came to join me in Aix-en-Provence.

"And that nice mechanic of yours?" I asked.

"We don't know," they replied, "apparently, he's been reported missing."

23

The headquarters of the AASF, to which I had been assigned, was moved from Rheims to Troyes, where it remained from May 31st to June 3rd; from Troyes, we went to Nantes, where the remnant of the RAF's ground crews in France vanished. They went to Brest where they embarked on the night of June 15th. At midday on the 16th, a Sunday, I watched the last English aircraft take off from their secret base at the château belonging to the du Chaffault family. Hundreds of Rolls-Royce engines, still packed in their crates, were burning, as well as mountains of wings and fuselages, the hangars and the men's hutments. Everything had been sprayed with gasoline. Everything was crackling and crumbling in the flames.

I was the sole witness.

Throughout the entire morning, I had been watching the squadrons passing swiftly overhead, on their way back to England. As I saw the very last airplane disappearing into the distance, I admitted to myself, at last, that we were beaten. Five minutes earlier, I would not have wanted to leave. I still believed in a possible recovery.

"France? No, it can't be! Verdun..."

My farewell to Wing-Commander Smoke had been very touching. "God bless you, Sir. You're lucky to be able to go on fighting, to continue the battle from England. France... I... I haven't the heart to abandon her... to leave France just at this moment, when the drama is going to be played out here... I feel it in my heart, and every Frenchman must stand his ground..."

I was traveling south. On the *route nationale,* the exodus had reached its peak. So, as usual, I took all the little by-ways where there was not a living soul except for the magpies. There were incalculable numbers of these birds of evil omen, fluttering from hedge to hedge, perching on the vine-props, beating their wings, rising up, startled—never had I seen so many of them! Their jittery flight and their black and white plumage made me think of Gilles de Rais, that damned soul, and his guilty conscience. I had just passed through Machecoul. I was driving slowly. Toward Bordeaux. I was driving through the beautiful vineyards of Cognac, with my eyes full of tears...

The following day, a Monday, there were scenes of hysteria in Bordeaux. Everyone looked distraught. Everybody who was anybody had left Paris and come there. They were all arguing. And bickering. And suddenly we were all struck dumb. Pétain had just appealed for an Armistice. They announced it on the radio. It was June 17th. Fifteen minutes past noon...

I could close this chapter with a formula Kipling was fond of: *"But that is another story..."* But, Jesus Christ, it was *not* another story!

Although the adventures that befell me during my dizzying peregrinations with the British Forces in France form no part of this account, and I prefer to say nothing about the harrowing scenes, or the laughable mix-ups that occurred due to my being everywhere mistaken for an Englishman, because of my uniform and my flat steel helmet ("Clothes Maketh the Man!"), and to pass in silence over the hallucinatory images that assailed me at every turning of the road, as well as the surrealist poetry of Christ— His commentary on a page out of the Apocalypse, or the film He was shooting of it, on location in France—nevertheless, these daily adventures condition the rest of my story, and its ending, just as the conditions of the Armistice, in that great, general calamity that overwhelmed the French people, had an immediate effect on my individual fate and, as for so many others, turned my life upside down and dictated my line of conduct for the years ahead.

So, on the evening of the next day, I found myself under arrest in Marseilles, because I was the last Englishman in town still in uniform!

The interrogation was very funny, and the Superintendent of Police was a good sport.

When I had explained my situation to him, this jovial southerner said, "Well, but what are you waiting for, Monsieur, why don't you simply take off your uniform?"

The evening before, in Bordeaux, I had already had a run-in with a superior officer whom I met taking his ease on the terrace of a large café he patronized.

"Cendrars," he said to me, "I advise you to put on civvies. It's time you unfrocked yourself. The English betrayed us in Belgium, they didn't want to fight... you won't be very popular."

Furiously indignant, I answered this unspeakable creature: "What do you know about it, Colonel? Where the hell were you on the tenth of May? And what have you been doing even since, the whole pack of you in your brass hats and each as big a hypocrite as the next? Shut up! I despise you!"

Already, people had taken sides, and this situation was to last right up until the Liberation.

24

In my letter to Édouard Peisson, which I quoted at the beginning of *L'Homme foudroyé,*[9] I explained how and why I began writing again on the 21st of August, 1943. But today, after further reflection, I am aware that I had other reasons for taking up my pen again and resuming my activity as a writer after such long, agonizing years of silence.

The dramatic battle of Stalingrad was over, Rome was about to fall. Ever since the 14th of July 1940, I had been in Aix-en-Provence, where I had retreated into absolute solitude, and, little by little, as events became more complicated, and police regulations and police repression ever more sinister, I had spent my time burning papers, clearing a space in my hideaway, so much so that, in 1943, when an informer for the Gestapo came to live on the same floor, next door to my furnished apartment, it occurred to me that, if they made a search, this in itself would be suspicious: a writer without papers, without notes, without files, without a card-index, without a book in sight. My clean sweep was, in fact, extremely compromising.

So then I started frequenting the library in La Méjanes, to provide myself with an alibi. Immediately on their arrival in Paris, the Boche had seized and pulped my last book, *Chez l'armée anglaise* (with the English Army), which was to have been published by Corrêa, and for which, naturally, I had not been able to supervise the publicity on the 10th of May, as agreed in my contract. Throughout the Occupation, the Boche went regularly, every Tuesday and Friday, to my home on the Avenue Montaigne, in Paris, to see whether I had come back, and good old Mother Lampen, who owned the building, used to send me an "Inter-Zone" postcard each time saying: "Aunt Amélie came to visit you again at lunchtime," and, although this was not a prearranged code, I understood at once what it meant. On their first visit to my place, they made a thorough official search, but found nothing, as I had not left a single paper behind, and it was again old Mother Lampen who had to face the chief of police when he asked, "Don't you know where Monsieur Cendrars is? He's still one of Germany's number-one enemies!" In 1943 (and I have good reason to believe that it was the result of a denunciation made against me by a charming little fellow-writer), the Boche put my name on the *Otto List* and I was banned as a Jewish writer—the bloody limit! In 1944, at Aix, the "militia" came to visit me twice on the Rue Clemenceau, but, each time, I happened to be in the country with my little goddaughter. I had been warned in good time.

La Méjanes turned out to be a very good hiding place, although it was right in the belly of the beast, for the library was housed in the same building as the Town Hall, which was swarming with police of all kinds and descriptions, all more or less "Bochified," but luckily not one of them was inquisitive enough to climb up to the first floor and see what was going on there.

It was under these circumstances that I opened a new file, made up of notes from my reading and references taken from the *Acta Sanctorum Vol. V. September,* in which I recorded all the flying achievements of the aviator-saint, Joseph of Copertino.

My dear little Saint Joseph!

I had almost forgotten him.

Only once during these long years of despairing hope had I seen his name in a newspaper, I forget which one it was, and the exact date. I am negligent, I did not make a note of it. By this time, I was in such a pessimistic mood that I thought I would never take up this work again, and in fact, I had already thrown my first file concerning him in the fire, so I had quite a shock when I saw his name in print in a daily paper; I cut out the article and pinned it to the kitchen wall, among the maps on which I was impatiently following the fluctuations of the battles on the various fronts.

Here is a copy of that yellowed and flyspecked cutting:

25

"AN ITALIAN MONK WHO ROSE INTO THE AIR SEVENTY
TIMES BECOMES THE PATRON SAINT OF AMERICAN AVIATORS

"*New York, 28th October {1943(?)}*—Following in the footsteps of
French journalists, who have recently chosen Saint Jerome as their Patron
Saint, American aviators have just placed themselves under the aegis of a
saint. Of course, we are speaking of the Catholic aviators.

"In Europe, men who fly already have a Patron Saint, Our Lady of
Loreto, but, unaware of this, the American pilots searched through the
hagiography to find a sacred personage to whom they could dedicate their
whole brotherhood.

"At first, they could not find anyone who had the slightest connection
with flying. But Miss Gretchen Green, a friend of the aviators, made a
careful study of *The Lives of the Saints* and discovered a Franciscan monk
called Joseph of Copertino, who was canonized in 1782.[10] According to his
legend, Joseph of Copertino levitated seventy times in the course of his
pious life, frequently rising as high as the topmost branches of the olive
trees, and from this altitude he preached humility, faith, and charity.

"The faithful, struck with wonder, even saw him flying above the high
altar of his church.

"It was on account of these miracles that he was canonized, and it is in
memory of them that Miss Green decided to make this St. Joseph the
Patron Saint of aviators.

"Already, medals have been struck representing St. Joseph of Copertino
flying, with the inscription, taken from the Bible: '*You have seen how I bore
you on eagles' wings.*'

"Nothing now remains but for Saint Joseph of Copertino to make himself as popular among fliers as Saint Christopher is among motorists, or St.
Barbara among gunners."

I do not know who this friend of the aviators, this Miss Gretchen Green
may be. In his own book, Olivier Leroy more than once quotes from an
American work, *Saint Joseph of Copertino* by Francis S. Laing (St. Louis,
1918), which proves that at least Miss Green did not get there first, even
in America! As for the medal mentioned in the newspaper (whose name
and date, alas! I do not know), I have searched diligently for it, and questioned American pilots, but I have never been able to get hold of one, nor
have I ever met anybody who was wearing one. But I know that it exists.

La Méjanes. This library possesses the finest collection of erotica in the world, including the original manuscript of *La Guirlande de Julie,* which the old curator, who died in 1941, had often shown me, adding his own malicious comments; old father Aude was my friend, a delightful, witty, and loquacious man, and he had read all the books and knew everything (how marvelous that was!). I met him in the aftermath of the First World War when I was making my first visit to Aix, in company with the Roosevelts and the Destroopers and a whole gang of young people who were living it up because we had come out of the war victorious, and what a racket we kicked up at the Grand Hôtel des Thermes Sextius! We plunged into the pool morning, noon, and often at night, too, although some of us had no need of the stimulating virtues of its waters—quite the opposite, in fact!—virtues that the Romans engraved on stone and that could still serve as an advertising slogan:

Venustas mulieri:
Priapus viro.

Old father Aude, who liked young people, often came to join in our smoking and drinking sessions, which did anything but induce melancholy. It was in this library that I read—just as I did in the Imperial Library in St. Petersburg, in 1907, during the most prosperous time of my life, and in the New York Public Library on 42nd Street, in 1911, when I was utterly down-and-out—Migne's *Patrologie* and the Bollandists' *Acta Sanctorum,* and in the evenings I would emerge from the La Méjanes Library with a large folio tucked under my arm, and carry it across the courtyard of the Town Hall surreptitiously, as if it were a shield I had stolen to protect myself and to reinforce my home defenses, which consisted of two thousand kilos of firewood, the logs piled up to form chicanes in the passage inside my front door. My revolvers were hidden in secret caches I could reach quickly in case of emergency and, if I had been arrested, I would have blown up the building having already prepared a mine of innovatory design, which I kept in my bedside table, because I could not bear the idea of being a prisoner... and both my sons were prisoners! Moreover, I had my dose of cyanide, just as in 1914!

And, as Kipling would say, here begins another story, the story of "The Dog Adolf," which I have not yet announced on the flyleaf of the present volume, for I do not yet know when I will have the right to recount this true story. A certain man has not yet returned from Germany. What is it about? Liberty, secrecy, and silence, or, simply, claustrophobia and anemia?

> ...A Frenchman must live for her,
> For her, a Frenchman must die...

Even the 84-year-old Parisian woman who was living with me at the time, and whom I was sheltering, never suspected a thing, and an English woman and an American woman (who were "living together") who came to spend the night at my place from time to time, without knowing who I was, declared: "That old lady who acts as our chaperone... thinking of that was sheer genius, Monsieur! Even a novelist couldn't have thought it up..."

Saint Joseph of Copertino...

Ah! The Saints, those *enfants terribles* of the Church! The only true things that prevent you from cursing and reviling life are saints, children, flowers and birds, lunatics, the gratuitous gifts that come to you from God knows where, harvest workers and innocent souls. Without these, life would be impossible. And so I read... and on the day of the Liberation, I hoisted a Chinese flag at my window, the only one flying in Aix. The poor Chinese, they had been at war for ten years and nobody was sparing them a thought, even though the war had been fought to liberate them! And today, they are still plunged in the same misery.

So, here are the extracts I picked out from my reading at La Méjanes, but, since I am not inclined to adorn myself with peacock's feathers, nor to puff myself up like the frog in the fable (I do not drink water!), I hasten to add that, to avoid overburdening my account, I am giving only brief extracts from the Bollandists, picking these out from the selection already made by Olivier Leroy in his aforementioned work, *La Lévitation,* and using the actual text of his summaries. I have done no more than check his translation, add a comma here, a statistic or a date there, and I have not touched the etymology, since the translation by this master is so accurate, so intelligent, and succinct. It is like cinema:[11]

27

"One day, on the Feast of Saint Francis, Joseph, who was wearing the cope and walking in the procession, was seen by the other monks and some of the inhabitants of Copertino to fly up to the pulpit of the church, fifteen spans high, and come to rest on the edge. He remained balancing there for a long time, on his knees, with his arms outstretched as if on a cross." *(Acta Sanctorum*, Vol. V. September, p. 1021 B/u)

"On the Thursday before Easter, while he was praying before the pyx standing on the High Altar, he soared into the air, right up to the tabernacle, without knocking anything over, and came back to his place by the same means when his Superior ordered him to do so. He was also seen sometimes, during the recital of the litanies, to fly to the altar of Saint Francis and the Virgin of La Grottella." *(A.S.,* ibid., p. 1021 B/x)

"Seeing some workmen struggling to set up a tall, heavy cross of Calvary on a little hill between Copertino and La Grottella, Joseph flew from the gate of the convent to the cross, some eighty paces distant, and, lifting it as if it had been a simple wooden stake, planted it in its hole. Later on, he was often seen levitating in ecstasy before this cross, at a distance of ten or twelve paces from it." *(A.S.,* ibid., p. 1021 C/ac)

"While describing how the Holy Ghost descended on the Apostles, he went into ecstasy at the sight of a monk passing by with a lighted candle in his hand. He flew through the air to a distance of about fourteen paces." *(A.S.,* ibid., p. 1021 C/bb)

"Another time, he flew up into an olive tree, because a priest, Don Antonio Chiarello, had said to him: 'What a beautiful sky God has made, Brother Joseph!' And he stayed there for half an hour, kneeling on a branch which was seen to sway slightly, as if a bird had alighted on it." *(A.S.,* ibid., p. 1021 cc). "When he came to," adds Bernino, "he could not climb down and they had to fetch a ladder." (Bernino, p. 285)

"On the 10th of July, 1657, while on his way to the convent at Osimo on the orders of Pope Alexander VII, he climbed up to a terrace from which it was possible to get a glimpse of the cupola of the church of Our Lady of Loreto, and there he had a vision, fell into a rapture and flew as far as an almond tree standing some thirty meters away. During this flight, he rose to a height of about two and a half meters off the ground." *(A.S.,* ibid., p. 1041 E/1)

"On another occasion, at Fossombrone, he went into a transport that carried him over the trees in the garden. It was the evening of the Sunday on which the Gospel of the Good Shepherd is read, that is, the second Sunday after Easter. This ecstatic flight was caused by his seeing a lamb, which reminded him of the words of the Gospel." *(A.S.,* ibid, p. 1038 E/u) Here is Bernino's version: "It was on the evening of the Gospel reading: Ego sum Pastor bonus; after supper, Joseph went out into the garden with the brothers and came across a lamb; he stopped to look at it and, as it seemed as if he would like to hold this animal, a young monk put it into his arms. Joseph embraced the lamb and held it tenderly against his chest, then, holding it by its hoofs, laid it across his shoulders. Almost imperceptibly, by slow stages, the saint became inflamed with the spirit of God; he quickened his pace and began to run across the garden. The monks and the pious laymen who were with them followed, curious to know how this rapture would end. Soon, they saw Joseph and the lamb in the air. The saint had launched the lamb into the air by virtue of some supernatural force and, almost at the same instant, had flown up in the wake of the lamb and was soaring through space on a level with the crowns of the trees in the garden. He remained there, kneeling in the air, for more than two hours, that is, until half an hour after sunset." (Bernino, p. 212)

"Several times, it happened that he carried someone else into the air with him during one of his raptures. The first time was in the Church of Santa Chiara at Copertino, where this event caused great terror. Joseph was attending Vespers in this church, and when he heard them singing the Antiphon, 'Veni sponsa Christi,' he sprang out of the corner where he had been kneeling in prayer and, in his ecstatic intoxication, rushed up to the Father Confessor of the convent, seized him by the hand, pulled him off the ground and began to revolve with him in the void." *(A.S.,* ibid., p. 1021 C/dd)

"During another levitation, he carried a lunatic, who had been brought to him to be cured, up into the air with him. This man, a certain Baldassare Rossi, had been brought in tied to a chair, for he was dangerous and would hurl himself at people, claiming they were mad. Joseph untied him, made him kneel down, and, laying his hand on his head, said: 'Fear nothing, commend yourself to God and His Holy Mother!' As he pronounced this phrase, he seized the man by the hair and, letting out his customary shriek, rose into the air together with the lunatic, and thus they stayed for some time. Then, having regained the earth, he sent Baldassare away with these words: 'Be joyful, cavaliere!'" *(A.S.,* ibid, p. 1022 D)

"While making a brief visit to Nardo, he had one levitation in the church of Saint Francis and another in the home of a sick man he had gone to visit. He came to rest on his knees on a table cluttered with medicine flasks, yet he did not disturb anything. The same thing happened to him in May 1649, in Assisi, at the home of old Gabriele de Caravaggio, who was dying. At the moment of extreme unction, Joseph was lifted up and hovered over the deathbed." *(A.S.,* ibid., p. 1021 E/ff)

"Passing through Monopoli, on his way to Naples, where he had been summoned by the Holy Office, who were troubled about his reputation as a thaumaturge, Joseph was taken to the church to see a new statue of Saint Anthony of Padua. As soon as he saw it, his feet left the ground, he traveled through the air and crossed the fifteen spans that separated him from the altar where this statue was standing, then he came back to his point of departure in the same manner. *(A.S.,* ibid., p. 1021 E/ii)

"In Naples, in the church of Saint Gregory the Armenian, he let out a cry and launched himself from the spot where he was praying. He came to rest on the altar, among the candles and the flowers, to the great terror of the Sisters of San Ligorio, whose convent was annexed to the church. Then, with another cry, he flew back to the center of the nave." *(A.S.,* ibid., p. 1021 F)

28

"For Joseph, everything was a pretext for rapture: a holy image, a religious chant, a blade of grass, the leaf of a cherry tree whose texture he admired. The acts of his process for canonization recorded fifteen levitations in the presence of images of the Virgin, and, during one of these, he rose to a height of over ten meters.... His ecstasies while saying Mass were daily events, and often accompanied by levitation." (Leroy p. 132)

On several occasions, Joseph's levitations took place in front of distinguished witnesses: Pope Urban VIII, the Grand Admiral of Castile, the Pope's legate, his wife, who fainted with fright, and Maria of Savoy, daughter of Charles-Emmanuel and Catherine of Austria, who came to stay near Assisi so as to converse with this holy man on spiritual questions, and saw him levitate. One may legitimately wonder, therefore, to what extent the Superiors of the convent exploited these ecstatic flights, with an eye to propaganda and conversion. The episode of the Duke of Brunswick is one of the most telling:

"John Frederick, Duke of Brunswick, then aged twenty-five years old, visited the principal courts of Europe in the year 1649. Having reached Rome, he wanted to push on as far as Assisi, for he was attracted by the saint's renown. The day after his arrival at the convent, the Duke, accompanied by his two chamberlains, attended a Mass at which Joseph was officiating. He saw the latter rise from in front of the altar, move through the air in a kneeling position for a distance of five paces, and come back to the altar in the same manner. On the following day, during the consecration, Joseph rose one span off the ground and remained thus for more than five minutes, hovering above the steps of the altar, holding the host in his upraised hands. At this sight, the Duke began to weep. As for one of the chamberlains—a Lutheran, like his master—he declared that he was sorry to have seen such a spectacle, because it threw all his convictions into doubt. The Duke, after a conversation with Joseph, not only declared himself a Catholic, but, after attending Compline and following the procession, enrolled himself as a novice in the Franciscan order. He then returned to Brunswick to settle his affairs and, the following year, came back to Assisi to make a solemn abjuration under the hands of Joseph and in the presence of Cardinals Facchinetti and Rappaccioli." (*A.S.,* ibid, p. 1024 P) "The Lutheran chamberlain, H.-J. Blume, was also converted, in 1653." (Quoted by Leroy, p. 136, after Laing)

29

And now I come to the most sensational of all Joseph of Copertino's flights:

"The monks responsible for guarding the treasure of the convent of Assisi were more than a little astonished when they saw Joseph, who had been entrusted with the dusting of the reliquaries and Saint Francis's habit, passing over their heads, backwards, and landing on the flagstones behind them."

This world record, unique in the annals of aviation, is so important that, in honor of this great achievement, I will quote the testimony to it in the Latin version: "Non absimilis fuit eorum stupor, qui ipsum sublimi volatu super capita sua RETRORSUM VOLANTEM conspexerunt, quando ad lipsanothecam expoliendam, vestemque sancti patriarchae Francisci reponendam, operam suam conferebat." *(A.S.,* ibid, p. 1022 B, C pp)

This first aerobatic flight took place in ANNO DOMINI MDCXLV.

30

The bull published by Pope Clement XIII on the 16th of July, 1767, for the canonization of Joseph of Copertino, mentions the levitations and the ecstatic flights of this areobatic saint:

"...Hoc ille nempe quamdiu vixit, non tam verbis quam re ipsa pulcherrime docuit, quum terram veluti dedignatus, frequentes ac prope quotidianas, extases patiens, SUBLIMIS IN AERA FERRETUR AC MODO EXULTABUNDUS CELERRIMO IMPETU CIRCUMVOLANS, CHOREAS VELUTI DUCERET, MODO ALIOS QUOQUE SECUM SUBLIME RAPERET..."

31

On the other hand, the Roman Breviary, which gives the 18th of September as the Saint's feast day, makes only one rather vague allusion to his flights, soarings, suspensions, ascensions, bodily transports, and fits of ecstatic jubilation:

"Die XVIII septemb.—In festo S. Josephi a Copertino, Confess. Lectio V.: Eluxit praecipue ardentissima ejus caritas in extasibus ad Deum suavissimis, stupendisque raptibus, quibus frequenter afficiebatur."

II

THE MIRACLE OF THE YEAR 1000

"Faith is MIDNIGHT *and God, it is*
the COMING DAY.*"*

St. John of the Cross

32

According to an ancient, continuous, and almost universal tradition, the human body, in the case of certain individuals and at certain moments, is capable of raising itself into the air, and sometimes of moving about in the void without visible support or the apparent action of any physical force.

Today, this phenomenon is called *levitation.* It is a word of English origin, invented by spiritualists, and, according to the Oxford English Dictionary, only came into use in 1875.[12] But, although the term may be recent, the thing itself is not. It is the rapture, the orison, the ecstasy—*raptus, oratio, extasus*—of the Bollandists; the theologians and hagiographers who succeeded them define the aerial acrobatics of the saints as *elevation, suspension, élan, ecstatic flight, ecstatic ascension, ecstatic elevation, corporeal ravishment, or the fire of divine love,* according to their degree of virtuosity and perfection.

As far as the levitation of the saints is concerned, manuals of mystical theology do no more than skim over the surface, although the examples cited are officially held to be authentic. But when a process of beatification is initiated in Rome, cases of levitation are examined and analyzed down to the last detail, and, nine times out of ten, rejected as manifestations of magic, illusion, or fraud, and that is why the Church only very rarely takes into account the agility of these glorious bodies and only gives them credence when constrained to do so by the patent sincerity and high moral character of the witnesses; even then, they are mentioned only in vague and enigmaic terms, often just the barest allusion, and always with the greatest prudence and modesty, because the Church is aware of the illusions of the senses, the artifices and evil spells of the devil, the false claims of sorcerers and magicians, the antics of the insane, the feats of hysterics, the trickery of so-called mediums and somnambulists, and the possible confusion between ecstasy and possession; and that is why, out of the approximately 14,000 saints whose biographies figure in the first six months of the Bollandists' writings, one finds only about sixty, that is 0.4 percent whose *indices morales* mention proven levitations, recorded and duly acknowledged only after being subjected to all the skeptical inquiries, depositions, and processes, clandestine investigations, cross-checkings, criticisms, judicial calls to order, and the famous *animadversions* of the Promoter of the Faith (The "Devil's Advocate"), which continue throughout the ages and are ceaselessly revised.

The list of levitating saints contained in the work by Olivier Leroy is the longest ever published, yet there are only just over two hundred names: ninety-three women and one hundred and twelve men.

This shows that the phenomenon is rare, extremely rare, and only grudgingly admitted by the Church, which, contrary to popular opinion, is not eager to ratify miracles, but is skeptical and deeply suspicious of them. And while it is true that the acts of the venerable are subjected to rigorous inquiries in which their lives, their conduct, their words, their humility, their faith, and even their intentions (prayers and orthodox practices—fasting, confession, and communion—are equated with invocations to the Devil if their aim is to acquire supernatural powers)[13] are passed through the fine sieve of dogma, tradition, and the Catholic experience after their death, it is also true that, during their lifetime, all these ecstatics, and more particularly the levitators and stigmatics, were closely observed, studied, mocked, chastised, envied, punished, put on the Index, made to do penance, banned, locked up, submitted to cruel tests of their genuineness, spied on, burned and pricked with needles by their brothers, suspected of hypocrisy and simulation, despised by their own communities and accused of trickery or of magic arts by their superiors, who willingly handed them over to the Inquisition, whose tribunals censured them, condemned them, put them under an interdict, held them prisoner secretly (like St. John of the Cross, who was forgotten in a tiny cell in the lower depths of a convent in Toledo), threatened them with excommunication and death, and, in fact, treated them like the innumerable sorcerers throughout Europe who were imprisoned, judged, and executed through the tender mercies of the Holy Office, and their number is so considerable, and the documents in the archives so convincing in their pathos, their horror, or the dryness with which they enumerate the facts and the appalling confessions extracted, that one has to admit that in neither case is it a question of credulity or superstition or complaisance or propaganda or artificial mise en scène, but proof that there exists in Man a strange and marvelous ambition to be an acrobat of the air, in profound contradiction to the physical possibilities with which nature has endowed this "featherless biped,"[14] and that in all these processes for canonization and all these trials for sorcery, the Church was doing its utmost to establish, through a body of well-defined and well-authenticated data, the knowledge and the technique, the science of the phenomena of spiritual life, its behavioral patterns and its various stages, and, in fact, the Catholic hagiography is today the only body of knowledge that has an ancient written tradition of levitation, in its various and continuing manifestations, supported by precise and doubly verified documents that permit it to trace a distinction between the divine prodigy and the demonic artificer, or the lunatic, between the charismata of the saints and the sinister, burlesque, or hysterical parody of the possessed, between contemplatives and charlatans, between heaven-sent gifts and venal exhibitionism, between the interior phenomena of mystical life and the impassioned transports of neurotics, or the publicity-seeking trances of mediums, between moral truth and extravagant lies, between the pure humility, the passive waiting, or the fugue of an ascetic filled with fervor and the psychic and physiological trickery of loud-mouthed mesmerizers and mountebanks, between the forgetfulness of self and vainglorious boasting, between prayer, which is a knowledge of God, and telekinesis, which is the triumph of Satan, between saints and the damned, to say nothing of present-day addicts who smoke, swallow, or inject themselves with large doses of hashish, stupefacients, and other drugs that reduce their bodies, muscles, and nerves to nothing but a film-clip, speeded-up or in slow motion, while their souls and their consciousness suffer total breakdown and their minds become deranged, and this is true whether they are free individuals or vain guinea-pigs confined in clinics, those complaisant prisoner-patients who have become putty in the hands of materialistic psychiatrists and vivisectors, having yelded themselves up and abdicated all personality to promote the apotheosis of science, and it is science that keeps them enslaved, or makes them dance to his tune by graduating or varying the toxic doses of datura, ether, or nitrous oxide, or by subjecting them to electric shocks; nor have I yet spoken of the positive power of poetic metaphors, the exaltation and legendary enthusiasm of popular myth, its cantilenas and fairy tales, its wonders and triumphs, nor of folklore, the Icarian myths of pagan antiquity, the inverse religion of the magicians of Babylon, the perverted or obscure traditions of prehistoric India and China, the tricks of the fakirs (the Indian rope trick performed in front of an audience of tourists armed with cameras!), nor of the antics of expatriate yogis on the radio who advocate pranayama—a return to the intrauterine breathing of the fetus; one sees so many people who train themselves to the point of maximum dilatation of the thorax and then have no idea what to do, the aim of this mechanical exercise being to achieve peace of mind as a preparatory stage to spiritual illumination, whereas all these sectarians, far from being wise men, are nervous wrecks, troubled souls, and political protesters, they are all Americanized, and there is nothing sacred about them except the badges they wear in their buttonholes, for they are all members of various clubs—freethinkers, vegetarians, tee-totalers, or spiritualists—and they are very often the spokesmen who open the endless debates in their societies, as if these jokers needed to use up immediately all the surplus energy they have acquired that morning by doing the exercise, sitting cross-legged and stark naked in front of their radios; nor have I breathed a word about the occult life of the last surviving savages, who are our contemporaries.

33

Saint Dunstan, the Archbishop of Canterbury who played such an outstanding role in the religious and political history of England, levitated on Ascension Day, just three days before his death on the 17th of May, 988 A.D. According to one of his biographers, he was seen to rise right up to the vault of the cathedral. This is what I call the "miracle of the year 1000," for the second levitator was Saint Stephen (Istvan), King of Hungary, who died on the 15th of August, 1038. His biographer writes that he was seen hovering above the ground one night while praying in his tent, the King, at that time, being encamped with his army; he had just taken command and was about to fight Conrad II, Emperor of Germany.[15]

Before the year 1000, we must go back to the Old Testament to find cases of levitation in the Christian tradition. The classic ones were: Enoch, who was carried off from the earth alive; Elijah who, while walking with Elisha, was snatched up by a whirlwind in the form of a chariot of fire; Habakkuk, who was transported through the skies of Judea to Babylon, to bring food to Daniel in the lions' den, and brought back to the spot where the Angel of the Lord had picked him up, and according to the text, held him by the hair throughout the flight. In the New Testament, we have, for example, the Deacon Philip who, after baptizing the Queen of Ethiopia's eunuch on the road between Gaza and Azot, was suddenly lifted up and disappeared from view; and the supreme case, the levitation that ended the terrestrial life of Jesus Christ: having led his disciples in the direction of Bethany, he rose into the air and disappeared from their sight; and we have the ecstasy of the Apostle and his announcement that, at the Last Judgment, the elect would be drawn up into the air to meet the Lord. The primitive Christian church reports only a few rare cases of levitation: according to the Provençal tradition, Saint Mary Magdalen, who lived in solitude on the hill of the Sainte-Baume, was transported seven times a day for thirty years, and this "chrysalis of the sky," with her body etherealized by mortifications and her mind exhausted by continual prayer, flew as far as the Saint-Pilon, though not with the aim of astonishing whoever might happen to see her prospecting her aerial desert, for she was ashamed to make a spectacle of herself and even embarrassed before the angels who came to meet her each time, not because she needed to be supported in her frailty and inexperience, but simply to escort her and defend her modesty. According to the historical tradition, we have Saint Ammon (d. 350), who was miraculously transported from one bank of the confluence of the Nile to the other; Saint Anthony the Great (251–356), who was ravished in spirit and felt himself raised up into the air of the Nitrian desert, circa 340; Saint Mary the Egyptian (354–431) who, with her skin cracked and blackened like an old, dried-out goatskin winebag, and clothed in nothing but her wildly disordered hair, was discovered lost in a trance of penitence and floating one cubit above the ground by Zosimus the priest, who gave her his cape (this scene is illustrated in a stained-glass window in the Cathedral of Bourges); Saint Schenute (333–451), the most picturesque personality in Egyptian monasticism, who, together with his monks, organized what were virtually raids against the pagan temples, and, as a result, was indicted and brought before the Praetor of Antinoë, whereupon he began to pray, rose up into the air, and remained suspended above the tribunal, at a height from which he could still make himself heard, and from there pleaded his cause at length before descending little by little to be acclaimed by the crowd, who hastened to receive his blessing;[16] etc.

From 1000 A.D. on, the levitation of holy persons has been reported uninterruptedly down to our own times, first by the old chroniclers, then by the *Acta Sanctorum* of the Bollandists and the official hagiographers, and finally, in modern times, by those well-informed historians and biographers who are most conversant with church affairs.

And here is a rich selection taken from the list drawn up by Olivier Leroy and published in his work *La Lévitation,* a list that includes 205 names of male and female ecstatic saints to whom the charism of levitation has been attributed and records a thousand years of Catholic experience:[17]

34

From the Year 1000 to the 13th Century

"The biography of Saint Ladislaus (1041–95), King of Hungary and descendant of Saint Stephen, contains precise details of a levitation similar to that of his ancestor. One evening, in the monastery at Warasdin, Ladislaus remained at prayer until a late hour; a servant, who was waiting for him at the door, began to wonder why he was so long and went into the chapel. There he saw his master, devoutly praying, elevated above the ground."

"When passing through the town of Castro, Saint Dominic, the founder of the Friars Preachers (1170–1221), stayed as a guest at the Benedictine monastery. As he forgot to come to the Refectory for a meal, and Prior Matthew and the other brothers were waiting for him, one of the monks was sent to look for him; he found him in the chapel, praying, at a height of one cubit above the ground. Allegedly, he had had previous levitations, one on the day when he miraculously brought Cardinal Orsini's nephew back to life after a riding accident, and another at the Church of Saint Sixtus in Rome where, at the moment of elevating the Host during Mass, he was raised off the ground to a height of one cubit."

"One day, Saint Christina the Astonishing," says her biographer, Thomas of Canterbury, who was writing eight years after her death and had consulted a great many eyewitnesses at Saint-Troud, in the diocese of Liège, Christina's birthplace, "one day, in the midst of her own funeral service—for everyone thought she was dead—Saint Christina flew right up to the vault of the church and remained suspended there. From that day on, her own community subjected her to a life of endless torments, because they believed her to be possessed. She shunned all society, taking refuge in deserted places, in trees, or at the tops of towers and churches. She would perch on the slenderest branches of the trees as lightly as a bird. Sometimes, she was discovered on the very tip of a post, singing psalms."

"It is said of Saint Francis of Assisi (1185–1226) that toward the end of his life, when he was in retreat on Mount Alvernia, his raptures multiplied.

It was the duty of Brother Leo, his favorite disciple, to bring bread and water twice a day to the grotto in the flank of the mountain where the saint had retired. Now, it happened at times that Brother Leo found Saint Francis in ecstasy, outside the grotto, his body elevated to a height where his disciple could still reach his feet. At other times, he found him half way up the great beeches, and at others again, he was so high that he was almost out of sight. In certain raptures, he appeared enveloped in a luminous aura."

"The Blessed Ivetta (Jutta), who died in 1226, lived as a hermit not far from Kulm (Prussia). Her refuge was an old, abandoned house. Her ecstasies took place twice a day and were accompanied by levitations witnessed by the people in the neighborhood. "...*instar Moysis vultu coruscante...*" say the *Acta*. "Her face was radiant.""

"Saint Elizabeth of Hungary (1207–31) was the daughter of King Andrew II, who married her to Louis, son of the Landgrave of Thuringia and Hess. On the death of this prince, Saint Elizabeth entered the third order of the Franciscans. She was canonized by Gregory IX, four years after her death. One of her recorded levitations is rather like that of Saint Dominic at Castro. A nun, on going into the choir to fetch Elizabeth, found her prostrated at the foot of a statue of the Virgin, then she saw her rising up to a height of one foot."

"The Blessed Gerardesca of Pisa (d. 1240) belonged to the Order of the Camaldolites. On one occasion, on the Feast of Saint John in the Church of San Giacomo of Podio, a Pisan woman saw her rise to a height of ten cubits. She was terrified, but the sweet singing of the ecstatic Gerardesca reassured her."

"Saint Edmund (d. 1242), who was Archbishop of Canterbury at the time, was seen by his friend and counselor, Saint Richard of Chichester, in a state of levitation in his chapel."

"Saint Lutgard (1182–1246) entered a Cistercian convent at the age of twenty and became the Prioress in 1215. On a day of Pentecost, as Saint Lutgard was singing the *Veni Creator Spiritus* with the other nuns of this enclosed order, she was seen to rise two cubits above the floor."

"The Blessed Giles of Santarem, son of the governor of Coïmbre (Portugal), went to Paris to study medicine, but, instead, gave himself up to magic. Then, he reformed his life completely and entered the order of Saint Dominic, later founding a monastery at Santarem. His biographer, Father Resendio, reports a levitation he experienced in curious circumstances: Stopping for the night at Lerena (between Coïmbre and Scalabis),

Giles went to lodge in the house of a lady called Pichena. He retired to his room, which he was sharing with a Dominican from Scalabis, and began to meditate, sitting on the edge of his bed. After a few seconds, his companion noticed that he was in a state of bliss and had risen above the bed. This Brother Andreas, being very surprised, called their hostess and some other people who were in the house and showed them the strange spectacle. He tried to move the entranced man, but could not do so, not even by one centimeter. News of this event having spread all around the neighborhood, people came running from all directions. The crowd was so eager to see Giles in this state that some of them, who could not get into the room, climbed up onto the roof in an attempt to look in and did a great deal of damage to the tiles (*tectum ipsum effractum*). When Giles learned what had happened, he left the house in the middle of the night."

"Saint Douceline (1214–74), a Beguine nun from Provence, was the sister of the famous Hugues de Digne, who was the Franciscan Provincial for Provence. She had frequent ecstasies during some of which she rose off the ground. 'One day, in the church,' says a 14th-century Provençal text published by Robert Gout,[18] 'she was carried away by the spirit of God. It was the evening of the feast day and the sermon was over. A noble knight by the name of Jacques Vivaud, who was Lord of the château of Cuges, was present with his son, for he had been told by his wife, Mme. Sancie, a noble lady devoted to good works, that the holy mother had been in a state of rapture ever since the morning, when she herself had accompanied the nun into one of the side chapels, where she had taken communion. On hearing this, the nobleman had very piously desired to see her. When he went into the church, he saw her in the air, suspended by the force of this marvelous attraction that drew her up toward God, hanging there without any support, without holding on to anything and raised to a height at which it was possible for the knight and his son, after removing their hats and reverently kneeling down, to kiss the soles of her feet with great piety.... Another man from Marseilles, Raimon du Puy, saw her in the same state. She was in the friars' church, in ecstasy before the altar where she had taken communion, lifted above the ground and in the same position in which Jacques Vivaud had seen her. Now, this very devout citizen knelt down, and he measured with his hand the distance that separated her from the floor, and he saw that she was elevated by a good hand-span. In great faith, he placed his head, which was giving him considerable pain, beneath her venerable feet and piously kissed them.'... "One day, on the Feast of the Assumption, she was also seen crossing the whole of the choir, above the floor, as if she were following an imaginary procession. At certain times, the ecstatic rose up, without actually leaving the ground, so that her big toes were still touching it. Yet again, she has been seen to hang with one foot a hand-span off the ground, the other holding on with only the tip of her big toe; and she has remained thus from the moment of taking communion until the evening, toward the hour of Compline."

"One would not expect to find Saint Thomas Aquinas (1226–74), the encyclopedist of the Church and author of the *Summa,* figuring in the list of levitating saints. However, his biographer, William da Tocco, who was his contemporary and intimate friend, says he saw him in ecstasy, raised above the ground, several times. The first occasion was in the Dominican monastery in Salerno: the saint was at his prayers before the High Altar, after Matins, when Brother Giacomo and another monk saw him elevated to a height of two cubits. Later, in a monastery in Naples, he was discovered in the same state by Brother Domenico. The latter, having noticed that Thomas was in the habit of going to church before Matins, followed him on two occasions. He saw him in ecstasy in the chapel of Saint Nicholas, with his body raised about two cubits above the floor."

"Saint Agnes of Bohemia (1203–82), daughter of Primislaus Ottakar, the King of Bohemia, refused to marry the Emperor Frederick II and entered the Poor Clares in Prague, later becoming the Superior General. Her biographer recounts that, during her meditations, she would soar above the ground. One Ascension Day, she was walking in the convent garden with Sisters Benign and Prisca, when she rose up and was lost to sight and did not reappear until an hour later. When questioned about this mysterious absence, she refused to answer. She simply smiled."

"Saint Ambrose of Siena (1220–86), while preaching to a congregation of both religious and laymen, twice rose into the air. Allowing his congregation to see him in this state was, he said, a grace accorded by God as a reward for their piety."

"The Blessed Franco Lippi, from Grotti near Siena (d. 1291), spent his youth indulging in the worst excesses, then was suddenly converted. After making a series of pilgrimages, he entered the Carmelite order. Goerres recounts the following anecdote about him: one day in his cell, Franco had a vision of the Madonna. In his bliss, his body began to exude a light so brilliant that the other monks came running, believing there was a fire. When they entered his cell, they saw Franco with his eyes raised to heaven, his mouth half open and his hands joined in prayer; he was oblivious to his surroundings and his body was raised off the ground."

"Saint Margaret of Cortona (1247–97), a Franciscan tertiary, spent twenty-three years expiating the wantonness of her youth by cruel mortifications. In his biography, Father Chérancé[19] gives this account of her first rapture, which was accompanied by levitation: Margaret was in the house of Donna Diabella, where she was taking care of a young, newly delivered mother, who was related to the lady of the house. Profiting by a moment when she was at liberty from her duties, she withdrew into a corner of the room to weep for her sins. As her prayers reached a peak of fervor, the spirit of God suddenly swooped down on her, drew her to Him, and carried her up into the air. The saint's body was lifted to a height of several cubits. Two eyewitnesses, Donna Mechtilde (the young mother in childbed) and a workman with whom the devout Tertiary often shared the bread of charity, attested to the truth of this event."

35

14th and 15th Centuries

"The Blessed Peter Armengol (1238–1304), who belonged to the family of the Counts of Urgell and was related to the Kings of Castile, led a rather unedifying life in his youth and even became the leader of a band of brigands. Stricken with remorse, he asked to be admitted to the Order of Mercy, and was invested with the habit in 1258. He chose to lead a life of cruel penitence and also devoted himself to the ransoming of captives taken by the Moors. Hanged at Bougie, Algeria, he miraculously escaped death. Witnesses declare that they saw him during his prayers, hovering above the ground."

"Saint Catherine of Siena (1347–80) was an ecstatic even as a child. She was only six years old when she had a transport accompanied by a sensation of levitating. J. Joergensen gives this account of her first rapture:[20] It was in a grotto at the gates of Siena, where she had gone with the intention of living as a hermit. She had taken a loaf of bread with her and, thus provisioned, began her solitary life. As she fell to praying, she found herself in that strange state where everything around her disappeared and she seemed to be soaring in a world of dazzling light. She had the feeling that, little by little, she was being raised from the ground, higher, ever higher, until finally her head knocked against the roof and this woke her up. She realized that she must have been in the grotto for a long time, since the sun was now low, the cicadas were shrilling in the figtrees and up there, at San Domenico, they were ringing the bell for Vespers. Later, this famous Dominican nun levitated in the presence of witnesses. Caffarini, for one, affirms that he saw her rise several meters above the ground."

"The life of Saint Colette of Corbie (1381–1447), a reformer of the Order of Saint Clare, abounds in marvels, but little is said about her levitations. At least, they are related with a dryness that is quite incomprehensible, seeing that the bodily transports of the saint were of a prodigious nature. And in fact, the entry in the *Acta* says that the other nuns, on more than one occasion, saw her soaring in the air and reaching such a height that she was lost to their view *(ab eorum oculis evanescens)*."

"The Blessed Peter de Geremia of Palermo (1381–1451) belonged to the Dominican order. He worked particularly on reforming the monasteries of his order in Sicily. His life has been written by one of his companions in the Monastery of Saint Zita, and this biography states that, while saying his prayers, he was often elevated above the ground. At such times, his body became extremely luminous. One day, his Superior, seeing the brilliance through the cracks in the door of his cell, thought it must be on fire. He forced the door open and found nothing but the saint in a state of bliss."

"Saint Peter Regalado (1391–1456) emitted a vivid light when he was in ecstasy. He also rose from the ground and sometimes remained suspended in the void for several hours."

"One levitation inspired Murillo to paint a famous picture, *The Angels' Kitchen,* which can be seen in the Louvre. A little to the left, the ecstatic Saint James (d. 1463) is seen floating just above the ground. His hands are joined in prayer and his eyes are raised to heaven. His body is enveloped in a faint nimbus. On the right, the angels are carrying out the various kitchen duties which had been allotted to the ecstatic saint."

"The biographers of Girolamo Savonarola (1452–98) credit the famous Dominican with a certain number of miracles, and levitation is cited among them. Even in his prison cell, writes F.-T. Perrens,[21] Savonarola worked miracles. Several times, the jailer found him freed of his manacles and his shackles; often, the door was open, but the prisoner did not take advantage of this to escape; finally, he was seen soaring in the air and surrounded by a luminous aureole. These prodigious feats touched the heart of the jailer, who was converted and became a perfect Christian. The biographers unanimously affirm these facts."

36

16th Century

"On Good Friday of the year 1505, the Franciscan Ladislaus of Gielniow (d. 1505), was preaching in Warsaw Cathedral. His theme was the Passion, and when he came to a description of the flagellation, he fell into a transport and, carried away, remained for some time hanging above the pulpit, causing great emotion among the congregation. Then he came down slowly, in a state of exhaustion; he took to his bed and died a month later, on the 4th of May."

"There are a considerable number of testimonials to the corporeal transports of Saint Francis of Paola (1416–1507). When Sixtus IV ordered this thaumaturge from Calabria to go to the court of France, he passed through Naples and there he was given lodging by King Ferdinand I. It was the latter who, observing him in secret, saw him in a state of ecstasy, with his luminous body suspended in the air. He was again seen in this state in the church at Plessis, near Tours, where he several times rose to a height of five or six cubits. Louis XI's daughter, Anne of Beaujeu, is mentioned as an eyewitness to these feats."

"Father Bouhours[22] relates that Saint Francis Xavier, the apostle of Japan and India, would sometimes break off in the middle of a conversation and retire to contemplate. Later, when they went to look for him, they would find him either in front of the Holy Sacrament, or in a solitary place, lost in profound meditation, often hanging in the air, with his face suffused with beams of light. Several eyewitnesses attest to these facts. Some say that, at the beginning, they saw the saint kneeling motionlessly, then they noticed that he was rising very gradually from the ground, and finally, they were seized with holy terror and could not look at him fixedly because his face was so luminous. Others claim that, when he spoke to them about the things of God, they saw him suddenly move away from them, and his body then rose up of its own accord. These bodily ravishments sometimes occurred immediately after the consecration, when he was celebrating Mass. This happened particularly in Malacca and in Meliapore. He was elevated again several times in Goa, while giving communion, and what makes it more remarkable is that it was his custom to give communion on his knees, and it was in this posture that he seemed to rise from the ground. These traditions have received official recognition. *(Die III Decembris, lectio IV)*."

"Only a single levitation is mentioned for Saint Thomas of Villanueva. One Ascension Day, say the acts of canonization, Thomas, then Archbishop of Valencia, was reading the Antiphon: *Et videntibus illis elevatus est,* when he went into an ecstatic trance and was lifted off the ground. He remained there, motionless, hanging in the void, for twelve hours *(ab hora quinta matutina ad quintam vespertinam)* in full view of the Archbishop's staff and various inhabitants of Valencia. Thomas of Villanueva joined the Augustinian order at about the time that Luther left it. The saint had accepted the Archbishopric of Valencia in obedience to the wishes of Charles V, who held him in the highest esteem."

"Ignatius Loyola (1491–1556), was thirty-three years old when he began his belated studies in Barcelona. He lodged with a lady, Agnes Pasqual, whose son, Juan, has reported various details of the saint's life. He had watched him, secretly, when he was at prayer. Sometimes, he relates, the room where Ignatius was in a state of rapture filled with light, while the saint, kneeling, and with his arms stretched out, rose to a height of four or five spans."

"Saint Francis of Alcantara (1499–1562), founder of the Friars Minor of the Strict Observance, was a contemporary of Saint Teresa, who regarded his *Treatise on Mental Prayer* as a masterpiece of mystical literature. During his transports, this contemplative remained suspended in the air at the height of the panelling in the choir. He was often seen soaring above the monastery garden, at the level of the topmost branches of the trees. It is said that one of his levitations lasted for three hours. Sometimes he was carried into the air by the impetuous movement known as ecstatic flight, and some of his levitations were accompanied by luminous beams of light."

"The Blessed Salvador of Horta (1520–67) was a Franciscan lay-brother. His reputation as a thaumaturge led to his being persecuted. His biographer, Dinas Serpi, recounts the following story: One day, when Brother Salvador was begging in Maella (Catalonia), he was invited to lunch by a citizen of the place, Antonio Vughet by name. As Salvador was cutting open a pomegranate, the sight of the crimson seeds, in perfect symmetry beneath the rind, seemed to him such a marvelous symbol of divine order that he fell into a blissful trance, crossed his arms over his chest and rose bodily from the ground. Instantly, his host left the table and went out to call his neighbors in to see this curious spectacle."

"Saint Louis Bertrán (1526–80) was a Spanish Dominican. After spreading the Gospel in the Caribbean, he came back to Spain, sickened by the barbarity of the adventurers who were plundering South America. This was in 1569. During the remaining eleven years of his life, he spent his time preaching and organizing the various houses of his order. His life has been written by Bartolomeo Arignoni of the Friars Preachers, who was the postulator of his cause for canonization. His biographer states that Louis Bertrán was lifted off the ground during his ecstasies. One of his levitations is described thus: one day, the saint was returning from Moncada (a few kilometers from Valencia) accompanied by a servant. On his way, he came across a field of ripe corn and asked his attendant to wait for him at the side of the road. The saint then disappeared into the field. An inhabitant of Moncada, Bautista Ferreri, came along and asked the servant whom he was waiting for. Intrigued by the man's reply, Ferreri climbed a hill to search the surrounding countryside. From this high point, he saw Louis Bertrán in a transport of bliss, with his body floating above the ears of corn. Some Arabs witnessed a similar spectacle at Tubara. They saw the saint praying, suspended in the air... *corpus ejus spicas segetis tolleretur in aerem."*

"With Saint Teresa of Avila (1515–82) we have, for the first time, a personal, firsthand account of the phenomenon of levitation. Explaining the difference between union and ravishment, the saint writes:[23] 'In these ravishments, the soul no longer seems to cleave to the body. And it is impossible to resist the divine attraction. In union, finding yourself still, as it were, in your own familiar country, you can almost always resist, although it is painful and requires a violent effort. It is not the same as ravishment, which you can hardly ever resist. Giving you no time to think, or to prepare yourself, this often falls upon you with such swift and forceful impetuosity that you actually see and feel this cloud that seizes hold of you and this powerful eagle that carries you off on his wings. I have said "see and feel," you know that you are being carried off, but you do not know where you are going and so, at the beginning, in your human frailty, you experience indescribable terror at this movement which, otherwise, is so delightful. Here, the soul must show far more resolution and courage than in the preceding states. It must, in fact, be ready to risk everything, come what may, and to abandon itself unreservedly, and with good grace, into the hands of God, letting Him guide it wheresoever He will; for, however painful it may be, one will be lifted up. Very often, when I was alone, but more especially when I was in public, I felt such lively terror, and such fear that I might be deceived, that I tried to resist with all my strength. Sometimes, I succeeded to some extent, but, as it was rather like wrestling with a muscular giant, it left me broken in body and prostrate with exhaustion. At other times, all my efforts were in vain; my soul was lifted up and my head almost always followed this movement, without my being able to restrain it, and, at times, even my whole body was carried off and no longer touched the ground. It was only rarely that I was transported in this manner. It happened to me one day when I was kneeling in the choir with all the other nuns, ready to take communion. It was extremely distressing to me, knowing that such an extraordinary thing would soon cause a great sensation. As this event happened very recently, since I became Prioress, I forbade the Sisters to talk about it. At other times, perceiving that God was about to renew this charism (and one day in particular, on the titular feast of our monastery, while I was listening to the sermon in the presence of some ladies of high rank), I suddenly threw myself on to the floor; my Sisters ran to hold me down but, in spite of this, the ravishment could not pass unnoticed. I begged Our Lord not to favor me any longer with these graces, since they were betrayed by external signs, for I was already weary of the circumspection to which they condemned me, and it seemed to me that He could accord me the same graces without anyone knowing of them. Apparently, in His goodness, He has deigned to hear my prayer, for, since then, nothing of this sort has happened to me, although, to be truthful, it is only a little while since I asked Him this favor. Whenever I tried to resist, I thought I felt beneath my feet the astonishing forces that were raising me up; I know of nothing I can compare them to. No other operation of the spirit about which I have spoken, comes anywhere near this forceful thrust. It left me shattered. The combat is terrible and serves little purpose. I confess that, at the beginning, I was seized with excessive fear on seeing my body thus lifted off the ground, for although (when you offer no resistance) the soul follows after the body with inexpressible delight, you do not lose consciousness. Speaking for myself, at least, I was fully aware and could see that I was elevated above the ground....'

"It is to Bishop Yepes, who knew Saint Teresa personally, that we owe some complementary details concerning the ravishment that surprised her when she was about to take communion: Don Alvaro de Mendoza, the Bishop of Avila, was giving communion to the nuns through the opening in the wall of the cloister when the saint, seized with rapture, was lifted off the ground and, rising higher than the level of the embrasure, could not receive the Host. One day, immediately after taking communion, Saint Teresa, feeling herself being wrenched off the ground, seized hold of the bars of the cloister grille, imploring God to spare her these favors, which could be seen by other people. On another, similar occasion, she grasped the rug that covered the tiled floor of the choir and carried it up into the air with her.

"The first official depositions regarding these events began in 1595, thirteen years after the saint's death and thirty years after the publication of her autobiography. There were still some eyewitnesses living. Saint Teresa's levitations are mentioned in the *Acta authentica canonizationis,* which recalls that these phenomena had been the subject of numerous depositions, and adds that her ecstasies were sometimes accompanied by luminescence."

"Saint Catherine dei Ricci (1522–89) is a famous stigmatic. At the age of twenty-five, she was elected Prioress of the Dominican monastery in Prato (near Florence). Saint Philip Neri held her in the highest esteem and carried on a spiritual correspondence with her. She was canonized by Benedict XIV, who had a summary of her life published. This compendium mentions that, when she was in ecstasy, Catherine's body sometimes remained suspended in the air, and that this phenomenon was observed by numerous witnesses."

"Regarding Saint John of the Cross (1542–91), the famous mystical doctor and poet, we will speak of the levitation he experienced at the same time as Saint Teresa at the end of this account. I do not think there is any mention of his levitating other than on the occasion of this double phenomenon."

"In his life of Philip Neri (1515–95), Father Bernabei, who took his facts from the acts of the process of canonization, says that the saint frequently levitated. It generally happened while he was saying Mass. He would then rise up to a height of five to six meters. A young girl who saw him in this state thought that he must be possessed. Cardinal Paul Sfondrati is cited among the witnesses to these events. The latter told Pope Paul V that he had seen Philip, at prayer, almost touching the ceiling *(ad cubiculi).* Another time, while he was praying for the recovery of a sick man, several people saw him rise up to the ceiling *(ad lacunar)* with his body bathed in light. Gregory Ozes saw him one day in this radiant and suspended state, as he was praying before the tomb of the Apostles in the basilica of the Vatican. Father Antonio Galloni, one of Philip's favorite disciples, has handed down to us an account of the sensations the saint experienced during his levitations: he felt as if someone had seized hold of him and lifted him into the air by force. Philip was very embarrassed when these things happened to him in public, and, when he went into church with another person, he made an effort to curtail his prayers so as not to fall into ecstasy and make an exhibition of himself."

37

17th Century

"Margaret Agullona (1536–1600) is known as an ecstatic and a stigmatic. In the entry for December 9th, in the Franciscan martyrology by Arturus, one reads that, during Vespers one Sunday in the octave of Ascension, when they were celebrating the Feast of the Holy Crown in the Franciscan church in Valencia, Margaret saw a picture illustrating the crowning with thorns, became ecstatic, and rose from the ground. Her body, upheld in space, swayed gently in the breeze that was coming in through the main door. Many citizens of Valencia, as well as the Franciscan nuns, were present and witnessed this scene."

"In the *Palmier Séraphique,* a biographical anthology of the Franciscan order, we read that Alphonsus Rubius of Valencia, a lay-brother who died in 1601, was sometimes elevated so high during his transports that the other monks could pass under his feet without touching them."

"The Carmelite Mary Magdalen (1566–1607), who came from the illustrious Florentine family of the Pazzi, is known as a stigmatic. Her life was written by her confessor, Virgilio Cepari, an esteemed hagiographer who was also known for his sagacity as a spiritual director. This biographer states that, on the 3rd of May 1592, the day of the feast of the Invention of the Cross, the saint rose up to a height of fifteen *aunes* (about eighteen meters) to reach a crucifix and lift it off the wall *(Crucifixum sumpsit, clavisque extractis).* When she climbed staircases, she moved so swiftly and lightly that her feet did not appear to touch the treads at all."

"The life of the Blessed Passitea Crogi (1564–1615), a Franciscan better known as Passitea of Siena, was written by a compatriot, Father Venturi. Maria de' Medici had this biography translated from the manuscript.[24] It tells us that Passitea was an ecstatic from a very early age: no sooner was the child freed of her swaddling clothes and put into dresses than her confessor reported that angels began appearing to her and holding her in converse. He added that, very often, these blessed spirits lifted her into the air, and she felt such happiness in her soul as cannot be described. Another biography, by L. Maracci, again refers to matters of this kind and gives us further details: According to the intensity of her rapture, she was lifted off the ground to varying heights: Sister Felice declares that she has seen her three spans above the floor, Sister Maria Francesca has seen her more than four spans up and, at the same time, her body was resplendent with light.

This levitation lasted for two or three hours. Once, in the home of the Sforza Duchess at Santa Fiora, in the presence of the Duchess herself and many other people, Passitea had a transport that lifted her up to the height of a man's head. The Duchess made all the witnesses sign a testimonial to this event. Sometimes, she was transported from one place to the other without any visible movement of her feet; she seemed to glide lightly over the surface of the ground."

"The Jesuit Bernardinus Realino died in 1616 at Lecce (south of Brindisi). During the inquiries for his cause of beatification, in Naples in 1621, Signor Tobias da Ponte swore on solemn oath that he had seen this monk in a state of levitation. Signor da Ponte had gone to Lecce in 1608 to consult Father Bernardinus on some spiritual questions. One Saturday in April, he was sitting waiting in the corridor outside the good father's chamber when he noticed that the door was ajar and there was light coming through the crack. Intrigued by this light, he stood up and pushed the door half-open. He then saw Father Bernardinus on his knees, with his eyes closed and his face turned up to heaven, and with his body suspended about one meter above the floor. Having contemplated this sight with a mixture of reverence, fear, and stupefaction, Signor da Ponte quietly withdrew. Here are the words of his deposition as written down in the report:[25] After being warned to consider well whether everything he had written might be nothing more than an hallucination, or imagination, and the transport he had glimpsed simply a reflection of the sunlight, an optical illusion or the result of some other natural cause, the witness replied: 'The thing was so clear, so certain, and so real that, not only does it seem to me I can still see it, but I am as sure of it as I am of speaking to you now, and seeing all that is around me at this moment. I noticed the light filtering out through the crack in the door not once, but two, three, or four times before arriving at any kind of hypothesis. Then I started wondering how there could be such a bright fire in that room, for the rays of light could only have come from a very large and intense fire, such as you see in the blacksmith's forge when he hammers red-hot iron on the anvil. So I got up and pushed the door open and saw Father Bernardinus elevated above the floor, as surely as, at this moment, I see Your Illustrious Lordships....' The witness was once again warned to take extreme care not to exaggerate the facts out of a misguided sense of devotion, and to describe them without altering them in any way, since saints have no need for their causes to be upheld by misrepresentations of this kind, which are, indeed, abhorrent to them. He was asked if he wished to modify any part of his deposition, and answered as follows: 'What I have stated is the whole truth, pure and simple, without invention or exaggeration.'"

"Francisco Suarez (1548–1617) was also a Jesuit and the author of some classic works on theology. In his biography we find the account of a levitation which is based on a detailed document. This was a declaration by Brother Jeronimo da Silva, the doorkeeper at the college of Coïmbre, written by order of Father Morales, the confessor of both Suarez and Brother Jeronimo. The document had been sealed in an envelope bearing the words: Confessional matters. Not to be opened before the death of Father Francisco Suarez. Here is the gist of it:[26]

"'I, Brother Jeronimo da Silva, a monk of the Company of Jesus, certify that I have written this document on the orders of my confessor, the blind Father Antonio de Morales, and that this same Father has commanded me not to disclose its contents, nor allow anyone to read it, but to keep it sealed in an envelope bearing an absolute prohibition against opening it until after the death of our Father Francisco Suarez. This have I done, because the said Father de Morales asked it of me, judging that the sanctity of Father Suarez, whose works have brought such light into the church of Our Heavenly Father, should not remain forever hidden, and adding that God might very well carry me off from this world in an acute attack of the infirmities from which I suffer. Thus, and for these reasons, he made me write this paper, under the conditions that I have stated above, and I swear under oath to all that follows, in order that it may be read with greater faith and credence.

"'Firstly, while I was keeper of the monastery gate at the college of Coïmbre, Don Pedro of Aragon, who was then Rector of the University of Salamanca, came to stay with us as our guest. On one occasion, he asked me to summon Father Francisco Suarez to him, but, when I arrived at his apartments, I saw that Father Suarez had placed a stick across the door. I thought he must be resting, but, as our guest might grow impatient if made to wait too long, I removed the stick, went in, called Father by his name and several times made a noise with my feet. I received no answer. The shutters in the first room were closed; I went into the second room and again called out and shuffled my feet. As there was more light in this room, due to the shutters being imperfectly closed, I could see quite clearly that Father Suarez was on his knees, with his hands upraised and his head bare, in front of the crucifix. As he made no move at all, I approached him and tugged three times at the sleeve of his soutane, but still there was not the slightest response and he did not move; this left me, as it were, stunned, for the space of a quarter of an hour. I went out to look for Brother Aquilar, his companion, but, as I could not find him anywhere, I waited until Father Suarez had finished. Some half or three-quarters of an hour later, he emerged from this very profound prayer, and I gave him the message without telling him that I had been in his apartments.

"'Another day, at the same time—it must have been two hours after noon—Don Pedro of Aragon again commanded me to inform Father Francisco Suarez that he very much wanted him to accompany him to Santa Cruz, to visit the monastery there. And, as Father Suarez had recommended me to call him whenever this noble gentleman required his presence, I went to him at once. As was usual at this hour, I found the stick across the door. Relying on Father's own instructions to call him when needed, and being unable to find his companion, I removed the stick and went into the apartments. The first room was dark. I called out to Father Suarez but he did not answer. The curtain over the entrance to his study was closed, but there was a gap between this curtain and the door jamb, and there I saw a great radiance. I lifted the curtain and went into the study. Then I saw a great light coming from the holy crucifix, blinding me when I tried to look at it and so brilliant that I could not remain in the room without being dazzled. This light, flowing from the crucifix, filled the room and shone on the head and chest of Father Suarez. In its radiance, I saw him kneeling in front of the crucifix, his head bare, his hands joined and his body raised five spans above the floor, at the level of the table on which the crucifix was standing. Seeing this, I withdrew, but, before I went out, feeling overcome and, as it were, beside myself, I had to stop and lean against the frame of the door. I rested there for the space of about three *credos.* Then I went out, my hair standing on end like the bristles of a brush, and I was obliged to hold on to the outer door of the first room, for I was completely disoriented. A good quarter of an hour later, I heard a sound from within, and Father Suarez, coming to remove the stick from the door, became aware of my presence. I told him that the nobleman was waiting for him. He asked me why I had not summoned him earlier. I replied that I had gone into the study and called him, but he had not answered. When Father Suarez heard that I had been in his study, he seized me by the arm and led me back into the second room, then, clasping his hands in supplication and, with his eyes full of tears, he begged me to say nothing of what I had seen, at least for as long as he lived. I asked his permission to speak to my confessor about it and he gave his consent willingly, since we shared the same confessor. As I have already explained, my confessor advised me to write this account, in the manner aforesaid, and I did so, and signed it with my name, because every word it contains is the truth. And if it should please God to take me to his bosom before Father Francisco Suarez, you can believe everything I have stated, as if you had seen it yourself; but, if it pleases Our Lord to let Father Suarez die before me, I will be able to confirm everything upon oath, for as long as necessary.—(signed) Jeronimo da Silva.'"

"The Blessed Ursula Benincasa (1547–1618), founder of the Theatines, was an ecstatic from the age of ten. Sometimes she was bodily transported, and this happened to her in a church, in the presence of the congregation. Because of these phenomena, she was suspected of possession and exorcised accordingly. Once, she levitated while Cardinal San Severino was performing the rites of exorcism over her."[27]

"The Blessed Mary of the Incarnation (1566–1618), better known under the name of Mme. Acarie, introduced Saint Teresa's order of the Discalced Carmelites into France, as well as contributing to the foundation of the Ursuline order and the reform of the Benedictine monasteries. The popularity of this remarkable mystic has been revived, thanks to the Abbé Bremond, who wrote about her in his *Histoire littéraire.*[28] André du Val, Professor of Theology at the Sorbonne, who was Mary's spiritual director for many years, albeit somewhat intermittently, published her biography three years after her death. In it, he describes a levitation that took place at the home of Cardinal de Bérulle's[29] mother: 'Father de Bérulle, Superior of the Congregation of the Oratorians, once saw her in such a powerful rapture that her body rose two or three feet off the ground, and she remained suspended in the air for a long time, which caused a drastic weakening of her body.' A later biographer specifies that this transport lasted three hours. Chancellor Séguier's mother learned of the event from Monsignor de Bérulle himself."

"Domingo Ruzzola, called Dominic of Jesus and Mary (1559–1630), was born in Catalayud (Aragon). When very young, he entered the order of the Discalced Carmelites and later became their General. It is said that he predicted the defeat of the 'Invincible' Armada and so became rather unpopular. His *Life* was published by J. Caramuel de Lobkovicz, twenty-five years after his death. According to this account, Dominic experienced several levitations in which he rose so high that the other monks could barely touch the soles of his feet; these took place in 1593, during the days that follow Ascension. In an attempt to avoid transports in public, he would throw himself to the ground. It is related that, one day, in Valencia, at the moment when he began to levitate in ecstasy before the Holy Sacrament, a bystander caught him by the feet and was pulled up into the air with him. Taking fright, this man let go and fell heavily to the floor. It is also said that, in Madrid, he went into ecstasy and was lifted bodily off the ground in the presence of Philip II, the Queen and their courtiers, and that the King, simply by blowing on him, made his body move like a feather in the wind."

"John de Massias (1584–1645), a one-time shepherd, entered the Dominican monastery in Lima as a lay-brother and became the doorkeeper. He was in the habit of going to the church at night to pray. He had several ecstasies accompanied by levitation. One evening, a novice went into the church, which was in darkness, and had a great fright when he bumped into the feet of the Blessed John, whose body was suspended in the void."

"Saint Mariana de Paredes (Mariana of Jesus) (1618–45), a pious daughter of Ecuador known as the Lily of Quito, was canonized in 1850. According to her legend, many people saw her in ecstasy, her face luminous and her body no longer touching the ground."

"Margaret of the Holy Sacrament (1618–48), a Carmelite from Beaune, had numerous levitations according to P. Amelot, who published her *Life* in 1651. On the 21st of November, 1631, on the eve of taking her vows, she had a levitation in the true and proper sense of the word: 'In order to prepare herself for the simple vows she was to make on the day of the Presentation to the Holy Virgin, Sister Margaret withdrew the evening before into a hermitage dedicated to the divine Mother. While she was at prayer there, she was suddenly ravished and lifted up to the level of the altar. On another occasion, an invisible force, which she could do nothing to resist, lifted her off her bed and held her suspended in the air, between the mattress and the canopy.' A later biographer reveals two more feats: 'One day, when Margaret had gone to gather grapes for a sick person, the other nuns saw her rise from the ground to pick a bunch that was out of her reach. This does not necessarily mean that it was very high up, because Margaret Parigot had stopped growing when she was about twelve years old. Finally, on Good Friday of the year preceding her death, she had been praying for several hours at the foot of a crucifix when she was lifted up, her body rigid, her arms outstretched, and her head inclined to the left. She remained thus for an hour, in sight of the other nuns.'"

"Juana Rodriguez of Jesus and Mary (1584–1650) entered the Order of Saint Clare after forty-five years of marriage. She was then sixty years old. She was an ecstatic and also bore the stigmata. Every week, for many years, she would mime the scenes of the Passion during her raptures. She used to lie down on a large wooden cross, and the other sisters declared they had seen her rise up on this cross without touching the ground. One day, when she had become extremely frail and was hobbling along painfully, supported by Alfonso and Francisco Ruiz, she heard the sound of some religious music coming from nearby. All of a sudden, she was carried off, as if by an impetuous force, to the Convent of the Augustinians, a distance of some two hundred meters, from which a procession was just then emerging. Her two escorts, who had not been left behind, could not understand how they had been transported with her."

"The Spanish Jesuit, Pedro Claver (1589–1654), is known as the Apostle of the black slaves of Bolivia, and spent forty-four years in that country. It is said that he had bodily transports during which he became luminous. His servant recounts having seen him rise from the ground on one occasion, lost in contemplation of a crucifix he was holding in his hand. During his final illness, the saint again levitated. By then, he was so feeble that the friar who was taking care of him, and who saw him in that state, had to put him back to bed when he recovered consciousness."

"Joseph (Giuseppe) Desa, known under the name of Saint Joseph of Copertino (1603–63), occupies an important place in the history of levitation. The phenomena started immediately after his ordination (March 28, 1628) and lasted up until his death (September 18, 1663). During this period, his superiors generally banned him from processions and from the choir and the refectory because of the disturbance his extraordinary transports caused, and which, in certain circumstances, were rather more comical than edifying. One of Saint Joseph's last levitations, one of the strangest and most fully described—although it is not often quoted—took place during the course of an operation. Here is the deposition made by the surgeon, Francesco de Pierpaoli, who observed the event: 'At the time of Brother Joseph's last illness, I had to cauterize his leg, in compliance with the orders of Dr. Giacinto Carosi. Brother Joseph was sitting on a chair with his leg resting on my knees. I was already applying the iron to carry out the operation; I saw that Brother Joseph was in a state of bliss, unconscious and completely abstracted. His arms were extended, his eyes open and gazing toward heaven, his mouth was agape and his respiration seemed to have ceased completely. I observed that he was elevated about a span above the chair, but otherwise in the same position as before the rapture commenced. I tried to lower his leg, but without success; it remained stretched out. A fly had settled on the pupil of his eye, and the more I tried to chase it away, the more obstinately it seemed to come back to the same place; in the end, I had to leave it there. In order to observe Brother Joseph more closely, I went down on my knees. The above-named doctor was also examining him, and we both recognized the fact that Brother Joseph was very visibly transported, out of his senses and, furthermore, he was indeed suspended in the air as I have already said. This situation had been going on for a quarter of an hour when Father Silvestro Evangelista, who lived in the convent at Osimo, came in. After observing the phenomenon, he commanded Joseph, by his holy vows of obedience, to come back to himself, and he called him by name. Joseph smiled and came back to his senses.' According to Bernino,[30] the last levitation took place the day before his death, while Saint Joseph was saying Mass. It was the Day of the Assumption."

"Mary of Jesus (1602–65), a Franciscan gray nun, Mother Superior of the Convent of the Immaculate Conception at Agreda, is known above all for her visions. Her process of beatification was abandoned in 1771, on the orders of Clement XIV, because of the over-imaginative character of its revelations. Father J. Ximenes Samaniego, who knew her personally, wrote concerning her raptures and levitations: 'The ecstasies of this servant of God took the following form: her body was deprived of its senses, as if she were dead, and became insensitive to all kinds of ill-treatment; it was raised a little above the ground and was as light as if it had no natural weight, so that even a breath was enough to move her some distance, like a feather. Sometimes these raptures lasted two hours, at others three. They would come on her while she was reading some spiritual text, or when someone spoke to her of the grandeur and beauty of God, or other divine mysteries, or when she was listening to the singing in church, but, most frequently, it was immediately after taking communion.' The nuns were in the habit of allowing the public to see Mary in this condition, in the hope that they would be edified by the sight, but when she heard of it, she shut herself up whenever she wanted to pray and meditate. However, they took a plank out of one of the walls of her chamber and carried her in front of the grille of the choir. When they did so, they found her body was as light as a feather."

"Bernard of Corleone (near Palermo) (1605–67) spent thirty-five years as a lay brother with the Capuchins. Goerres gives this description of an ecstatic flight of his: 'One Corpus Christi, before the procession started, Saint Bernard of Corleone was kneeling in the choir of the main church with the other monks; as he raised his eyes toward the high altar to contemplate the Blessed Sacrament, which was displayed there, his soul was inflamed with such fervor that it carried his body with it in a mighty bound toward God, and, in sight of all present, he flew through the air and remained suspended in front of the object of his love and adoration. Filled with amazement, everyone came running to see this marvel at close quarters, to kiss the monk's feet, or at least touch his clothing, but the great concourse awoke him from his ecstasy and he descended gently to earth.'"

"Sister Maria Villani (1584–1670) of the Dominican order, who founded the monastery of Santa Maria del Amore Divino in Naples, has described her own levitations. This is what she says in a letter to her spiritual director: 'Once, in my cell, I felt a new sensation; I felt that my ecstasy was carrying me away with such force that I was drawn right up off the floor, just as a scrap of iron is drawn by a magnet, and yet it was also very gentle. At first, I was filled with a great terror, but afterward I was left with a sensation of extreme gratification and joy. Although I was transported out of myself, I was still conscious of being elevated above the ground, and of my body remaining suspended there for a considerable time. Up until last Christmas (1618), this has happened to me five times.' Sister Villani confided to her confessor that she had prayed that these special favors should never be known to anyone, and her prayer had been granted."

"Another Dominican, the lay sister Teresa of the Cross, could not hear of the love of God nor pronounce certain sacred names without entering into an ecstatic state and levitating. Wherever she happened to be, in the choir, in the cloisters, in her cell, or even in the refectory, her body lost its natural weight and she would rise up into the air without letting go of whatever was in her hands. Sometimes she stayed suspended like this, out of her senses and motionless, for five or six hours at a time. Because of these phenomena, Teresa was sent to another convent, treated as a sorceress, and, finally, sent back into the world. The convent in Liège, where she had taken her first vows, finally accepted her back into the fold. She died there in 1673."

"Saint Francis of Saint-Nicholas (1608–78) had such frequent ecstasies during Mass that his altar boy had to tug at his chasuble, or even prick his heel with a needle to prevent the Mass becoming interminable. These ecstasies were sometimes accompanied by levitation. Once he levitated while officiating at Mass in the chapel of the Escorial. And once he flew right up to the vault of the church."

"Another Franciscan, Blaise of Caltanisetta (d. 1684) presented the most curious symptoms during his levitations, and these have been described by

Imbert-Gourbeyre:[31] 'His heart beat as if it were full of boiling water, his thorax visibly swelled, he trembled from head to foot as if in an attack of ague and cried out several times as he rose into the air, in sight of numerous spectators who could see his chest swelling and hear emerging from it a sound like two stones striking against one another.'"

38

18th Century

"The Blessed Joseph Oriol (1650–1702), reports the Abbé Daras in his work on the saints and blessed ones of the 18th century, often rose into the air during his raptures: 'Has he not been seen many and many a time, in the Church of Santa Maria del Pino (Barcelona), kneeling in the air and no longer touching the ground? He would hang as if suspended between heaven and earth for hours on end. One day, after having been to confession, he was transported while praying at the foot of the altar, and he remained in this condition for a long time, with his body elevated about six inches off the floor. In 1698, when he was on board a Catalan ship taking him from Marseilles to Barcelona, he had an ecstasy on the deck. His body rose rapidly into the air, astounding the sailors, who tried to follow his ascent by climbing up the rigging. Raphaël de Baladas de Blanes, the owner of the ship, was so moved by this scene that he could not speak of it without weeping.'"[32]

"Charles Lavagna (1651–1711), from Potenza (Basilicate), entered the Conventual Friars Minor and took the name of Brother Bonaventure. He wanted to remain a lay brother, but his superiors raised him to the priesthood. 'While saying his first Mass,' writes the Abbé Daras, 'he burst into tears and his body rose from the floor, as if wishing to come nearer to God.... When he spoke of Our Lord's sufferings, and of His love for mankind, his eyes seemed to throw forth flames, his feet no longer touched the floor, and the very chair on which he was sitting floated up with him.' One day in 1711, as the priest, Don Francesco d'Amato, handed him an apple, remarking how good it smelled, the perfume of the fruit reminded him of the ineffable sweetness of God, 'and he could not master his rapture [says the same author]; he changed color, lost the use of his senses, and his body rose about eight to ten inches off the ground and remained in the air for some time.'"

"The Dominican, Francis de Posadas (1644–1713) used to rise off the floor while preaching or saying Mass. As soon as he began speaking, his voice made his vast congregation tremble; then, the love of God that inspired him seemed to inflame his soul and beam out through his body; his face became radiant, he was uplifted, and on several occasions it was seen that his feet no longer touched the ground. One day during Mass, just at the moment when he was elevating the Host, his soul flew up to God, followed by his body, and he remained suspended in the air. When he came down again, a great number of people saw that he was entirely surrounded by light. Francis was not aware of what happened to him during his levitations: 'I do not know,' he said to his confessor, 'I do not know whether the ground falls away from under me, I do not understand what happens to me....' Similar feats are related in a biography by Sopena, published after the Blessed Francis's death."

"John Baptist of Mastena, a Franciscan, after spending some time in monasteries in the Holy Land, returned to his own convent in Como, where he died in 1713. On the 17th of November 1700, reports Dr. Imbert-Goubeyre,[33] 'He was busy sweeping, and deep in contemplation, when he found himself rising up, more than a span above the ground, but still holding the broom in his hand.' Another time, his confessor saw him rise to a height of four spans and remain in that position. And once he was found in his cell elevated to the height of a man's head."

"Saint Pacificus of San Severino (1653–1721) entered the Franciscans of the Regular Observance in 1670. After being ordained a priest in 1678, he spent his time preaching, but serious infirmities soon interrupted his ministry. He retired to the convent of Forano. In the course of the inquiries made for his beatification, the inhabitants of San Severino reported having seen Pacificus in ecstasy during the consecration; at these times, his face became luminous, he stretched out his arms and his body rose several spans above the steps of the altar. Father Felix Pascal, the postulator of his cause, also has this to say: 'In the month of December 1714, Pacificus was saying Mass in the chapel of the Crucifix at San Severino when, following the consecration, his body began to exude a resplendent light and rose one span above the altar steps. He stayed thus, in ecstasy, without touching the ground, for about five hours. The boy who was serving Mass went to fetch the Superior, who ordered the ecstatic to come back to his senses and finish the Mass....'"

"Ursula Gouliani (1676–1727), who took the name of Veronica when she joined the Capuchins in Città di Castello, was the subject of such strange mystical phenomena that the ecclesiastical authorities, who suspected her of imposture, made her undergo numerous tests and trials. She was dismissed from her position as Novice-Mistress, treated as a witch and threatened with death at the stake. Saint Veronica's ecstasies were almost continuous and she was often seen in the garden, rising off the ground and floating above the topmost branches of the trees."

"One day, when the Blessed Thomas of Cori (1655–1729) was giving communion in the church of Civitella, he was seized with rapture and rose right up to the vault with such speed that the servers were afraid he would crack his head. After floating in space for several seconds, he gently came down to earth again, still holding the ciborium in one hand and the Host in the other. On the eve of his death—the 10th of January 1729—he rose horizontally from his bed. The monk who was nursing him declared he had seen him thus, suspended at a height of about two feet and surrounded by brilliant light. These events were reported by the postulator of his cause, Father Luca of Rome, who based his biography (published in 1786) on the documents of the process. The Blessed Thomas of Cori belonged to the Friars Minor of the Regular Observance."

"Gerard Majella (1726–55), a Redemptorist lay brother, fell into an ecstatic trance one day while listening to a blind beggar playing a popular canticle on his flute:

> *Il tuo gusto, e non il mio,*
> *Voglio solo in te, mio Dio...*
>
> (Thy will, my God, not mine,
> I have no will but Thine...)

and in this state he was lifted off the ground. This took place in Caposele, in the presence of Dr. Santorelli and of some poor people who had come to receive a distribution of alms. The blind man was called Filippo de Falcone. Another time, he rose up into the air as if of his own volition:[34] 'Gerard, accompanied by two young workmen in the service of the monastery, was returning from Deliceto; at the side of the road that led from the little town to the monastery stood a small chapel dedicated to the Holy Virgin. Gerard took it as a pretext to turn the conversation to the subject of the mercy and goodness of Mary. Suddenly, he stopped, seized a pencil, feverishly wrote several words on a piece of paper, then threw it into the air, as if he wanted to send a message to heaven. At the same instant, the two workmen saw him rise off the ground and fly with the lightness of a bird to the spot known as *Il Francese,* about five hundred meters away. There, he came to earth and quietly returned to the monastery. The two witnesses to this strange event, who both died around the year 1804, would tell the story to anyone who would listen to them, and they never varied the account of what their astonished eyes had seen.' Another ecstatic flight took place on Good Friday, April 20, 1753, when the traditional procession went to Corato; on the return journey, when they were bringing back a picture of the Crucifixion from the Benedictine church, Gerard was again seen to rise to a considerable height off the ground. He died very young, in 1735, and was canonized by Pius X in 1904.'

"Paul Francis Danei, founder of the Passionists, and known by the name of Paul of the Cross (1649–1775), was returning one winter's day from Monte Argentaro, where he lived in a hermitage. He felt so exhausted that he was afraid he would succumb, so he lay down on the ground and prayed. Then, he felt himself being lifted up and, in a moment, he was transported to a spot near his convent. At Latera (in the diocese of Montefiascone), while he was exhorting the ecclesiastics in the sacristy, they saw him rise up into the air. On the island of Elba, while he was delivering a sermon, he left the dais, where he had been walking up and down as he preached, and began to walk in space above the heads of the congregation; he then returned to the dais in the same manner. In the latter years of his life, during a pious conversation in the sacristy of the church of Saints John and Paul, in Rome, his face was seen to become radiant and his body to tremble. Warned by these premonitory signs, Paul, who was sitting down, pressed himself hard against the back of the chair and clung to its arms. 'In spite of these efforts,' says a witness, 'he began to rise up, still in his chair, the legs of which reached the height of my head, and this made me think he must have risen to seven or eight spans. He remained in ecstasy for a very long time. When he came to himself again, I noticed a slight trembling in the upper part of his body, then he came down, gradually, still sitting in the chair.' The levitations of Saint Paul of the Cross are mentioned in the Breviary (Die XXVIII aprilis, lectio VI)."

"No actual levitations are credited to Saint Benedict Joseph Labre (1748–83), the pilgrim beggar. However, it is worth noting that those who were present at his transports declared that his body, without losing contact with the ground, seemed to escape partially from the laws of gravity, since it could get into, and hold, the most extraordinary positions."

"Saint Alphonsus Liguori (1696–1787), founder of the Congregation of the Most Holy Redeemer, had some public levitations in the course of his preaching. The most famous of these took place at Foggia, shortly before Christmas, 1745, while he was giving a sermon in the cathedral. At a certain moment, a madonna, known as the Madonna of the Seven Veils, or the Old Image, and venerated at Foggia since the 11th century, seemed to become luminous and project a beam of light on to the preacher's face. Quite beside himself, Alphonsus stammered: 'O Holy Mother... I am yours... all yours!' And soon he entered into a holy trance and all the people saw him, with his eyes fixed on the Madonna and his arms held out toward her, rise several spans above the dais as if he were about to take flight. The two thousand people who made up the congregation were at first struck dumb with amazement, then they cried out 'Miracle! Miracle!' and their enthusiastic exclamations resounded beyond the sacred precincts and, being taken up everywhere, attracted crowds of the curious to the environs of the cathedral, to such a point that the Sisters of the Annunciation, whose convent was not far from the cathedral, thought a riot had broken out.

"A similar event—so similar, in fact, that, if it were not for the witnesses, one might think it another description of the same occasion—took place in Amalfi in October 1756. Saint Alphonsus had another levitation while preaching a sermon on the Blessed Virgin. Casanova writes, 'Alphonsus exhorted his listeners to recommend themselves to her in all their spiritual and temporal needs, then, all of a sudden, as if inspired by God, he cried out, "You do not have sufficient confidence in your Holy Mother! You do not know how to pray to her from your hearts! I... I will pray for you!" And his ardent soul was uttering the most touching supplications when, all at once, a ray of light, coming from the image of Mary which was placed on the righthand side of the pulpit, struck the preacher's face. We then saw him with his face beaming, his eyes staring, ravished with bliss, rise two spans above the pulpit, like a seraph flying up to heaven. This rapture lasted more than five minutes, during which, in the midst of indescribable emotion, the sobs of the congregation mingled with cries of "Miracle! Miracle!" from every corner.' Four eyewitnesses made statements about this feat at the process: the Canons Casanova, di Luca, di Stefano, and Father Criscuoli. It was to this miracle that the latter attributed the extraordinary effect the mission had on the morals of the inhabitants of Amalfi: 'I was present every evening at the mission to Amalfi, and it will ever be dear to me, because it was the immediate cause of my entering a religious community. I therefore have positive and certain knowledge of what happened there. Now, I particularly remember how two parts of town, which had been full of prostitutes, were completely transformed. By an act of grace, these creatures given up to vice were all totally converted after listening to the servant of God.'

"Other levitations received less clamorous publicity: 'One morning, early in 1762,' recounts Brother Verdesca, 'I went to our Father Alphonsus to recite the office with him, as was my custom. On entering his cell, I saw him raised two or three spans above his chair in the attitude of a man half-sitting and half-kneeling. His arms were outstretched, his eyes open and raised to heaven, his face was luminous, as if transfigured. I went quietly into the cell and knelt down between the armchair and the bed, so that, by turning my head, I could contemplate his face. The ravishment lasted nearly a quarter of an hour but, for me, that quarter hour seemed but an instant. While I, with my eyes bathed in tears, was observing this wholly celestial spectacle, the servant of God let out a deep sigh and cried: "My God, my God!" At that moment, he came to his senses and found himself sitting, quite naturally, in his chair. I burst into tears and, thus becoming aware of my presence, he was covered with confusion. He turned toward me and said with an air of gentle reproach: "Wretched man! So you were there! Whatever you do, do not tell anyone what you have seen..." And we began to recite the office. However, he appeared to be dazed and still under the effect of this long transport.'

"Father Tannoia also had occasion to observe one of Saint Alphonsus's levitations and he gave a detailed description of it: 'Finding myself at Pagani in the month of October 1784, I went to attend Holy Mass; while Alphonsus was sitting in front of the Blessed Sacrament altar, I heard him moving his feet, as if they had slipped on the tiled floor; a few seconds later, I heard this sound again, and, suspecting that something supernatural was happening, I threw a sidelong glance at him and saw Alphonsus rise up into the air above his chair, and this occurred several times. Now, in his normal state, it was only with great effort, and with the assistance of his servant and the brother who attended him, that he could move at all, whether to go to church or simply to get up from a sitting position. After Mass, having placed myself at the far end of the choir to say my act of thanksgiving, I noticed that the same rising movements were repeated more than once. In order to study the phenomenon more thoroughly, I placed myself, for several consecutive days, in the same position, from which I could observe him well, and I saw the same levitations occur, always with the speed and lightness of a feather.'

"Saint Alphonsus had levitations right up until the last days of his life, even when he became helpless and had to be taken about in a wheelchair, and even on his deathbed. Cardinal de Villecourt records these facts as follows: 'One day, when he was being pushed along the corridor in his armchair, it was noticed that, like a man in delirium, he was talking to himself about certain obligations that he had not fulfilled. Father Volpicelli, wishing to take his mind off these painful thoughts, said to him that, at his age, and in the poor state of his health, he was no longer obliged to do anything, and that, by a single act of love, he could satisfy all that was required of him. "Yes," said Alphonsus, as if waking out of sleep, "by an act of love!" Father Volpicelli repeated: "An act of love satisfies all." Since Alphonsus was hard of hearing, Father Volpicelli came very close to him and said loudly: "My God, I love Thee!" and at once, in a perfect rapture, Alphonsus rose up into the air, and his head knocked Father Volpicelli on the chin, for the latter had bent down to make himself heard. Another time, Alphonsus again begged Father Volpicelli to let him make an act of love to God, but this time the good father took the precaution of not bending too close, so as to avoid the jolt he had received before, and it was as well he did so, because the old saint was lifted up in the same manner.'

"When the Bishop-Saint was close to death, Joseph de Mauro, the King's architect, came from Naples to Pagani to inspect the work being done on the Redemptorists' church, and he paid his respects to Alphonsus. The latter asked him if the theaters were crowded, and whether his nephew went to them. 'Monsignore,' said the architect, 'it is now quite common in the world.' Alphonsus was silent for a moment, then he asked, with greater vehemence, 'And the chapels, do many people go to them?' 'Yes,' replied Joseph, 'and you wouldn't believe how much good it has done, and with what ardor the lower classes attend them. Nowadays, one sees coachmen who are veritable saints.' At that particular moment, the Monsignore was lying on his bed, seemingly at death's door. On hearing that coachmen had become saints, he cried: 'Saintly coachmen in Naples! Gloria Patri!' As he spoke these words, he rose more than a span above his bed and repeated three times: 'Coachmen in Naples who are saints! Gloria Patri!', So powerful was his emotion that he was unable to sleep the whole night long, and kept calling his servant, or the monk who attended him, and saying to them over and over again, 'In Naples, there are coachmen who are saints!'[35]

"In the office dedicated to him *(Die 2 Aug., S. alph. de Ligorio, Lectio V),* there is no allusion to his levitations. The events at Foggia and Amalfi are simply recorded in these terms: *'a Virginis imagine in eum immisse miro splen-*

dore totus facie coruscare et in extasim rapi coram universo populo non semel vissus est.'"

"Saint Mary Frances of the Five Wounds (1715–91), a tertiary of the Franciscan branch of the Alcantarines, was remarkable, so it was said, for the precocity of her religious fervor. From the age of four, she was seen to fall into raptures. At Christmastime, when her parents made a Nativity scene, she could not be dragged away from it. She prayed there for hours on end, even after her family had gone to bed. One night, her sister surprised her in a ravishment, elevated almost two feet off the ground. This is the only feat of levitation cited by the Abbé Daras. He simply adds that, being frail and sickly, she normally walked slowly, but one day she was suddenly seen to assume extraordinary agility and run through the countryside at such speed that one would have thought she was flying. However, in her office in the Breviary, her levitations are referred to as, if not frequent, at least repeated: *'Coelestibus rebus intenta, frequenter in extasim est rapta et quandoque a terra subtala* (6 Oct.).'"

39

19th Century

As we approach the present day, traditions regarding levitation by mystics continue without interruption and are no rarer than before. Here are some data concerning the 19th century which Olivier Leroy managed to collect:

"Claude Dhière (1757–1820), rector of the large seminary at Grenoble, is said to have levitated during his ecstasies. 'Father Dhière,' says his biographer,[36] 'was very often led from prayer into rapture by the violence of the Divine Love that consumed him. On these occasions, his pupils saw him lose his senses, stretch out his arms, as if he were nailed to a cross, and rise up from the floor. If some words escaped his lips during these moments of exquisite ardor, they were generally texts from the Holy Scriptures or outpourings of divine love. When his soul returned to itself after these pious trances, he humbled himself and begged forgiveness of those around him, calling these transports of fervor *oublis,* states of oblivion. His ecstasies during Mass were nearly always mentioned in the prayers for the living and the dead, and those of his pupils who served him habitually assure us that, once carried away by God, his feet no longer touched the earth.'"

"Anne Catherine Emmerich, a famous clairvoyant and stigmatic (1774–1824) did not have levitations, properly speaking, but claimed feats of abnormal agility that must be cited here: 'While I was carrying out my duties as sacristan, I was often lifted up, very suddenly, and I soared, or climbed up and stood in the highest places in the church, on the window ledges, on the ornamental sculptures, or on projecting stones; I cleaned and set in order all the things in places which were humanly impossible to reach. I felt myself lifted and supported in the air, and I was not in the least uneasy, for I was accustomed to being assisted by my guardian angel, ever since childhood.'"

"Andrew Hubert Fournet (1752–1834) was beatified in 1926. The following details are borrowed from the painstaking biography dedicated to him by M. Jules Saubat. The author drew them from the informative process that followed the preliminary inquiry ordered by the Bishop of Poitiers in 1853: 'A. H. Fournet's first levitations took place in 1820, while he was staying at Issy, in the convent of the Congregation of the Daughters of the Cross, an order he had just founded. He was then sixty-eight years old. During his time there, the servant of God celebrated Mass, and, at the moment when he elevated the sacred Host, Sister Marie-Alexandrine saw him rise from the floor and float in the air. Filled with emotion, and fearful that she might be mistaken, or deceiving herself, she called the attention of the other nuns to this phenomenon. Thereafter, they never failed to observe Father Fournet closely, and joyfully confirmed the prodigious event, which was repeated for a whole week, each time the good Father officiated at Mass.

"'A certain Lafleur-Peignon, from Paizay, had acted as altar boy to the Blessed Fournet in his early youth, and he related that sometimes, in front of the altar, the Blessed Father seemed like a bird taking flight, and his feet did not touch the floor.'

"The nuns in the Convent of La Puye (Vienne) saw him praying in the church, on his knees, but in the air. The sister who made a deposition to this effect during the informative process had heard the story from Sister Monique, an eyewitness. She made the following declaration: 'Our dear Sister Monique has declared to me that once, when she was in the Church of La Puye with five or six other nuns, she saw the servant of God on his knees, with his arms held out as if on a cross, right up under the bells.'

"Another time, he was seen to levitate while making the Stations of the Cross in the same church. Sister Ludvine, who belonged to the Daughters of the Cross, relates the event as follows: 'I will report what I witnessed in the Church of La Puye. The servant of God was making the Stations of the Cross in the presence of our whole community, and preaching at each station. I was walking behind him, carrying a candle, and there was another Sister with me who had been assigned to the same task. At the tenth station, as Father Andrew was beginning to preach, I saw him rise off the ground. As I was close to him, I could clearly see the light between his feet and the tiles of the church floor. He was elevated to a height of more than six inches, but not quite a foot. Seeing the servant of God thus detached from the floor, I was utterly amazed and could not contain my emotion, so I said to the nuns who were near me: "Oh, look! Father Andrew is in the air!" The other nuns made signs to me to keep quiet and not disrupt the service. I do not remember the names of the nuns who witnessed this levitation with me. But, in any case, I was able to contemplate this extraordinary feat at my leisure and it lasted all the time Father Andrew was preaching before the tenth station.'

"There are more numerous and more detailed depositions concerning another levitation that took place while A. F. Fournet was preaching. Once again, it is the nuns from La Puye who make the statements: 'On the feast day of Saint John the Baptist, which, at La Puye, is also the day for taking First Communion, the servant of God was preaching in front of a cross which had been set up on the ancient road that leads to Paizay. Some parishioners, and the children who had just taken their first Communion, had been led there in procession. Suddenly, the children began crying out to Sister Saint Vincent de Paul, who was leading them: "Oh, Sister, do look at Father Andrew, he's up in the air!" The nun ordered them to be silent, saying: "I see him quite well, but you are not to say a word about it!" Then she came, very quietly, to tell me of it, because I had cast my eyes down as I listened to Father Andrew, who was speaking with great animation and fervor. I looked up and saw him raised a foot and a half above the ground, but he was by then coming down, very gradually.'

"Another nun gives this account of the same event: 'As usual, we went in procession toward a cross that stood at the end of the sisters' enclosure on the road to Paizay. We stood in a circle around this cross: the men and the children who had taken their First Communion in the front row, then the nuns and, lastly, the women of the parish. We, the little boarders, were behind the nuns. Father Andrew was preaching to us from the foot of the cross, which was set into a stone standing on a small mound of earth. He was speaking about the joys of heaven; we could hear him very distinctly. I cannot recall whether, at the beginning of his discourse, I could see him as well, because I was not thinking about it, but, on account of my short stature (I was then about twelve years old) and the people in front of me, it is unlikely that I would have been able to see the priest. While he was speaking, I heard a woman beside me exclaim that the good Father Andrew was rising up to heaven. She seemed very moved and was in tears. Her exclamation made me look up to see what was happening. And then I saw Father Andrew very clearly, for he had risen above the people who were in front of me. I could see right down to his knees, and then even the edge of his surplice. It would have been impossible for me to see him like that if he had not been elevated well above the ground. And then, being very naive, I began looking up at the sky as if expecting some angel to descend and carry Father Andrew off.'

"And here is Sister Saint Vincent de Paul's deposition: 'The servant of God arrived, with the procession, at the foot of this cross; as was his usual custom, he immediately prostrated himself, singing *"O crux Ave!"* and then the canticle: "Long Live Jesus, Long Live His Cross!" Then he stood up and, mounting a narrow ledge that encircled the base of the cross, he began to preach zealously, his words full of fire. I was leading the children who had taken First Communion, and I positioned them in the circle. I was listening to the teachings of the servant of God, but not looking at him, when one of the children, who happened to be beside me, cried out: "Oh, Sister, Father Andrew has risen off the ground!" I looked and, in fact, I saw that the servant of God was no longer touching the ground, but was about a foot above the little stone ledge on which he had been standing. I could see him very clearly, for I was only some five or six paces away from the priest and there was nobody between us and nothing to impede my observing him in this position. I went to tell one of my Sisters, who was just a few steps away from me, and said: "Do look at Father Andrew, he's in the air!" This nun was Sister Saint Martin, and she then began to watch with me. However, at that moment, the servant of God was already beginning to descend toward the ground. From the moment when, alerted by the child, I saw Father Andrew raised above the earth, until the moment when I saw him coming down imperceptibly, and finding himself on his feet, on the earth, ten or twelve minutes had passed.... The servant of God was facing the children who had taken First Communion, among whom I was standing. The parishioners of La Puye could not see him because they were standing behind the cross.'"

"The Blessed Joseph Benedict Cottolengo (1786–1842) lived in Turin as a secular priest; he devoted himself to numerous charitable works and founded various institutions to initiate or support them. He was beatified by Benedict XV in 1917. A good many levitations are recorded in the documents of the process for his beatification. Here are some of them, according to the depositions of an eyewitness: 'At dusk, one evening in the year 1836, Joseph was returning to the Piccola Casa (the Little House of Divine Providence) where he lived, when he was attacked by some ruffians. He escaped, thanks to the intervention of two policemen. The nun who acted as doorkeeper stated that she saw Joseph come in looking pale and distressed. She was surprised to hear him ask for a cup of coffee. After drinking it, Joseph went up to his room. The doorkeeper nun was still rather anxious about him, although she did not know what had happened, and she was surprised not to hear him moving about upstairs, since his room was directly above the porter's lodge. Fearing that the Blessed Joseph might be ill, she went up to his room. She knocked at his door several times without eliciting any response, so she decided to open it. Then she saw Joseph Benedict praying in ecstasy before an image of the Virgin. He was standing with his arms stretched out, his face was radiant, and his feet had left the floor.'

"The same nun was able to contemplate similar scenes on several other occasions. One day, in particular, when some visitors at the lodge gates asked to see him, she went up to call Joseph and, receiving no answer to her knock, opened the door and found the ecstatic in a state of levitation; he was gazing at an image of the Virgin that hung over the door, so the nun had a perfect view of him: *Rapito in estasi, fuori dei sensi, sollevato da terra, colla faccia accesa, aria ridente, occhi scintillanti e rivolti al cielo.* He was in a kneeling position in the air, and the witness noticed that his soutane no longer touched the floor. His ecstasies, said the Sister, coincided with certain liturgical feasts, or else occurred when the Blessed Joseph had been subjected to some humiliation.'"

"Saint Mary Magdalen Postel (1756–1846), founder of the Sisters of Mercy, was canonized in 1925. At the time when she was still only a Venerable, Monseigneur A.-M. Legoux wrote a voluminous biography based on the documents of the various canonical processes, over which he had presided in the capacity of Judge. The facts that follow are taken from this work. 'One day, her pupils surprised her in ecstasy before the tabernacle in her oratory. She was on her knees, but floating above the floor. Her arms were held out at each side, as if on a cross, her face was shining with celestial light and her eyes seemed to be contemplating infinite beauty.... Thereafter, moved by an understandable, and indeed, a forgivable curiosity, they wanted to enjoy this ravishing spectacle again. They would get up at night, tiptoe silently to the oratory and look in through the cracks in the door or through the keyhole. Often, the saint was elevated above the floor, kneeling in the air, her eyes turned up to heaven and her face transfigured.... She was again seen in this state by two nuns, Sister Xavier and Sister Aimable, kneeling unsupported in the air with her hands clasped in prayer; she was murmuring passionately: "I suffer a great deal, my God, but it is all for Thee.... O God, let it be still more!"'

"After Mass, Mary Magdalen Postel would remain in the chapel to prolong her act of thanksgiving. When the nun who helped her take care of the sacristy came back after breakfast, she often found her on her knees in the void, her face radiant with divine light.

"Another transport, which must be added to her feats of levitation, is described thus: One afternoon, she went to a neighboring parish called Gatteville, which, like Barfleur, was situated beside the sea. She wanted to see her confessor who, in recent days, had been keeping himself hidden away.[37] On her way there, the tide was low, so she took the shortest route, along the beach. By the time she was ready to return, night was drawing in and the tide was high. She was therefore faced with the necessity of taking a long, lonely, and dangerous road, but suddenly she heard a voice saying to her clearly: 'Have no fear!' Then God put the wings of the wind at her service, and, in the winking of an eye, she found herself transported to the other side of the bay, several kilometers away; she was already back in Barfleur.

"Forty-five years later, her superior, Father Delamare, who knew of the miracle, wanted to hear it confirmed from the lips of the Venerable Mary Magdalen herself, for she was not expected to live much longer. It was a delicate matter—how could he overcome the scrupulous humility that caused her to hide the favors she received from God more carefully than a miser hides his treasure?

"After agreeing among themselves, Sister Marie, the bursar, recalled the event in the presence of Father Delamare and the Chaplain, M. Lerenard, who then interrogated the Mother Superior closely and put very specific questions to her.

"'God be blessed! He knows everything.'

"That was her only reply.

"Wishing to extract a fuller admission, M. Lerenard again asked, 'Are you sure that Providence didn't send you a boatman, who ferried you across, or a man with a horse?'

"The holy woman answered with a certain asperity: 'There was neither a man, nor a boat, nor a horse. When God wants something, it is soon done. After hearing the voice, I was carried across in less than the winking of an eye.'"

"In his short treatise on levitation,[38] A. de Rochas lists the Curé of Ars, Saint John Baptist Vianney (1786–1859) among the levitating saints. He refers to the abridged biography by the Abbé A. Monnin for a description of the relevant events. In this work, we read: 'One night, the Curé of Ars awoke with a start and felt himself being lifted up into the air. "Little by little, I was rising from my bed," he said.'"

"Maria-Domenica Barbagli (1812–59), an Italian ecstatic, was said to have very frequent levitations. Dr. Imbert-Gourbeyre obtained an eyewitness account concerning her. One of his patients, whom he was then treating at Royat, told him she had been present at a bodily transport of this ecstatic in the following circumstances: 'In 1855, I saw the ecstatic of San Savino, near Siena Longa in Tuscany. She was known as Minichina, a diminutive of the name Domenica. She lived at home and was greatly renowned for her sanctity. It was on a Friday that I saw her in ecstasy. She was kneeling, with her arms outstretched and her body raised two feet above the bed. This ecstasy lasted an hour. I put my hand under her knees, she was as light as a feather, and I could lift her still higher. When I blew on her, her body swayed slightly in the air, like a leaf gently moved by the wind. I had been told of these phenomena in advance, and now I had experienced them. On the following day, during Mass, she went into a rapture three times, and levitated once. Thousands of people witnessed this kind of transport.' *Per lievissimo soffie ondeggiava quasi sottilissima piuma,* says P. G. E. Bini, another biographer who alluded to her levitations and her lightness.'" (quoted by Leroy)

"Mary of Jesus, better known as Mère du Bourg (1787–1862), founder of the Sisters of the Savior and of the Holy Virgin, was the aunt of Monsignore d'Hulst. The latter told Father Bulliot that his aunt had risen from the ground on several occasions, and in sight of all the nuns of her community; this occurred especially when one spoke of the love of God in her presence. Father Bulliot made a statement to this effect to the Société des sciences psychiques (meeting of February 3, 1897). Both Mother Mary of Jesus's biographers, the Abbé Bersange and G. du Bourg, give us some further details: 'It was almost always at the end of her rapture, notes the latter, that Mère du Bourg was suddenly lifted off the ground. She tried to resist, but a superhuman force bore her aloft. Then, helplessly, she abandoned herself to this supernatural attraction.'

117

"Dr. Imbert-Gourbeyre knew this holy woman personally. Several members of his family had seen her floating above the ground while praying. He has this to say concerning her levitations: 'Her ecstasies rarely ended without Mère du Bourg being suddenly lifted off the ground and crying out: "O charity! O sacred love!" Then she would try to defend herself from the divine attraction. After vainly trying to hold on to her chair or her prie-dieu, she crossed her arms over her breast, or stretched them out, with the palms of her hands turned slightly upward, and surrendered to the force that lifted her swiftly. She invariably remained in the air in the posture in which the rapture had fallen on her, whether kneeling, sitting, or standing.'

"According to the same author, these aerial transports occurred regularly: 'Every evening, when the community was saying prayers, Mother Mary found it impossible to hear the Act of the Love of God recited without immediately being ravished. She then rose into the air above her chair and fell back abruptly on to her prie-dieu. One day, her fall was so violent that she broke the step of her prie-dieu.'

"This last is also reported by Mère Marie de la Croix, who witnessed the event on the 7th of April 1856, and, next day, went to see her: 'They keep asking me about my knees,' said Mother Mary, somewhat flustered, 'but they are not hurting at all.'

"'The prie-dieu could not say as much,' I said.

"'My heart was simply bursting and flew away,' answered Mère du Bourg. 'It was a purifying love and it made me suffer a good deal.'

"A few minutes later, she went quietly down to the chapel to see what had happened to her prie-dieu. Bending over it to see where it was split, she said very softly: 'O you miserable, wretched creature! Now look what you've done!'[39]

"On the 24th of October, 1854, during a period of retreat, Mother Mary had an ecstasy lasting two hours, in the course of which she was twice lifted off the ground.

"It is said that, on the day when she learned of the death of Pope Gregory XVI (in 1846), Mother Mary knelt down to pray and was bodily carried off."

"Marie de Moerl (1812–63), the celebrated stigmatic from the Tyrol, had almost daily raptures, and although there are no reports of her ever being lifted up into the air, it is recorded that often she did no more than touch the surface of her bed with the tips of her toes. M. D. de Moy, professor of law at the faculty in Munich, wrote a letter to Monsieur Boré describing the position in which he himself had seen the ecstatic: 'Her hands were joined together, her head and eyes raised toward heaven, she was on her knees, her body leaning forward as if supported by the invisible angels who held her up, for the angle of her body was contrary to all the laws of balance, and her knees left hardly any impression on the coverlet of the bed.'"

"Sister Mary of Jesus Crucified (1846–78), an Arab Carmelite, on the other hand, rose very high into the air, but her levitations never took place without some kind of support. In her ecstasies, she rose to the very tops of the trees in the garden of the Carmelite convent in Pau, but she began by hoisting herself up with the aid of some small branches and never floated freely in the void. Her last biographer, R. P. Buzy, almoner of the Bethlehem Carmel, alluded to these facts. In a letter to Olivier Leroy, he gave the following details:

"'Sister Mary reached the summit of the trees via the extreme tips of the branches. She used to put her scapulary in one hand and, with the other, grasp the leafy tip of a small branch, then in the winking of an eye, she would glide up the outer part of the tree to reach the highest branches. Witnesses insist on this point: that she climbed up instantaneously. She would even cross from one lime tree to another via the tips of the branches, which, in normal circumstances, would have been far too fragile to support a person of her weight.'"

Here are some of the statements made by witnesses at the process:

"Sister E. has declared that, chancing to be in the garden one day with the servant of God, the latter said to her: 'Turn around!' She barely turned her head away, and when she looked around again she saw Sister Mary already seated at the top of a lime tree, balancing on a small branch like a bird, and singing of divine love."

"Another person declares: 'I saw her once, in ecstasy, at the top of a lime tree. She was sitting on the tip of the highest branch which, normally, would not have been strong enough to support her. Her face was radiant! I saw her come down from the tree, flitting from branch to branch like a bird, with extraordinary lightness and modesty. It occurred to me that, since the branches of the lime tree were very small, they would normally have snapped under the weight of the servant of God, who was rather heavy. When she came down again, she was still in ecstasy.'

"When she came down from the tree, notes another witness, she moved from the tip of one branch to the tip of another, as light as a bird, and her habit trailed behind her, as it does when one is coming down a staircase.

"Only once did she have difficulty in descending: the Prioress had ordered her to come down, as she often did. Sister Mary hesitated for a moment. Then she came down, but with great difficulty. She attributed this physical lapse to her slight delay in obeying her Superior. 'If me obey quick,' she said, 'tree become little, like that!' and the saintly girl put her hand down almost to ground level."

"In July 1898, the transatlantic liner, *La Bourgogne,* sank off the coast of Newfoundland. This tragedy produced a scene which has its natural place in this account," writes Olivier Leroy: "The hero of the story is a Dominican, Joseph Baumann (d. 1898), brother of the novelist Emile Baumann,[40] from whom I have borrowed the following extract:

"'Regarding my brother's last moments, here is an unlooked-for testimony that came to me not long ago, as if sent from On High. While I would refrain from claiming that this strange and miraculous occurrence was supernatural, in the true sense of the word, it nevertheless bears witness to the state of ecstasy in which he passed from the dark terrors of the sea to the light of eternity. During the last moments of the *La Bourgogne,* a Protestant lady—one of the few women to be saved—was in a lifeboat moving away from the scene of the disaster. Turning back to look at the ship, which was now listing so badly that the rail was almost touching the water, she saw the three Dominicans on their knees among the other shipwrecked souls; the eldest of them, the Prior, was holding his rosary and his crucifix out toward them, while the youngest, my brother, with his eyes raised to heaven, seemed to her to be levitating above the deck, and around his head there was *a circle of fire.*

"'I heard of this incident from the Reverend Father Hugon, Professor at the Angelicum College in Rome, who is a level-headed theologian, hostile to Illuminism. While in a hospital in New York, the Protestant lady had revealed the story to a certain Mother Henri-Joseph, a nun of the order of the Bon-Secours de Troyes, who was a woman of sound judgment and quite incapable of inventing a miracle. She wrote to Father Hugon about it. The latter begged her to keep it to herself, and not divulge it to anyone, even in her own convent. He wanted to avoid the reckless placing of a halo around the head of a young individual who had died prematurely. He recalled that there had recently been some discussion in his hearing about Brother Joseph of Copertino, and he felt it his duty to communicate the facts to me and tell me the exact sources of his information. There is no doubt that the shipwrecked woman certainly *saw* the scene as described, but, as she is the only one among the survivors to have done so, we cannot establish whether she herself was in a state of exaltation that gave rise to the phenomenon, or God, to enlighten her, vouchsafed her an anticipatory vision of the glory of an elect soul.'"

40

20th Century

"Gemma Galgani, of Lucca, who died in an odor of sanctity in 1903, had several levitations."

"With Mary of the Passion, of the order of the Adorers of the Crucifix, we again have a case, not of true levitation, but of ecstatic agility. Sister Marie Prassede, of the same community, reports in a letter of the 3rd of June, 1913 that, one day, she was told to take Mary of the Passion back to her bed, for she had come down to the chapel to take communion and was too weak to return alone. 'Hardly had we left the choir when I saw the servant of God, in spite of being very ill, climb the stairs in an instant, as if she were flying. I, who was in good health, could not keep up with her. She did not seem to touch the floor at all, and veritably flew up the staircase leading to her room.'"

"A Breton ecstatic, Marie-Julie Jahenny, from La Fraudais, who is still alive, had frequent rapturous transports over a period of more than two years, according to Dr. Imbert-Gourbeyre. He adds: 'I had been told by competent persons that she possessed ecstatic lightness.' I tried to verify these statements, but the present curé of Blain, the parish on which La Fraudais depends, could not give me any personal corroboration."

The above extract closes the list of the ecstatic, levitating saints compiled in 1928 by Olivier Leroy, who also quotes numerous cases of semi-levitation and agility during sleepwalking, as well as enumerating the most famous mediums of the nineteenth and twentieth centuries: Daniel Dunglas Home, W. Stainton Moses, Eusapia, Paladino, Ruggieri, French, Maria Vollhart, Willy Sch... (his brother, Rudi Schneider, has been the guinea-pig medium of the Institut Métapsychique in Paris since November 11, 1930), and the Brazilian, Carlos Mirabelli. Leroy also studies in parallel (and analyzes in the form of synoptic charts, with the aim of making an objective distinction between the two) both the flights of saints and the similar phenomena manifested by hysterics and frauds, insofar as these have been ascertained or discovered by chance through clinical observations, pathological descriptions, laboratory experiments, and the minutes of the meetings of pseudo-sicentific academies of spiritualism and metapsychism; Leroy also includes in his study a great many related phenomena: tricks and theatrical props, manipulations, mesmeric passes, showmanship, infra- or ultra-red rays, black phosphorescence, indirect lighting, false mirrors, veils, illusions, photographs, transparencies, ectoplasm, doubles, dead souls, evocations, table-turning, table-rapping, automatic writing, annun- ciatory voices, telekinesis, bilocations, and all the other monkey tricks and exploits in the repertoire of the fiends of Hell and of the Devil himself in the guise of the touring managers and impresarios of the five continents. But, for all that, the miraculous life of the mystics does not end with the century, and in spite of all the technological progress made in this century, sanctity and Christian humility remain the same, the Pope's Pronotaries Apostolic are still active, the Promoter of the Faith continues to inveigh against the candidates for sainthood, and his animadversions are still going full speed ahead: reviling, arguing, recording, ratifying; either damning and "ploughing," or beatifying and canonizing the ecstatics, the levitators and the stigmatics, and always with a healthy caution and a wise lack of haste that maintain and vivify the Holy Tradition, for neither Time nor publicity for the Church is of any account when it comes to the work of Eternity and Truth.

I do not know how many cases are currently under consideration in Rome, nor how many processes have been lost or won there since the year 1900, for the Roman Curia does not publish any statistics, in spite of the fact that Vatican City has been steadily modernizing itself since the begin- ning of this century, and now has a railway station, a tunnel, its own radio station and antennae, an important independent newspaper, a power sta- tion, white airplanes (with the keys of Saint Peter on their fuselage mark- ings), postage stamps for collectors, and, most recently, an astronomic observatory, a biochemical laboratory, telescopes and microscopes, film stu- dios to provide up-to-date propaganda, and even an up-to-date American Cardinal, as is only logical;[41] but the proof that the mystical life is not dead is that, in spite of the hurly-burly of two world wars, and their economic, social, and intellectual after-effects, problems of morality and nationality, racist threats, the triumph of the proletariat, revolutionaries who blow hot and cold, hot jazz, swing, bebop, poverty, full frontal nudity, sexual aberra- tions, industrialization that is killing the planet, widespread famine, the shifting of populations, concentration camps, tinned foods, secret weapons and molecular atomization, it still happens that unknown beings, lost in ecstasy in their obscure convents, wake up one fine morning to find they have made it in the newspapers, and there are their names in the headlines, dazzling and outshining the usual stars of the press: artists, painters, literati, politicians, soldiers, inventors, engineers, stockbrokers, bankers, industrialists, socialites, snobs, boxers, dancers, aviators, speculators, and publicity whiz kids, along with all their contraptions, their exploits, their championships, and their records, eclipsing them, stealing the limelight, making a deep impression and coming into close-up, to the consternation of the masses, who do not understand these sublime but alien brothers, although they kneel down and worship them and follow them to the end, for these men and women are the saints of the 20th century: little Saint Teresa of the Child Jesus, from Lisieux (Normandy), about whom not a great deal is known and who perhaps never did anything really wonderful except appear in a dream to Teresa Neumann, the stigmatic of Konnersreuth (Bavaria), and lead her blindly along her *via dolorosa;* the latter herself, the daughter of simple Bavarian peasants, who is still alive and works miracles in her village, where she is visited by hundreds of people every Friday, and on Good Friday by thousands of the curious, believers and unbelievers alike, foreigners, Jews, enemies, compatriots, cops burdened with bad consciences, and sick people who are hoping she will cure them of their sores and their ulcers, she, Teresa Neumann, who has kept herself alive for years and years on teaspoonfuls of sugared water, and is nailed to her bed not so much by her own sufferings and lamentable accidents as by the sins of the world, this servant of God who, for thirty years, has been the victim and the butt of commissions of inquiry, experts, wise men, psychiatrists, materialistic experimenters, doctors of theology, members of the Hitler Youth and of the German Communist Party, as well as the clergy of Ratisbon, and whose long spiritual, ideological, and scientific martyrdom is far from being over, and indeed, one asks oneself, compassionately, how it will all end for this woman, on whom the Church has as yet made no pronouncement, but whom the unbelieving newspapers of the entire world made famous overnight by publishing her photograph (without her knowledge and without the approval of the Vatican, who have a horror of such practices and are not in the least modernized in this respect) slap in the middle of the page and in close-up, showing her eyes weeping tears of blood, and it was this sensational photograph, published by *Paris-Soir,* that launched Teresa Neumann in France, in 1936, at a time when there was intense euphoria for the "popular front," and this was not at all the usual habit of the press, not even of those newspapers that, in France, are known as *"d'information";* and a third saint, the humble little sacristan of Santiago, Chile, who, although he himself did not levitate, casually caused a mason to levitate when he fell off the scaffolding during repairs to the tower of the cathedral, directed his fall from a distance, as if by remote control, slowed him down, stopped him in midair with a gesture, broke his fall and caught the unfortunate workman in his good hand, while the other, the maimed, the crazy hand, remained tucked into the belt of his trousers, for the sacristan, although sickly and feeble-minded, a simpleton, a half-caste—the son of an Italian woman and an Indian—was an active healer of the poor among whom he lived, and was much sought after, especially by barren women who desired to have children, and on whom he would blow by way of a cure, to the great shame of his curé, the Dean of the cathedral, who, thunderstruck and far from reassured by this latest miracle, enjoined him not to work any more without his consent, because he did not want to have *any trouble with Rome*; and this sacristan was the subject of a first hagiographical notice I took the liberty of sketching in my *Histoires vraies;*[42] finally, another unknown whose renown has just this moment reached me, Padre Pio, the ecstatic who performs "prodigious prodigies" [sic] in the fastness of a remote convent in Apulia, and whom I first heard about from a film producer who stepped off the plane from Rome when it landed at Saint-Segond, Villefranche, this very morning, the 5th of May, 1948.

And we are only halfway through the twentieth century! Today's newspapers are full of the Italian elections, but, no matter what the results, the Congregation of Rites will still carry on its task, and the journalists will once again make front-page news of those lean-faced ascetics and weightless ecstatics who, at the moment, are still anonymous, held in the spell of sanctity, wholly immersed in it, giving themselves up to macerations and wearing hair-shirts, men who, perhaps, will escape all unwittingly from the destruction of the world by bombs, layers of noxious gases, the action of atomic denuclearization, spontaneous radiations, total and instantaneous incineration, because their hallowed bodies will rise, will levitate from among the patented machines and the robots and the whole dirty, infernal, legalized bag of tricks man has stored up for himself, and they will be annihilated by love, carried off by the Holy Spirit, the Nameless One, GOD, with whom, forgetful of all else, they jubilantly identify in prayer.

"In principio erat Verbum!" murmured Saint Joseph of Copertino, exalted in prayer, losing touch with the ground, adoring, overcome, dazed, idiotic, letting out a deep sigh, crying out his *"Amen!"* as he was ravished in ecstasy and flew away.

III
THE RAVISHMENT OF LOVE

Y a cabo de un gran rato se ha encumbrado
Sobre un abrol do abrio sus brazos bellos,
Y muerto se ha quetado, asido do elios,
El pocho del amor muy lastinado.

A long while after climbed he up into the tree
And wide outspread his splendid arms
Then, hanging there, he died,
His heart pierced through and through with love.

Saint John of the Cross
Canción VIII
("A Lonely Shepherd Boy Feels Sad")

41

And the monk arose at night to pray.

42

Once God has set your feet upon the arduous path of solitary contemplation, once you are lost to the world, with no one to guide you but a
Job's comforter or a builder from the Tower of Babel, what could be more
disillusioning, more hallucinatory, more distressing than to find your spiritual life languishing, impatient, drying up, dying of thirst for an intimate
understanding, your prayers undermined by doubt, your tongue itching,
paralyzed, burned alive by the unpronounceable and the unnameable, your
concentration disrupted by its own feverish emanations, which bombard
you with chimeras, fantasies, visions, discarded illusions and obsessive
ideas, while your body refuses to go on, jibs, bridles, sweats, froths at the

mouth before, at last, surrendering and letting itself go, exhausted, falling down as if dead, dead to the world, distracted, giddy, absent, buried in its own excrement, exposed on the altar of sacrifice, a secret victim, or one crucified at the crossroads, crushed, turned to dust, the dust that cements the trampled paving stones, used up, wiped out, split, and everything cracks and everything crumbles at the resurrection of the bones and of the flesh?

43

Thus, it is as a beggar, a blind man, a cripple, an invalid, a soul mad with love that the ascetic presents himself before the Holy Spirit, and it is the force of this mad love of God that carries him away, just as it is his stubbornness that drives this vagabond to haunt the crypts and the catacombs, where his wanderings as a simple, feeble fellow, sick in spirit, staggering among the debris and the ruins, lead him along tracks and footpaths that twist and turn down a thousand detours that constantly turn back upon themselves, through vertiginously lonely places and troughs of despair before bringing him, at last, to contemplation, and it is the repeated falls of this sublimely intoxicated wanderer, who falls down at the approach of God, by Whom he is possessed, and Who, in turn, possesses the upstart and gives Himself to the rash but daring pilgrim in His Embrace, that bring down upon him all the Glory that falls from heaven upon the earth, day and night, swallowing him up and burying him in the scorching heat of its love more surely than the sand that runs through a clepsydra into the mute throat of time, or the agitated waters of the deep ocean, for this Glory is the kiss of the Eternal: the Trinity, *la Vita Nova*.

44

The newborn babe has no need of either the zodiac or a horoscope, He is the child of Love, the Child lost among the Doctors, the Savior: his Mother is his star and his planet.

45

Thy lips. Burning, stigmatizing, indelibly tattooing. Thou speakest without words. Thy mouth, a scar. I am melting in this insulted, slapped, and sealed-up mouth. Thy smile. AMEN!... Thine eye. AMEN!... Thou art the All-Powerful and the All-Forgiving. *They know not what they do.* Already, Thou turnest away. Thy thoughts are of something else on the other side of the world, in the other world, in the New World. The Cross flies away. O my love, let me follow Thee! They are playing at dice. Thy crown... The nails... Thy garment without a seam... The ignominious placard... Thy shroud... Heaven.

46

The heart of the saint, lying exhausted at the side of the road, makes a little hump like a beggar's scrip, but it contains nothing but the gift of tears, charity, humility, and love, and the dogs of night surround him with bared fangs and bristling hair, growling, yet reluctant to throw themselves on this forgotten pilgrim who has a strange smell and who, dead to the wide world, has lost his staff.

47

The skin of the Leper crucified at the crossroads is like the Milky Way that swoons above the ripened corn. His sores are stars in the dawning light. Soon, the daylight will shine on the old, broken pots and the shards glinting amid the brushwood and the thorns at the foot of Calvary. You stumble on. One step at a time, one step forward.

48

The Way of the Cross. The wall. One more step. A bell tolls in the monastery chapel. One stroke. One more step, the last. A door is pushed open. It creaks. The bell tolls and your heart is its clapper. The sound fills your skull. Your head listens to your heart. You fall down, out of breath. The door closes behind you. You are shut in. The bell tolls, a solitary stroke. Another. It is the last. You listen to the silence. The soul is a fly that cannot find a place to settle, so it settles everywhere, irritating and useless. It is searching for a corpse.

49

A candle is burning. The flame gutters. A shadow glides in front of the altar. A monk's habit flaps its wings. Arms to your sides! It is the wind of prayer. Attraction. The gaping mouth. Flight. On your knees! Throw back your cowl. Bare feet in sandals. Your hands tug nervously at your rope girdle. Clasp your hands! Other hands officiate. Bare hands. Naked, delicate fingers which fan out like rays of light. The ring. A dart, and the heart is pierced. The Host, and a somersault into the Eucharist. The flight of a wasp. A waxen tear. A burning drop. The lips are sealed. Tears. The pain is searing.

50

Death. Life. Deglutition.

51

Sustentation.

52

One can never become sated with Love.

53

The conflagration of divine love, the golden bough, the flower of Jesse, Jacob's ladder.

54

The Blessed Ones.

55

In the cell, the spirit is afraid. The tonsure touches the ceiling. A stroke. Dizziness. A stroke. The shiver of dawn. A stroke. The bell tolls. A long drawn-out stroke. The white monk is disciplining himself. A stroke. A stroke. A stroke. Matins. Stay on your knees!

56

The conscience is strangled by obedience, as if it were a cord, and the will is a hanged man.

57

A rigid habit. Bare, sandaled feet, floating and luminous. A halo on the ceiling. The ecstatic hovers, his neck outstretched, his hands clasped in prayer or held out at his sides. Kneeling. In the air. Lying on his side. Offered up. His eyes upturned. His heart laid bare.

58

When he came out of his ecstasies, still white-faced, stammering, and trembling with inward jubilation, Saint Joseph of Copertino was in the habit of saying: "Obedience is the knife that cuts the throat of man's will…. 'Obey!'… At this word, God draws back the curtain…" Certainly Brother Joseph always expressed himself in a comical way. Saints are like children, they play with fire, have a taste for danger, and like to laugh. They have no shame. They love to lose themselves. They are confident. They do not belong to themselves. No matter where they choose to perch in heaven, their Father will always find them again. And Heaven makes puddles everywhere, as after rain and tears.

59

The day is dawning and the first rays of sunlight, entering the narrow cell like a jolly workman entering his workshop, finger the hairshirt of prayer.

60

Every craft guild has its favorite tool. The soft fleecy curls of the Lamb's wool are tangled in the carders, and there are drops of blood on each of the sharp points.

61

"Good morning! Beautiful, wild sweet briar, companion of my solitude, you have flowered at my door during the night."

62

The morning is all perfumed with the bonfire of the cut vineshoots and armfuls of dead thorns.

63

Abraham is preparing.

64

Isaac is bound.

65

The sacrificial Lamb.

66

The shepherd's knife with its curved blade.

67

Immolation.

68

Ecstasy.

69

The flame of the holocaust crackles and rises straight into the air. The sacrifice is consummated. All the sins of the world blow away in the smoke. Cain and Abel. Again. It is enough. All around, the sheep are bleating. Adam prepares his flute. Eve, the shepherdess, is not there. A turtle dove coos in the ravine. Beneath the trees, a sound of running water...

70

The Tree.

71

The Forbidden Fruit.

72

This morning, creation gleams like a fruit left behind by the harvesters, like an orange in the dense foliage of an orange tree—one sees nothing else now!—like a kiss on the cheek of an Innocent, on the breast of a Virgin, beneath the robe of an Angel who blushes with pure joy, in Thy beard of flowering rosemary, O my Father Who art in Heaven, my Father who will never abandon me, fruit in my mouth, Succulence, a prolonged Kiss that I swallow, O Benediction, O Perfume, O Light, O inexhaustible Effusion of prayer, AMEN!

73

I no longer know what I am saying in this rapture that pours out of my mouth and lifts me up to Thee, flowing beyond Thy mouth to be lost and engulfed in Thine ear, where it makes its nest—a nest made of mud, like a swallow's, or of fine down, the long threads from a spider's web and the hair of the Virgin, like a robin's, or of rumpled straw, like a sparrow's. I cheep, I twitter, I cackle. The birds of the field are no longer carefree, nor is the nightingale in the orchard, nor the blackbird in the garden, nor the skylark who trills merrily in the air, nor the lowly wren who chirps in the thimble-shaped sage flower, nor the enormous ostrich who forsakes her egg in the African desert, nor the the Australian bird of paradise, who dances and arranges pebbles and bits of silica more brilliant than his own plumage in circles in a clearing in the bush, nor the anchorite kiwi, who resembles an anthill, a walking haystack, or a coolie paddling in the rice paddy in the pouring rain, nor the thieving magpie, nor the royal eagle, nor the absurd and touching penguins who look like nuns and bray like donkeys in the polar ice, nor the starlings in the acacias, nor the thrushes in the rowan tree, nor the cuckoo, the bird of echo who is answered by another, phantom cuckoo, and who lays her eggs in a neighbor's nest, nor the secretary bird, that dazzling creature who sits on the cactus and decoys the traveler, leading him away from springs, wells, and all sources of water, nor the *paille-en-cul,* who dives far out at sea, nor the vigil bird who rides on the back of the elephant or struts along the saw-toothed spine of the most sated crocodile and cleans the corners of his eyes, his tear ducts and the teeth of his monstrous smile for him, nor the waders—the ibis, the pink flamingo, the familiar stork—nor the albatross, who rides the storm, nor the wrathful serpent-eater who strikes with his spurs, nor the hoopoes, the pelicans, the swans, the peacocks, all of whom swagger, display, and fan out their tails on the mosaic parterres around the Shah of Persia's pool, nor the seventy-two thousand species of pigeon in India, nor the ducks strangled in Chinese brothels or left to choke and bleed in barrels, nor the yellow vultures, the carrion-eaters who perch on the Towers of Silence and the stinking terraces of the Parsees (who are all bankers in Bombay), nor the condors of the Andes, who inscribe themselves against the sky like a series of black notes, nothing but semiquavers and demisemiquavers, *presto, prestissimo,* between the parallel ranges of the Cordilleras, whose snow-clad volcanoes are the white notes in arpeggio or the accompanying chords, the figured bass, the organ stops, nor the colibri, who flies so fast he is almost invisible to the human eye, and who, because he hums, is called the hummingbird in English, while, in Latin America, this little scrounger is called the *chupa-flores,* the *beija-flores,* which means the kisser-of-flowers, an apt name for this fly-cum-bird, of which there are thousands of species, the smallest being the sturdy little *Pygmornis rubra,* which is no bigger, although ten times swifter, than our own bumblebee and weights no more than two grams, and whose wing-vibrating flight is like an arrow, a crystalline glitter, a spark, a burning cinder, a mote of dust in the sunlight, a shooting star, a diamond, a tear, a flash, nor the quail squatting in the stubble, the startled partridge, the honking wild goose, nor the silent raptors of the night with their velvety flight, the birds of prey who swoop down from the heights of heaven and rise up again with a great beating of wings, the rustling of the capercailzie, who clucks and utters his cry of alarm, the blue kingfisher, the jackdaws of the snows with their red beaks, the crows on the cathedrals, who shit on the statues and bespatter the stained-glass windows, the owls and the screech owls who haunt ruins, laugh like demons and have such tender, human plumage around their eyes, shaped like a circumflex accent, and, under their hoods, a medieval profile like a question mark, nor the parrots and chattering parakeets on whom the Impressionist painters wiped their brushes, nor the toucan, that comical scarecrow of Amazonia, nor the egrets, those tropical fans, nor the mockingbird of the Argentinian pampas, nor the squawking eider-ducks of the Norwegian fjords, nor the thousands of squabbling sea birds on their guano islands off the coast of Chile, nor the grouse of Scotland, who come and perch on your shotgun in the dense fog, nor the turkeys of the prairies, who are impaled, scandalized and protesting, on the end of a long, sharpened stick and carried alive to the roasting spit, nor the pheasants and their chicks who get entangled in the net, the ortolans who are trapped with a loop of horsehair or a drop of bird-lime, the plump warbler caught in the snare, nor the ever-surprised woodcock, who never suspects the trap, nor KRA (which means "Tomorrow! Tomorrow!" in Armenian), the croaking crow of Saint Expedite, that tough Legionary who carried a small iron cross with the word HODIE (Today) engraved on it, and brandished it as if it were a tomahawk, and this same misanthropic old crow, one of whose ancestors refused to feed Elijah, comes back *today,* winging swiftly out of the night of time, to accompany his saintly master when he is invoked in desperate and urgent cases, so anxious is this bird *today* to participate in good works and make up for lost time... *hodie mecum eris in paradiso...,* nor the cock that crowed when Peter the Apostle denied Christ, nor the village weathercock, the totem of the Gauls which, in France, has been cooked in wine ever since Henri IV's famous *poule-au-pot,* Paris being well worth a Mass,* nor the first pair of doves from the Ark, the male, which was lost forever by the drunken Noah, and the female, which was found again, O miracle! with the waters of Baptism, returning, descending, being present at the same time as the Holy Spirit, the bird of fire, nor the psalms, nor the canticles, nor the popular litanies, nor roundsongs, nor the sequences, those learned processionary poems of the Christians, nor the Antiphon, nor the euphonium, the horn, the trumpet, the serpent, which are birds without feathers, but with cut-glass throats, smooth hips, amplifying horns, swelling mouthpieces, beaks curved or elongated, or straight and narrow as a straw, ivory flutes, ebony clarinets, bagpipes made from a perforated calabash or a rolled-up strip of bark, a little pipe made from a spring shoot of the hazel

---

*Henri IV said every French peasant should be able to put a chicken in his pot on Sundays. Being a Protestant, Henri had to convert to Catholicism in order to ascend the throne of France. Hence his saying, "Paris is well worth a Mass." (Trans.)

tree or a sheath of the elder, the burning bush, a cluster of pipes with three, five, or seven holes, leather bellows that feed it with air, Breton pipes with motley, streaming ribbons, wind instruments shaped like birds, organs containing all the warblings, all the music of the spheres: "Noel! Noel!"— the little symphony of the angels and the rejoicing shepherds, the recitative of the boatmen as they beach their boats, the savage onomatopeia the men chant to set the cadence as they shoot the rapids in their pirogues, the obscene, nostalgic shanties the old-time sailors sang as they set sail on voyages of discovery in the South Seas, the whip that cracks and farts on board the Roman trireme or on the king's galley in the Mediterranean, the drinking songs of pirates and slave traders in the ports of call in the Antilles, the processions, the gifts, the idolatrous homage of the Three Kings, the Magi, the airplanes that today, in 1948—the year 1367 of the Hegira and the 5708th year of the Biblical era—fly over Bethlehem, firing off a chaplet of tracer bullets or a rosary of incendiary bombs, the taciturn Archangels who watch over the gates of the celestial Jerusalem like eternally wakeful lions, and whose polished eyelids are throbbing propellers, and whose pupils the uranium lightning, the *Song of Songs* with its sighs and its swoonings, no, there is nothing as carefree as I am, I, myself, the singing madman, the supremely absent-minded dreamer, who alights and does not alight in my prayer, my perpetual prayer that carries me away, my dazed adoration, my stammering words, Thy word that falls like seed, this chaplet, this rosary, this endless cascade, this association of images, of ideas, of causes, effects, and identifications, this chain, this necklace Thou hast hung about my neck to set me free, and from which thou ART suspended like a precious jewel, a garnet that strikes me with lightning at point-blank range and magnetizes me, Thine arms, Thy hands, Thy fingers, Thy unbearable caresses, Thy breath, which tickles the tip of my tongue, Thy Respiration which makes it move and vibrate in Thy PRESENCE, and this is not a confession, for Thou, O Ineffable One, knowest everything already, and I, I no longer know what I am saying, THY mouth seals my lips like a burning coal, I cannot speak, I am exploding, ejaculating, *the new Life:* HALLELUJAH!

74

    The virtue of prayer is that it enumerates all the things in creation and calls them by their names in an effusion of the spirit. It is an act of thanksgiving.

75

It is not a matter of moving your lips or clacking your tongue or making it flap. The words are not to be spoken.

76

Only God speaks.

77

That is why the saint who falls into ecstasy falls into the abyss, floats On High, levitates, gyrates in a transport, breaks out, and is no longer in possession of himself. At the most, he lets out a cry or a last sigh. Then he lets himself go and plummets into the very depths of the Word of God. He soars...

78

Dead to the world.

79

Mental prayer is the aviary of God.

80

Tell me, my handsome Bird-Catcher, my Falconer: Is there a greater diversity of souls than there is of birds, are there greater numbers living in the Oneness of God than there are fish in the ocean—fish, those birds of the abyss, who move their lips perpetually yet are mute, for their mouths are tactile, and the body of the fish, that rises and descends and gyrates, and is shaped like a double spindle, is the sacred symbol of CHRIST; tell me, handsome Fisherman, Thou who seekest men's souls in the rumblings of their bowels and in the soundings of their kidneys, are there more fish in the sea or heavenly bodies and double stars in the universe to sing Thy Glory?

81

Thy Glory is the Respiration that animates Heaven and Earth, and the Ocean is Thy black Lung.

82

Dense shadows darken the day. The night is transparent, like the Holy Ampulla, and I circulate in the globules of Thy effervescing Blood; Communion, Resurrection, Life, the self-consuming heart, the bleeding forehead, the halo on the ceiling, the robe hanging down, bare feet radiant in their sandals, kneeling, prostrate. I lose myself On High.

83

A blow of the spear and the body empties itself, is extinguished.

84

The body prostrate, running with sweat and blood.

85

A stroke. A stroke. A stroke. Another, the last, and it is the Angelus. The arm is weary. The bell has a feeble sound, the bell is cracked, the bell and its exhausted clapper. The bell. The Passing Bell. One step backward. In fear. It is the summons. The gravedigger. Back! Back! The bell has stopped ringing. Silence. And the fly returns to find the fallen corpse.

86

Each craft guild has its favorite tool. The hand, the painful hand touches, feels. The fingers explore. It is Thomas. Where is the Lamb's curly fleece? He has nothing but a dirty comb, stinking of coagulated sweat. Can that be God's tool? He is doubtful. He wants to laugh! The body comes back to life, panting heavily, and suddenly he has a horror of intimacy and is bewildered by the joy he feels.

87

The saint also has his migraines and his despairing lassitude. His short-comings. His aversions. His lapses. His doubts. Fever. The sweat of anguish. He is suspicious of illusions, of somnambulism and dreamlike states; he distrusts the acrobatics of certain drunkards and the fits of exalta-tion and the nervous breakdowns of certain epileptics and neurotics. A mystical grace is a free gift and he is afraid that it may manifest itself in public, so he resists. He is ashamed of his triumph, because he feels he is unworthy. It violates all his feelings, and his vows of humility. Macerations, mortifications, cruel penances, unnatural abstinence, death to the world, all these bring in their wake the most diverse ways of life, both internal and external, which are the theurgical virtues of asceticism and can-not be controlled. Asceticism is a secret discipline that has its virtuosi. All the individual's faculties are directed toward the heroic realization of cer-tain moral and spiritual ends; perfection, mystical union. Ecstasy is God's affair.

88

Levitation is linked to ecstasy. Unlike many ecstatics known to History, who were doctors, theologians, poets, missionaries, mystical explorers, valiant architects and builders of the Church, her lawyers and her soldiers, Saint Joseph of Copertino, the most famous of them all because of the fre-quency and the prodigious nature of his levitations, and of whom one can reasonably say that he spent half his life in ecstasy *in the air*, distinguished himself by a singular inaptitude for all the work of body and mind. But his taste for the refinements of asceticism was epoch making and has been recorded in the depositions of contemporary witnesses, together with his obedience, his love of God, his daily raptures, his spiritual transports, his trances, his bodily levitations, his astonishing cry and his "AMEN!", his joy, his good temper, his simple sense of humor, his stammering, the words of the beautiful prayer attributed to him and his memorable prowess, the feat that created a unique record in the annals of levitation and aviation: his flight backward! This is what the *Acta Sanctorum,* Vol. V, September, pages 1017 and 1018, has to say about his ascetic practices. I give the Latin text so as not to be accused of exaggeration or showing off and impudence:

137

89

Page 1017, *marginalia* E/F/G: "Verum quo majus erat internum gaudium excommunicatione cum Deo, eo durius corpus sum tractabat; ut spiritui subjectum contineret. In hunc finem post adeptum sacerdotium quinquennio numquam pane usus est, nec decennio vinum bibit; folis herbis contentus aut siccatis fructibus, fabifve intolerabilis amaritudinis pulvere conditis, uti exparti fuerunt quidam Religiosi, qui illum piper esse crediterant. Herba vero, qua feriis sextis vesci solebat, adeo erat insipida et nauseosa, ut, cum guidam Religiosus eam extrema lingua libasset, totum sibi stomachum commoveri senserit, nec sin nausea per triduum ullo cibo vesci potuerit. Continuis jejunis addictus... et observabat cum tanto rigore... ideo que antequam hunc sumpsisset, palidus ac debillisimus apparebat, sed eo sumpto, rubicundus et robustus."

90

Page 1018, *marginalia* A/B: "Hinc factum est, ut deficiens stomachus carnem jam amplius ferre nequiret, quas tamen ex superioris imperio semel comedit, sed mox etiam rejecit. Hinc quoque fancibus ejus interdum arcte constrictis, qualemcumque cibum aegre potuit transmittere. Ad tam insolitos effectus concurrebat praeterea somnus brevissimus, (quem capiebat in lecto, qui non quietis, sed doloris poterat appellari) et dura carnificina, quam in corpus suum per flagella, acubus, aciculis et stellulis chalybejis intexta, exercebat, cum tam copiosa sanguinis effusione, ut muri in cella, allisque praedictis locis, in quae soluerat se cedere, eo tincti, imo incrustati etiam aliquor post annis apparuerint. Ad hasce flagellationes, et ad catenam atque cilicium, quibus jam a multo tempore cruciabatur, grandem laminam ferream addidit, quae, cum cilicium et catenam magis magisque stringeret, in ejusdem carnem tam horribili modo penetravit, ut ipse aliquando a superiore jussus sese exuere, non nisi unum vulnus appareret. Quam ob rem superior ipsum eo redactum conspicetus, ut exiguum ipsi vitae superesset, jussit horrida ista poenitentiae instrumenta a suo corpore, amovere."

91

In the mystic, it is *ecstasy,* in the medium, *trance.* Both phenomena may show certain organic symptoms in common: alienation of the senses, coolness of the extremities, slowing down of the rate of breathing, and often rigidity, anesthesia, catalepsy.

In the case of mystics in a state of ecstasy, the cessation of the heartbeat, and tachycardia, reveal the movements of the soul and its transports (cf. Blaise of Caltanisetta, page 125); in the case of mediums, cramp and turgescence, often accompanied by orgasm, denote a profound moral disturbance (cf. Willy Sch., *vide* Leroy, page 273).

The mystic enters into ecstasy spontaneously; he is taken by surprise, often without any premonitory symptoms, whereas the medium must be hypnotized by a third party or put himself into a trance at prearranged times and through special techniques (which are often sexual), manipulations, and moves.

The individual's state of health does not have the same influence in both cases. In the medium, poor health, or even a slight indisposition, generally paralyzes his or her abnormal powers, which are dependent on short-lived magnetism or auto-suggestion; in the mystic, it is not enough to say that poor health is no obstacle. One must go further and say that the levitating saints are marked by a particularly rigorous asceticism; they all fasted and denied themselves sufficient sleep.

The lightness of certain ecstatics, particularly stigmatics and levitators, is proven, whereas mediums present all the normal phenomena of weight.

In the same way, it is impossible to compare the luminosity of mystics with the alleged luminosity of mediums, because the latter has yet to be proved, and there has been more trickery, more phony stage effects and clever mechanical illusions unmasked in this field than in any other. Mediums always perform in semi-darkness, amid small gatherings of sympathizers, and in a special atmosphere, a setting decorated with a certain studied refinement, hung with Oriental trappings or abstract paintings, whereas, in ecstatics, the phenomenon of luminosity is produced without their knowing and has been observed both by day and by night, in artificial lighting or broad daylight, in secret, in the solitude of the cell, or in public, in the vast naves of cathedrals and churches, or in the open air, in gardens, and in fields, in front of a handful of witnesses or in the presence of thousands and thousands who, whether true believers or skeptics, have come running to see the event.

Throughout the ages, a great many sorcerers have complained that, whenever they had occasion to invoke the Devil, there was a chilling of the atmosphere, which they compared to an icy breath, the "kiss of Satan," and they declare unanimously that, while his trident is rigid and forked, it is made of ice; moreover, this kiss gave them the terrifying sensation of being driven down the first steps to the tomb; it was overwhelming and congealed their blood. Now, this *current of icy air,* coming from they knew not where, and which accompanies all the phenomena known as "psychic," never occurs during the external manifestations of the mystical life. Quite the contrary, a great many ecstatics—and again it is more particularly the stigmatics and the levitators—present a phenomenon known as the *fire of divine love,* sometimes accompanied, not by the frenzy of repressed passions, but by a positive warming-up of the surrounding atmosphere, which can be registered on a thermometer.

But, above all, ecstatics and mediums differ *morally,* so much so that the two types could be called antipodean.

The moral life of the saint is entirely informed by an ideal of perfection; the moral life of a medium is drab and colorless. While the saint always remains the man of faith, and is fortified by his unique love, the medium generally suffers from mental disintegration and gives himself up to licentiousness. The saint submits himself to an inflexible ascetic regime; he makes heroic efforts to repudiate the natural man and replace him with the will of God, whereas there is not a trace of asceticism in the sorcerer's apprentice, who is usually a showoff, a liar, a coward, a sensualist, a swindler, and a boaster, equally inclined to run away, in case of failure, or to brag about some dubious success. The saint has a fierce repugnance for all the spectacular manifestations of saintliness; the magician is devoured with ambition and a jealous desire to prove his supernatural powers.

The mystic considers his gifts to be the result of *divine pleasure,* like the graces and the charismata of which he is unworthy, and whose effects on his humility he dreads; the medium believes his successes are due to the influence of *the spirits* he invokes (or has invoked in his name by other hell hounds and agents of the Devil) and whom he hopes to master and manipulate at will for his own greedy and ulterior motives. One is dead to the world; the other makes a public exhibition of himself. And it is only insofar as both the one and the other take occult forces into account, and are aware of supernatural realities and of the Being who personifies them, and in the respect they have for HIM, the honor they show HIM, in their public conduct as well as in their most intimate feelings, in their prayers or in their underhand schemes, that the ascetic and the sorcerer possess something in common morally: a resemblance. The Saint. The Monkey.[43]

92

Saint Joseph of Copertino never expressed himself personally on the extraordinary subject of his ecstasies and their phenomena, and we do not even know whether he was aware of his levitations, since the details of these have come down to us only through trustworthy witnesses. But he must have had at least some idea about them, since he apologized publicly for them, as if for some physical weakness. The carrying off of Baldassare Rossi is evidently a premeditated act: "Fear not, Cavalier!" he shouts cheerfully as he grabs the lunatic by the hair. He foresaw, therefore, what was about to happen, and must have remembered his previous flights: horizontal spins, banking, falling like a dead leaf, and climbing like a rocket, since he warns his passenger to sit tight in the saddle, thus implying that he is going to put him through his paces, otherwise, why should he call him *Cavalier?* Certainly, it is not merely a polite form of address! But as the flying saint never said a word about it, we know nothing of what his personal sensations may have been when he soared, circled above the tops of the trees, came to roost on a cross, floated in ecstasy in front of the tabernacle, or flew impetuously into the distance, just as we know nothing of his preparatory techniques, although the episode of the lunatic allows us to suppose, and to conclude, that there was some preparation, some training, and indeed some impatience as he waited for the order to take off: "Anchors aweigh!" and that he was ready and, on occasion, even knew how to take command, to take the controls, at least in this particular case, to use the self-starter at will, press his foot on the rudder bar, and handle the joy stick, with his eyes on the control panel... which is rather disturbing.

93

En el principio moraba
*El Verbo....,"**

exclaims Saint John of the Cross, the subtlest and most precise guide to asceticism, the greatest mystical poet in the Spanish language—perhaps in all Christianity—Angelical Doctor and spiritual Vicar of Carmel, of whom Saint Teresa of Avila wrote, after their first meeting:[44] "I have found a man after God's heart and after my own. We understood one another at the first words." Many years later, she declared: "He is the father of my soul!" in

---

*In the beginning died the Word. (Trans.)

allusion to the spiritual conversations she held continually with the holy confessor at each of their meetings, as well as in an exchange of letters that lasted for fifteen years, and in their almost daily contact at the Convent of Carmel, where, through the grille, she communicated to him her plans for reform, her disappointments, her desires, and her hopes, and consulted him on a thousand questions of a practical nature, telling him of her scruples, sharing with him her agonies, confessing to the grace with which she had been touched, opening her ardent soul and her manly heart to him and keeping nothing back.

In the *Cantico,* when he wishes to describe the painless flight of the purified spirit, whose activity is totally absorbed in God, Saint John of the Cross, that great master of the word, does not hesitate to call it *el arrobamiento de amor,* the ravishment of love.

In *Llama,* the mystical doctor tries to define what this *arrobamiento de amor* is, and to come to grips as closely as possible with the process by which the soul, overflowing with joy and drunk with the love of contemplation, relieves the body of the weight of sin and prompts it to fly; Saint John of the Cross describes the warning symptoms: "At God's touch, the soul rejoices according to its powers and its substance. Much more strongly, its overflowing felicity gushes out on to the body and fills all the sensitive matter, the limbs, the bones, and the marrow, with rejoicing, not gently, as at first, but with a feeling of great happiness and glory, and this is felt right down to the joints of the extremities, the feet, and hands."

But, like other saints, the great contemplative, the poet of *The Dark Night of the Soul,* does not wish to say a word about his personal experiences during prayer, experiences that carried him on from alliterating rhymes to the supreme stammerings of love in the face of the Word, which is pronounced aloud in the highest Heavens, as in the Womb of Things, and when the ecstatic returns to earth, restored after his rapture, recalled to reality and the world, Saint John of the Cross writes in secret, faithful to his vow of humility, but with magisterial intelligence, for he is a fine psychologist, a prudent analyst of the spiritual life, and weighs his words carefully: "This would be an appropriate place to define the characteristics of the different types of ravishments, ecstasies, levitations, and flights of the spirit that have been observed in contemplatives, but, remaining faithful to the plan I have laid out for myself, I will leave this task to others more competent than I. Our Blessed Mother, Teresa of Jesus, has dedicated some admirable pages to these various states and I hope that, by the grace of God, these will soon be published." And Saint John of the Cross hands the pen to Saint Teresa, whose statements regarding her personal sensations and her repugnance for flying are, in effect, unique in the annals of levitation.

94

And here are the declarations of Saint Teresa of Avila, a strong woman who never recoiled from a daring act and went further along the dark and difficult path than anyone else; she even built dwelling places and set up staging posts and shrines along the route; she was a vagabond hunted by God, her quaking soul abandoned itself, her body was broken, but her hand held the pen firmly and she seems to be the only one among all the heroic ascetics of the West who did not lose her human reason, although she risked certain feminine avowals, and this tells us a great deal about the softness and the pity of her heart, which comes as no surprise in this enterprising woman, whose energy constructed the vertiginous towers of perpetual worship and the wells of silence and prayer in Carmel, that realistic establishment founded by a great lady of the world, and of Spain, whose most splendid jewel she is. Since her statements are unique and important, I do not hesitate to quote them a second time, so that the reader may have a true idea of the phenomenon of levitation and be further initiated and better-informed, and really know what it is about:

"In these ravishments, the soul no longer seems to cleave to the body. And it is impossible to resist the divine attraction. In union, finding yourself still, as it were, in your own familiar country, you can almost always resist, although it is painful and requires a violent effort. It is not the same as ravishment, which you can hardly ever resist. Giving you no time to think, or to prepare yourself, this often falls upon you with such swift and forceful impetuosity that you actually see and feel this cloud that seizes hold of you and this powerful eagle that carries you off on his wings.

"I have said: See and feel, you know that you are being carried off, but you do not know where you are going and so, at the beginning, in your human frailty, you experience indescribable terror at this movement which, otherwise, is so delightful. Here, the soul must show far more resolution and courage than in the preceding states. It must, in fact, be ready to risk everything, come what may, and abandon itself unreservedly, and with good grace, into the hands of God, letting Him guide it wheresoever He will; for, however painful it may be, one will be lifted up. Very often, when I was alone, but more especially when I was in public, I felt such lively terror, and such fear that I might be deceived, that I tried to resist with all my strength. Sometimes, I succeeded to some extent, but, as it was rather like wrestling with a mighty giant, it left me broken in body and prostrate with exhaustion.

"At other times, all my efforts were in vain; my soul was lifted up and my head almost always followed this movement, without my being able to restrain it, and, at times, even my whole body was carried off and no longer touched the ground.

"It was only rarely that I was transported in this manner. It happened to me one day when I was kneeling in the choir with all the other nuns, ready to take communion. It was extremely distressing to me, knowing that such an extraordinary thing would soon cause a great sensation. As this event happened very recently, since I became Prioress, I forbade the Sisters to talk about it. At other times, perceiving that God was about to renew this charism (and one day in particular, on the titular feast of our monastery, while I was listening to the sermon in the presence of some ladies of high rank), I suddenly threw myself on to the floor; my Sisters ran to hold me down but, in spite of this, the ravishment could not pass unnoticed. I begged Our Lord not to favor me any longer with these graces, since they were betrayed by external signs, for I was already weary of the circumspection to which they condemned me, and it seemed to me that He could accord me the same graces without anyone knowing of them. Apparently, in His goodness, He has deigned to hear my prayer, for, since then, nothing of this sort has happened to me, although, to be truthful, it is only a little while since I asked Him this favor. Whenever I tried to resist, I thought I felt beneath my feet the astonishing forces that were raising me up; I know of nothing I can compare them to. No other operation of the spirit, about which I have spoken, comes anywhere near this forceful thrust. It left me shattered. The combat is terrible and serves little purpose.

"I confess that, at the beginning, I was seized with excessive fear on seeing my body thus lifted off the ground, for although (when you offer no resistance) the soul follows after the body with inexpressible delight, you do not lose consciousness. Speaking for myself, at least, I was fully aware and could see that I was elevated above the ground.[45]

"Often, my body became so light that it no longer had any weight at all; sometimes it reached a point where I hardly felt my feet touching the ground anymore."[46]

95

The famous double ecstasy, or double levitation, at the Carmel of the Incarnation in Avila, mentioned by all the biographers of Saint John of the Cross and of Saint Teresa, is the most remarkable known example of spiritual exaltation and the ravishment of love, because it was double, that is to say, two people were lifted into the air, in ecstasy, at the same time, and both were plunged into such deep reciprocal contemplation behind the bars that separated them that neither Saint John, who clutched hold of his chair, nor Saint Teresa of Avila, who rose in a kneeling position on the other side of the grille, were aware of the unprecedented feat, nor did they become dizzy, intimately united as they were in the mystery of the Holy Trinity, which they had just been discussing, and both believed, quite simply, that they were carrying on their conversation as usual. Contemporaries adjudged this to be so extraordinary and prodigious an event that it should not be kept secret, especially in view of the status and the virtue of the two people involved, and so the following inscription was placed beneath the picture illustrating the scene in the parlor of the convent:

> "Siendo priora de este convento de la Encarnación
>   nuestra Santa Madre,
>   y vicario de dicho convento
>   S. Juan de la Cruz,
> estando en este locutorio hablando en el misterio de la
>   Santissima Trinidad,
> se arrobaron entrambos, y el Santo subió elevando tras
>   si la silla,
>   COMO SE VE EN LA PINTURA."[47.]

96

The *Acta Sanctorum*[48] also gives an account of this sensational encounter between two souls lost in a pure contemplation that caused them to levitate simultaneously: "Cum quadam die in locutorio monasterii Incarnationis altissimos ac pro more suo fervidissimos de Sanctissimae Trinitatis, mysterio, sermones miscere coepissent, et Johannem sublime loquente Teresia in genua provoluta per cancellos auscultaret; adeo utriusque animus divino igne incaluit, ut primum puidem Johannes una cum sede in qua resia, genibus uterat flexis, rapti fuerint sursum versus. Testem hujus rei habemus Beatricem a Jesu (filiam Francisci Alvarez,

145

patruelli S. Teresiae) tunc ad Incarnationis monacham, sed posteaad Excalceatas cum aliis pluribus transgressam; quae ipso ecstaseos tempore locutorium ingressa fuerat ad nuntium aliquod sanctae ferendum, atque ex ea postmodum tam miri spectaculi causam et occasionem didicerat. Idem non semet contigisse consendum est, dum est, tum ex fide historicum, tum maxime ex eo quod ferunt. S. Matrem dictirare solitam, caute de Deo collo-quendum esse cum P. Johanne a Cruce; quippe qui non solum raperetur ipse, verum efficeret ut alii quoque raptus paterentur."

This ecclesiastical Latin is like an organ accompaniment!

97

Leroy[49] summarizes: "One of the most famous of Saint Teresa's levita-tions is the one she had at the same time as Saint John of the Cross. He had come to visit her at the Convent of the Incarnation and, through the grille of the parlor, Saint Teresa was listening to him speaking about the Holy Trinity. Suddenly, the saint rose up into the air in a transport, carrying his chair with him. Saint Teresa, who was on her knees, was also lifted off the ground. By chance, Sister Beatrice of Jesus, the daughter of Francisco Alvarez, Saint Teresa's first cousin, came into the parlor at that moment and witnessed the spectacle."

98

In his fine book on Saint John of the Cross,[50] the Reverend Father Bruno brings to life the atmosphere of the convent and makes the story ring with a note of family intimacy and emotion: "One day, on the Feast of the Most Holy Trinity, Father John of the Cross was in the parlor—it was a little parlor, two and a half meters high and five feet long by five feet wide, the floor was paved with red brick, the walls were of gray stone and the ceiling was supported by brown beams. Father John was sitting on a chair and the Reverend Mother, on the other side of the grille, was seated on a bench. He was speaking of the mystery, 'his favorite mystery,' and his soul plunged into this ocean of fire. The ardor of the Spirit carried off the body, and, as Father John clutched his chair, it carried away the chair, too. He rose up to the ceiling. Teresa of Jesus was ravished by the same impulse of love. Doña Beatriz de Cepeda y Ocampo, the future Beatrice of Jesus, opened the door and came in to give her relative a message, and so witnessed this truly transcendental rapture. 'There is no way one can speak of God to my Father John of the Cross, because he immediately goes into ecstasy and causes others to do the same,' said Teresa very charmingly, by way of excuse."

99

Can't you just see them, these two, in their little parlor, separated by a grille, chatting away, ascending face to face like a couple of hummingbirds, or like those birds of whom the poet has sung:

> ... they have but a single wing and fly in couples...

in ecstasy, lost to the world. Can't you see them as *beija-flores,* kissers-of-flowers, in ecstasy before a curtain of jasmine, hovering there, their wings beating so fast that they create a shimmering aura around them, these two, our two hummingbirds in their tête-à-tête, each in ecstasy before the mouth of the other, as if in front of a half-open corolla, and, between them, each little white flower in the quivering curtain of jasmine like a translucent Lilliputian star, exhaling its perfume, each dazzling the other, each becoming incandescent and melting in the act of thanksgiving, of contemplation, of jubilation, of impulse, possession, and joy, and the pure love that surrenders itself impetuously and is consumed in *the fire of divine love?*

100

It is God's moment.

101

Midday.

102

It is time.

103

The cannon on the citadel, ignited by the burning glass of the perpendicular sun, fires its single, noonday shot.

104

Hence the cries of Saint Joseph of Copertino when he flew away. Questioned about these cries by Cardinal de Lauria, Brother Joseph replied: "When the powder in the arquebus catches fire, it bursts with a great noise, and so does the heart ignited by divine love... AMEN!"

105

He cried out and flew away.

He hovered in front of the altar, not like a bird who gazes into a mirror and knocks his head against his own image, but in ecstasy before the face of God.

...EMISSIO SUSPIRIO CUM MAGNU EJULATU...

modulates the organ accompaniment of the Bollandists' *Acta Sanctorum*, page 1023, Vol. V, September, *marginalia* B/C, published *apud Bernardum Albertum Vander Plasschi,* ANTVERPIAE, MDCCLV, *in folio.*

Postscript for businessmen.—If a producer ever feels like making this prodigious film, I—I, who have sworn never again to waste my time making films—will drop everything, give up my solitude, my tranquility, and my writing, to make this film about Saint Joseph of Copertino, in memory of my son, Rémy, the pilot, and as a souvenir for his sometime girlfriend, the out-of-work baker's girl, with whom I lost touch in wartime Paris.

Notes

1. Bernino (D): *Vie de Saint Joseph de Copertino, de l'ordre des frères mineurs,* Paris, Poussielgue, 1856 (translation of *Vita del ven. Padre F. Giuseppe de Copertino dei Minori Conventuali, descritta da D.B...., etc.* Rome, 1722).

2. A variable Italian measure. "Five perches," that is, about 25 meters, according to the Latin text by Angelo Pastrovicchi, whom Benedict XIV ordered to write a biography of the greatest ecstatic in history.—Note by Leroy, p. 125.

3. Biographical note by Leroy, pp. 123—24.

4. Died on the 12th of October, 1946 in San Francisco.

5. A propaganda tract *Pour le succès dans les examens,* published by les Frères Mineurs Capucins, 26, rue Boissonnade, Paris, XIVᵉ.

6. *Zambo:* a half-caste of mixed black and Indian blood.

7. Paris, 1919.

8. See Blaise Cendrars: *Chez l'Armée anglaise,* a war report, with photographs, Paris, 1940.

9. Paris, 1946.

10. An error, in 1767. see p. 89 para. 30.

11. Leroy, chap VI, pp. 123–39.

12. Leroy, p. 6.

13. *Sum.* 2.2. *q.*96, *a* I, quoted by Leroy, p. 345. This was also the teaching of Buddha.

14. Leroy, p. 198.

15. Quoted by Leroy, p. 61.

16. Quoted by Leroy, p. 55.

17. This section is composed of extracts from the monograph by Olivier Leroy. As with Chapter 27 of the present work, dealing with Saint Joseph of Copertino's most famous flights, I have made use of Leroy's published translation of the Bollandists' *Acta Sanctorum*, although not always in full, and I have followed his chronology, which was not always easy to establish. I reiterate here my homage and my gratitude to the author for his conscientious and magisterial work, which really exhausts the highly controversial subject of levitation and studies it in all its aspects and all its manifestations, whether legendary, hypothetical, fraudulent, or genuine. I have checked Leroy's quotations from the *Acta Sanctorum,* and found they contain no major errors. See Leroy's monograph for these cases, and, for others, his Bibliography.

18. Bloud and Gay, 1927 (quoted by Leroy).

19. Quoted by Leroy.

20. Quoted by Leroy.

21. Quoted by Leroy.

22. Quoted by Leroy.

23. From Bouix's translation of the autobiography of Saint Teresa, chap. XX. Cf. *Oeuvres,* vol. III, chap. V (quoted by Leroy).

24. Quoted by Leroy.

25. Quoted by Leroy, after Thurston.

26. Quoted by Leroy, after Scoraille.

27. Quoted by Leroy, after Imbert-Gourbeyre.

28. Quoted by Leroy.

29. Quoted by Leroy.

30. Quoted by Leroy.

31. *La Stigmatisation,* Vol. II, p. 247, quoted by Leroy.

32. The Persian poet and mystic Jalal al Din Reumi (died 1273) tells of another levitation at sea in his *Mathnawi.* A certain sheikh, suspected of

having stolen some pearls, demonstrated his innocence by majestically levitating from the deck of a ship (quoted by Leroy, p. 22, after Wilson).

33. Quoted by Leroy.

34. Quoted by Leroy, after Tannoia.

35. Anecdotes quoted by Leroy, after Berthe.

36. Quoted by Leroy, after Franclieu.

37. This was during the Revolution (note by Leroy).

38. *Recueil de documents relatifs à la lévitation du corps humain,* Paris, 1897.

39. This piece of furniture has been preserved, without repairs, in the chapel of the mother house of the Congregation, in La Souterraine (Creuse) (note by Leroy).

40. Émile Baumann: *Mon frère le Dominicain,* pp. 391–92 (Paris: Grasset, 1927). And to think that Émile Baumann's name was on the same "Otto List" as mine, in 1943, and that we were banned by the Germans as "Jewish writers living and working in France." what bloody nerve! But perhaps it was just stupidity, or the result of a denunciation.

41. The United States had everything, except a female saint. This lacuna has now been filled. Recently, Pius XII canonized the first North American woman to become a saint, Mother Francesca Saverino Cabrini (1889–1917), of order of the Sacred Heart of Jesus, of which she was the founder. On this occasion, the illustrated daily paper *Cavalcade,* for August 15, 1946, published photographs of the Yankee saint, whose body, like Saint Catherine Labouré's, remained in a perfect state of preservation without embalming and is now the object of the first pilgrimage in the history of the United States. The newspaper gives the twelve requisite conditions, and details the procedure, for all canonizations:

"THE TWELVE CONDITIONS

"1. The candidate for sainthood must be postulated locally.

"The Bishop, or a Superior of a religious community, must make the first proposal after having organized a 'Diocesan process' and carried out a local inquiry.

"2. The saint must have been proclaimed 'Venerable' by the Congregation of Rites.

"The results of local inquiries are sent to Rome and examined by the Congregation of Rites, which, after studying them, either rejects the cause or declares it to be initiated by proclaiming the candidate 'Venerable.'

"3. The saint must be a Christian and a member of the Roman Catholic Church.

"The saint cannot be other than a son or daughter of the Catholic community. In primitive times, the faithful were called 'saints,' as is shown by the expression 'the communion of saints,' which indicates the solidarity among members of the church. Furthermore, Pope Benedict XIV laid down that 'even though one can find pagans who display true moral goodness, capable of reaching heroic heights, men who are called heroes among their own people on account of certain virtues, they are nevertheless lacking in other virtues and cannot be called heroes in the Christian sense.'

"4. The saint must display Christian virtues to a heroic degree.

"These virtues are faith, hope, and charity. The aspirant saint must also be without stain. He must be united with God: sanctity presupposes a special favor from God. he must be neither 'quietist'—passivism not being heroic—nor suspected of falling into the mystical heresy of Meister Eckhart, for whom the soul in ecstasy identifies itself with God, a sin of Pride. The true saint exercises his virtues in difficult circumstances, promptly, and with joy, and this must be so on every occasion, not just as an exception (Benedict XIV).

"5. The saint must have accomplished at least two duly verified miracles.

"In our era, miracles are considered as apparitions witnessed and confirmed by several believers, and, above all, the curing of the sick or the infirm. Mental and nervous diseases are particularly mistrusted. Every miraculous cure must be attested by doctors, the testimony of unbelieving doctors being not only admitted but actually sought. Stigmatics must also undergo medical verification.

"6. The saint must first have been 'beatified.'

"When the Congregation of Rites has reached a favorable conclusion concerning the preceding points, it proposes to the Pope that an act of beatification should be signed. The Blessed one then becomes the object of a cult restricted to his or her own diocese. There are two kinds of beatification: formal or ordinary: When it is a question of an aspirant saint who is the object of an 'immemorial' cult attested by the Bishop, this is the equivalent of beatification and, in this case, the Congregation of Rites has only to give its approval to the episcopal decision, and the papal brief is then called the brief of approval.

"7. The saint must have been the subject of a secret process in consistory.

"A consistory held by the Pope must re-examine the cause, the writings, the acts, the life, the virtues, and the miracles of the candidate. A representative of the Congregation of Rites keeps the dossier up-to-date. A promoter of the faith (devil's advocate) presents the objections (animadversions) and questions whether the miracles have really been brought about through the intercession of the Blessed one.

"8. The saint must pass through a double, semi-public process.

"The conclusions of the consistory, if they are positive, are submitted to two other analogous processes, but in a semi-public consistory where new objections may be raised.

"9. The saint must be the subject of a favorable proposition by the Sacred College.

"To conclude the foregoing procedures, the Sacred College of Cardinals must hold a solemn meeting at which they give their favorable opinion and propose the candidate's canonization to the Pope.

"10. The saint must be designated by the Pope.

"According to the opinions expressed at the last meeting of the Cardinals, and after the final examination of all the documents, the Pope makes his decision and fixes the date for the ceremony of canonization, which takes place in Rome with great pomp. It may also be the occasion of a ceremony in the saint's own diocese, in the presence of a papal legate.

"11. The saint must be proclaimed by a papal bull.

"Once the ceremony has been carried out, a papal bull notifies Christianity of its purport and its terms. This bull constitutes the decree of canonization.

"12. The saint must be inscribed in the canon of saints.

"This is the last stage. When the decree is presented, the new saint is added to the list of the canon of saints. He then has the right, throughout Christianity, to the cult known as the cult of dulia (the cult of latria being reserved for God and Christ). This cult of dulia consists of: an office on the saint's feast-day; mention of his name at the sacrifice of the Mass; external homage to the image of the saint; the gift of the saint's name at baptism; the patronage of towns, states or churches. The Holy Virgin is in the first rank of the saints and receives a special cult known as hyperdulia."

42. Paris, 1936.

43. In Leroy's *La Lévitation,* you will find all the details and the historical examples that illustrate this thesis of the antinomy between ecstatics and mediums, plus a parallel study of the phenomena manifested by neurotics, which have been clinically observed and classified and are nowadays considered as classic. This study is still far from complete, not because there is any shortage of tests, but because the most objective minds have difficulty in admitting the thousand years of Catholic experience as concrete *facts.* Even the best-documented historical dialectic is reluctant to take it into account! The first to laugh at it were the Encyclopedists, and since their time (man being descended from the apes), innumerable bastards have been born to them in various Faculties and Laboratories. I think that, today, Voltaire—who particularly mocked the legend of Saint Joseph of Copertino—would be the first to laugh at this degeneration of the Sorbonne-ites and other official scientists in every country, the intelligent schoolmaster having replaced "that ass, the curé," and the primary manual of compulsory education "that idiotic catechism," which had, however, proved its value. In any case, I laugh at the Protestants and Anglicans who triggered off this modern spiritual poverty, which began in the nineteenth century with the spiritual and metaphysical sects who recruited members to their church as if it were a cultural melting pot of all the fiends of hell! That's progress.

... veni, Creator spiritus...

44. Teresa de Ahumada y Cepeda was fifty-two years old; Juan de Yepes, twenty-five. She had founded her second convent of the Reformed Carmelites; he was a poor little monk on vacation. This was at Medina del Campo, at the end of August, 1567.

45. *Sainte Térèse: Vie par elle-même,* translated by Bouix, chap. XX, pp. 190–93. Cf. *Oeuvres,* vol. III, *Sixièmes demeures,* chap V., p. 400.

46. Yepes: *Vida, Virtudes y Milagros,* vol. I, chap XV (quoted by Leroy, after Thurston).

47. Inscription reported by Leroy, p. 100.

48. Vol. VII, October, p. 239/BC.

49. P. 100.

50. Fr. Bruno de J. M.: *Saint Jean de la Croix,* p. 133, Paris, 1929.

Para a mais linda Paulista do mundo

THE SIDEREAL EIFFEL TOWER
(Rhapsody of the Night)

"It is true that we love the world,
but that is because we have grown
accustomed to love, not to life."

Nietzsche

I

LEFT BANK

Since reading all the books that mention the colibri (the hummingbird, the *beija-flores*), from Buffon to the most recent,[1] I have had the opportunity to observe this tiny bird and its flight at the *fazenda* of the Morro Azul, a paradise for birds where the Emerald, the Garnet, the Ruby-Topaz, the Golden Belly, the Rainbow, and that little creature with golden crests, the winged jewel the natives call a Star and naturalists, more prosaically but just as evocatively call a Fly-Bird, and even the Avocet, the most dazzling and the rarest of all, could be seen in considerable numbers flying around the patio and the verandah; some had straight beaks, some downward-curving beaks, and others, incomprehensibly, beaks that curved upward. The reason for their presence was that Dr. Oswaldo Padroso, the owner of this old, exhausted plantation, a kind of hermit living in solitude, a lay saint, a free-thinker with a gentle soul, and, like his master, Auguste Comte,* a positivist touched by love, had forbidden hunting and shooting throughout the whole extent of his property, and so the valley of the Morro Azul (the Blue Mountain) had become a refuge for birds.

The Morro Azul!

In the tropics, night falls swiftly and, on the road that runs along the crests to join Campinas to Glaréola, I had lingered to admire the throng of blue mountains facing me and the Rio Tiété, which wound its way among them, the last pools of light caught in its meanderings amid a jumble of banana trees, tufts of bamboo, and giant trees that were the last vestiges of the primeval forest, the forest corridor that, not so long ago—barely a century—had been so overgrown with parasitic plants that the banks of the river were inaccessible.

---

*(1798–1857) French mathematician and philosopher, founder of Positivism. (Trans.)

The landscape was grandiose and ravaged, the road scorched, railroad tracks had been laid and charred tree stumps gave evidence of the thinning of the forest, for they were in the process of electrifying the area, and I wondered in which fold of those mountains on the right bank the *fazenda* I was heading for nestled. A friend in São Paulo had announced my arrival and taken the necessary steps to ensure a welcome for me, so they were expecting me, and I was due to arrive before nightfall.

"Don't miss this stop, Blaise," this friend had said to me. "I've had such a hard time persuading Oswaldo to put you up for the night. He's one of our old employees, it was our bank that arranged for him to get this *fazenda* cheap, and we advanced him the money he needed, so he can't refuse us anything. But he's a misanthrope and a bear, and if I hadn't insisted, telling him you were the greatest living poet, and from France, I truly believe he would have refused to receive you. So don't blame me, my dear friend, if Dr. Oswaldo bores you to death with his elegies, but the place is worthy of you, you'll see, and it's well worth making a detour to see the *fazenda*. It's the Emperor's *fazenda*, it's all built of marble, there's nothing like it in the whole of Brazil."

"The Emperor's *fazenda*, Caïo? I didn't know Dom Pedro had ever been so far into the interior. I thought he spent all his time in Rio and Petropolis, where he'd established his court."

"And you were right, Blaise. Dom Pedro traveled a lot, but not in this country, although it was more or less his own, as France was Napoleon's. He was always supposed to come to São Paulo and visit the coffee plantations in the interior, but he never did. Under the influence of Gobineau, who was the French Ambassador in Rio at that time, and dragged the Emperor all the way to the Caucasus, the cradle of the white race, which was his pet subject, Dom Pedro had nothing but contempt for the Paulists, although they were ardent patriots and they and their blacks were clearing the jungle and planting coffee, the source of Brazil's wealth today, and that's why the Emperor is so unpopular in São Paulo. The Paulists are very sensitive and always ready to criticize the authorities, and, in fact, that was the cause of his rapid downfall. It's much the same today, as more than one President in Rio, which has been our capital since we became a Republic, has found out to his cost. The Paulists are individualists and chauvinists and very proud of their achievement in clearing the forest and developing this immense country, and of always being at the forefront of progress and backing it financially. But, in expectation of the Emperor's visit, which was forever being postponed, the rich planters of the province, proud men but, at that time, gullible, ruined themselves in their reckless desire to build *fazendas* that would be worthy of receiving the Emperor, each one wanting to lodge Dom Pedro in his own home, and this rivalry created such a flood of follies and extravagances, such lavish spending, so many debts and mortgages, that the landowners in the Glaréola region never recovered from it, their *fazendas* fell into a ruinous state and, when everybody started going in for a single crop, the intensive and profitable cultivation of coffee, the great modern plantations were developed still deeper into the interior, around Ribeirao Preto, where you're going today, and so the area around Glaréola, which was once so flourishing, degenerated into an utterly bankrupt municipality. It was in these romantic circumstances that the Morro Azul came to be built. The Emperor's *fazenda* is all in rose-colored marble, and it's the last vestige of that great era of hope. Dr. Oswaldo will fill you in with the details of this great disillusionment, if you're interested. They say he's written a poem about it, a kind of Epic, because, you know, our poets are uninspired and way behind the times."

"So, he's a poet, your Dr. Padroso?"

"So they say. Well, what else could he do in his solitude? But, don't be surprised, Cendrars, the man's in love. Who with? I'll tell you when you get back, if Dr. Oswaldo hasn't already told you himself. It's a long story, it's been going on for twenty years, so it's an open secret and everybody in town laughs at him. Yes, it seems he's written some verses in the style of Edmond Rostand, verses that are passed round clandestinely, which is just as well because they're not very good. But what can you expect, the man's in love, and when a Brazilian is in love, he writes poetry. It's the national vice. You could say there are as many poets as there are male inhabitants in Brazil, and for some time now, even our women have been at it. A promising sign. Anyway, all this explains both the superabundance and the poverty of Brazilian poetry, official or otherwise, academic, religious, or whatever, and why it's always redundant and empty. But don't judge us by that. There are some exquisite popular songs. I'm ashamed to admit it, but the blacks are the only ones who know how to sing of love in this country, and they're the real poets, although they're illiterate!"

"That's nothing to be ashamed of, Caïo. Gobineau has already crowned the black man with the laurel wreath of poetry—yes, that same French Ambassador who had such a baleful influence on the destiny of your Emperor. But, tell me, is this Dr. Oswaldo Padroso a doctor, too?"

"Him? Not on your life! He's like me, he only took the first two exams for his degree. You're forgetting that, in Brazil, everything is exaggerated,

159

including titles. They call him 'Doctor' because he's been to the University, just as they call the planter who is totally uneducated but has made a fortune out of coffee 'Colonel,' and the same goes for retired men, while the pimps, here in Rio, are nearly all deserters from the navy, so they call them captains in slang, *caftens*. It's the climate that does it. Look at the exuberance, the lushness of nature all around you. Open your eyes. But don't be fooled. Everything in this country is exaggerated. I wouldn't wish it on you to fall in love with a Brazilian girl, Blaise. What a drama! You have no idea..."

What a malicious tongue! He was initiating me and I liked him very much. In Paris, a spiteful, caustic, coldly mocking dandy like Caïo, a jealous poseur full of intrigues, would have given me the creeps in no time at all, but in São Paulo, where there is no entertainment and the circle of social relations outside the Automobile Club is very restricted, this debunking banker's son, who played at being a well-informed cosmopolitan, amused me with his worldly wisdom and his indiscretion, and the stories that Caïo de Azevedo told me, often very risqué and always elaborately embroidered, in spite of his detached and couldn't-care-less way of telling them, taught me more about the country and its social customs than dozens and dozens of weighty tomes written by distinguished economists and historians. His grasp of the facts was as perfect as his disrespect for them, and none of his scandalous propositions was ever made without some ulterior motive, this man of deadpan humor, being so perfidious, putting ideas into my head, setting me on the right track, that is, the forbidden track, with malice aforethought, and full of secret jubilation when he saw me entangle myself, take the bait, make outrageous gaffes, and fall into the trap.

Men of this type are not uncommon in Brazil, where snakes abound. It is the Indian blood, as noxious as cocaine. And yet I was congratulating myself on having Caïo as a companion, indeed, I could no longer get on without him, for this disconcerting hypocrite was so useful to me in this country where everything, as he rightly said, is pushed to extremes, human feelings are as exaggerated as hostile nature, and friendship as impure and as disturbing as the orchids, those exquisitely beautiful parasitic flowers which, paradoxically, are poisonous and bring bad luck, so that, unlike the North American varieties, no Brazilian woman would dream of wearing them as a corsage, and even the brainless hummingbird gathers no honey from them, although naturalists explain the often outlandish length of the hummingbird's beak, with its absurd and surprising curves, as being necessary for the collecting of nourishment from the depths of the irregularly shaped or curved and saw-toothed corollas of these diabolical flowers, as if this irrationally shaped beak was a cutting or penetrating tool, a brad awl, a scalpel, a lancet, a pair of fine tweezers, whereas, in reality, it is his protractile tongue that the hummingbird uses for sucking honey out of the deepest calices, his triggered tongue that flaps, snaps, sucks, whips, and churns, for it is a sounding lead, a fishing line, a long wriggling worm, a detector, an inhaler of fragrances, a titillator, the most effective ravishing tool conceivable, voluptuous as well as efficacious, and one sees the flowers of sensitive plants and foxglove swooning, while the half-closed petals of the citrus blossom open out; the beak is an empirical weaving tool and serves, above all, for nest building; only exceptionally is it armed with serrations like the teeth of a comb, and this occurs in the more exclusively carnivorous species, who also make use of their tongues, hinged and sprung like a fly-swat, or like a kind of sticky lasso, to capture the mayflies and the spiders they love to eat, and which these inveterate scroungers pick off daintily as they flash past, without pausing in their flight and without tearing the webs; all species, with a sure instinct and with the reflexes of an insect rather than a bird, avoid orchids, no matter how alluring they may be in shape, color, or perfume, probably because these monocotyledonous phanerogams are bottles of poison.

A seductive country, full of simultaneous contrasts, and highly dangerous, to judge from the unanimous discussions of the Brazilians, those feverish chatterboxes whose garrulousness masks the profound melancholy to which man is a prey in this torrid climate, feeling himself lost in the vastness of the country and utterly powerless and impotent in the face of the immensity of his task, and, in spite of the stimulus of his most exciting successes, which he knows very well to be meretricious, he tends, generation after generation, to fall back into a morbid apathy, a discouraging weariness, like his ancestor, the hardy pioneer who stretched out exhausted in his hammock and who often let himself die in the wilderness, completely disoriented, his head empty, and the rich Brazilian of today eagerly fills this emptiness with words, before falling asleep, taking his siesta in the clubs and roof gardens of the capital cities, annihilating himself with well-being, befuddling himself with self-indulgence, coddling himself with sporadic fits of melancholy and lethargy, handling immense business projects in the way that some people abuse aphrodisiacs or narcotics.

Creole mentality or Portuguese atavism? Long ago, the anthropophagous Tupís were already noted for their deep-seated sadness, their funereal songs, their macabre dances, the weeping they indulged in, even on happy occasions! And what are we to think of their women, with whom the Paulist *bandeirantes* founded families? They were tattooed Indians, often splendid-looking creatures, but melancholy and always bursting into tears. The Brazilian women of today are throwbacks. They are passionate. In the tropics, love is a mental illness. Never have I seen so many little wooden crosses as I saw along the tracks that penetrate into the solitudes of the interior. These are not the victims of brigands and outlaws, the *salteadores* of the highway, but of jealous men. And the jealous villain, the killer who "avenges his honor," the Lusitanian, proud of his exploit, is quite content to lose himself and die in the jungle. Sometimes, you come across his skeleton. Suicide haunts the virgin forest where, among other horrors, the proliferation of life—totems, animals, snakes, vegetation, vermin, rottenness, and phosphorescence—is both a nightmare and a hideous daydream.

I thought about all this, and I asked myself whether the most highly evolved representatives of modern Western European civilization are not, in fact, worthy reflections of this half-caste mentality of Creole millionaires on the other side of the ocean, with their pessimistic optimism, their carelessness and indifference, their lassitude due to an excess of comfort, luxury, hygiene, mercenary concerns, and, ultimately, to a lack of faith in what has been achieved so far, which is patently demonstrated by the continuance of wars of extermination and the fact that these have become more and more frequent ever since the dawn of the nineteenth century, when the civilization of the old world began to devote itself exclusively to the discovery and scientific conquest of matter, and now, like the *conquistadores* who, at the beginning of the sixteenth century, devoted themselves to the discovery, conquest, and exploitation of the fabulous riches of the New World, our materialistic experts and our leaders dream of exploiting the universe, but in cold blood, without personal risk, without rushing into exotic adventures, and our captains of industry, who have neither balls nor charisma, are working hand-in-glove with our politically conscious and asexual proletariat at the trituration of the secrets of the cosmos, all working together toward a financial reward that has been calculated in advance, worked out statistically, and which, thanks to the closed circuit of a managed economy, a five-year plan, for example, or a gigantic trust, a state monopoly, can be realized in record time, just as, in the seventeenth and eighteenth centuries, it was possible to get rich in the colonies, without too much effort and in a relatively short time, thanks to the concessions granted to the great trading companies of the East and West Indies, to the Hudson Bay or

Minas Gerais companies, and by dint of practicing a controlled economy and the small-scale, one-product cultivation of sugar, conchineal, spices, tobacco, or treasure-hunting, prospecting for precious metals and... man-hunting, rationalizing the workforce by using black slaves as forced labor, which was a precursor of ruthless mechanization and work on an assembly line.

The astounding and catastrophic results of this first triumphant applica-tion of Reason to the management and regimentation of men's lives are well-known: This first attempt at rational economic order created all the disorders that led to the explosion of the French Revolution, and our own efforts, from which we are already reaping the "benefits," will be a verita-ble planetary cataclysm, because when applied on a universal scale, our frail reason will not be able to withstand the blow, as is proved by the last war, by our ideologies and our current world, split in two by fanatics who are equally materialistic but divided as to the methods of applying a scientific formula destined to ensure, not happiness, as the adherents of the two antagonistic parties claim, but the swift decline of the human race.

As if, since the Earth began to revolve, we had ever succeeded in doing anything large or enduring for the happiness of Mankind! Even Dante failed, and did no good at all with his tiresome *Paradiso*. Adam was chased out, I mean out of the "earthly garden," for this world has never been a par-adise. Without Christian charity, man is a wolf to his fellowmen. Pontius Pilate washed his hands of him. "After us, the deluge!" said His Most Christian Majesty, King Louis XV. Words, attitudes that illustrate the paradoxical behavior of our modern white women, the most sophisticated of whom go half-naked, dressed like savages in feathers, furs, or animal skins, their complexions adulterated, the napes of their necks shaved, weighed down with jewels, their bodies as thin as men's on the pretext that they must "keep their figures," an aesthetic affectation that is nothing more than a masked rejection of maternity (some take it to extremes, even undergoing ablation of the breasts!), and these midnight women go in for aggressive polyandry, cocktails, smoking, and dance halls, claiming the right to "live their lives," as if nature had made them unique and indepen-dent! That is degeneracy. I thought about all these things...

"You and I, like all our contemporaries who are very proud of being up-to-date, coddle ourselves as if we were tubercular, we avoid the least draught, treat ourselves like invalids, and yet we're healthy, even if we don't go in for sport, like some of our friends. What are we to do with all this excess of health, how can we invest this idle capital?" Caïo asked me

163

one day. He was an ex-pupil of the Jesuits, and, although he financed the sports stadiums, he did not like to be seen there.

And he added, with a most provoking cynicism that gave one an insight into his private inhibitions:

"I wonder what use we could put our good health to? What do you say, eh?"

I thought about it. There are examples from history. The words of the blasé and debauched Louis XV are a testimony to it. But there are also zoological examples.

I thought: Gigantism is the order of the day, and it was gigantism that rapidly condemned the ichthyosauri and the plesiosauri to death and led to the extinction of the species whose monstrous skeletons are found in the lias and in the friable, sandy red rocks of the Jurassic period, gigantism, said to have been the most formidable surge of animal life ever and calculated to have taken place twenty million years ago, when these colossal creatures, great, stolid brutes, apparently quite devoid of intelligence, lorded it over the earth with their prodigious strength, but gigantism, then, was nothing more than an external morphological phenomenon, whereas the gigantism that is taking over today, having reappeared unexpectedly in our consciousness, is of a psychological order, an internal monstrosity, an aberration, a psychosis, the most prodigious *folie de grandeur* man has ever known, a brainstorm, an inordinate attack of pride, knowledge, skill, and technology with its tentacular cities, the multi-media onslaught of publicity, competing trusts, industrial complexes, holding companies, anonymous networks that encircle the world several times in all directions, in the air, on the ground, underground, on the water, under the water, in the stratosphere, and through the airwaves, and whose ambition is to capture the entire universe, propaganda for the exclusive use of the masses, dictatorship of the proletariat, imperialism, monopolies, and this mania of *Homo sapiens* in the laboratory, making *Homo faber* slave away and proposing to throw even the nucleation of the atom out of gear and to make money with the vital and, up to the present, beneficent (since it is unknown) energy of the cosmic rays, this new scourge, this new Gold-rush which is about to gush forth from the retorts, the test tubes, the spectrographs, the electroscopes, the transformers of matter into energy and the ovens of the state cyclotrons. And here they are, already announcing the mesons[2]... industrial cosmic rays, a byproduct engendered by cyclotrons at Berkeley!

Oh, yes, I thought about all these things.

GOLD.

In the recent historical past, the Great Work of alchemists in the pay of kings and emperors impoverished by wars was to find SYNTHETIC GOLD, christened the PHILOSOPHER'S STONE to make people believe it was a pious work destined to ensure the future happiness of the human race and a *return* to the GOLDEN AGE; in the same way, our modern experts, technicians, and technologists in the service of capitalist or communist regimes, equally impoverished by wars, proclaim in unison that they are working in the name of great democratic principles and exclusively for the universal happiness of mankind, for this famous GOLDEN AGE, which political economy, under a pretense of sharing the riches of the earth, and in the name of the Equality and Fraternity of all men, places squarely *in the future,* while the very fact of scientific progress makes that future less and less certain and causes all our hopes to recede further and further into the distance.

Liberty, the happiness of the human race? But it is all a matter of dough and nothing else, dough to finance THE WAR, to feed it, for the human race can always be left to die of starvation, men being nothing but slaves to the machine, and under the heel of politicians and officials who no longer brandish the whip, like the masters of earlier times, to make backs bend, but who have developed robots that can grind rebellious individuals between their automatic jaws and which, instead of shitting blood or excrement, eject from their equally automatic anuses a series of gold discs, clean, polished, gleaming, hypnotic, precisely calibrated, and all of the same weight: Uniformity.

The metal Eucharist of political economy!

GOLD.

Unity.

Union.

ECONOMIC UNITY = POLITICAL UNION

The U.S.A. = The U.S.S.R.

Giants, geographical colossi, certainly, but as fragile as money. CAPITAL = WORK or WORK = CAPITAL.

Today, one cannot condemn capitalism without condemning communism, unless one is prepared to falsify the concepts and upset the balance of truth, nor can one opt for one or the other, since these two minters of counterfeit coins put exactly the same false currency into circulation.

MAN = GOD.

And it's a toss-up.

Heads or tails?

And it's war, the war to end wars.

What is the difference between a golden louis and a rouble from Soiuz-Zoloto,* can you tell me? Between the Communist International lantern of revolution and the "Statue of Liberty"? They would have us believe the moon is made of green cheese, on both sides. And whatever the stamp of the coin, whatever effigy is on it, the death mask of the embalmed Lenin or the phoenix arising from the ashes, or the eagle, the emblem of Roosevelt's New Deal, or the red star of the Soviets or the forty-eight stars, the luminaries on the American flag, and no matter what the symbol, the exergue, the monogram, the motto, the device, the slogan, the initials, and the date of minting engraved on it, it is a lie (and a lie so blatant that there can be no possible historical dispute about it. For example: the "A.E.I.O.U." still within living memory—and I am not talking about Arthur Rimbaud's colored vowels:

A black, E white, I red, U green, O blue...

but about the magic letters that sanctified the privilege and the monstrous primacy of the Archducal house of Austria over all the kingdoms of the West: *"Austria Erit In Orbe Ultima!"*, the proud device of the Emperor Frederick III, ancestor of Charles V, who, in competition with François I and Henry VIII, was the first to achieve that world empire on which *the sun never sets,* that short-lived universal domination—and what is left of it now, twenty-five years later, and what of the million crowns, now worth less than a Poincaré† sou? and even if this gleaming gold coin bears the Sun device of Montezuma I, called Huehue (the Elder), or of Montezuma II, called Xocojotzin (the Younger), it is a dead star, absolutely valueless, a disc in the void.

GOLD is a decoy.

And to think that, since the dawn of time, social man has constantly let himself be hypnotized by this artifice and has never learned better!

In the dust of all men's tombs one finds, not monumental bones, such as those of the ichthyosaurus and the plesiosaurus found in the red lias, but gold coins, which leads one to believe that all the defunct civilizations, however glorious, however ancient and powerful they were, succumbed to this maggot in the brain, to GOLD, and to the false idea of the intrinsic value and redeeming virtue of this conventional symbol, the ring and the heart of the anus!

Ah! In practice, a fat lot of use all man's intelligence has been to him!

---

* A Soviet goldmining company. See note 31, below. (Trans.)
† Raymond Poincaré, President of France, 1913–20. (Trans.)

The intelligence of which man is so immeasurably proud, and which was so cruelly lacking in the monstrous saurians of the Jurassic age, acephalic giants, they say, who did not know how to think.

It is a poison. A bloat. A grotesque exaggeration. A bad dream uncoiling its Saturnian rings.

And if the ultra-cultivated man of today, who has already blindly knocked everything to bits, now takes it upon himself to dismantle the Universe, it is because he senses that his long hypnosis is coming to an end, he feels the approach of the final crisis. Man is an evil, destructive animal, that is the truth his conscience is unwilling to admit and his intellect rejects, camouflaging it in an infinity of ways so as not to have to face it. If ever he regains his sight, his awakening will lead to a collective suicide. It cannot be otherwise. That is the logical outcome. Today, O Modernity, we are already bankrupt! The human race is done for. Yes, I thought about these things...

Have you never seen laymen visiting a laboratory, walking on tiptoe and so impressed that they display a religious awe that no cathedral, not even the basilica of Saint Peter's in Rome, can arouse in the breast of the vainest trade union leader or the most ass-licking member of the cell? In a lab, they make themselves patently ridiculous, with their respect and their sanctimoniousness. Soon, people will be visiting industrial sites and shutdown factories in the same way that, nowadays, we visit deconsecrated cathedrals or the Kremlin of the Czars. They will be like museums of barbarianism and superstition.

Belief in the benefits of science and the humanity of physicians is just as stupid, narrow-minded, and widespread among intellectuals today, in this new between-the-wars era, as it was at the end of the eighteenth century when the Encyclopedists, those first busybodies and men without God, inaugurated the cult of Reason, worshiped an undefined Progress, preached the infinite Rights of Man, and believed, poor brutes, in the innocence and virtue of the "noble savage"; meanwhile, Voltaire was toadying to the King of Prussia, Diderot* was cuddling the Semiramis of the North, and Jean-Jacques* was sacrificing to Onan in the groves of Les Charmettes, right under Mme. de Warrens' windows unbeknownst to her gardener-lover, Claude Anet, who would have pulled his ears for him, for our three great men were thinking of nothing but earning a comfortable income and assur-

---

* Denis Diderot (1713–84), French philosopher and playwright. He was rumored to be the lover of Empress Catherine the Great of Russia (Cendrars' "Semiramis of the North"). (Trans.)

ing their places at table, and in bed, and not giving a fuck for the human race... and the same thing happened in 1940, this attitude being typical of men of letters who feel not the slightest shame at their public conduct in the face of the enemy, nor at the contradiction between their alleged convictions and their behavior, since they are producing Literature! And this makes "commitment" legitimate, that is to say, the conformism of the last generation of writers who dedicated their pens to the cause of one or the other of the two reigning ideologies. To hell with the whole bunch of humbugs! What are they doing to liberty? But bread and butter comes first[3]... And perhaps that is why, seeing all this coming on, I had left France and, since 1924, had been tramping round Brazil[4]... Happily, in France, there were some young people who were not fooled! By their lack of desire to do anything, or to be anything, have they not *saved the essential,* as Paul Andreota asks in his moving little novel, *Hors-Jeu?*[5] My heart goes out to them, for their consciences are in a tragic situation. Why tragic? The good Rabelais would have laughed. But nervous people do not laugh, and these young people, boys and girls, are big, nervous children (I spent a day with them in Marseilles during the Occupation, just at the moment when the Germans were destroying the Old Port, blowing it up with dynamite...) . And perhaps that is another reason why I fortified myself in solitude, seeking direct action and detachment from things, according to the precepts of Saint John of the Cross:

> To achieve knowledge of all things,
> Desire to know nothing at all.

> To experience the taste of all things,
> Desire to taste nothing at all.

> To gain possession of all things,
> Desire to possess nothing at all.

> To become the totality of all things,
> Desire to become nothing at all.

I thought about all these things...

"Don't forget to let me know, Blaise, if you need to see a member of the government when you get back from your excursion into the interior. I know everybody in Rio. Our bank is at your disposal. Make yourself at home there. You can count on me," Caïo de Azevedo had said to me when

---

* Rousseau (1712–78), Swiss-born French philosopher of Romanticism. Stayed at Les Charmettes, the home of Mme. de Warrens, in Savoy. (Trans.)

he came to say good-bye. As he gave me a fraternal hug, an *abraço*, clapping me hard on the back at the same time, he congratulated me, somewhat ironically, on renewing the tradition of disinterested travelers, such as Alexander von Humboldt, von Spix and von Martius, Saint-Hilaire, Debret, and Lund, who came to Brazil out of curiosity, for love of the country or to write a book, and not as businessmen or swindlers like all the other Europeans and Yankees and the poor immigrants and out-of-work intellectuals and the unemployed of all classes at the end of the nineteenth century.

"Thanks, Caïo, I'll take you up on that when the occasion arises," I had replied, in the same tone. "When I get back, maybe I'll ask you to get me a concession for a gold mine, or a diamond mine. One never knows! Then your bank will get the usual commission and you'll get a rake-off. You can be sure I won't forget you."

"You're not intending to write a book, Cendrars?"

"No!"

"You know, I could get our newspaper to publish it. The bank..."

But I had already pressed the starter, I was off, sounding my horn, for I preferred adventure.

I was on the qui-vive, with all my senses alert and receptive, on the lookout as I bowled along.

My head was humming like my engine, my state of mind, nihilistic and skeptical, was carrying me forward.

I had already lost an arm in the war.

I was wildly undisciplined.

The wilderness, the Brazilian *sertão*, the bush, and the interior, suited me.

No women. But, in case of a pleasant encounter, alcohol and a well-stocked refrigerator on board, and, in case of an unpleasant one, my Colt, with its wooden butt that could be adapted in the twinkling of an eye and fired from the shoulder like a carbine. My camping kit was neatly stowed. And my feather hammock. Cigarettes. Books. A phonograph, with blank discs for recording. A spare can of gasoline. A whole battery of cameras, large and small.

I was trundling along the brand-new, deserted road made of beaten earth, the *terra roxa,* or red earth, which is the famous diabase of coffee, the crests of the mountains were tinged with violet beneath the blazing sky, and already I had got sunburned, under my chin, on my chest, and on the underside of my arms, where the sun had reflected through the opening in my shirt as I was strolling about, taking photographs all afternoon, on this

169

road that ran along the crests of the Cachoeira do Cachorro, a bare sierra, a slope that looked like a fortress boldly etched between earth and sky and whose spine, naked and polished, stood up from the mound of debris that cluttered its lower slopes like the penis of a porphyry dog projecting from its sheath, the foreskin all shriveled, soiled and wrinkled like spilled butter that has melted and hardened again, in an ejaculation that has given its name to this mountain chain, and already, just a short drive from the great city of São Paulo, I felt a desire to lose myself in these solitudes of the *campos*, where the ravaged landscape and the strong odor of bulls sweltering behind barbed-wire fences enchanted me. I wanted to push on to the very limits of the civilized world.

What romanticism!

Yes, what romanticism, but also, what a drag having to stop at the Morro Azul and be bored to death (as I imagined) listening to the grievances and tales of woe of this old *schnook,* Dr. Oswaldo Padroso, forgotten in his lost *fazenda.*

What a pain in the ass!

God, how difficult it is to cut yourself off from everything, break all your ties, once and for all!

Why had I agreed, why had I promised to go there? And now they were expecting me at the Emperor's *fazenda...*

I was thinking about the old man's mistress. Who was she... a negress or a whore? Or some old cow, one of those nagging harpies, those servants who get their hooks into a bachelor, or perhaps some kind of tight-fisted housekeeper, in possession of all the keys, battening on to him and making him pay dearly for not having married her and for not letting her appear when there were guests in the house?... Oh, these old students! Socrates, with antique serenity, managed to put up with Xanthippe right up until the end, and Schopenhauer with his cantankerous dressmaker up until the day when our modern philosopher chucked the woman out of a ground-floor window and she broke her bones on purpose, so that he was condemned to pay her a pension for life, which served to confirm our pessimist in his misogyny...

And Caïo, the banker, with his maid-of-all-work, Juana the Mad, whom he liked to dress up as a purple Archbishop, or a Legate in cardinal red, as an androgynous page or a sailor... Was this arrogant, butch girl, this accomplished *cordon bleu* cook, his mistress or his succubus?... For Caïo de Azevedo also wrote poetry...

Night was falling fast.

II
RIGHT BANK

That night, as I let my Alfa-Romeo roll down from the heights of the crests, right down into the already darkened valley, I was thinking about all these things. The engine was purring quietly, the very sensitive carburetor sneezing as I passed through the orange groves, which were like one immense orchard stretching away to infinity, gleaming as the last rays of the setting sun varnished its fruits, while, lower down, in the dense cloud of mosquitoes hovering over the river and the cocoa-brown smoke curling up through gaps in the roof tiles—it was the hour of the evening meal— the lights of Glaréola suddenly lit up all at once in a festive orgy of electricity.

It was the first time they had switched on the current in this old town in the countryside.

"*A luz! A luz!*" the people were shouting as I turned into the main road, honking my horn and, from all the alleyways, horsemen came galloping at full tilt, overtaking me and deliriously firing their revolvers into the air, while the blacks, all dressed in white cotton, and the sunburned, barefooted urchins acclaimed me joyfully, for I had just switched on my headlights, and the young girls, leaning out of their first-floor windows, or standing on the doorsteps of their parents' little houses so as not to miss the dazzling inauguration of the fairy-like electricity, smiled at me or laughed in amazement, for even a little Ford or a Chevrolet was still an object of curiosity in this region and the inhabitants of Glaréola had never yet seen a car like mine, a "grand tourism" torpedo, pointed at the front and back, a convertible with a blue lamp on the dashboard, red parking lights, a *Stop!* signal, a luminous French license plate, headlights that shone either red or amber, and an adjustable spotlight which I could turn either horizontally,

171

to project a dazzling cone of light along the road well ahead of the car—which made the horses rear up and the mules lash out—or perpendicularly, toward the sky, which made the mosquitoes rain down, the moths fall like snow, and the hideous bats capsize, or obliquely, on to the windows on either side, which redoubled the laughter and the exclamations of surprise from the excited virgins, as if I had been the good genie of the feast, and they came crowding around the car, for I had also turned on my radio, to hear the eight o'clock broadcast of chamber music from Paris—the Poulet Quartet was playing—and it was almost impossible to drive on, to forge a way through the crowds and reach the bridge at the exit from the town, an old wooden bridge across the River Tiété, which was to serve me as a landmark so that I should not miss the start of the wretched, hollowed-out road, a couple of miles further on, on the right bank, which climbed up the massif to reach the isolated little valley of the Morro Azul.

"You can't miss it," Caïo had told me, pointing out that it was the old mule track that had served the *fazendas* on the plateau in the old days, before the construction of the *Paulista* and the regular train service, and he had added, teasingly: "It's a wild neck-of-the-woods. It's more like the dried-out bed of a torrent, full of big round stones, than a real road, but I'm not worried about you, with that car of yours! Nevertheless, I advise you not to set out on it in the dark, on account of the treacherous hairpin curves, right on the edge of the precipice. That's where they used to ambush the convoys of coffee at one time. There have been plenty of murders on that pass. Good luck!"

Suddenly, the lights of Glaréola's first cinema were turned on and the whole town rushed towards a hoarding lit with blazing multi-colored bulbs. It was advertising *The Mysteries of New York,* with Pearl White. The street having emptied, I put my foot down on the accelerator, left the town to the accompaniment of my exhaust backfiring and shot across the rickety old wooden bridge, then, some seven hundred meters further on, on the right bank, I entered a deep ravine and began climbing up the escarpments, all studded with thousand-year-old tree stumps and the half-charred trunks of huge, solitary trees, zigzagging, turning on the very edge of the sheer drop, constantly veering to the right, climbing up and up at a crazy speed, drawn onward and upward, cutting the corners very close, on two wheels, as in a car chase in the movies, rocking, bouncing through the ruts and potholes, climbing, turning back on myself, winding up like a corkscrew, shooting like a rocket, my engine filling the mountain with the racket of its lightning accelerations, which echoed off the rocky walls of the narrow defile, and leaving behind it a trail of castor oil whose smell intoxicated me as much as the melisma of its six cylinders, which announced far and wide my spiraling ascension; I kept accelerating, and the night was so dark and the road so ill-defined that I only just managed to avoid the scattered rocks, tree stumps, uprooted trees, fallen giants, craters, thickets, bushes, and landslides and was very nearly thrown out of my seat on one of the sharp turns, while the tires squealed, the springs and shock absorbers creaked, the brakes screeched, the wheels shuddered as I raced on as if trying to make up for the time lost in the afternoon, on the opposite face of the mountain, but the higher I climbed, the less desire I felt to arrive at the top, time no longer being of the slightest importance in this wild nocturnal solitude—halfway up, the forest had become dense and under the mighty trees and the high, fantastic foliage illumined by my headlights, the darkness, hot, solid, and unyielding, was breached by my headlights and stirred like fur when you run your fingers through it to test its thickness and its downiness, and I buried my burning face in it and closed my eyes, for time no longer has any importance when you let yourself be carried away in the night by the genius of music, and the Poulet Quartet was playing, secretly, for me alone and, like me, they were sure of their instruments, and, being virtuosi, of their own reflexes.

The last rise, a straight embankment rising steeply and stretched taut, like a tightrope walker's wire attached to the top of a steeple on market day or on the day of the village fair, a wire along which the fairground artiste wobbles uncertainly, hardly reassured by his balancing pole... walking the tightrope! A feat I had often dreamed of in my childhood and, when I arrived at the top of the steeple, I would heave myself up on to the arms of the cross, or do a pirouette on the weathervane, dangle with my head down and my feet in the air, and the earth would disappear, the earth, the steeple, the roofs, the square, the fairground, until there was nothing down there but a void, but I was not giddy, I soared deliciously in the void, like an upside-down moon, with my feet in the air! The last rise, very steep, debouching into the sky, on to a balcony, a sort of esplanade hanging in space, a bald rock-table dominating the valley of the Tiété where the sparkling lights of Glaréola swam reflected in the meandering waters of the river, a thousand meters down; the horizon opposite me, on the other bank, was filled with the silhouette of the Sierra of the Waterfall of the Dog, which, outlined like the back of a stranded whale, made a blank screen against the starry sky, and when I turned my back on this western pocket teeming with electric lights and stars, to try and get my bearings, I found myself lost in the depths of an arena filled with moonlight, in a *tête-à-tête* with the frowning mountains in the foreground, a whole massif with an amphitheater of forests and plantations nestling in steps on different levels and on different planes, and I could only guess at the distances and the perspective, into which the somber black ravines and the flow of the coagulated forest, like the flow of petrified lava, must lead, shoring up the contours of the different levels, like terracing, and all this chalk- and coal-smeared massif beneath the diffused light of the moon was compartmentalized and arranged like the solitudes of Camaldoli in an old Italian engraving, or the mountain of the thousand Buddhas on an ancient Chinese print, baroque scenery, tormented, churned up, where the roads, the tracks, and the paths, all dappled with moonlight, wound in all directions, disappearing into the distance, and, through a wide gap, as if looking through a perfectly adjusted lens, I discovered another level of the sky sprinkled with stars, but tarnished, dusty, as if painted on an old worn-out backdrop, wrinkled, bulging, and sagging for want of fresh size, and between the cracks of this backdrop and its frame, equally worn from having been rolled and unrolled too many times, like a panoramic picture in the window of a travel agency, I saw the scintillation of some tiny winking lights, which were not the small multi-colored bulbs of some advertisement nor the glow of the millions of fireflies fluttering everywhere in the darkness, wherever I looked, but those of a train traveling along the far end of the northern horizon, moving along the successive crests, which were invisible until delineated by the winking, caterpillar-like progress of the train in the far distance, and I even believed I could hear the puffing of the engine—I had stopped dead on the lunar esplanade and, by a reflex action, had switched off my engine and my headlights, but the Poulet Quartet was still playing softly—I believed I could hear the puffing and the hoarse panting of the locomotive as it crawled along the ridges at the far end of the northern horizon, leaving showers of sparks behind it.

It was the Nocturno 17, not a Nocturne by Chopin, which the Poulet Quartet might well have been broadcasting (but they were, in fact, playing Mozart's Andante with five variations in G major), but the night express, *o nocturno,* as they call the night trains in Brazil, the weekly Nocturno 17, the only luxury train that runs on this railroad track, which penetrates the solitudes of the hinterland and goes as far as the terminus, crossing successively the rivers Tiété, Turvo, and Grande, the waterways up which the Paulist *bandeirantes* traveled when they first penetrated into the interior in the sixteenth century, the slow-flowing rivers that wind into the interior of the inhuman virgin forests—the mysterious rivers which run east to west from the Serra do Mar, the Serra do Paranapiacaba, and the Serra do Mantigueira on the borders of the ocean to flow into the north-south basin of the rivers Parana and Plate, which means that this enormous mass of water drains into the interior of the continent and has no connection with the Atlantic Ocean—long detours which the *descobridores* were forced to follow, interminable watercourses, going on and on, one flowing into and engendering the next, carrying a whole world of vegetable detritus torn away from their constantly crumbling and constantly reforming banks, carrying the pioneers of Brazil, crews who were stunned, terrified, suffering from fever, miserable, exhausted, killing themselves with paddling month after month, capsizing in the rapids, dropping dead during the portages, when the thresholds of the basins overflowed and ran into one another at the end of the rainy season and they had to carry their pirogues overland (one giant hollowed-out tree trunk could hold up to forty men), getting drowned in the boggy and pestilential marshes or in the *paranas,* those luminous gaps in the forest, where the heavy boat was bound to sink if they let themselves be caught in the unleashing of the hurricane, which always explodes with unbelievable violence just when the good weather is at its peak, exposed day and night to the treacheries of an infernal climate and cannibalistic Indians, and it is an inexplicable mystery how a handful of lost men—and often they died of inanition at the moment when they were about to turn back to harvest the rice or the maize they had planted on their way out, along the treacherous banks of these heartbreaking waterways that lead nowhere—could have unified this vast, disparate country without any knowledge of its hydro-and orography, which are unique in the world, and today, the railroad tracks into the interior ignore the ancient routes of Portuguese civilization, the cosmopolitan luxury train crosses them and leaves them behind in a flash, the Nocturno 17, which I was now losing sight of as it threaded its way full-speed ahead along the crests to reach Uberaba; Uberaba, the center for adventurers, gold prospectors, and diamond miners, half-caste mule breeders, and *vaqueiros,* who own enormous wild herds; Uberaba, a little station where the Syrian peddlers get out to try their fortune hawking their cheap wares (Coty eau-de-Cologne and Japanese preserves!) around the miners' camps scattered throughout the hinterland of Minas Gerais, the high, desert-like plateau of Goyaz, Matto Grosso, and where the rich Hindu merchants come to sell their bull Zebus to improve the indigenous stock of cattle, the *caraculs;* Uberaba, the terminus, Uberaba, at the back end of the world, at least five hundred kilometers from São Paulo as the crow flies, and to reach it the express takes an uncomfortable night and a never-ending morning that often stretches on into the evening of the next day, and, while the track is normal gauge at the beginning, it becomes narrower and narrower during the course of the journey, so you have to change trains three times and finish up in a Decauville, whose last wagon, the restaurant car, has become so long and narrow that the passengers have to sit one behind the other in single file and the steward has to perform acrobatic prodigies to pass around the plates and bottles (a lousy Bordeaux!); Uberaba, situated at the source of the river Tejuco, where you can again join the traditional route of the *bandeirantes* of former times, and embark, like them, on a pirogue which will take you up the river Paranahyba and into the heart of the *sertão,* as far as Santa Rita de Paranahyba, its legendary capital, where the classic peons, the autochtonous hunters, the taciturn nomads of the forest, and even the *cangaçeiros,* those extraordinary bandits who haunt the highways of the area, go to church once a year, attend Mass on horseback, and confess without ever setting foot on ground... *O Nocturno 17!* the only train I would have taken if I had truly wanted to lose myself in this virgin country, since the highway, which I virtually christened, went barely halfway, no further than Ribeirão Preto, the terminus of the Mogyana on the river Pardo, which is the center for the intensive cultivation of coffee, and therefore in the heart of modern civilization in spite of its remote geographical location, its exoticism, its actual picturesqueness, its marginal situation, and the inevitable absenteeism of the immensely wealthy planters, and now that the family plantations are evolving toward the formation of limited companies, its fortunes depend on the ups and downs of the Stock Exchange and the general march of the times, and, as happens everywhere when an essential product is in the hands of a trust, it is already beginning to decline, simply by virtue of its being a one-crop system, suffering from overproduction, rational methods of exploitation, technology, progress, banking, credit, advertising, a rocketing rise in consumption linked to a fall in prices, the rewards of publicity...

So many slips between the cup and the lip!

I had studied all the maps, every one of them inaccurate, incomplete, riddled with blatant errors in spite of the fact that there were blank areas and dotted lines to indicate doubt and uncertainty; the only good map was given to me by the Vicomte de Taunay, not an explorer but a bookworm who, after analyzing the tons and tons of archives on the subject, in both Brazil and Portugal, had retraced the itineraries of the *bandeirantes* who traveled through these lost regions for three centuries, and drawn the map of their day-to-day travels. I was haunted by this lonely wilderness.

(...In 1927, when I finally disembarked from the Nocturno 17, there was a revolution in full swing and Uberaba was occupied by the followers of a certain Dr. Armand Schmitt, a German veteran from the battle of Verdun, who had emigrated to Brazil and set himself up as dictator in these unsettled regions, where he hunted down the wandering population and tyrannized over the apathetic inhabitants of the little town. The time for the presidential elections was drawing near, and Dr. Schmitt was giving the soldiers of the federal government plenty of trouble with his bands of men recruited among shepherds, hunters, miners, and the nomads of the forest, who are all more or less outlaws, and whom Schmitt had armed and trained in German style—*gedrillt!*—and toward the end of 1936, just as I set foot in Santa Rita de Paranahyba, having traveled from Cadiz to Buenos Aires by ship, the malcontents of Santa Rita de Paranahyba, who were all men of the hinterland and the bush, proclaimed *O Fronte Verde,* the Green Front, like *El Frente Popular* proclaimed by the Spanish proletariat, and plundered everything in the legendary capital of this remote wilderness: the stockades, the corrals, the racks for smoking meat and the *giraos* for drying it, the *matadouros,* or slaughterhouses, the stores of rawhide, the humble little houses built of adobe with blue-painted doors, the primitive church and its magnificent palm trees, the miserable little booths of the Syrians, who were also pawnbrokers, the gold prospectors' casino, the bandstand and the dance hall, and clouds of mangy, carrion-eating *urubus,* or black vultures, swooped down on the smoking ruins. Ah! What a fine state of affairs, and what tears and grief! for all these European antics were utterly without rhyme or reason in the vast wilderness of the *sertão,* where the lazy river, flowing beneath an empty sky, emerged from the virgin forests and the savage mountains to swell and pour itself over the unreclaimed *campos,* its steep banks crumbling away in the heat and the caymans yawning in the sun on the dried-out mudbanks, while the chattering birds on either bank made even more senseless din than the yelling lunatics who were waving flags and placards in the red dust of the one and only street in Santa Rita! And if the exuberance of the birds was an expression of their *joie de vivre,* the members of the Green Front, the picturesque and good-natured *Lumpenproletariat,* looked pretty grim, as if they meant business, in spite of the *tiroteio,* the rifle shots they were firing off at random, and their wild gallops. Two or three days later, everything was calm again. This was due to neither politics nor the police, but the inevitable victory of the tropics, always triumphant in this climate, for it was because of the crippling heat that the exhausted men gave up shooting and, in the end, simply disbanded. And then, throughout the whole region, men started rioting again, more sullen than ever, every man chewing his wad of tobacco, salivating, and, in camp in the evening, relaxing with his feet up on a tree stump and gazing into a wood fire as he sucked up his maté tea... Ah! What a good yarn to tell, in the future, at the end of a long day's journey... for this is the kind of tale men tell around a campfire, boastfully embroidering it, for they have ruminated over it for a long time before telling it... and that is how legends... and heroes... are born, and songs become famous. In spite of everything, I managed to record a few discs.)

III
BETWEEN MOUNTAINS — BETWEEN WORLDS

That night, when the Poulet Quartet had fallen silent (it could only have been nine o'clock, then), I sat in my car with the engine off and the headlights extinguished, smoking cigarette after cigarette, and each time I inhaled, or flicked my lighter, the tip of my solitary fag-end or the flame of my lighter added to the light of the millions of fireflies scattered through the clearing like a milky way, to the winking lights in front of and behind me in the darkened, confusing landscape, to the will-o'-the-wisp light of the stars blinking on and off in the depths of the sky, to the light of the fixed stars that stared at me and obliged me to tip my head further and further back as the lower regions of the sky became progressively blacker with the rapid decline of the moon, which was in its first quarter, while in the high, infinite regions, the "blue immensities" of the poet, cold little suns, double stars, and shooting stars, with their tails and trails, multiplied, together with the familiar planets which are the three-cornered milestones of space, and around which the comets and meteorites run their chariot races, cutting the corners as tightly as possible in the ether, and raising a cloud of diamond-dust, sparks, glinting hubs and wheel rims, socket-less eyeballs, flying eyes, flapping eyelids, squinting eclipses, eccentric ellipses, an impalpable pattering that disturbs the best-known configurations, stirring them into a whirlpool at the zenith and settling like a fine powdering of glacial wheaten flour on the subsoil of the sky, whose wrinkled bas-relief one discovers with amazement, glittering transparently through the classic constellations, and whose forms one can admire in the background, like the skeletal ribs of dead leaves which fall, gleaming intermittently, from a burning bush or a bonfire on the Feast of Saint John on to a carpet of rotting, phosphorescent humus, the very bottom, the most profound depths, the subsoil of the heavens.

179

I had given up trying to find my bearings in this labyrinth of brilliant luminaries burning themselves out in the darkness.

All these dead suns, these posthumous rays which take millions of light-years to reach us, asteroids, fragments of dead worlds, shattered and exploded, old moons, gnawed and cankered, crusts, sores, blotches, cold lupus, devouring leprosy, sanies, and that last drop of pearl-like light, the purest of all, sweating at the highest point of the firmament and about to fall... is not a tear nor a dewdrop, but a drop of pus. The universe is in the process of decomposing and, like a cemetery, it swarms with becoming and smells good. The stars are unguent-bearing and throb feverishly, each ray carries seeds sown in the brain of man, and they are the seeds of destruction. Gray matter contains sunspots that eat into the whole circumference of the brain. It is an index of disintegration. Thought is a pestilence.

I had let down the back of my car seat to make a sleeping-berth and lay stretched out on my back in the bottom of my sarcophagus-shaped vehicle, like an embalmed Pharaoh in his hypogeum, facing the mirror of the sky, but I was not awaiting the predictable return of my birth star—it was so silent now that, in the depths of the night, I could have heard the wheels turning and the purring of all this automatic machinery, regulated like the clockwork mechanism of the planetarium in Jena, which I had visited meticulously on the day of its inauguration, after seeing Goethe's brain preserved in a jar in his house in Weimar on the previous evening, O dreaming and romantic Germany of Jakob Boehme,* which your learned professors perpetuate in formidable and mathematical surrealizations, but which break down regularly, thank God, and I say this without irony, and without going so far as to ask these Fausts of the University to demonstrate that they can actually make Goethe's brain think, for this extremely well-preserved organ is nothing but a dead brain in a jar, like a calf's brain steeped in refined alcohol or spirits of wine, and these convolutions and lobes give no key to the genius of the man, and even if they could run electric filaments through it in little tubes of mercury, which would release by induction a whole Morse alphabet, this would in no way reproduce the living genius of the poet, nor the free play of his spontaneous ingenuity, and the vault of the planetarium has to be wound up again periodically, since it is not, in any case, the perpetual motion of the heavens, nor is the squaring of the circle the Word, and all this ingenuity and scientific display are sim-

---

* German theosopher and mystic, 1575–1624. (Trans.)

ply a bluff, for the universe is not a puzzle, nor is life a crossword for Sunday newspaper readers, that would be too silly, and that is where the error lies, the error of the Germans ever since Luther, of the *Herrenvolk* and of their pragmatic modern epigones, the Russians and the Americans, for there exists, thank God, the Holy Spirit of the Apocalypse: Asia!—no, I was not awaiting the return of my birth star but contemplating the abyss, a crater, a black mouth from which escapes, according to a popular belief of Indian, or perhaps Inca origin, which is very widespread among the *cablocos* of the interior, who are all of mixed blood, the wind that creates the tornadoes and the typhoons that periodically ravage and uproot the virgin forests, causing havoc like a tidal wave, while the furiously churning clouds pour down waterspouts; this mouth is not a celestial body but a hole at the zenith of the sky, a funnel, an inverted pyramid, the orifice of an upside-down well, the projection of a black cone, it is the abyss that the people of Brazil call the "coal-sack," as if to say: It is the entrance to Hell, the Cavern of the Devourer of the World.

In these latitudes, the Southern Cross is the mistress of the hemisphere. The coal-sack is situated immediately below and slightly to the left of the hypothetical point where the two arms of the cross of the symbolic southern constellation meet. In fact, there is a black pocket there. And the more you gaze at it, the deeper it seems. It is such a hypnotic gulf, and of such an intense black, that it seems to recede, to detach itself, throwing into relief all the stars in fission that flare for a moment in the foreground and, the more you gaze at this hole, the hollower it seems to become, and the more it draws you into its depths, into its unfathomable profundity. It looks as if it has been polished with a velvet cloth, it shrinks and swells, tightens up and slackens over and over again, spilling a patch of oil, or rather tar, at the back of the sky, and getting steadily denser, so that, in the long run, all the stars in the sky are reduced to nothing more than smoking candle ends melting into this intense blackness which absorbs them like blotting paper, or felt, or the porous wall of a water cooler or an earthenware jar, of a gourd in the shape of a fabulous beast or a calabash with black poker-work patterns, and, to the mind's eye, they finally disappear, one by one, as if by slow osmosis.

Such is the abyss, the abyss of the sky, this vertiginous, this absolute and deglutitious black, this stain, this damp mildew, this black beast, blood, throat, lung, gland, glairy matrix, rubbery brain, soft tumor, or polypus. Imbibition. A living sponge. The sky is a blackboard. Not a single algebraic formula, written in frost-rimed chalk, nor stardust in suspension, nor the faintest sparkle remains on its surface. All is effaced!

I have seen this sponge, seen it with my own two eyes. It is an enigma.

IV
THE COAL-SACK

The coal-sack does not appear on any celestial map. I questioned scores of people in Brazil. The people of the interior knew exactly where it was and pointed it out to me with their arms, their index fingers stretched out, making me follow its wake, its folds, and its dark eddies, interpreting its black patches in the way that fortune-tellers interpret ink stains and telling me about their peasant superstitions while repeatedly making the sign of the cross. "It's the Devil," they said, "the Devil in the sugarcane and among the cattle. Once again, the coffee harvest will be poor and, this year, there's worm in the maize, the manioc will be black, the bananas are rotting on the trees, there will be floods." The good folk were worrying about their crops, their wasted labor, having no other thoughts in their heads than the anxieties of men who are always bent over the soil, with their backsides pointing up to the stars, and who only rarely look up from their labors to inspect the sky distrustfully and stand with their hands on their hips, feeling all the aches and pains in their backs.

The people of the littoral, the large cities, and the capital had all heard of the coal-sack but they could not locate it exactly and would spend hours discussing the reality of its existence, like the bourgeoisie at home in France who, after a weekend trip to the seaside, argue about the green ray, which they know of only from Jules Verne (and, even then, only by hearsay!), and claim to have seen, or not seen, each one offering his hypothesis and holding fast to his opinion as to whether it is possible or impossible to perceive the phenomenon in certain meteorological conditions, just as, in Nice, both winter and summer visitors claim that, from the Casino or from their hotel rooms, they can, or cannot, see Corsica, outlined on the sea at twilight, and bet each other rounds of apéritifs, bottles of champagne, or a splendid dinner on this score, but, in fact, what they actually see, when they see anything at all, is not the island but—but, in optimum conditions, when the atmosphere is extremely limpid, and then only from a very high vantage point such as Peïra-Cava, and if they are exceptionally lucky, at dawn, and most probably in the month of February—the shadow of Corsica projected into the air to make a blot on the sea at the horizon, exactly as Dan Yack saw the shadows of the Earth, projected on to the screen of the sky by the Sun, making a bolt on the ice-pack of the Antarctic, as, little by little, the luminous planet moved down below the northern horizon, to emerge no more, but to announce, through this phenomenon, the end of the long polar night, a grandiose spectacle which the eccentric Englishman compared to a lesson in celestial mechanics in which, to demonstrate the complexity of the circulatory movements of the heavenly bodies, the teacher walks with a lighted candle behind spheres made of paper, and Dan Yack, the killjoy, to avoid becoming infected by the delirium of his companions at the end of the long over-wintering, concluded: "It is only shadows one sees moving, and never the sun!"[6]

The night, shadows in the darkness, ghostly beings that move, the *camera oscura,* the dark chamber of the imagination... one cannot speak of these secret things except to children, for they alone know what it is all about and take it seriously, lying in their beds waiting for the creeping shadows, which they follow with their eyes closed, and that is why all the children in Brazil listen to you without saying a word, but with their eyes bright with intelligence and a spark of surprise at hearing a grown-up speak of these things with interest, when you ask them about the "coal-sack," which, for them, is not the entrance to Hell, but the exit from the World, the mouth of all that is wonderful, the fairy-tale world their Nannies, whether white, black, or half-caste, have told them about: *Once upon a time, there lived an ogre...*

It is the strict truth. The Universe is a monster. Life an ogre. And the Nannies are quite right to frighten little children. I am thinking of my Egyptian Nanny who, while teaching me the zodiac, deified Death.[7] Let those who still remember understand!

> The star on high,
> The fire below,
> Coal on the hearth,
> The soul in the eye,
> Cloud, smoke, and death!

says a Negro poem.[8]

V
THE WORLD IS MY THEATER

"Behind the Milky Way, there is an Eel, or some kind of Serpent of the Sky. It nourishes itself on the suns that teem in the primeval slime of the Depths. Its eye is like the four-leafed clover of Space, and worlds in eruption, tied to its tail like rattles, mark the passage of Time. When it sloughs its skin, a comet falls from each of its scales. And the digestive process of this beast is the Light. Like an earthworm in a root, it is caught, and almost entirely hidden, in a Sponge, which it gnaws continuously. Every pore of this Sponge breathes and whimpers like a human in the act of procreation. It is the Sponge of Darkness. A tuft of Tongues. The Organ of Origins. It is cast in the primary Mold, like a brain in a cranium. It is the simplest primary prototype, the most elementary of a family of nameless and unspeakable inverted beings at the Antipodes of Unity."[9]

...The night. Shadows in the darkness. Creatures of the Spirit-World. Beings that move. The dark chamber of the imagination...

VI
THE NIGHT

In 1917, when I was writing *L'Eubage* for Monsieur Doucet, the couturier on the Rue de la Paix, I had not yet seen the "coal-sack" with my own eyes and, in fact, I had never even heard anyone speak about this enigma in the starry skies of Brazil, a rebus that becomes blacker and more and more disturbing the further you push on into the interior of the country. I had, however, just escaped by the skin of my teeth from the "coal-scuttles," as the French troops, the *poilus,* nicknamed those homely projectiles, the huge aerial torpedoes surmounted by a ululating copper rod that the Germans rained down on us. They exploded in our trenches with a racket like a whole wagon load of explosives blowing up. Many of them were duds; they made a lot of noise but did little harm. The greatest danger was that you would be buried alive and die of suffocation, for the weight of these filthy swines and the blast of the air they displaced when they went off was terrific, their hot breath, their venomous spittle and the poisonous yellow smoke of the chlorine in their charges turned you into a hussar in madder-red breeches or a trapeze artiste in sky-blue. But my number was not up. I came back from the front. I had been invalided out, minus one arm. They were short of beds, so they had turned me out of the hospital and, for a year now, I had been roaming the streets of Paris like a miserable beggar, trying to pick up a few sous. It was shameful. My amputated arm gave me a lot of pain and I was drinking too much. To avoid becoming embittered I felt, as a man, that I needed to go and live in the country and, as a poet, that I needed the refuge of solitude.

Some other time, in another book, I will write about that crucial year. But it was at precisely this moment, when I was desperate and in despair, that Monsieur Doucet sent me his manservant. Someone had told him that

I was a highly talented letter-writer (I have never been able to find out who it was and, to this day, I am baffled by it, for I have always had a horror of writing letters!) and he asked me to address one letter a month to him for his collection of hand-written manuscripts, sending word at the same time that he would pay me one hundred francs a month and explaining that he could hardly come and rummage through a poet's papers in the way that one goes to a painter's studio and selects a painting off the walls.

It was true that it would have been downright indecent to let anyone come and ferret through my papers, but, on the other hand, since M. Doucet was not a friend of mine, there was no reason why I should write him letters—and what would I write about, not even having the honor of his acquaintance? This is what I explained to him in my reply, adding that he was already getting a bargain, for here he was, receiving a first letter for his collection, free, gratis, for nothing! My letter informed him, moreover, that I would accept his proposal on condition that I could write a book for him, sending him one chapter a month.

Not an hour had gone by when M. Doucet's manservant came back and handed me an envelope containing a brand-new one-hundred franc note and, written on a visiting card, a very friendly word confirming our agreement. I replied with a word of thanks, not forgetting to point out to M. Doucet that, as a collector, he was pulling off a real *coup,* for here was a second missive on the same day, and again for free, like the previous one! At the same time, I did not omit to lay down precise conditions, telling him that, for one hundred francs a month, he would understand that I could not write more than a certain number of pages, at so many lines per page and so many words per line (I have forgotten the figures, but they were pretty small!) and that, consequently, the little book I was going to write for him would be very short, although it would lose nothing as to quality, and the subject was to be the itinerary of a voyage in the hinterland of the sky, at the Antipodes of Unity. (The title, *L'Eubage,* I only found much later, one night when I was thumbing through my Petit Larousse and happened to come across this word.*) As a postscript, I insisted on being paid in advance, that is, one hundred francs on the first of each month, whereas I would not post the few pages of my manuscript until the 30th or 31st. A second P.S. laid down that, since there were only twelve months in a year, our agreement would be valid for the duration of one year only, that I

---

*From Petit Larousee: *Eubage:* A priest of Gaul who devoted himself to the study of the natural sciences, astronomy, and divination. (Trans.)

would undertake to finish the little book within this period and that under no circumstances would I prolong or renew the experiment, no matter what the results, the entreaties of my patron, his appetite as a collector of autographs (who liked to see his dossiers snowballing), the omissions in his catalogue or in my writing. A third postscript specified that I would remain sole proprietor of the copyright and sole judge of the date and occasion for publishing my little masterpiece. (I swear I used this phrase "little masterpiece," although at the time I had not the faintest idea how I was going to fill up these pages, written to order for an unknown patron!)

I can only assume that the collector was delighted at having convinced me, for, far from being annoyed at my intransigence and the bad-tempered tone of my missives, this amiable man sent his manservant back to me, for the third time that day, to give me two hundred francs on the spot in payment of my two preceding letters, and once again they were new-minted hundred-franc notes, which the man pulled out of a bundle that had been pinned together, and held out to me hesitantly, obviously very impressed by my miserable hovel, and saying there was no need to sign a receipt.

So then I invited the young man—he was a chubby little fair-haired goiterous fellow from Isère, he had neither forehead nor temples, his hands were clammy and he had flat feet, one could see at a glance that he would never make a soldier—to come and have a drink with me at the bar on the corner. I bolted the door, gave my address to the concierge, and, after we had had our drinks, I went to the station and took the train. By midnight, I was busy writing for M. Doucet by the light of a candle stuck into an empty one-liter bottle, my backside was perched on a bale of hay in an abandoned barn, and I was using one leaf of the door, which I had lifted off its hinges, as a table. The yawning opening of the double doors gave on to the sky and, every time I raised my head to take a drag on my cigarette, my eyes were lost among the stars, and I strained my ears to hear the guns rumbling in the depths of the night, coming to disturb the sleeping department of Beauce, importuning me, marking the passage of time in my solitude. I was at La Pierre, near Courcelles, not far from Méréville, Loiret. The guns I could hear were on the Somme. The offensive to recapture Verdun had begun. Our boys were hitting back. Like an old war horse, I was drawn to the threshold of the barn and even took a few steps outside to listen in the night...

By dawn, the first chapter of *L'Eubage* was written and, thanks to M. Doucet, I had nothing to do till the end of the month but dawdle through the fields, lie down in the grass, smoke, dream... and, when the year was over and my "little masterpiece" written, when the collector could wring not another word out of me, M. Doucet and I became good friends, in spite of all his arguments and entreaties. He was a gallant old gentleman, my stories amused him and I, in turn, was amused by him as an old man-about-town who knew the ways of the world and was no fool; he could tell an anecdote wittily, adding his own dash of spice to it, and, at table, he liked to surround himself with elegant women whom, as a couturier, he had dressed, and with girls from the theater whom he was kind enough to help, when necessary, with certain small services regarding their *toilette.*

This entertaining old beau was not cynical and, like all true Parisians, he cultivated romance, in the form of a caged bird that he liked to tease and squabble with, tormenting her and making her ruffle her feathers and sing, a bird who had once been an *equestrienne,* an old mistress he had married late in life and whom he kept tucked away in a secret basement, where he would bring only a few intimate friends to see this rare bird preening herself in her gilded cage. She was an elderly lady and nothing remained of her erst-while fame and florid beauty except a necklace of pearls seven and a half meters long. (One day, M. Doucet did me the honors of his celebrated collection of modern autographs. "I am very proud of this short work," he said, showing me the slim manuscript of *L'Eubage* preserved in a sumptuous cover. "You are the only one of all my authors, Cendrars, who had the sense to stop in time, that is to say, before the hour of my death, so that I still have a little while left to enjoy my collection, and I do so love to put it into worthy bindings. How can I thank you? Look at the others, they carry on writing, overwhelming me, for years now they have been almost crowding me out of the house. You were right, the snowball becomes an avalanche." And he showed me boxes and boxes, stuffed to bursting, in the cupboards in his library. "They will never stop writing!" sighed the old gentleman, half-opening the files of this or that already famous writer, or the poems of a young hopeful, flipping through the pages with hands that were well-manicured but clumsy and trembling, knotted with rheumatism. There were a great many letters from my contemporaries, but very few works, and most of those were duplicate copies or reworkings, manuscripts embellished or overloaded with corrections to make them into collectors' items. A whole world! The forbidden extracts from *Fleurs du Mal* and Baudelaire's notebooks, Verlaine's school exercise-books, Pierre Louÿs's notebooks, an unpublished work by Rimbaud, another by Proust, the usual rareties carried off by dealers, who outbid everyone else at the auctions at the Hôtel Drouot, a lot of junk in the form of pages from illuminated manuscripts, not to mention the masters of the day who are well-known for faking "unique" pieces and "other versions" for bibliophiles... and the rigmarole of the dadaists, who were neither one-armed nor one-legged and off whose backs their manager was making a nice little nest egg for himself, having finally got hold of the old man—who had lost his caged bird—exploited his senility, and crowned this honest man with the New Spirit, O vanity of vanities! and the old couturier was enjoying a last triumph before dying, finding himself among the avant-garde, at the very forefront of Parisian fashion!)

All this prolegomenon to explain the circumstances and the occasion that induced me to write *L'Eubage,* to evoke the atmosphere I was immersed in at the time and explain the tone, the style, and the form of this little piece. I have mentioned these things, more than once, in *L'Homme foudroyé*[10]—nature, the sky, the plants, the underground water-courses, my occupations during the day, the speech of the people around me, the absolute simplicity of the life I was leading in this narrow watery valley on the confines of the contemporary world, in the subsiding land of the watercress-growers, which has a varied and very characteristic flora and fauna of its own, half wild and in distinct contradiction to the culture and the monotonous aspect of the surrounding department of Beauce, which is a land of corn, an infinite plain—I mentioned these things to give some indication of the state of mind I was in when I said good-bye to Paris and Poetry in 1917, with no wish to return, and perhaps all this will give the key to the vocabulary and the source of the poetic images in *L'Eubage,* but it will not explain the choice of subject.

But did I choose?

I am a great devourer of dictionaries, and I was looking for words. The subject is implicit in the words, or rather, the words crystallize around it, just as, when you dip a glass rod into a supersaturated solution and move it about, the crystals form around it. And I had the subject at my fingertips.

VII

SHADOWS IN THE DARKNESS

At night, at the front, when I was not out on patrol, the universe came pouring through my de luxe loophole, a loophole cut through an armored plate, a slit, a Judas-hole, through which I could take a look at the world beyond or fire a rifle at the enemy or lob a grenade over the top like a child who kicks a big stone into a ravine and listens excitedly, as it bounces down and down until it reaches the bottom, so as to judge the depth of the gulf; this is not so paradoxical as it seems for a contemplative who did not yet know himself, a young man who had just devoted two or three winters to the study of the terminology of Kant, who defines the notions of the subjective and the objective better than anyone else, an enthusiast whose metaphysical love had crystallized around Schopenhauer's pessimism, an apprentice to life who had just discovered man and men (I was twenty-seven years old in 1914) and was busy shooting at them and exposing myself to danger, for fun, out of a taste for taking risks, or out of some remote atavism, using the fact of being a soldier as an alibi, seeing just how far it could go, where this game would lead me and whether it would hold up morally, taking a morbid pleasure in holding my life cheap, for I had nothing but contempt for myself, as an individual, and, in general, took a sadistic joy in despising the human condition as I saw men trampled underfoot, pounded, asphyxiated, bleeding, offered up as a holocaust on the greedy and violent altar of the nations, the flag unfurled to cover the ignoble merchandise offered up to auction, sacrificed to no purpose, thrown out with the garbage, for there were always plenty of replacements to fill the trenches. What a mess! I was right, but I was ashamed of it.

The pain of living, the anonymous suffering multiplied by all the millions and millions of soldiers in the firing line, each with his registered

number, the generations of living dead on the borders of no-man's-land...
what an absurd, and yet perfectly logical, synthetic image of the great
farce that is human life on earth! One could hardly conceive of a better
symbol of the nothingness of man's spiritual life, a more manifest illustration of the uslessness, the impotence of his intellectual activity. It was
indescribable, and I can find no words to describe it except the chorus
sung by the Foreign Legion, a refrain that carries you beyond the parapets
of reason:

> Let down your trousers,
> Grognon, old man,
> Look, here's a blood-sausage, blood-sausage, blood-sausage,
> For the Swiss, the Alsatians, the men of Lorraine.
> It's no use giving it to the Boches,
> Cause all their assholes are perfectly square,
> Perfectly square,
> It's no use giving it to the Boches,
> Cause all their assholes are square![11]

But, since then, what a lot of ground has been covered! For now, the
whole world has set out to follow the drums and bugles of the Foreign
Legion into No-Man's-Land, the country that belongs to nobody, this dark,
unique reality, this total blackness that I could plumb with my eye, touch
with my finger, and into which I could fire off rifle shots from my loop
hole, the "square asshole" of the historic chorus, a hole made in the thickness of an armored plate, a loophole, a Judas-hole, a narrow fissure through
which my mind could venture out, in the twinkling of an eye, in the
instant during which an Allied or an enemy flare tore the opaque tissue of
the night (which, with the speed of a zipper, immediately formed a scar) to
grasp and comprehend the great age of the Earth, her deep wrinkles, her
face, her scars, and a section of ravaged forest like a painted backdrop for
the Grand Guignol, a bit of road that ended in a frieze of horsemen in a
row, a hoarding, a furrow, a hedge, a village in ruins, a battered barndoor,
the corner of a devastated landscape, barbed-wire stretching to infinity
and, in closeup, a corpse strangled in a chicane, every detail illumined by a
magnesium flare and recorded as if by flashlight.

It was stupefying. What good was this animated photography? Who
clicked the shutter, and who would frame it, to what purpose and for
whom? Such precise definition, and so many vivid and down-to-earth
images! They stunned me. I could not drag myself away from my loophole.
I spent hours and hours there. I took my comrades' turns of duty and they

were only too glad to get out of it, and they laughed at me as a crazy poet. Did these good-natured fellows guess my secret, then?

A poet with his rifle resting in a loophole, a poet who did not write and who was searching for words to define the things that came crowding in from out there, crowding in to engrave themselves forever, as if on a little mirror or a portable screen. It took my breath away. An eyewitness? An accusing, conscience-stricken observer? An automaton? One could hardly remain neutral! But how to name the shadows in the darkness? The men were unanimous about it: nothing on earth was as black as the darkness of night at the front. They were stupefied and overcome by it. They lost themselves, infuriated. You could hear them swearing, blaspheming, cursing existence, calling her a filthy whore, bumping into things, stumbling, picking up a dropped shovel, clattering their mess tins, playing dead, our men as well as those on the other side, and it was only then that these revealing flares were let off, followed by the rattle of machine guns in the blackness that closed in again on all sides and forged ahead like a herd of elephants. But there was never silence. Silence is not human.

I could not find the words I wanted. I have never understood how Guillaume Apollinaire was able to write such beautiful poems at night at the front, nor how Aragon, who was equally inspired by war, could have done the same in May and June 1940. The fact that it was spring and the weather was fine (the meteorological office had forecast an anti-cyclone to last for forty days and that swine, Hitler, had taken advantage of it!) is no excuse, for Aragon was not naive. Did our poet really not guess what was to follow? In any case, *Les Lilas et les roses* is a fine piece of work.

The most haunting metaphors of Lautréamont, that evil genius of the night, were of no help to me in classifying the shadows in the darkness that my brain photographed and my mind developed and tinted, automatically storing up, at a crazy rate, these fugitive forms that were all intertwined, tangled up, swirling around, melting into each other and expiring with a powerful death rattle, while my imbecile tongue failed to summon up the creative Word to name them, but I recited to myself, mentally, the formulas of the *Fourfold Root of the Principle of Sufficient Reason,* that touchstone of all thinking minds, *Über die vierfache Wurzel des Satzes vom zureichenden Grunde,* that bunch of keys that opens all the locks of the understanding and double-locks all the hypotheses, the bitter little treatise by Arthur Schopenhauer, the last of the metaphysicians, the most intelligent of the modern philosophers, the first, and perhaps the only European philosopher since Descartes, for photography and the cinema are abstractions, and, like everything in black and white—writing, printing—outside time and not in space.

Before the war of 1914, I had already been involved in the cinema, shooting documentaries for Pathé, reels which formed part of a series entitled *Nature at Home,* but it was not so much a way of earning a living, God help me!, as of seizing the opportunities it offered to spend time in the most paradisiacal corners of the planet and illustrate this sentence, which I had written in the Golden Book in a teahouse in Kyoto and signed with my name:

"The mere fact of existing is a veritable happiness..."

Poor me! That had been around 1911, only a few years before, and now here I was, standing at my loophole, exposed to the risk of receiving a bullet in the head and stuffing and unstuffing my brains, awaiting the lightning stroke of sudden death or the lingering death of a dubious trepanning, like Apollinaire, like René Dalize, who had his head blown off by a shell, like that idiot, Bikoff, who camouflaged himself as a tree, like my comrade in the Foreign Legion, Hernando de Bengoechea,[12] who was also a poet, although, to my shame, I only discovered this thirty-three years later, in *Les Nouvelles littéraires* of August 26, 1948, whereas I should have guessed, since he, too, haunted his loophole in the sector known as the White Earthworks, to the north of Arras, and it was in this loophole that he was killed on either the 9th of May or the 11th of June, 1915, I cannot remember which, alas! And I wonder whether he was struck by a bullet between the eyes, or by an illumination as Rimbaud called it!

The uninterrupted cannonade that came from the north, from Bapaume, was like the breathing of the ocean in the night, its ebb and flow, crescendo and decrescendo made one think of some cosmic ballet in the sky, invisible but registering on the membrane of the eardrum like the music of the spheres. It was stunning. So then I started thinking about the chicken's heart that had been beating for years and years in a glass dish on the thirty-seventh floor of the Rockefeller Institute for the Advancement of Science in New York, and I counted, as one counts the seconds between the firing of a shell and its explosion on landing, the pulsations of this plucked-out heart, of this "heart laid bare" by Dr. Carrel, who kept the organ alive by watering it every morning with an artificial serum manufactured in his laboratory (it seems this heart has just stopped beating—or should I say, it has just died?—because, while the doctor was away for a weekend, the laboratory assistant who stood in for him forgot to water the heart on Monday morning, or so I read recently in the American newspapers, but they forgot to say that the heart had been beating for more than thirty years in its deep dish, that is, six times longer than it would have functioned naturally as part of the viscera in the breast of a living cockerel or a mother hen! But what sex was this heart?... A handsome reward offered to anyone who can tell me!).

And many other things besides these passed through my loophole, most of them rendered absurd by association: On nights when there were air raids on London and Paris, I was reminded of old naval charts, where one sees, engraved in one corner, a cherub with puffed-up cheeks, an angel from whose puckered lips the North Wind emerges as he blows up a storm, for, all of a sudden, a storm of tearing sounds and vertiginous melismas blew down on me from the heavens and five, six or seven great dark, spindle-shaped shadows fell on me—they were the shadows of those mastodons, the zeppelins, with all lights extinguished, taking their bearings on my loophole and passing on, hedge-hopping through my perpendicular slit, no sooner seen than vanishing again (and, afterwards, I understood the parable in which a camel can pass through the eye of a needle more easily than a rich man. The technical term "chas" or the common "eye of a needle" is not a lapsus on the part of the translator, as Monsignor Duchesne, director of the École Française in Rome would have us believe, according to his critico-historical exegesis, but the logical sequence of a poetic image, to be taken literally and in its secret sense!); in winter, and in his season, I saw Orion, that giant hand hung up like the sign of the glove maker on the Avenue de l'Opéra (I am almost sure it is above the Gant Perrin boutique that you can see this red hand, in the rain, set in a triangle of neon lights and standing out against the Parisian night like the hand of God), in front of my loophole, and that is why, today, when my hand hurts too much, I say that my amputated hand has gone up to heaven, to the constellation of Orion (which is just as childish as saying it had gone to Perrin's to get itself fitted with a glove—Alas! A disabled man cannot afford such luxuries. All the state generously awards him, by way of elegance, is a wooden hand, gloved in floss-silk and officially known as *the parade hand,* priced at one hundred and twenty-five francs, which is deducted from the ex-serviceman's gratuity, unless he renounces his right to the hand by signing a declaration of discharge in due and proper form! It is not a hand to boast about, and it's utterly useless!); etc., etc....

My loophole reminded me of the hole my friend, Robert Delaunay, the painter of the Eiffel Tower, made in the shutters he had had put over the windows to transform his studio (a very bourgeois drawing room) into a darkroom during the day, for certain problems of modern painting were beginning to torment him mentally, notably his new technique of painting which he called "simultaneous contrast," to make a pendant to "reinforced concrete," a term which had made a great impression on him and which the architect-aesthetes of the new spirit were using more and more frequently.

Delaunay was starting from scratch and this is how he worked:[13]

"He closed the shutters and shut himself up in his darkroom. Having previously prepared his canvas and ground his colors, he made a little hole in the shutter with a brace and bit. A thin ray of sunlight filtered into the darkroom and he began to paint it, to study it, to break it down into its components, to analyze all its elements of form and color. Without knowing it, he was doing spectrum analysis. He worked for months like this, studying pure solar light, reaching the sources of emotion without any subject matter whatever. Then he enlarged the hole in the shutter a little and began to paint the play of colors on a transparent and fragile material, such as glass. Reflections, crystalline glints; his little canvases took on the synthetic look of jewels and Delaunay started grinding precious stones into the colors he used, especially pulverized lapis lazuli, like Fra Angelico. Soon, the hole in the shutter became so large that Delaunay opened it wide and let all the broad light of day enter the room. The canvases of this period, already a little larger in format, represent closed windows with the light playing on the glass panes and on the white muslin curtains. Finally, he drew back the curtains and opened the window: Now one can see a luminous gaping hole, and the roof of the house opposite set against the light, hard and solid, a first clumsy, angular, sloping form. Progressively, Delaunay is attracted by what is going on out there, outside, and he rediscovers the minuscule play of light he has studied in a sunbeam, but on a gigantic scale, in the ocean of light that washes over Paris. The painter is faced with the same problems, but the proportions are different, the scale vast. Then he paints his enormous canvases, five or six meters high, *La Ville, Les Trois Grâces sur Paris,* in which he attempts to bring together academicism and all the painterly novelties he has just discovered: the spire of Notre-Dame, with the Seine flowing into the suburbs of Paris. Charenton and Alforville. Finally, he finds a new subject, which will allow him to apply all his discoveries and new techniques: the Great City. But this sets him a multitude of new problems: analogies, poetic correspondences, physical and spiritual contrasts, questions of perspective, of materials, abstract questions of unanimism and synthesis. And the whole personality of Paris penetrates and pervades him. More and more, Delaunay, who now spends months contemplating Paris from the heights of her towers and churches, turns his eyes toward the Eiffel Tower, that extraordinary form."

In *Aujourd'hui,* I recounted the drama of Robert Delaunay's struggle with the Eiffel Tower, for I was Robert Delaunay's poet (before the war of 1914, each of today's masters had his own poet: Picasso, Max Jacob; Braque, Pierre Reverdy; Juan Gris, Riciotto Canudo; Léger, Chagall, Roger de la Fresnaye, Modigliani—excuse me, but it was Blaise Cendrars; and the entire School of Paris, cubists and orphists, Guillaume Apollinaire; it was not the art dealers, nor the critics, nor the collectors who made these painters famous, it was the modern poets, and people forget it rather too easily, and so do all these painters who, today, are millionaires and are still indebted to us, the poor poets!). Robert Delaunay was my pal, a tough guy who deserted France on the declaration of war, which I can accept because I understand the fear of bullets, but what I cannot accept is his coming back to Paris from Spain, once the war was over, and thrusting an official certificate of insanity under my nose, a document written out in his name by the French Embassy in Madrid, and his exhibiting it proudly, trying to prove to me that he had been within his rights—no, that was too much! To me, this gesture excused nothing, and I did not bother to question him about it, for I could not understand this strange moral courage that had made him act in this perverse way, and, in fact, I never again saw the painter, or his paintings, after that...

So much wasted moral courage, just like all the physical courage squandered by those of us at the front!

At the time, I had a theory that the boys in my patrol took for a rather exaggerated tall story. I declared that I preferred the shirker behind the lines to the one at the front who, while pinching the booze and tobacco rations, hypocritically boasts of his glory as a soldier on campaign, whereas the reality is that, in Paris, it is really dangerous to pass in front of one's concierge's lodge two or three times a day, and it certainly takes courage for the war dodger to go to bed with the wife of a mate of his who is fighting in the front line, and I added, moreover, that I greatly preferred a deserter to a behind-the-lines shirker, for the deserter who goes overseas is, in his own way, a hero, a man who has had the courage to say No! which is manly and shows character, it is the action of a generous soul; all this, of course, based on the given premise that the *poilu,* the rank-and-file soldier was the most ridiculous Frenchman of all, because he knew perfectly well that he was just a jerk! My paradox made my comrades laugh, for the joke was on them, and they were pissed off about it.

Among the deserters, there were some who went to endless lengths to save their skins, but they did not always succeed. For example, there was the poet, Arthur Cravan, whose wartime history I am now going to tell. Cravan, Delaunay, and I were a trio, we used to go to the Bal Bullier, where we danced the tango in silk socks that did not match, Robert sporting a half-red and half-green dinner jacket, Arthur in black shirts with the dickey slit right open to reveal his bleeding tattoos and the obscene inscriptions on his skin, his coattails flying free and daubed with fresh paint (before going to the dance hall, Cravan invariably managed to sit down on Robert's palette, which made the artist yell at him because the lapis lazuli cost a fortune, and this ruined more than one of our evenings out!) and me wearing ties from Chicago that were as corrosive as tomato ketchup and American pickles and more garish than a parrot's plumage. We dressed up like Orphic harlequins to create a scandal, but also to outdo Marinetti's futurists, whose permanent delegate in Paris, Gino Severini, telegraphed the details of our bizarre get-ups to Milan every evening, and the news was noised abroad, even as far as Saint Petersburg, where it influenced the rayonism of Larionov and Gontcharova, the couple who designed the decor and costumes for Diaghilev's ballet company, and even the futurists in Moscow knew about us and imitated us, Mayakovski's celebrated chrome yellow shirt being the last fashionable echo of our nocturnal follies in Paris. The poet, Arthur Cravan, had immense talent, but he used it as badly as he did his immense physical strength, Arthur being a champion athlete, a boxer, but morally weak, like many semi-professional sportsmen who exhaust themselves with intensive training, being slaves to their beautiful bodies, victims of their torsoes and the muscles they love to show off, flexing their biceps to seduce women and earn themselves honors, prize money, comfort, luxury, and, ultimately, the flabbiness that overtakes them before they are thirty years old!

On the 2nd of August, 1914, the day war was declared, the poet Arthur Cravan, "nephew of Oscar Wilde," "poet and boxer," "the poet with the shortest hair in the world," as he liked to describe himself in his magazine, *Maintenant,* and on the posters outside the Noctambules where, several weeks previously, he had given a lecture, announcing with a great deal of ballyhoo that he was going to commit suicide in public, replace the usual carafe of water with a bottle of absinthe, and, in honor of the ladies, or perhaps some sister-soul, wear nothing but a G-string and put his balls on the table (in the end, he did none of these things, he was so embarrassed that he emptied the carafe of water without even realizing it, for he must have been thirsty, jabbering on and on, taking the mickey out of Victor Hugo, and not daring to brandish the revolver with its chamber empty—not even loaded with blanks!—that was lying on the table, and giving such a boring lecture, spouting so many platitudes that it should at least have gained him a *succès de surprise* with the audience of snobs and aesthetes whom he had had Van Dongen round up for the occasion, and who were expecting a crazy session, for his friends, long aware that the actions of this giant, this lazy man, had the fatal quality of the pricked balloon about them, had not bothered to come, being quite confident of seeing him again, still alive and still weak-kneed, so poor Arthur wallowed and floundered, ill-at-ease, without moral support, intimidated in spite of his boasting and his crackpot ideas). Well then, the day war was declared, Arthur Cravan was in such a funk that he threw himself into the river, swam tirelessly across the Bidassoa, with its shallow water but shifting sands, and made a beeline from Hendaye-Plage, where he had been staying, to Fuenterrabia, where he rejoined Robert Delaunay, that other Big-Mouth having crossed the international bridge at Béhobie the previous evening, before the frontier was closed, and hurriedly taken the train to Lisbon complete with bag and baggage, that is to say, with palette, brushes, tubes of color, rolls of virgin canvas, his pictures and his entire household, his wife, the baby, the Lithuanian nursemaid, and Mme. Delaunay, his mother—quite an uprooting!

Arthur unhesitatingly joined the Delaunay caravan, but he did not feel at ease in Lisbon because he was a British citizen and Portugal was Britain's ally. And so, when Portugal declared war in her turn and became a belligerent, Arthur crossed illegally into Spain and lived for some time in Madrid, where Robert was not long in joining him. Sonia cooked for them all and managed to get on all right with her mother-in-law, the two women having opened some boutique or dressmaking establishment.

Sponging off these two women did not worry Cravan unduly, but he did not feel quite safe in Europe. He wanted to get to the United States, where he had some relatives and useful contacts, but he was penniless, and the money he was hoping for from England and Ireland failed to arrive, his brother, Lloyd, having been enlisted in England, his sister-in-law Alice choosing to turn a deaf ear to his appeals, and all the other relations, friends, and acquaintances refusing to reply. Arthur did not know where the devil to turn. At first, he had managed to ingratiate himself with Mother-in-law Delaunay (a sharp-tongued Parisienne), wheedling her into

199

lending him the money for the desperate appeals and the telegrams he sent off in all directions, but now, having let her down, abused her generosity, cheated and *empapaouted*.[14] her, he had finally put her back up. Then, one day, he slipped off quietly to Barcelona to join the famous boxer, the world champion, Jack Johnson, a magnificent black who enjoyed the high life. Arthur had had occasion to meet him in the boxing rings and training gymnasiums and, at one time, had shown him the sights of Paris and Berlin, trotting him around all the bars in La Chapelle and on the Alexanderplatz, indulging in riotous living at Johnson's expense, swigging champagne in the nightclubs of Montmartre and the Kurfürstendam, smoking fat cigars in the gay and decadent company of a crowd of drug addicts and homosexuals—all for the fun of it, naturally!

In Barcelona, Jack Johnson was up to his old tricks in the port and in the Barrio Chino. At that time, the black champion had been more or less disqualified because of some involvement in prostitution, and he had already run into trouble with all the police in Europe. He was sick of it. He dreamed of going back to the States and carrying on his career as a boxer, but he could not quite make up his mind to it, for he had a ball and chain round his ankle, a German baroness who used to come and hunt him out in the shady bars where he took refuge. Besides, he was not in good shape and, as with Cravan, funds were low. I do not know who first thought of the idea, but the two accomplices soon came to an agreement. A sensational boxing match was arranged, and it was announced as the world champion's comeback, his return to the ring, a bout in which the great Jack Johnson would defend his title against the challenger, Arthur Cravan, the "nephew of Oscar Wilde, poet and boxer, the poet with the shortest hair in the world, etc. etc." The Spanish organizers of the event did things in grand style. There was massive publicity, as if for a *corrida*, with posters in the streets of Barcelona, articles in all the Catalonian newspapers, and soon the curiosity and excitement of the public were worked up to a climax, prices for seats soared and… and it was a lamentable disaster. Big Jack did not lose his title, but he lost whatever was left of his honor and never again appeared in the ring. As for Cravan…

The handsome Arthur took up a defensive stance, his gloved fists in front of his face…

I learned the details from an eyewitness of this epoch-making encounter, which is unparalleled in the annals of the noble art. As is the usual practice, both contestants had a guaranteed purse. The victor's, obviously, was larger. On the eve of the fight, Cravan had persuaded his managers to pay him an advance, let's say five thousand pesetas, and he had gone at once to book his berth on a steamer that was sailing for New York on the following evening. He did not breathe a word about this to his comrade, but, as he was in no shape to survive more than three rounds, he begged the black man not to knock him out and not to hit him too hard!

After the event, Jack Johnson took the opportunity to express, in public, his contempt for this great white coward, the "nephew of Oscar Wilde etc. etc.," who had brought him bad luck.

It seems that, in New York, Johnson searched for the poet-boxer in all the bars in the Bronx, which, at that time, were frequented by sportsmen in training. He wanted to teach him a lesson, but the poet with the shortest hair in the world had let it grow so as not to look like a man who was eligible for mobilization, in fact nothing about his person must suggest such a thing, and now the heavy, thick-set, but still seductive nephew of the dandy Oscar Wilde no longer kept company with sportsmen, but with all the lily-livered funks of all kinds whom the European winds of war had blown away to New York, like Arthur himself, and the handsome poet was a big hit in the salons of the Stieglitz, the art photographers, and with other art dealers, proclaiming his own war, dada, DADA, and becoming the spokesman for men of bad conscience, launching his blustering and anodyne thunder which neither killed nor wounded but which filled his mixed audience, made up of European deserters, internationalists, pacifists, neutrals, and 100 percent pure-blooded Americans, all fiercely isolationist, with enthusiasm, and lording it over all this loud-mouthed rabble. This was in 1915. "Art has no country!"

The encounter in Barcelona took place one Sunday afternoon, but I do not know which disused arena they used. In the ring, once the presentations and the announcements were over, and the referee had shouted "Fight!" the handsome Arthur stood on guard, holding his gloved fists up to his face, lowering his head, pulling in his stomach, pressing his elbows tightly together and leaning forward so as to cover his heart and await the fatal blow; with his neck pulled right down into his shoulders and his back humped, he made not the slightest sketch of a gesture, not even a feint, a sham to make it look as if he was at least playing the part, but contented himself with marking time, dancing on the spot, *trembling visibly* while the big Negro circled around the vain white boy like a large black rat around a Dutch cheese. Three times Johnson was called to order, because three times Big Jack kicked the poet-boxer in the ass to try and unfreeze the nephew of Oscar Wilde, then the black man pummeled his ribs, punched him,

201

laughed at him, egged him on, insulted him, and, losing his temper all of a sudden, laid him out flat with a formidable slap on his left ear, a blow worthy of a slaughterer in the abattoir or of a cut-throat, for he was really pissed off! Cravan did not stir. The referee counted out the seconds. The bell rang to end the contest. And Jack Johnson was proclaimed the victor by a knockout. The whole thing had lasted less than one minute. Then the black man started insulting the Catalan audience, who were protesting vehemently, invading the ring, demanding their money back, wrecking the arena, setting fire to the barriers. The police came to the rescue and evacuated the place, and, the riot having spread to the streets outside, they had to call in the *carabineros* to take the world champion to the central police station, while the managers had to give in and reimburse the spectators!

Big Jack was furious, he spent the night in the *calabozo,* yelling for Arthur, swearing to have his blood, and the sergeant on duty had to threaten him several times with the strait-jacket.

While the Spanish managers were hunting all over town for Cravan, who had managed to make himself scarce, the handsome Arthur was already shut up in his cabin on board the liner that was setting sail for America. He was sponging his left ear, which was inflamed, not from shame, but from the violence of the blow he had received. But, knowing him as I do, I am sure he didn't give a shit about it, he would have said to himself: "Saving face, that's OK for the Chinese! As for me, my beauty is intact, and that's all I care about, my dear old phiziog!" And he must have smiled at himself in the mirror as he leaned over the hand basin and carefully applied a compress. He would have thought of his wife, too, a Burgundian woman whom he had left behind in Paris, and perhaps he already knew that he was going to get married again in New York, for Arthur Cravan died a bigamist.

To recount Arthur Cravan's life in New York would be to write the history of the foundation of dadaism, but I am not going to write about that now, and nor, up to the present time, has that flashy adventurer, the apostle of art for art's sake, Francis Picabia, written a word about it; in New York, Picabia saw Cravan every day and, inspired by his example, had the great moral courage to provide* Leonardo da Vinci's Mona Lisa, who was too surprised to protest, with a pair of mustaches just like Kaiser Wilhelm II's; nor has anything been written as yet by the inventive Marcel Duchamp (and what did this malicious Parisian do in New York? He taught love,

---

*Actually, Marcel Duchamp... painted the mustache on the Mona Lisa. (Trans.)

that game of chess!), who also saw Cravan every day in New York and who, submitting to his influence, had the great moral courage to provide the chamberpots on sale in a bazaar with the following guarantee: *"I declare that this household article is an authentic work of art!"* and underwrite this declaration with a facsimile of his signature, in a form only the initiated understood: *Rrose Sélavy;** nor has anything been said up to the present time by the Grand Mufti of Zurich, who did not know Cravan and who, to his confusion, received the investiture of the new church from the hands of Picabia, in 1917, for, in the meantime, the United States had entered the war and Picabia, although he was a Cuban, had taken refuge in Switzerland, allegedly to nurse an attack of shingles and take a detoxicating cure, but, in fact, to indulge in frantic propaganda, for his cases were packed with DADA, plans of campaigns, manifestos, bombs, and works written by Cravan's bad conscience, in other words, all the paraphernalia of the new faith which the Grand Mufti, Tristan Tzara, hastened to communicate to his followers at the Cabaret Voltaire and which the epigones of the dancer from the Bal Bullier and the stammerer from the Noctambules received as reverently as the Apostles received the Holy Spirit. (N.B.: the members of the Cabaret Voltaire in Zurich were mostly Germans who loved France too much to take up arms against her, and almost all the others were Jews from Eastern Europe who had fled from the wearing of any uniform whatsoever. Second N.B.: At that time, Switzerland was the Promised Land for spies and aesthetes, pacifists and Zimmerwaldians. Bolo, Dada, Romain,† Lenin, a famous cocktail which added to the Babel of languages, an amusing cockade of eidelweiss attached to the Red Bonnet, folded like a gendarme's hat, which was sported by all these weathercocks whose heads turned with every wind that blew.) "Dada! Dada!" shouted the neophytes of Zurich, kicking up a hell of a racket, with their eyes fixed on Paris, for they wanted a war of their very own. *"Art has no country!"* As for Cravan, he had vanished.

But the wartime adventures of Arthur Cravan do not end with the invention of dada, quite the contrary, it is only now that his misadventures as a deserter begin to gather momentum.

---

*Duchamp adopted the pseudonym Rrose Sélavy (That's life) in 1920. Man Ray photographed him in drag as Rrose in 1921. (Trans.)

†Zimmerwaldians: Named after the Swiss town, Zimmerwald, where Swiss and Italian socialists held an antiwar conference in 1915. Bolo, Paul or Pascha: variously described as a French traitor or German agent, convicted of treason, died 1918. Romain Rolland (1866–1944), Nobel laureate, pacifist, novelist (*Jean-Christophe*). (Trans.)

When the United States entered the war, our poet, who did not want to have his pretty face spoiled, was in such a blue funk at the thought of being caught and flung into the maelstrom that, without further reflection, he slipped over into Canada, since that happened to be the nearest frontier and he could reach it in a single night. It was only after he had made it over the border that Arthur Cravan realized his head was in the lion's jaws, for Canada was a British Dominion, and therefore at war, and Arthur, although a conscientious objector, of course, was also a British subject, an Englishman who wanted nothing whatever to do with this imperialist war, for God's sake!... *Quos vult perdere Jupiter, dementat prius.*

The hare-brained idiot took refuge in a farm, and there he remained quietly for some time, not knowing what to do nor how to get himself out of there. What gave this great strapping fellow the idea of dressing up as a woman I do not know, but probably he was thinking of the homosexuals he had seen dancing together in the night clubs on the Kurfürstendam and at La Petite Chaumière in Montmartre when he was living it up at Jack Johnson's expense in Paris and Berlin, for these are things that come back to you when you are all alone and keep hashing over your past while you whistle a popular tune to keep your spirits up.

I do not know how he got hold of female clothing in that remote farm in the woods, but the Canadians are not very quick on the uptake and probably the farmers saw no harm in this big joker who knew how to make himself agreeable and who must surely have given them a hand here and there during the day and entertained them and made them laugh in the evenings. The Canadian winter is long, there are not many amusements in the country, and the passing stranger who has an interesting tale to tell, and can make jokes, such as an out-of-season traveling salesman, is welcome. Moreover, many of these little farms are clandestine distilleries and Cravan may well have dropped a few hints among the gangsters who ran them and the smugglers who patronized them, for he would have known some useful addresses in New York, where there was big money to be made. But perhaps, quite simply, Arthur managed to seduce the daughter of some farmer, or a maidservant who gave him shelter, for he was a handsome hunk of man, a liar, and an arrant flatterer.

I do not know how he managed to get to Montreal without arousing suspicion, and on to Quebec without getting arrested, nor how he embarked on board ship and landed up, high and dry, in Newfoundland, still dressed as a woman, but what I do know is that he disembarked without out a cent and immediately (just time to change his costume behind a

fence somewhere) had to look for a job, which proves that his flight in trav-
esty must have cost him dearly, for Arthur had left New York with his
pockets full. He had passed the hat around among all his friends and
acquaintances and he had carried away with him all his young American
wife's jewelry. I have reason to believe that he had false identity papers
made, for he found work at once, as a sailor, in Bonavista, Newfoundland,
on board a Danish boat that was setting off to fish for cod on "the Banks,"
and Arthur must have sweated his guts out, that's for sure! Oh, that
blessed Cravan!

This cod-fishing expedition was the hardest period of Cravan's life. A
fisherman's lot is no joke and, in Newfoundland, it is sheer misery. Arthur
had a rough time of it. For the first time in his life, Oscar Wilde's nephew
had to soil his hands with work, and the poet-boxer did not like to spoil
his beautiful hands any more than he liked to spoil his pretty face. I
remember a letter he wrote from Newfoundland to his wife in Paris,
expressing his bitterness, his disgust at the life he was living, his despair,
and begging her to do the impossible, to pawn all her possessions and cable
him a money order by return. Even allowing for the exaggerations, the
pathetic tone of a missive like that, full of emotional blackmail, written in
such conditions and in a moment of the blackest depression, I must admit
that life cannot have been a bed of roses "on the Banks," and that Cravan
must have been sick to death of it. The Burgundian girl sent the money
order "care of the Danish Consulate," as Arthur had instructed her in the
letter he had signed with a false name. But this money order was never
delivered, it was returned to Paris, via Copenhagen, with the words:
"Addressee embarked on board the 'Santissima Madre de Dio,' a Mexican schooner"
written on it. I have forgotten now what false name Cravan used in
Newfoundland, for he used several others in Mexico, before he finally
found the moral courage to sign his letters to his Parisian wife in his own
name. He was afraid of being extradited. He thought the Great War had
been unleashed against him personally. Oh, that blessed Cravan!

A first letter arrived from Mexico, then another. Then there was a long
silence. Then, several months later, three bundles of letters came in rapid
succession, one after the other. Cravan was traveling in southern Mexico,
prospecting the silver mines. Then, several more months of silence followed by one last letter from Mexico City. He announced that he had
opened a Boxing Academy in the city, and that it was a great success. He
was also giving lectures, his fame was at its peak, the "nephew of Oscar
Wilde," the "poet and boxer," the "poet with the shortest hair in the

world," etc., etc., the same old bluff and ballyhoo as in Paris, Barcelona, and New York. He was jubilant. His affairs were prospering and he was anxious to know what people in Paris thought of his success. Then, nothing. Five, six months passed, and suddenly the rumor began to spread through Montparnasse, without anyone's knowing where it had come from or being able to verify the truth of it, that Arthur Cravan had been murdered in a dance hall by a dagger-thrust to the heart...

The stuff of cinema!

To have gone through all that, done all those things to save his skin during the war, and then to cop it right at the end, on the very eve of peace, and in Mexico of all places!

None of this detracts from the immense talent of the poet, and it really seems that his stay in Mexico, his travels in the south, the prospecting for silver, might well have been the "road to Damascus" for him, if he had not done a right-about-face in the wilderness. During that period, he wrote extraordinary letters to his wife in Paris, they were full of emotion, of intense but restrained poetry, hymns to the night as profound and fluent as any of Novalis's, and there were some stunning insights, as prophetic and rebellious, as desperate and bitter as those of Rimbaud. He had found his true climate. But this regeneration, this catalysis of his genius on coming into contact with Indian life and the great savage nature of the country did not endure. When he returned to the capital, the corrupt life of the city, and its modern, sophisticated atmosphere got its claws into him again and he was too vain, too inwardly deranged to resist success, money, women, fame, the facile scandal of dadaism, and his own vicious and congenital puerility, for one cannot be a handsome young man and the nephew of Oscar Wilde with impunity! I do not doubt that, one day, the letters Arthur Cravan sent to his wife in Paris will be published (there are about sixty of them), and that they will be added to the three or four promising poems that marked his debut, poems for which I have a tender affection, such as a man feels for his younger brother.[15]

To dada! To dada! To the madman! What cinematic stuff!

"Square-ass," my luxurious loophole in no-man's-land, could equally well have been equipped with a "cat's eye," which is not only an accessory for the camera, but also, and more particularly, a gimmick that has a distinct psychological effect, like other tricks and professional artifices of cinema technique, such as the dissolve, the traveling or panoramic shot, the close-up, the play of mirrors, the use of gauzes, veils, velvet backgrounds for certain process shots, speeding-up or slow motion, filtered or direct lighting, makeup, simultaneous montage, the rhythm of sequences, the cadence and timing of images, highlighting, the inhuman beauty of a face lit by such high voltage that it looks like porcelain fired and refired in the kiln and even acquires a crackle glaze, or lit by transparencies, so that it seems to be illumined from within and shines like the Holy Grail, and, since the invention of talkies, the graduated and startlingly dynamic use of silence.

But, in a projection room, I often look away from the screen to follow with my eyes the dark rays that quiver in the cone of white light that beams from the projector to the silver screen, above the heads of the spectators; these black rays are the shadows released by the shutter and set in motion by the movements of the handle, which turns at such a rapid tempo that the conscious mind is not aware of it, only the retina receives the impression, thus giving the eye a rest from the animated images that the shutter serves both to link together and to separate; black rays, but also the screw-threaded axes around which the characters gyrate, as they are projected on to the screen by the cone of light, turning in a prodigious spiral, which I have tried in vain to capture by shooting horizontally instead of vertically, as is the universal practice: a pathetic spiral of living beings— world-famous stars, stars with sex appeal!—whom I imagine following one another, not upright as on the screen but lying down, stretched out, intertwined, crawling in this cone of shadow that seeks perpetually to reconstitute itself—and if one projected the film backwards, these drawn-out shadows, mixed up, tangled into corkscrews, coiled like snakes, would have to re-enter the lens in a dark, compact mass, a nest of vipers, a black ball, a plug... But this is not the case. This abstract black that I seek, remains... A projection of the fall from Heaven, nothing but mental confusion.

With my loophole, it was my mind that acted as the shutter. My heart was the lens. Focus. Close-up. Long shot. A question of degrees, of meshing gears, angles, setups, strips of film printed with key numbers.

At night, at the front, everything is distorted. The universe came pouring through my loophole, which was equipped with a shutter: me!

My mind, my heart—were they just *ad hoc* patented accessories?

In contemplation, all is mental confusion. Where is understanding? I could not find my words, those sacred monsters, I was just a poor poet in a steel helmet, or a forage cap, or bare-headed, with a bump on my forehead where I'd been hit by a rifle butt.

VIII
CREATURES OF THE SPIRIT WORLD

I no longer remember where I read this story, but it must have been in an old book read after the midday siesta, or while keeping vigil at the campfire one evening and then lost somewhere along the way:

Around the year 350 A.D., a pilgrim was traveling from the leafy convent in Bethlehem, where he had been initiated, to Egypt to follow the teachings of the great Saint Anthony and his anchorites. Losing his way in the deserts of the south, or of Zin, he fell into the hands of a tribe of nomads who carried him off into the desert of Pharan, where they kept him prisoner for ten years.

These nomadic brigands were fire worshipers and, every evening, when they set up their tents, they lit oil or kerosene lamps and attached them, in clusters, to an immensely tall mast, fitted with numerous branches or yard arms, where they were left to burn all through the night; these lamps were arranged to correspond to the shapes and sizes of the various constellations, their positions changed according to the fluctuations of the seasons and the passing of the hours, for their rotating globes imitated the movements of the heavenly bodies, their gravitation, their inclination, their differences of light intensity and coloration, and it makes me giddy to think what this traveling show, this huge mast equipped with all the constellations, must have looked like in the midst of the desert, in the heart of the Oriental night, with its two night watches of acrobatic lamp lighters running up the shrouds, hanging from the ropes to feed the revolving lights of the luminaries, from which the nomads read the auguries that enabled them to plan their itineraries for the next day, the ephemeral tracks through the dunes that were all these men of prey and plunder left behind them.

In another sector of the front, we were only separated from the enemy facing us, who were just as uncomfortably lodged as we were, by a parapet made up of three or four layers of corpses, and we spent the nights lying on our stomachs among these stinking, putrefying bodies, spying on and listening to those on the other side as they cursed this same son-of-a-bitch existence in their own guttural language, swearing raucously and stamping about in their heavy, iron-shod boots, like tethered horses; every now and then, one or the other would get himself shot, the living being unable to keep still among the dead. But, as for me, I spent the night on my back, without moving, contemplating the cold stars of March like a dying man who, forgotten and abandoned on his deathbed, watches the flies on the ceiling ceaselessly revolving like tiny black stars, crossing and recrossing each other in the void, eddying, letting themselves drop as if on the end of an invisible thread, hovering, buzzing, settling on the nose, the hands, the forehead, the temples of the dying man, gathering at the corners of his lips, irritating, monstrous, insidious, and unclean, crapping into his eyes, leaving flyspecks spattered across his parchment eyelids, tickling, stinging, devouring him until the moribund man turns over between the sheets and exhales his last breath, whereupon the flies exultantly suck up the good smell of the spirit as it flies toward the infinite Spirit.

"Behold even... the stars are not pure in his sight" (Job 25:5). And the Spirit entered me and I could not tear my eyes away from the sky, and this Trench of Carrion offered neither shelter nor dugout nor cover of any sort. *"Behold, he putteth no trust in his saints; yea, the heavens are not clean in his sight."* (Job 15:15)

And so, I lost myself in contemplation of the heavens, deciphering the constellations, reconstituting them, tracing them one after the other, according to the hour, reminding myself of their names, and I was astounded at the poverty of the nomenclature of the stars, you would think they had been named, not by heroes and geniuses but, at first, by cowherds and later by junior schoolmasters, teachers of rhetoric (they might just as well have baptized them with serial numbers, as they once did with railway engines and, in more recent times, with taxis, since they had such dull minds and such short memories and were lacking in faith—like the geographical scholars who lived at the time of Marco Polo and simply could not believe in his travels, in spite of the routes the great Venetian, in his prison cell in Genoa, freely described for them, telling them where to procure silks, textiles, damask, gauzes, embroidered cloths, muslins, brocades, satins, carpets, precious gems of every color: sapphires, rubies, emeralds, topazes, amethysts, beryls, turquoises, diamonds, pearls, and the whole gamut of spices: cinnamon, nutmeg, ginger, cloves, white pepper, black pepper, and chilis, as well as scents and unguents, from jasmine to civet and kohl, from incense to musk, camphor, palm oil, sandalwood, and holothurian or sea-cucumber, a royal aphrodisiac, and, in spite of the immediate rush of European merchants who, impatient to enrich themselves, were flooding along the new roads into Asia, the cartographers of the time remained faithful to the classical tradition inherited from Ptolemy and continued to represent the world in the form of a flat disc surrounded by water, and to distribute the nations schematically around Jerusalem, which they considered to be the center of human habitation, and these wise men, these specialists were the last to react (long after the Church, which hastened to make use of this guide to practical commerce which Marco Polo had put at her disposal, for *The Million or The Travels of Marco Polo* was not only the account of a journey, but also a kind of voluminous Yellow Pages full of useful addresses, and to send missionaries to evangelize the idolators and gather souls all along the new routes) and it was only after a long, long delay that these contrite scholars were at last obliged to revise their world maps of the fourteenth, fifteenth, and sixteenth centuries—the first map of Asia, by Giacomo Castaldi, dates from only 1561—and report the news of the overpopulated cities and the teeming nations discovered by Marco Polo! and I wondered why not one of the heavenly bodies bears, even by chance, the name of a boat, or of a crew who set out on a voyage of discovery, since the sea is the only mirror of the stars, and the stars are the only guide for mariners, those world conquerors.

"I intend to declaim in a loud voice, but without emotion, the cold and serious strophe you are about to hear..... I salute you, old Ocean!...
"...O stern mathematicians,[16] I have not forgotten you..."

(*Lautréamont*)

The poverty of imagination is incredible! In the northern hemisphere we have the Whale, the Dolphin, and the Sextant, in the southern hemisphere: the Whale, the Southern Fish, and the Ship; then, in the zodiac, we have Pisces, the Fishes, and Aquarius, the Water-Carrier, and these are the only allusions to the oceans and to sailing in the whole calendar of the sky; the other names are nothing but bric-a-brac, the mythological dregs of antiquated classical poetry, such as Berenice's Hair, the Centaur, Cassiopeia, Perseus, Hercules, Regulus, Antinoüs, Andromeda, the Phoenix, the Hydra, etc., etc., pretentious terminology to provide a little relief from the common vocabulary of the primitive cowherds who gave such prosaic names to all the other stars: the Dog, the Bear, the Goat, the Lion, the Eagle, the Ram, the Bull, the Dove, the Hare, the Great Dog, the Little Bear, etc., etc., clichés that have been in use since Time began. Every exceptional name in the astrologers' almanacs, or in the alchemists' books of spells, tells us much more about the geography of the sky and the enigmas of the universe than any of our modern astronomers' and physicists' maps, charts, slides, and photographs of a sidereal pullulation they have not yet had the courage to number, classify, catalogue, and rationalize with a view to a practical horary, since they prefer to cling superstitiously to that pastoral tally of the poultry house, the sheepfold, the farmyard, and the hunt, and to that artificial schoolroom poetry, in spite of the fact that we are on the eve of an astounding adventure—interplanetary travel, no less!—and ready to take all the risks involved in this long and perilous navigation.[17]

Even the Chinese mandarins, who, a thousand years before the Christian era, invented the telescope and the compass for the use of navigators (which enabled the Jesuit Fathers to establish an astronomic observatory in Peking as long ago as the seventeenth century), gave animal names to the stars: the Dragon, the Serpent, the Crab, the Scorpion, the Unicorn, the Peacock, the Crane, etc., and we have to go back to Lemuria* to find a significant word in the sky, at the time when Man, a newcomer, a magical being who had arisen from the universal waves, was fixing his attention on the optic nerve, which was unfolding like the fiddleheads of the arborescent ferns and the quivering tips of the giant monocellular grasses that surrounded him, and, at the same time, becoming aware of the burgeoning of his eye and of his other eye in this mutation, for, thanks to the effects of a first ray of light and a tear from the first wave of fresh water, he now saw his brain maturing, swelling up like a slobbering gland and becoming congested to form a third eye, the pineal gland, an inward-turning eye, turbid, bloody, and soft, but with magnetic short-circuits, an eye that was to be reabsorbed into him, to unbind his tongue and thus bestow upon him the gift of POETRY. And, in his mounting fever, magical man began to call things by their proper names, to identify with them, to domesticate animals, to make his choices, as one searches for rhymes and assonances, to select from the uniform opacity of the carboniferous strata those aquatic mosses that would eventually bear grain—rice, millet, and corn—to cook his food and prepare his pharmacopeia according to the essences and the hidden virtues of things and their correspondences (for he had a very fine sense of smell and seven ossicles in his ear which gave him

---

*Mythical, Polynesian island, submerged like the continent Atlantis. (Trans.)

the power of divination, and, thanks to his ability to move his ears and open and close them, a sense of direction), to make fire, to distinguish between the sexes, to procreate secrets through the Word: God, the four cardinal points, the spirits, the orbits, and the mathematics of the heavenly bodies, which celebrate the festival of eternal return, the earth and the ocean, the high and the low, what is before and what is behind, to the right and the left, as they appear in our dreams, and, in order to maintain the high temperature of his cerebral fever by artificial means, he got a familiar snake, against whose venom he had been immunized, to bite him, and dressed himself in a mask of psychic lightning, so that his life became a phrase formulated by the enigmatic "I," which consumes and perpetuates itself on the appearance of that accompanying phenomenon, THE GREAT ANCESTOR and his phases, a shooting star in the instinctive unconscious and in the sperm ejaculated from it like thunder and lightning, like fucking, in the belly and in the Word: *"O my love!...,"* the cry *"Ouch, you're hurting me, dear..."* (dear being an onomatopeic or imitative harmony like *Ouch!* and meaning *you bastard!* or words to that effect...)

But who, nowadays, knows the cosmogony of the Lemurians and their phantom metaphysics, and who could decipher their tattoos, which are hieratic and hierarchic scars, the marks and the insignia of their magical surgery, their INVENTION, their cruelty, their sacred operations which ranged from incisions, grafts, and ritual trepanning to sacrifice, spiritual communion in the drinking of blood and the eating of flesh, circumcision of the phallus, enucleation of the vulva, and, most frequently, the cutting, dislocation, and amputation of the thumbs and the big toes, or sometimes the forearm and the thighs, the stumps of which were cut into the shape of a whistle or a bird's beak or the barb of a harpoon or the point of a needle or a fishbone or the head of a pestle or a club in the case of a particular elite, or a family of male sorcerers, in memory of the TOTEM that came out of the midst of the waves and danced in whirling spirals, humming like a top, on the beaches of light, pivoting on his atrophied fins, whipping himself around with his tail, furiously shaking his head adorned with crackling external gills, shouting with joy-bursts of ferocious laughter, madness, foam, snapping jaws—and leaving everywhere in the universe HIS radiant imprints in the form of letters and scales, the runes at the edge of the sea, mother-of-pearl shells, indelible carapaces riddled with patterns of fire, the bluish blotches, the progressive traces, the profound itchings, the lesions, the cracked skin, the tumors, the livid scabs, the squama of a hereditary syphilis, the aura, the starry night?

A strange genealogy for the God of Lautréamont's *Chants de Maldoror,* a God who, while washing his feet on a Saturday night, absent-mindedly strangled his creatures with his big toes, which were armed with nails like spatulas, and who, on coming out of a brothel, left a hair from his head in an anonymous bed (it does not matter who used it, nor for what purpose) and who is nothing but a very distant cousin, many times removed (like the giant Patagonians, the wild Indians of the pampas, who terrified the Spanish chroniclers for a long time and were believed to be cannibals), of the Great Ancestor, that double of the magical man who came out of the cosmic waves, and the hair that fell from his head (which was coiling and uncoiling itself and making one hell of a row in an unsuccessful attempt to batter down the door of a room belonging to a prostitute who was temporarily absent, having gone to the bathroom to wash her vulva, her "octopus with the look of silk"), is only a pale, town-bred caricature of the concentric tattoos that the Lemurian man sported on his everyday face, and of the SPIRAL, which was on all the festival masks used for initiation rites and is a symbol of life's free fall into the expanding universe.

Nobody practices MAGIC anymore, for this poetry in action, highly charged with opposing currents of electricity, is too dangerous! (It is a fact that the citizens of Montevideo, where the werewolf, Isidore Ducasse, known as the Count of Lautréamont, was born, have become nice, smiling bourgeois citizens who love to get together and do a little table-turning, to frighten and amuse themselves, for they are bored, nothing ever happens in their town, and their little republic on the eastern side of South America is on the fringes of the world's great traffic!) And nobody wears the forbidding mask that used to terrorize the enemy within and congeal him in a hypnotic trance, in HEREDITY. Epilepsy and *grand mal* have become shameful. It is not that magical man has been forgotten, his psyche has not been rendered powerless, nor has the source of his creative vision dried up, but, today, the REAL is under lock and key. TABOO. It is forbidden. *Verboten!* Not to be touched, for fear of blowing everything sky high! That is rational. The tongue is the reflection of the human consciousness. Language moves from the concrete to the abstract, from the mystical to the rational. The languages of savages are rich in detailed and concrete expressions, the languages of civilized man have very few of these left and tend to become more and more generalized and abstract. We no longer speak of the self: the "I." The poetic "I" is proscribed. Through speculative analysis, the atom has risen to the surface like an atoll. It *is* today. A detonator. A button. Close your eyes. Blink. Press the button with one finger. Instantaneous explosion. The voice of guns and bombs. Nothing means anything any-more. We take refuge in an automated war of the robots to avoid facing the reality and the shock of our internal contradictions. We are afraid, abjectly afraid, of the Word. The sky is about to fall! We turn somersaults. Glossotomy. Our breath is vivisected. SILENCE follows, heavy and mute. Horror. Stupor. Loss of consciousness. Convulsions. THE SPIRIT. It is the falling, or comitial sickness. The meeting is over. Someone cries out...

...A shell crashed down beside me, burrowing, floundering, and wal-lowing in the mud, but it was a dud, it did not explode. I was bursting for a piss and I had rolled over on to my side...

...Where was I?...

In my daydreams, I was attending the revels of the Lemurians and the intuition suddenly came to me that it was an initiation rite.

From a distance, I saw them forming an immense circle in the twilight, then a dissolve brought them into close-shot and I became aware that what I had taken to be a large, scattered village, or an agglomeration of dwellings built on piles, was in reality an armada of tribesmen and family groups crowded into, not the migratory pirogues that were to come much later in the course of the ages (these Polynesian pirogues, artistically carved out by hand and bearing on their stately bows a figurehead similar to the huge stylized statues you see planted in the sands of Easter Island, majestic and serene, masked and tattooed, and with fine spirals drawn around their eyes, formed the proudest and the most daring war flotilla ever to set sail, cleaving the waters of the Pacific Ocean from New Zealand to Honolulu and the almost-island of Malacca in Chile),[18] but, like shipwrecked souls, into a mass of branches, leaves, algae, submarine and half-floating roots, tufts of grass, faggots, fasciae, a mattress of sponges and seaweed, and this long train of rafts was stranded in the shallows of a lagoon that flowed out of the marshes after high tide, and a freak current, full of detritus, was dragging it imperceptibly out to sea in a slow, ragged convoy, disjointed but little by little forming itself into a loop like a submerged atoll. There was no swell. The sky was overcast, the atmosphere murky and nebulous, the clouds were leaden and charged with heat lightning, the water like pewter. The rays of a fitful light shone between the emaciated legs of these strange, half-starved shipwrecked souls, who, dripping with sweat, were alternately gesticulating in a standing posture and prostrating themselves, all together, as if struck by magnetic waves that hit them in the stomach and made them fall down, until a trance jerked them upright again, with their spines cracking, their arms stiff with cramp, their legs apart, and then, from one sinking or marooned raft to the next, the men and women cried out to one another in alternating choruses.

From close to, every man seemed to be three-legged, for his familiar parasite, a kind of fat leech which came out of his backside at his cackling summons, was an integral part of him, and this disgusting annelid worm answered him with a gentle, purring rumble of the bowels and uncoiled itself, stretched right down to the ground, where it sucked up the primaeval slime, gorging itself and bending into a bow, forming the auxiliary leg of the unstable creatures who were the primitive men of that era, and making them look as if they were sitting down when they were actually standing up, like the kangaroo family when they rest on their tails, uneasy and adaptable, ready to jump into the water at the least alarm. Some of them still had the rudiments of external gills. All had extraordinarily mobile ears, which they turned constantly in all directions, but especially out to sea, for it seemed they were expecting some threat or danger to come from there, their looks and their eyes, the prominent eyes of nyctalopes, were fixed on a point drowned in the fog, like a cluster of bubbles at the center of small concentric waves, or like the gurgle at the mouth of a spring. I thought I saw something welling up out there, something inexhaustible emerging from the depths of the secret night to become a palpable presence, but the behavior of the women distracted me from the open sea.

The women, all of whom suffered from hemorrhoids, inevitably stood with their legs as wide apart as possible and were even more unstable than the men, for they were weighed down with clusters of sea grapes or gulf weed that flowed from their ovaries like spawn and itched so much that the women scratched themselves incessantly, drawing blood and rooting out the blisterlike pods, then throwing them overboard as if they had been aborted fetuses; these shapeless masses, these gelatinous curds became iridescent as soon as they touched the water and burst in a pale yellow cloud that gave off the stink of sulphurated hydrogen, of rotten eggs, in the wake of the floating islands overloaded with men and women.

The tribes, the families of Lemuria were all there, each clan in a heap like a colony of croaking frogs adrift on a giant water lily-pad, the whole flotilla of matted grass being carried out to sea by the imperceptible current, the rafts hooking themselves on to the train or drifting away and detaching themselves, according to the strength of the opposing electrical forces that were pulling them in two different directions to make them form, eventually, a perfect circle, a circle that would enclose a lagoon in the open sea and at the center of which there would be GOD, sitting there in his nuclear dream, God, fishing with a rod and line, his lumpish shadow cast upon an aerial shower of phosphorescent droplets and a whistling, flashing network of *moulinets* traced by the fishing line as he whirled it about his head before making his cast, a god who was probably Tangaloa of the Marquesas Islands or Nouka-Hiva, the only god of the Lemurian mythology whose legend and, perhaps, whose name, are more or less known to us, because the degenerate natives of Polynesia still speak of him today during their interminable palavers concerning the population of Heaven and the Islands of the Pacific, and these ancient Vikings of the South Seas also mention him, although he has obviously been distorted out of all recognition, when they relate their nightmares, which are full of flying wizards, sorcerers who commit suicide, vampires who glut themselves on human blood, and necrophages who feast to their heart's content on human flesh, and when the craziest of these natives relate their blackest sexual dreams. It is religious delirium, like the love they display for and in spite of everybody, day and night, although their souls are dead.

Here is the only human version of the legend of Tangaloa, and it is of recent origin. There are others, horrific variations all tainted with the macabre superstitions of nagualism:

While fishing with a line, the god Tangaloa caught the world and pulled it out of the waters.[19] At once, he burst out laughing and cast his line again, flinging it as far as possible, and again he fished the earth out of the waters. It was most amusing! He began to enjoy the game and threw his line still further out, for he was very strong and had a long, stout line, and he kept fishing out the world, the world, the world, and, again and again, the world! Then he stood up, laughing louder and louder and, with a supreme effort, made a last throw, cast his line beyond the horizon and reeled it in, hauling mightily; the hook withstood the strain and, again, he pulled the world out of the waters! And as fast as he pulled out the worlds, he threw them over his shoulder, till they piled up behind him, for he *must* have another, another, and yet another world. When he woke up, night was falling and he saw that he had caught nothing throughout all that day and was empty-handed. But that is how the Universe came to be populated with the stars in the Sky, the islands in the Sea, the mountains and the continents upon the Earth, with Comets and Volcanoes everywhere, and with Phantoms and Spirits drawn from the depths of Dream and each thing was provided with its soul and its reflection, and the Archipelagoes and the Nebulae formed little clusters. But when Tangaloa went back home in the darkness, his wife, the Moon, turned her back on him and began insulting him, and his children, who are Men, began to cry because they were dying of hunger. That is why the Moon no longer appears at the same time as the Sun, and why, ever since, we men—all of us—are crying and dying of hunger.

...I saw the sky populating itself with worlds that sputtered and caught fire; I saw the worlds falling behind Tangaloa's back to form mountains that piled up, burst, split open, exploded, froze, erupted; I saw the barely formed Earth beginning to melt from the heat of its interior fires, and I saw the moisture and the heavy mists covering it; I saw the surface cracking, cooked, and recooked, peeling over the course of ages, and I saw the squama that detached themselves and fell without haste, like the onion skins that mark the different epochs of its evolution, the primary, the secondary, the tertiary, the quaternary ... and each time a globe spun and fell a little short behind Tangaloa's perpendicular shoulder, I saw this new world crush one of the flotilla's rafts or capsize it in eddies of turbulent water from which geysers spouted, scalding and drowning, swamping the rafts of the shipwrecked souls in a churning, boiling foam, a squirting waterspout that fell back on the survivors in the form of diluvian rain, noxious droplets that made them grimace, a clinging dust of water that disfigured them and corroded their faces like vitriol; and at each new wave that lifted them up and threw them forward, to be steeped, inundated, thrown back, shaken by the furious waves provoked by the energetic activities of Tangaloa the fisherman, I saw the people of Lemuria raise their heads, their faces frozen with horror like a tattooed mask with livid spirals, and I heard the men apostrophize their god in the hopes of paralyzing his anarchic movements and stopping his game, which was creating typhoons, and I listened to their cries, straining my ears. They were not cries of distress that answered the laughter of the God, but a magic incantation, a charm to cast a spell on him, for all these cries that rose separately from the islands floating in the mud were reunited in the air, according to a strongly stressed rhythm, to form the syllables of a name that carried to a tremendous distance, and just as I was about to seize on, to comprehend this name and take possession of it... a second shell...

...A second dud shell crashed down beside me, burrowing, floundering, and wallowing in the mud, but it did not go off...

...And just as I was about to grasp this Lemurian name and learn the formula of the incantation, a third shell burst beside me, this time followed by a bellow, a howl of pain... Was it French or German?... I did not know... Someone was screaming as if he had been disemboweled... and I could not make out where the sound was coming from...

217

Now shells were raining down from all over the place and bursting very low, sprinkling the area with detonations and explosions, raising geysers of mud and earth, and the trench was filling with the acrid smoke that catches you in the throat and, suddenly, a noise like a lot of old saucepans and empty tin cans being rattled began to ring out everywhere like a carillon of cracked bells... then a startling voice, followed by other voices, yapping and yelling: "Gas! Gas!"... It was the gas alarm, and now there were scarecrows popping up everywhere, emerging from the stacked corpses of the Trench of Carrion and running all over the sector, shouting and bawling, dashing in all directions to vanish into a nauseous cloud that was getting denser and denser and overtaking the fleeing men... There was total panic... And when I at last dragged myself out of my dream and began to run, too, sneezing, spitting, suffocating, with my tongue hanging out, my throat burning, and my eyes stinging more and more fiercely, I had taken only a few steps when I ran into a bunch of fugitives huddled into a corner behind a bit of wall, a ruined corner with bricks scattered everywhere, all that remained of a semblance of a house or cattle shed that had been blown away in the disaster...

...Where am I?... In front, behind, to the left, right, north, south? ...I no longer knew who I was with... French or German soldiers?... Men of the twentieth century?... I do not know... Everybody was wearing the same mask: a pig's snout...

...And that is when I started to vomit. Overcome with vertigo, I flopped down. And I heard a voice saying to me quite distinctly: "It's the yellow cross.* I'm putting you inside on a charge. You'll be confined to barracks for a week, you son of a bitch! What have you done with your gas mask?"... They were speaking to me in French. But I... slid down into oblivion, just as, when I was a small boy, I used to slide down from a greasy pole when I had won a prize, and, in my swooning state, I believed that I had just stolen the last lamp from the truck of the vertiginous mast set up by the nomads in the desert of Pharan, and I had the impression that I was being pursued through the labyrinthine dunes, and they were furious with me for extinguishing this lamp... A last star... And I lost consciousness... The sand was burning my eyes, the mud filling my mouth, I was running and running, there was the smell of chlorine, a blanket of chlorine.

---

*World War I, German Bombs containing mustard gas were masked with a yellow cross. (Trans.)

VIIII
Beings that Move

As a child, I used to wait until my father's back was turned then sneak into his library, which was strictly forbidden.

I was knee-high to a grasshopper when I began this game that was to last for years and years, for children love to play games that frighten them. I would sneak into my father's library, the room would be silent, the venetian blinds always closed, and the parquet floor let out the merest creak when I stumbled and fell in the semi-darkness, having caught my foot where the carpet was rucked up. Then I let myself sink into the deep pile, I rolled over on to my back and lay there motionless, listening to the silence, plunged into a bluish atmosphere that smelled of encaustic, of crushed-out cigars, and some mysterious, subtle musty smell of alcohol emanating from the uncorked bottles, all stained and sticky, covered in dust, that lay under my father's work table, and from the leather armchairs where his business files were stacked; the glass fronts of the bookcases were multiplied to infinity in the mirror over the fireplace, which was full of the reflections of gilded and tooled bindings and I could guess the titles and the authors' names through these transparent reflections and in the profound depths of the books held prisoner behind a hanging bronze ornament, studded with cabochons, whose pot-bellied lamp floated in close-up and oscillated imperceptibly on its chains whenever a truck from the port, or a timber-cart, passed by in the street, shaking the whole house.

Could I read already? No, perhaps not, but it did not matter. The keys to each section of the library lay on top of the different bookcases. They shone in the penumbra. Nothing happened, nobody could have heard my fall on to the thick carpet, so, the house remaining silent, I climbed, I crawled up, I stood on tiptoe to reach the key, I turned it, and, with my

219

heart pounding, I opened one of the bookcases, always the same one, the one with the cracked glass-pane at the bottom that trembled in its frame when, with a thousand precautions, I opened the mahogany door on its fragile silver hinges. Then, I let myself fall on my backside and, holding my breath, contemplated the row of books on the lower shelf, the large ones in quarto, menacing, looming above my head. They were the *Géographie universelle,* by Élisée Reclus. Finally, I reached out my hand and, with a great effort, managed to make one volume topple over. It was always the same one, Volume IX, *L'Afrique équatoriale,* the lightest of all but the one that attracted me most, and, as it fell out on top of me, it always opened at the same page, the one with an engraving of a huge ebony idol crouched at the foot of a giant tree in the virgin forest, a stolid, four-square idol with monstrous eyes and grinning teeth that terrified me. Then I would run out into the passage, sweating, tottering, my teeth chattering with fear, until, I plucked up courage to creep silently back into the library, restore the volume to its place on the shelf, relock the glass book-case, shut the door of my father's library, and go and hide in the garden or shut myself up in my room or pretend to play on the terrace, but all this as if I were a sleepwalker or an automaton, rigid with terror, taciturn, and all the rest of the day I would savor my fear, and those were the days when my mother found me to be a real goody-goody, too much so, for I was habitually rebellious.

"Go and play," Mother would say, uneasy at this sudden change.

"I've played already, Mamma."

"When was that?" she would ask.

"This morning, Mamma."

"This child is very odd," she would say to my father that evening, "I don't know what to do with him..."

My father went and shut himself up in his library. My mother sat down at the piano. I was taken up to bed. I lay in bed with my eyes open, and, if I shut them, the black idol came and insinuated himself between my eyelids and myself. And he looked at me. I felt a chill run down my spine, and it was still worse when the idol began to breathe from his stomach, just like me, and, in the end, I no longer knew who was imitating whose breathng, nor which one of us, to try and fool the other, was the first to hold his breath and let it out slowly, slowly, till he was ready to burst. I was frozen stiff. I pressed myself against the wall behind my bed. I cried out in my sleep. I woke up with a start. I was naked. The sheets and blankets were on the floor. I was bathed in sweat. I picked up the sheets and blankets and wound them around me. I plunged into sleep. I stretched out like a yard of elastic. I curled up tight, I made myself small, like a little old man. In the morning, they had to search for me in the bed. I had disappeared into its depths. I was no bigger than a dead fly. I often dreamed about flies, flies and tree-trunks, I had nightmares about trees that crushed me. I was burning like a match... But, at the next opportunity, as soon as my father's back was turned, I sneaked into the forbidden library and started my game all over again, the game of frightening myself, the game that was to go on for years and years.

I do not know when I first played this secret game that afflicted me with such malaise and filled my nights with terror, but I remember that I was just a little mite, and that I played it, all alone, for a long, long time. This was in Alexandria. Nobody suspected a thing. Not even my Nanny.

Later, I played in the library with friends of my own age, but only little boys, I never took girls in there. I had warned them what they were in for. I opened the glass bookcase. I pulled down the book that opened by itself, always at the same page: the Negro idol!

We fled, pushing and tumbling over one another. Somebody bumped into Mamma's piano, a grand piano that now stood in Father's library, among all the other furniture that cluttered the room. But, no matter how many times we moved house, and no matter how we managed to arrange the mountains of furniture, fitting it into the most diverse and ever more cramped and reduced apartments and lodgings, in the most diverse countries, where the conditions of our existence became ever meaner and shabbier, the arrangement of my father's library invariably remained the same, and the Reclus was always the foundation of the ever increasing edifice of books.

Later still, I began to read. There was something of everything in my father's library. He had just bought the Complete Works of Balzac. For my tenth birthday, he had given me Gérard de Nerval's *Les Filles du feu.* I was allowed to read in his library now. So, I read. But for a long time, my little school friends and I, whether in Naples, Paris, or London, still preferred the Reclus to all others, and it was always the same volume, *L'Afrique équatoriale,* that tumbled out on to the floor and, as always, opened at the same page: the Negro IDOL.

Now that we were older and knew how to read, we might well tackle the other volumes, just leafing through them, but we always came back to the Negroes of equatorial Africa and to the illustration of the great black idol in Volume IX.

By this time, we were ferocious soccer players and thought ourselves tremendous heroes as we tried out the first bicycles, but still that illustration gave us the shivers. It was enigmatic. It had no name. There was no note, no caption, no commentary or explanation to tell us about its origin or the place where it was actually to be found. The text of the chapter in which it appeared contained nothing but considerations of a general order on the religion, morals, habits, and customs of the blacks. We lost ourselves in wild conjecture. The most courageous among us talked of going to find it when they were grown up. I do not know whether any of these boys ever realized the dream of becoming explorers that haunted us all. From Palestrina to General Leclerc, from Saint Vincent de Paul to Braque, Brancusi or Picasso, many, many a vocation has been inspired by an image, something read, an impression, a childhood memory, although not necessarily by an exotic idol lost in distant lands and illustrated in a quarto collection, for very often just a "penny picture" will do the trick: an exemplary image of devotion or charity, the subject of a military or religious picture, a scene from Roman history, an entertaining book, like Jules Verne's *Around the World in Eighty Days,* a simple anecdote even, and I wonder how many financiers have dreamed they were going to outdo the Rothschilds simply because they picked up a pin at a significant moment—as if pins were deliberately scattered over the earth at the very moment when they were applying for a job in a bank, at Laffitte's or elsewhere—for alas! there are so many of these failures! Speaking for myself, it was not the idol in Vol. IX of Reclus's *Géographie* that stimulated me to travel (in fact, it served rather to paralyze me), but, once I was on my way, it was this image, cubic and millenary in its solitude, that taught me to remain calm, and to mull over the why's and wherefore's of my presence, an inhibition that makes me feel like a stranger, an exile everywhere and, although I did not know it at the time, I have come to understand that I had that same feeling as a child in the bosom of my family.

Like all engravings, this image printed in the Reclus volume was influenced by the tastes of the period. It was not realistic. The idol, set in the center of the page, was framed by banana leaves, palms, and lianas that formed a clearing in the forest. The crouching figure stood out boldly against the trunk of the giant tree, which sprang from a single shoot, like the smooth bole of a Brazilian rosewood, although higher up, its branches were tangled and knotty, stunted and contorted, ramified like the branches of a baobab tree overloaded with monkey-bread, and from each knot, each elbow, each armpit hung plants, parasitic flowers, mosses, and tufts that trailed halfway down the tree. Its aerial roots were like those of a mangrove and through the spaces between them you could see the gaping jaws of crocodiles wallowing in a pool of black water or a swamp. The sky was obscured by foliage, so there were no birds visible, but butterflies fluttered in the air or rested on the corollas of the flowers, and, on the ground, there were lizards and toads. There was also a rattlesnake, coiled up between the square feet of the monstrous fetish, which was tightly caged in by candelabra cactus and nopals. The botanical and zoological fantasy of the engraver did not distract us from the arresting Presence. This romanticized fecundity of tropical nature did not deceive us, nor did it soften our morbid curiosity. The wooden idol had two breasts, and, when you looked at it closely, you could see that it was also equipped with male genitalia, with a prick like the clapper of a bell. One day, a boy whose father was an expert in old pictures brought a magnifying glass with him and the game, the innocent game of my childhood, which I had invented to frighten myself, rapidly degenerated into laughter and tickling. At night, my nightmares, my anguish, became obscene. Then, for a long time, I did not invite anyone into my father's library, nor did I touch Volume IX.

Still later, at Neuchâtel, when I was fourteen, and then fifteen years old—and ran away, escaped out of the window, and traveled all the way to China, having no desire to return to my parents' house, since my father had had the bizarre idea of enrolling me at the famous École de Commerce in that town—I shut myself up in my father's library as often as possible so as to avoid attending the courses at the school (that is, when I was not spending the day on the beautiful Swiss lake, sailing), and reading the twenty-four volumes of the *Géographie universelle,* which I had taken in hand again, this time with the intention of reading them, from the first page to the last, especially Vol. IX, which was by then worn, tattered, and broken-spined and still opened at the same page, although someone—it was certainly not me!—had torn out the famous engraving of the idol, for I had finally discovered a footnote at the bottom of a certain page, which gave the translation of a Negro fairytale, "The Story of the Elephant and the White Rats," which Reclus quoted as a curiosity, and this had been such a revelation to me that I had begun to search in all the secondhand bookshops in our little town, which was full of academics and religious bigots, and to read all the books containing black African legends that I could lay hands on, such as *Popular Tales of the Basutos* and *Songs and Tales of the Rongas,* collected and translated by the Protestant missionaries, Jacottet and Junod, and a book by an explorer, the adventurous, hell-raising Yankee journalist, the famous Stanley, who, on the pretext of going to rescue Livingstone and make a sensational scoop, conquered the Congo on behalf of the Belgians, and who, in the midst of the battles, found time to write *My Dark Companions and Their Strange Stories,* daydreaming tales that his black porters told him in the evenings, when they stopped to make camp around a brushwood fire, and which this man of action, willful, indeed ferocious and formidable when it came to beating a path through the territories of hostile peoples, massacring whole villages on his way, pushing on, forging ahead regardless of the violent protests which his armed intervention in Central Africa provoked in all the chancelleries of old Europe and of the far-reaching consequences of his actions, which could prove fatal to world peace, had had the humanity to listen to and transcribe; and the standard work, *Totemism and Exogamy* by Frazer; and the numerous writings by Father Trilles, who belonged to the community of the Holy Spirit and was responsible for evangelizing and converting the blacks. Being a shrewd and subtle man, he understood that, in self-defense, he must study the cosmogony and the metaphysics of the Africans, so as to be able to combat their animism and their devilries with their own weapons, and the wise Father Trilles finished up translating their legends and magical charts, which he published in Munich, after ten years in the heart of the dark continent, for the man of God had been so impressed by the lofty morals of the pygmies and the Fangs, and by the importance they gave to the word, although both these tribes were fetishists and cannibals! No one has penetrated so deeply into the consciousness of primitive peoples, and into the soul of the Negro, as this religious man.[20]

Since then, my passion for black literature in all its manifestations has never been appeased (and up to this day, I still feel the same secret titillation whenever I see an African figurine or a Negro mask, striking reminders of my childhood idol, the one that terrorized me and took possession of me at night) and, although I am no linguist and have never wanted to specialize, my knowledge of this subject became such that, in 1919, I was able to compile my *Anthologie Nègre*[21] lying flat on my stomach on the parquet floor of a room devoid of furniture, working by the light of a candle, and I wrote the three hundred and fifty well-filled pages of this fat compilation, which was to earn me only four hundred francs, in less than a month. But what a windfall! At night, when I was utterly tired out (during the daytime, I was doing research at the Bibliothèque Nationale), I had only to blow out the candle and wrap my overcoat around me two or three times before falling asleep in a corner, up against the partition wall and as much out of the draughts as possible, that is, when my amputated arm would allow me to sleep, and when it would not, and my missing hand was too painful, I would go and strike a few dissonant chords with my other hand on an upright piano that had been left stranded in this empty room and was all that remained of the former splendor of the old woman who had rented it to me, a widow from the war of 1870! Poor woman, I was only too delighted to be able to pay her one year's rent in advance with those four hundred francs, but... poor Blaise, too! I played these dissonant chords because I wanted to express as truthfully as possible my otherwise inexpressible pain, for there are no words to describe the agony I suffered from my amputated hand. Since then, I have never touched a musical instrument, it makes me ashamed, for the making of music is sacred. But I still feel pain in my stump. And, to avoid bawling day and night, I tell myself Negro tales. And I no longer suffer from nightmares. I have mastered them.

And that is why, at the age of sixty, I find that, like a professional night watchman,[22] I am fifteen years behind with my sleep, five of those years due to the Second World War and the Occupation when, I can truthfully say, I never closed more than one eye at a time, God help me! And to these I must add all the nights I have spent writing, ever since I started working regularly again... hence the overwhelming fatigue that engulfs and penetrates me from the top of my skull to the tips of my toes and all around my heels, and sometimes paralyzes me for an entire night when I am sitting in front of my typewriter, but it seems this is not a bad thing, according to the teaching and practice of the yogis, who say that lack of sleep, fatigue, and immobility enable you to see clearly and closely the dark and troubled things that lie deeply buried in the unconscious.

A funny kind of yogi!... The veil is torn... A starry night... Destiny... Men... My characters... Myself, the man of letters... I no longer understand anything. And I start writing again to recapture lost time, life itself, which is fleeting, men, who dance to the rhythm of the dance of the Gods of Creation and Destruction who are, most often, but one God and one Goddess, Siva and Kali, the sacred lingam and the great yoni, who are but a single body, who make the Beast with Two Backs... It is not possible, it is not I who have written this... these phrases that write themselves... these words that come to me from God knows where... these often incomprehensible words... these verbal windfalls... these marginal images... this unreal, parabolic light that brings everything to life again, the dictionary, the herbarium, the dead, one's own past, and all the beings one has loved or detested and lost sight of long ago, as well as those for whom one has been forever waiting and who will come today, or tomorrow, even if they are already dead, if they have committed suicide or been killed or are languishing in prison or in their mothers' wombs, and whom one admires, and for whom one sketches expressions of friendship, other words, other phrases, a whole network of description that outlines itself and becomes clearly delineated like the safety net spread out to catch the acrobats and the aerobats who fall or who jump from... shall I say, the floodlit vault? No, but from higher up, from the dark pinnacle of the Big Top, a whole crowd of tightrope walkers and trapeze artistes, men, women, and children of every nationality, and even a hilarious clown who glides down and deflates like a pricked bladder each time he touches ground, and then, to the accompaniment of thunderous applause, climbs up again, clumsily, and somehow gets entangled in the strings of the safety net; sick at heart, one acclaims them at the end of the show, this show that is a massacre, a massacre of legendary beings, of Olympians in panties, athletes, gymnasts, bare back riders, male and female trapeze artistes in clinging tights and leotards, sirens of the night, dragonflies, black- or midnight-blue-winged bats, red-gloved spiders, star dancers, the men nostalgic (often they are ex-convicts eaten up with pride), mustachoied, made up like brigands or clean-shaven like Don Juans, the women scintillating with diamanté, gold sequins, silver spangles, embroidered mythological emblems, crowned with aigrettes, artificial feathers, flowers made of glazed taffetta, their faces covered with lace masks or their smiles radiating through layers of melting makeup, the children blowing kisses, beautiful bodies panting, sweating, smelling strongly of horse dung and the lion's den, of the miraculous draught of fishes, but the show is tragically ephemeral, it is interrupted, for they are closing down now, the spectacle is over, the audience is leaving and the damned immortals are changing, taking off their glittering costumes and putting on their dreary everyday clothes in the dark, for the electricity has been switched off, and, outside, it is raining, the circus artistes button up their shabby raincoats and tomorrow they must go through it all again, play the same discouraging game, for the stake in this game is their bread and butter, their miserable livelihood, their need to make ends meet and earn a pittance to feed their families, and they must arouse the indifferent audience from its torpor and, if such a thing is possible, win their affection, and they would do the impossible to achieve this, gambling with death every evening, performing ever more dangerous tricks: Looping the Loop, the Wall of Death, the triple, the quintuple somersault, the Perilous Jump on a bicycle, the Leap of Death without a safety net, for even machines—motorbikes, cars, airplanes—play a part in their unhappy fate, as they do in mine, for strumming on the keys of a typewriter is no way to sanctify life, far from it.

To write... is to go down, like the miner who descends into the bowels of the earth with a lamp, protected by wire mesh, attached to his helmet, a lamp whose dim, uncertain glow distorts everything, whose flame constitutes a perpetual risk of explosion and whose flickering gleam, thick with coal dust, worries and gnaws so cruelly at his eyes that, when he emerges once more from the darkness, the great light of day hurts him, and the blinded man begins to rub his inflamed and bloodshot eyes and to stammer and drool and rave like a lost soul about the ghosts he has seen among the blocks of anthracite, although he will never say a word about the imprint of a woman's hand or a man's fossilized foot embedded in the coal face, traces that are more disconcerting than the footprints in the dazzling guano beach on the shore of Robinson Crusoe's island, unexpected revelations that leave the worker, the manual laborer, more stunned than a concussed man who has just escaped from an explosion caused by firedamp, and he thinks about it over and over again, on Sunday, while he is silently smoking his pipe among the sunflowers in his little patch of garden...[23]

Master of the night! Poor Blaise, you must know that, wherever the Unknown God holds sway, wherever a totem has been set up or an idol crouches on the ground—whether it is the pictographic totem pole of the redskins of Labrador or the *paraderos,* those mountains of detritus, the shell-mounts of Tierra del Fuego, or the pyramids of the Incas and the Egyptians, crumbling beneath their bestiaries, or the Great Fetishes, abandoned in the moonlit clearings of tropical Africa, America, Asia, and the East Indies, or assembled in the deserted halls of the British Museum, or the magical knucklebones whose auguries men read in the Provençal Alps, in the southern tip of California (which is the poorest and most backward place on earth, for the Indians wear dungarees, go to Uncle Sam's school, and drive old Fords, but still live like Stone Age man and have his same, primitive mentality), in the very progressive Basque provinces, in the Hungarian *puszta* with its stolid and unbelievably superstitious peasants, on the steppes of Mongolia where, moreover, as each caravan passes a tumulus, everyone throws a stone on to it, adding to the pile, in the tundra in the extreme north of Siberia, where these maleficent dice are as big as the vertebrae of mammoths, while on the littoral of the Sea of Ice they are whalebones or the molars of the elephant seal and very often cubes of fos-

227

silized ivory, which are decorated, carved, and engraved, each face bearing a design as plain and linear as the ones you see on the rocky walls of the caves of prehistoric man in the Spanish Pyrenees or the micaceous chalk of Périgord Noir, the *cuevas* of Altamira, or the grottoes of Les Eyzies-de-Tayac, in the Dordogne, or on the sides of the white earthenware pots of the high plateau of sub-Himalayan Asia, which date from before the invention of firing and still bear traces of the strings by which they were hung up to dry in the sun and wind, and of the artistic fingers that modeled them millions and millions of years ago, not to mention the subterranean devils of Tibet, the phonolitic statues of Easter Island, the Polynesian masks which hypnotize and bewitch enemies—wherever, in fact, the IMAGE is manifest, man does not sleep at night, for he suffers the anguish of the riddle of identity, of the Me and the Self, the inquietude of atavism, striving to decipher, as one draws augurs from the state of the sky and casts horoscopes according to the position of the planets and the stars at the moment of birth, the marks, the burns, the scars, the tattoos, so as to learn the age and origin of the prototype of the Great Ancestor, not hesitating to mutilate himself out of respect for a Taboo, or to adorn himself with feathers, scales, beak, and tail, to disguise himself as a Beast, to indulge in frenetic dancing and reckless drunkenness, in the belief that, in this way, he can escape from the human condition, from the miserable seed scattered profusely throughout the immensity of the Universe.

Vertigo! Eternity is no more than a split-second in space and the infinite grabs you by the hair and instantly blasts you with lightning. Time does not count. O the useless pain and unutterable suffering of beings in evolution! At each stage of the creative evolutionary process there is a God who is more and more jealous of his creatures. The cruelest is not necessarily the most advanced. In India, among a million others, there is one who does no harm. He is content with digesting. His belly is so full and swollen that it bursts the notches on his belt and, through constantly sniffing and snuffling at his food, his head has become elongated like an elephant's trunk and he uses it to forage in the burned offerings. No one knows whether he is the god of Life or Death. In any case, he no longer has a brain, it has run out through his nostrils. From his slanting eye, cut in the shape of the hole in a prick, drips a froth of hot fat. *I do not think, but I am. I am what is!* It is a nightmarish vision. He is made entirely of flesh, without a bone in his body! I wonder who could have dreamed him up? Alas! Not white worms, but men. You or I. It depends what has appeared to you in Sleep. Sleep, what horror!...

Before the confusion of languages and the dispersal of the races, religion, that *opium of the people* according to the slogan of the modern revolutionary proletariat, was nagualism, a form of individual totemism,[24] a condition in which a man feels himself to be living in close communion with a spirit, a being, or a thing. This may come about following a revelation in a dream, or in an ecstatic state induced by privations, famine, a long enforced fast, or the imbibing of a drug, a fermented drink or the juice of chewed plants, or, on the other hand, in a time of plenty or at the end of a happy hunting season, it may be induced by the excitements of war, massacre, slaughter, riot, or be due to an excess of fresh meat, a feast, sex, or the dance. Phantoms are invoked and men practice the necromancy of the shaman or sorcerer and consult the medicine men or the wizards and their poisons. Each man has his individual spirit: the jungle, the marsh, the prairie, the hinterland, the forest, the panther, the eagle, the antelope, the snake, such-and-such a phase of the moon, a star, water, the pelican, a fish, crustacean, the crocodile, the wolf, a singing flower, a wild herb, a certain stone, tree, bird, flea, or thorn. The totem with which one identifies is the origin of the thing that engenders the being, just as, nowadays, machines are not only the concrete embodiment of the genius of contemporary man but also contain all man's dreams of happiness and his spiritual aspirations for future salvation, and that is why the gas pumps all along the macadamed highways, for example, are so similar to the fetishes of the savage, with the same stylized forms, the same garish colors, the same ornamentation, glass, mirrors, copper, nickel, ampoules, or pearls, the same splashes, whether of blood or used motor oil, the same high polish, the modern electric adver-tisements replacing the sacred tattoos of primitive man, the trademarks of the different petroleum companies or the emblems of the rival trusts replacing the amulets of the initiated sect, the same spiritual need engen-dering the same esthetic to express the same terror, of GOD, God the Father, GOD, and that is why the gas pumps at the roadside and at the exits from the towns, to say nothing of the blast furnaces, factory chimneys, and all the rest of the industrial paraphernalia, the complexes of pipes, tubes, girders, gear wheels, cables, sparks, dense smoke, jets of steam, flashing lights and electrical discharges that make man's activity today such a tragic spectacle, stand in a circle, each wearing an advertisement like an African mask that lights up at night and stupefies the observer.[25] Idols do not laugh very often, but machines, with their clenched teeth, never do. It is terrifying. They are much fiercer and more vengeful than Jehovah, the avenging God of the Jews. Look at our war weaponry, for example; it exter-

minates everything indiscriminately, even to the last, the ultimate generation. It is the last word.

God created Man in His own image. He said: "Thou shalt make no
other God in thine image." But man is afraid, and each has made a God in
his own image and lives under his protective tutelage, and even Jesus, the
Son of Man, said familiarly in his prayers: "Our Father, Which art in heav-
en, hallowed be Thy name"... which leads one to suppose that man has
some influence on the majesty of God. And Jesus added: "Thy kingdom
come, Thy will be done on Earth as it is in Heaven..." which makes one
doubt the omnipotence of God. And he also said: "Lead us not into temp-
tation, but deliver us from Evil..." which is an accusation of complicity.

Now, one must not presume to judge ONE'S FATHER, otherwise all the
complexes and repressions of psychoanalysis, which are the totems, the terrifying idols, the grimacing masks of the Jews, the Anglicans, the
Protestants and the members of modern sects, all of whom are iconoclasts,
will get hold of you and devour you and drive you mad. This is the
vengeance of the Old. In China, one does not judge one's father, the
Ancestor. (*The child is father to the man.—Lao Tse*)

In China, in that ancient country of scholarly mandarins and intellectuals, one constantly comes across totems, erected along the sides of minor
roads in the country as well as on the Imperial highways; they are stylized
steles in the form of a monogram or a letter of the alphabet, a character
from a form of writing so ancient that no one understands it anymore, nor
even attempts to decipher it, the traffic rolls under it, the passerby walks
through it without raising his head, for this ideogram in stone or wood,
silhouetted against the sky, is an archway, an entrance gate. It is a symbol.
These entrances do not lead anywhere, they all debouch on to PEACE, the
Chinese peace, that is, the peace of cemeteries, for the landscape, riddled
with funeral mounds and tombs, which these arches lead to and frame like
absurd windows framing the void, is nothing but a vast, desolate waste-
land, a lake of mud from the twilight of evening to the twilight of dawn, a
slough of floods dating back to the Flood and still continuing, an
unplumbable slough in which you see the reflection of the nocturnal sky
and its constellations, including the Dragon, which holds the full moon in
its jaws, like a lighted lamp on the end of a bamboo pole, like a goldfish
bowl, transparent and shining, with monstrous fish swimming in it, a
goldfish whose tail and fin movements trace calligraphs and whose untir-
ing sucking movements of the lips spit out, not a cloud of ink like an octopus, which has only one orifice that serves as both mouth and anus, but a

universe of infusoria, the largest of which are the minute worms and the larvae of mosquitoes as slender as the feverish symbols of a mnemographic shorthand, undulating, vibrating, trembling, nervous, evanescent, penciled-in, gray, milky tracings that finally coagulate into a fleecy mass in suspension, thick and absorbent as blotting paper, the plankton of an immense and all too vast opium dream.

Nebulous convolutions of wreathing smoke.

The pill sputters over the candle flame.

It is night.

The nauseous Chinese night.

A blue and black gelatinous and wrinkled film.

The leprous face of an old beggar.

Only the coolies sleep outside, not under the beautiful stars, but sheltering under the printed cloth hoods of their rickshaws which, with their shafts sticking up in the air, are making the sign of the horns, a gesture of conjuration.

Chinese ink.

Dilution.

It is snowing.

X
The Dark Chamber of the Imagination

In the station at Tsitsihar or Harbin, at Tchita, Krasnoyarsk, or Irkutsk, while waiting for the train that was often more than a week late, so that we hardly knew whether we were catching the train for that day or the one due a week ago, we could hear the sound of dice being shaken, the rattle of knucklebones, mah-jongg and ouija coming from behind a blanketed sky like the door of a house of assignation, and this was followed at regular intervals by the dry clack of a wooden ruler on the lacquered counter, the sudden tick-tack of a scoreboard for billiards or an abacus as the Russian *chiotka* kept the score, then the clatter of the money changers' scales as they poured the winner's take into the pans: taëls, sapekes, piasters, thalers from the time of Marie-Thérèse, silver dollars and roubles, falling in a shower like rain. The teeming alleys of the Chinese quarter were full of posters and placards with their vertical calligraphy. From somewhere or other we could hear the quacking and squawking of ducks being strangled in a brothel. There was a stink of cooking and carrion and the all-pervading odor of human excrement and lice.

At the station, my boss, Rogovine, and I settled into our compartment on the Trans-Siberian Express. When we were traveling back from Central Asia, we left behind us a sky imprinted with Chinese monograms and, when we were returning from the far north, we left behind us the phantasmagoria of the polar sky, fringed and shaken like a theater curtain by the aurora borealis, a hail of aerolites, the tail of a meteor, the parahelia, the blaze of an eclipse and the plumes of Saint Elmo's fire, which had crackled even on the runners of our sledge when we were in the extreme north, at the mouth of the river Lena or the Yenisey, where we had exchanged a cargo of discs of rock salt against as many discs of pure silver and, on a second occasion, against fossil ivory, narwhal teeth (alleged to be unicorn), and the tusks of mammoth: thirty-six sledges in all. During the frosty, starlit nights of these northern regions, it was so cold that the horse's turds, gripped by the frost, exploded under his tail and went off like bullets before they had even reached the ground. Whenever we took our places on the Trans-Siberian Express, we were on our way to see the big boss, that is, Rogovine's secret boss, a man by the name of Lyouba, the richest jeweler in Saint Petersburg. When we reached our destination, we unpacked our bags, unwrapped our bales, returned the coffers with false bottoms, opened our sample cases overflowing with jewels, undid our body belts stuffed with precious gems, and Rogovine emptied his secret hoard, and reckoned up the profit on our purchases, our barter and exchange; then, delighted as any provincial at finding himself in the big city, Rogovine would take off and go to a good restaurant where he ate a splendid dinner, made the gypsies play all night long, and seduced the women of the capital in the private rooms, after which he would go home to his family in Warsaw and get another child on his wife. Meanwhile, Lyouba took me into the strong room of his stores, situated on the corner of the Street of Peas and the Street of Gardens, *ougol Gorochovaya i Sadovaya,* an old showroom converted into a vast safe containing millions and millions of roubles' worth of precious stones, the most beautiful collection of diamonds and pearls in Czarist Russia, where I was to remain locked in for a week, a fortnight, a whole month, classifying everything we had brought back, sorting the stones, weighing them, selecting them, grading them according to their weight in carats, their caliber, their size, their brilliance and purity, and, in the case of the pearls, their luster, their roundness, their whiteness and perfection, sorting them out, putting aside the *schtropps* destined to be cut in such-and-such a shape according to their impurities, their clarity, their faults, blemishes and flaws, putting them into matching pairs for earrings, grading them in sizes to make up a diamond or pearl necklace, selecting the colored stones to be set in brooches, crosses, buttons, escutcheons, pins, horseshoes, hearts, fans, pendants, buckles, knots, flower sprays, feathers or aigrettes, picking out the teardrops or the stones worthy of adorning a severely classical tiara or a barbaric goblet or a napkin ring or an erotic cigarette case, getting excited over the limpidity of a solitaire as I laid it away in a jewel case, separating out the rareties, such as the pink or black pearls and the superlative stones, a pure blue-white diamond from Golconde or a primrose-yellow carbuncle, a ruby like a pigeon's egg or a faceted emerald as big as my fist, which would be displayed in the showcases in Lyouba's shop windows, packing up, for shipment to Amsterdam or Antwerp, all those stones that needed to be corrected and improved in value by a skillful recutting and an additional delicate polishing, worn pearls that needed to be "skinned," and carefully wrapping up the whole ungraded lot of sapphires, rubies and turquoises in the softest tissue paper, which I folded up like a pharmacist's little sachets, tucking one fold into the next, to be addressed to the clockmakers in Geneva and La Chaux-de-Fonds, and the small granules of rose and white diamonds that would be sold wholesale to the manufacturers of cheap trash to make up the Pforzheim jewelry, and there I sat, busy, meticulous, conscientious, earning a lot of money (at the age of eighteen, I already had a bank account) but utterly unaware that one day these years of apprenticeship... (and all the journeys with my boss, Rogovine, in China, in Persia, in Mongolia, in the far north, in Tiflis, at the fairs in Njini Novgorod and in Manchuria, and my stays in Saint Petersburg with my boss's boss, the great Lyouba, who had confidence in me, but who nevertheless kept me under lock and key until the day when he finally entrusted me with the keys to his treasure house, and our rip-roaring sojourns in London and Paris, where Rogovine and I replenished our supplies of novelties and renewed our classic stock before once again taking the Trans-Siberian Express, stopping off in Berlin, where, on the way out, we deposited our investments with Mendelssohn at that time the only bank in the world that would handle Chinese paper, that is to say, bankers' drafts due to mature in three, six, or nine years' time, the profits on our sales on credit, and, on the way back, our order-book for all the Made-in-Germany rubbish we required, the Pforzheim jewelry and the tinplate, alarm and cuckoo clocks from the Black Forest, Westminster regulators with pendulums, clocks with counterweights from Frankfurt, round wall clocks, Swabian pipes, pipes made of artificial amber or fake tortoise shell, imitation Meerschaums, porcelain pipes, enameled iron pipes, the first phonographs, etc., etc., cargoes that had to wait for the thaw in Siberia or for the floods in China to recede before we could reach our various staging posts, contact our agents along the route of the Trans-Siberian Express or at the caravanserais, and our correspondents in Central Asia, cargoes for which Mendelssohn had opened new, unlimited credit) ...yes, I was totally unaware and would never have dreamed that these years of apprenticeship would serve me as years of apprenticeship in poetry!... and that one day, yes, one day, I would be a bloody poet!... and that then, I would begin to write in earnest!... But that's the way of life, and women will understand me, for women know that a cage, even a gilded or a magic one, and even if one seems to have settled in, made one's nest or one's home in it, is impossible to live in for long, and becomes unbearable once love has knocked at the door, or comes prowling around the house, and the ogre who holds you captive wants to gobble you up or give you his daughter in order to get his hooks even deeper into you. For what purpose, I ask you? It is an old theme of fairy tales and popular songs. (Lyouba wanted to adopt me, Rogovine offered me his only daughter in marriage, even my father wanted to keep me at home. I weighed up the pro's and con's, knowing my own idiosyncrasies, I listened to the voices of "my" demons, I tossed up, heads or tails, for my life, I shook the dice and, one day, I just dumped everything and escaped, in the belief that I was choosing freedom. At the beginning of my life, I consulted my own oracles. Today, God help me, I am a novelist! But that's the way it is.)

Shut up in my dark chamber, I read a great deal, sometimes all night long, and also during the day to distract myself when I was weary of making the stones glitter in the light of my portable lamp and of making the battens and the stage floodlights play over the large oblong table where I was sorting and classifying the stones, pouring the contents of the purple plush-lined trays of our traveling jewel cases out on to a square of green velvet, and where for days and days on end, for weeks, often for over a month, I sat perched on a stool as high as a bar stool and shaking a strange implement made of tinplate, an implement about the size of a large coffee percolator, and, like that kitchen utensil, divided into a series of filters in graduated sizes through whose holes the gems poured and so classified themselves in order of size, falling into the different detachable compartments, the largest remaining at the top, the smallest, which I then put all together into a bag, falling to the bottom. When one of these compartments, numbered from 000 to 21, was full, and when all these bowls or cups were full, I emptied them out, one after the other, on to the velvet square and sorted the stones, lining them up on the big table according to size, type, and color, and when the table, which had a surface of several square meters, was entirely covered with precious gems that sparkled in the electric light, I weighed the stones one by one in a diamond merchant's scales, which I took out of my professional kit, at the same time extracting the decigram weights, which were flakes of brass no thicker than a section cut through a catechu seed and had one corner folded down and stamped "2 dg" by the Department of Weights and Measures, with a pair of Brussels forceps, which I handled dexterously, loading the little weights into fragile cups made of calcined bone, and when all the stones had been weighed, one after the other, and arranged according to weight on other trays marked with notches, each of which represented one carat, I picked them all up again, one by one, between the tips of my forceps, with a jeweler's glass screwed into my eye (I used my right eye, others use the left) and played all sorts of tricks with the lighting, direct and indirect, turning the stones in every direction, inspecting every facet closely to detect any flaws, taking out my jeweler's glass to peer closely, then standing back to judge their clarity, their purity, and the general effect they made with the naked eye, turning them around and around again under a blinding bulb to study their transparency, their inner fire, the play of light and shadow on their facets, their iridescence and sparkle, so as to estimate their value before shutting them up in labeled jewel cases, which I then laid away in coffers.

Time passed. Days, weeks, a whole month. It was interminable. I was a prisoner. I read a lot, to amuse myself, and when I was tired of handling and rehandling my stones and of beginning all over again the operations for checking and re-calibrating and re-evaluating my classifications and estimates, I read the Classics in an English edition, but, also to amuse myself, I would sometimes unroll a map of the sky, lay it out on the big table and cover each of the constellations with the precious gems I was about to stow away in the coffers, marking the largest stars with the most beautiful diamonds, outlining the configurations with the most vivid stones, filling the gaps between the designs with a rivulet of the most beautiful pearls from Lyouba's collection, switching on the whole available battery of lamps, the stagelights, the electrolier, the inspection lamps, my pocket flashlight, and focusing and pivoting the portable reflector like a firehose, or rather, a garden hose, for, as I aimed it at each stone in turn, inundating it with harsh light, so that particular stone would dominate, as each plant blossoms successively in the cycle of the seasons, or as each girl appears in her turn during a round dance, advances, presents herself, is momentarily isolated, becomes the star, sings her piece, and returns to the dance, hiding herself and mingling with her companions:

...kiss the most beautiful of all!...

They were all beautiful! And I recited to myself Marbode's* immortal, and to me unforgettable, page on the symbolism of precious stones, which I

---

*The Abbé Jacques = Paul Marbode (1800–75), French scholar who wrote works on theology. (Trans.)

had just come across in Remy de Gourmont's gem-studded book, *Le Latin mystique,* a compilation, a translation, an anthology that turned my whole consciousness upside down and baptized me, or, at the very least, converted me to Poetry, catechized me and initiated me into the Word.

When the day finally came, the day on which the extraordinary and distrustful Lyouba (who appears in this chapter only as a shadowy figure, but who will be the central character in a later story, and whose full-length portrait I intend to draw, just as, presently, I am going to draw the living portrait of Dr. Oswaldo Padroso, the hero of the romance of the Morro Azul) handed me the keys to his treasure house, the first thing I did was go out and buy the aforementioned *Le Latin mystique* (I also stuffed Dostoevsky's *The Idiot* into my pocket, at the instigation of the very charming salesgirl); the second thing I did was go to the Imperial Library to examine a collection of tales written in the old Slavonic tongue about the town of Pskov and the conquests of Antar, a Russian cycle that is the Oriental equivalent of the romances of the Round Table (it is commonly forgotten that Russia is an Oriental country); on my third outing, I went to the Maryinsky Opera one evening with... (they were giving Mozart's *Magic Flute* and, ever since then, the big aria, *"Ich bin die Koenigen der Nacht!"* sings pathetically in my memory whenever I feel particularly happy; this must have been before 1907, for Lenotchka, my sweet schoolgirl, was hanged in Viborg that year, the same year in which I quarreled with my boss, Rogovine[26]). It was the girl in the bookshop who introduced me to my sweet and enthusiastic little revolutionary schoolgirl, in whose memory, and in memory of my first reading of *Le Latin mystique,* which I always associate with her in my thoughts, I buy a volume of Migne's *Patrologie latine* every year—the Latins and Greeks are too learned for me!—and also reread *The Idiot,* so as not to forget the beautiful Russian language, which I still speak very brokenly, and it was an old man, the librarian R. R., who was so fondly attached to me that he went to the trouble of supervising the reading of a frivolous jeweler's apprentice and urging him to write, and I had the audacity to show my first manuscript to this erudite linguist, and he was patient enough to translate it, without my knowledge, and generous enough to have it published at his own expense, sinking his last savings into this project before his death in order to give me a wonderful surprise and encourage me. It was *The Legend of Njini Novgorod: A Prose Work Translated into Russian by R. R.* (fourteen copies printed in white ink on black paper in a folio edition of 144 pages presented in a folder, typography by Sozonoff, Moscow, 1909), the story of the fair of Njini-Novgorod, a kind of humorous heroic epic, written in reminiscence of my readings from the medieval verse chronicles of the conquering Slavs. Today, I do not possess a single copy of this publication, nor do I even have a copy of my manuscript, for I have scattered my books to the four winds, in every corner of the earth, and the last lot I managed to gather together disappeared, along with all my other papers, when my country house at Tremblay-sur-Mauldre (Seine-et-Oise) was looted in June 1940, and after three wars in Russia and the Revolution in Moscow, this work is not to be found anywhere today. (All these characters and my adventures and encounters in Saint Petersburg, with Dostoyevsky's *The Idiot,* with Chekhov's circle, with the opium addict, Alexander Blok, as well as my temporary but active participation in the Revolution, out of love for Lenotchka, and in the founding of the first soccer club in the capital, and the introduction and advertising of this sport in Russia, will figure in my book about Lyouba and provide the atmosphere surrounding the central character. Here, I wanted to speak only of the virtue of precious stones.)

The Revolution. Time passed. One could have heard a fly buzzing in my shuttered room when I gave myself up to my passionate game with the precious stones, but, as time passed (I had already been traveling and trading with Rogovine for three years, and from time to time, between two long trips, I would come to stay in Saint Petersburg for a while), I heard rifle shots, machine-gun fire, and bombs exploding more and more often, accompanied by the dull roar of crowds tramping, gathering together or scattering and beginning to run from the *nagaikas,* and the raucous cries of the Cossacks as they urged on their wild little horses penetrated right through the closed iron shutters of my strong room to reach me, and the day came when I said to myself, each time I heard one of these demonstrations, that perhaps it was "the most beautiful of all" who was brandishing the red flag among the crowds marching in procession and singing the socialist-revolutionary songs just outside my barred windows.

These were troubled times. Some time ago now, Rogovine had given me a nickel Browning, which I counted as part of my professional equipment as a budding jeweler, and when Lyouba finally entrusted me with the keys, it was neither a spontaneous nor an entirely disinterested gesture. When he handed me his bunch of keys, he also gave me a large-caliber revolver, for this odd little body was frightened to death, not for his own skin, of course, but for the eventual fate of his jewels. Such a precious collection! He was literally sick with fear, and he had already installed a whole system of alarm bells at the doors and windows of his shop and store rooms, which he alone knew how to operate, and, more particularly, a secret network of electric contacts which all led into the strong room where I was imprisoned. On the day he handed me the keys, he also let me into the secret of the system, and it was by no means child's play if I wanted to go in or out at night: There were twenty-eight electric circuits that I had to break and reconnect successively, in front of and behind me, in the darkness and in strict order so as not to set off the alarm throughout the whole house, downstairs in the porter's lodge, in the courtyard, in the night watchman's hut, and outside, at the corner of the street, where there were always *gardavoies* on duty and, further off, in the local Police Headquarters, and, as the big boss had trained as an engineer at the École Centrale and had begun his career on the railways before making his fortune as a jeweler, he knew his business and had complicated the whole thing to his heart's content, laying the wires with his own hands, hiding the contacts in the most unbelievable nooks and crannies and under the most heteroclite objects; a chain of red and blue pilot or warning lamps, which flashed on for a second, served you as guidelines through the circuit, their dazzling bulbs suddenly lit up to blind and startle you, making you drop things and lose your wits, and then went out just as abruptly, plunging you once more into utter darkness, standing completely disoriented between one door and the next. Now that "expropriations" were becoming common everyday affairs, Lyouba had made me stow away his collection, and his rarest gems in the vaults of the Crédit Lyonnais, on the Nevsky Prospect, for he believed that, being a foreign bank, it was much safer.

"If there's a revolution in Russia, they won't touch that French bank. The Russian people owe it millions. Besides, the revolutionaries sing the *Marseillaise*. That's a guarantee. They wouldn't dare."

I do not know how the big boss envisaged the Revolution. But, as he gave me his big revolver, he charged me to go to the bank every morning from now on, fetch the jewel cases we might need that day, and take them back and redeposit them every evening. So I always went out armed, and Lyouba made me laugh, for I had tried, in vain, to point out to him that the socialist-revolutionaries were not criminals, they were only after the State Treasury, they had never yet attacked a jeweler's shop, and I explained that the aims of the Revolution were quite different, and much more far-reaching and that, in any case, the destiny of the capitalists and their property, including the banks, was preordained and that the Crédit Lyonnais did not offer any guarantee of security, not one ounce of extra safety, but that the revolutionaries might call on him, Lyouba, because of his professional competence and expertise, to make an inventory, should the need arise, of the treasures belonging to the Crown, and that he would then be peculiarly qualified to serve the Revolution as a specialist, a technician, an expert, but he treated me as a gullible simpleton and would not listen to reason, he did not want to go abroad on account of his clients, the Grand Dukes and three or four other madmen among his friends, Nicolas Linden, Eliseyeff, Chlokovsky, who, like him, had a passion for gems and fine jewelery, and I pitied the old man who was sweating blood every night as he cudgeled his brains, trying to think of some camouflage for the jewel cases I had to carry (as for me, I simply wrapped them up in old newspapers and tied the parcels with string) and who accompanied me as far as the door that gave on to the street, always asking me if I was sure I had my revolver on me and whether it was loaded, bombarding me with recommendations and appeals to take care right up until the moment when I settled myself, clutching all my badly tied packages, into the wretched fiacre or sled that then set off at a gallop in the thawing snow, throwing up a shower of mud and slush.

Gee up, horsey! Use your whip, driver! To the bank! I was carrying millions of roubles' worth. *"Birguiz!"* shouted the *izvoschik,* urging on his horse. I was happy to be out of doors. I breathed in deeply. Coming out of the Crédit Lyonnais, I wandered along the Nevsky Prospect. The very idea of having to manipulate all those damned contacts and the blasted alarm bells, which a moment's distraction, or forgetfulness, or a single false step could set off, discouraged me and I no longer felt like going back to the shop. In summer, the white nights of Saint Petersburg are long and people go to the Islands to have a good time; in winter, night life is in full swing at the skating rinks, in the cafes, at Philippoff's in the night clubs where people go to dance, in the cabarets, the gambling dens, at The Bear and at Palkine's. The concerts, the theaters, the first cinemas. I hesitated. I dawdled. I went and had a drink. I stayed out late. I went to the Library to talk to R.R., who was on duty until midnight. Often, I escorted my friend to his home over by the Liteinie Prospect and went up to his apartment stuffed with books and ancient icons, and it was marvelous—we drank tea, we smoked, we chatted all night long. R. R. made me talk, smiled up his sleeve, gazed at me intently. I made him laugh. I made him uneasy. On these lucky nights, I did not go back. That poor man, my boss, pined away in sheer terror, I swear it! Life was becoming impossible... And one day, for a joke, I played a dirty trick on him which brought on an attack of jaundice from which he almost died. I had never meant to do that to him.

What I wanted, more than anything else, was to get kicked out. Everything was going wrong. My sweet schoolgirl had been condemned to death...

The year before, I had already dared to play a similar trick. I was coming back from a trip to London and Paris, crossing Switzerland without stopping, and this happened on that straight bit of railroad track, after Lausanne, where the Simplon Express tries to put on some semblance of speed along the borders of Lake Léman. I was standing in the corridor, in front of an enamel plaque listing the regulations and instructions for using the Alarm Signal, and I had got as far as the article stipulating a fine of one hundred francs for improper use of the safety brakes, when my hand, of its own volition, took hold of the red-painted handle and pulled it down hard. I was curious to see what would happen. I had the one hundred francs ready, I was holding the banknote in my hand. I had imagined there might be a catastrophe but, even without one, I swear I got my money's worth! In fact, the train stopped violently after skidding on all its wheels for some hundred meters or so, emitting steam that whistled and poured out all over the place. There was a brutal jolt and then a rush of passengers all wanting to find out what had happened. Doors banged. People ran along the ballast. Questioning each other. The passengers from my carriage came nervously out of their compartments, rubbing their foreheads where their own cases had landed on their heads, peering up and down the corridor, asking each other questions, whispering, staring at me, and I guessed that they were all convinced I was the perpetrator of this prank, this practical joke, and knew I had done it just for fun. And suddenly the conductor erupted into the carriage and fell upon me, shoved from behind by a bunch of irate passengers who were crowding down the corridor shouting: "It was him! It was him! Somebody saw him!" The conductor, with his splendid red satchel on his belly and a pen and notebook in his hand, all ready to take down his report, was red in the face, the sweat was pouring from under his tall silver-braided cap and his eyes were out on stalks. He was overcome with emotion as he barked at me breathlessly:

"Was it you, young man? Did you do that?... Why, what's the matter with you? Are you crazy?"

The others would have given me a rough handling if the conductor had not been so bulky that he blocked the entire corridor, for I was laughing so hard I could not speak. I pointed to the regulations with my finger. I held out my one hundred francs. I flopped back into my seat. I was helpless with laughter. Splitting my sides. The tears were streaming down my face.

The conductor knew perfectly well it was his duty to do something, but he could not understand how I could just pay the fine without a word of explanation, he resented it as an affront to his dignity, and the passengers, who were trying to outdo each other, calling me all sorts of names, amused me beyond words—all these good bourgeois citizens, indignant, outraged, grimacing, glaring at me, furious at the thought that I had made fun of them. They looked like figures in a painting by Breughel the Elder. They were beside themselves. Each one felt personally offended, and the women were the most outraged of all. What joy, not to belong to that lot anymore! A brakesman had gone to tell the engine driver what was happening and the train had begun to move cautiously. The conductor put away the money. I had the cheek to ask him for a receipt, just to cock a snook at him. From Domodossola on, there was a constant procession of passengers coming down the corridor to take a look at "the madman," the perpetrator of such a stupid trick, and their comments were anything but flattering. I am convinced that, next morning, the good Swiss newspapers must have been full of the incident, and they would have castigated unmercifully the parents who had produced such a guttersnipe, such a delinquent brat... and... and... But I did not have a chance to read these papers. By the following evening, I was already in Abbazia, where I was to rejoin Rogovine, who occasionally indulged in holidays on the Dalmatian Riviera—what the boss called "taking a high-life cure." He had told me to meet him there before setting off again for God knew where.

So, one night—it was after two o'clock in the morning—when I came back to Gorochovaya Street, I purposely made a wrong move and stood quietly waiting in the stairwell. What an uproar ensued! But the Russians are understanding people. The *dvornik,* the night watchman, the porter, the cops from the corner of the street, who immediately came running with revolvers in their fists, proved themselves to be more human than my fellow travelers in Switzerland. They took it as a good joke, the gesture of a boozy young traveling salesman who, coming home late and walking on tiptoe so as not to make a noise, is so clumsy that he wakes up the whole house. The alarms were still ringing when the local Commissioner of Police climbed up to the third floor to rouse the big boss from his bed and plead my cause. I must admit I had handed out a good many tips and slipped a fat banknote into the hands of this police officer, a thing that is simply "not done" in Switzerland. Only Lyouba took the matter seriously and, as a result, was struck down by an attack of jaundice that nailed him to his bed for forty days. By the time he recovered, Rogovine and I had already departed on a little trip that was to take us to Tashkent, the city of silk and chebules and myrobalans, which are plums, melons, and other edible cucurbitaceae but taste of the chemist's shop, of iodine and camphor. On our return, nothing more was said about my escapade and there were no repercussions. In any case, it was over. One more journey to Persia, and then I was to part company with Rogovine.[27]

Everything was going wrong. I was reading an English edition of the Classics. This was during what proved to be my last stay in Saint Petersburg. I was shut up in the armor-plated room. I did not go out. At the beginning of the week, they had declared a General Strike. The electricity had been cut off. Nobody knew what was going on. The newspapers were no longer being printed. I was bored. Not a sound filtered in through the iron shutters. The city seemed to be dead. Not a carriage on the streets. From time to time, a whistle made me prick up my ears, it was an interruption to the day and, during the night, I would hear the galloping hooves of a patrol, a solitary shot, loud arguments just outside my windows, a cry of terror. Yet another poor wretch who had been caught, who would be taken to the hospital or to the police station, or who was being beaten up at the corner of the Sadovaya.

On the eve of these events, the big boss, seized with panic and no longer knowing which saint to pray to, had made me reorganize the jewel cases deposited at the Crédit Lyonnais and bring many of them back with me. And so, that day, to amuse myself, I went and opened the overflowing coffers. Never before had I had such an abundance of precious stones available for laying out the pattern of the sky in mosaic.

It was on that day, and precisely because of the fact that the current had been cut off, that I had a revelation of the virtue of stones, which Marbode has written about, and of their gentle and distant scintillation, like lost stars shining in the skies, in the immensity, the profundity, the void of the Universe; it was because everything was lit by candlelight, as if at the court of the Czar, and in this light, so soft, so warm, intimate, and discreet, as carnal as the emanations and the familiar odor of a human skin, the neck, the bare shoulders, the voluptuous nape of the neck, the disturbing décolleté of a beautiful woman, the perfume of her hair, gems are no longer ostentatious, the glitter of the stones is no longer diabolic vanity and satanic pride, for the jewels shine with a secret, intimate brilliance, and the cut stones do not blind you, they palpitate, they are alive, moist and tender, swooning with emotion and they seem to awake as if drawn out of a long, enchanted sleep and to celebrate the splendor of creation, like saints who, motionless in prayer, are unaware that they are surrounded by a nimbus of light, that they emit luminous rays and that their red and shining faces, which betray the concentration of their spirit, are a reflection of the Splendor they are contemplating in all humility in the Beyond; passive action, frozen fire, living death, an intermittent message from the sun whose light reaches us after such a long delay, and from such a prodigious distance that the cold beam that touches us, and comes from such a far-off, petrified past, is an annunciation, a promise, the future, a contingent future which may or may not be.

One issue of a sumptuous art magazine, *Wroubel* or *La Toison d'Or,* I forget which, had fallen into my hands and in it there were colored reproductions of Fouquet's miniatures, which are housed in the Musée Condé in Chantilly, and, for some time now, I had been taking the illuminated pages from the Book of Hours of Estienne Chevalier, Treasurer of France under Charles VII and Louis XI, as models, not for my designs, for I have never been able to draw, and the drawing of Fouquet, who was a great portraitist, is too realistic and much too subtle and delicate to be imitated in mosaic, but for the application of colors, their distribution and balance: red, yellow, green, blue, and the whites that are used with such sensitivity in Jean Fouquet's work and are almost impossible to copy, but the fact that I was using precious stones in my schematic counterfeits of his celebrated illuminations enabled me to equal him in brilliance and contrast and even to outdo him spiritually in my large-scale mosaics, which took up the whole of my worktable, for the pearls, rubies, sapphires, emeralds, topazes, amethysts, beryls, and diamonds sang in simultaneous opposition, like the different voices in a choir, and I filled in the parts of the design that, in Fouquet's illuminations, were in shadow, the areas that were opaque, the duller colors and the guilloches in their gilded, Renaissance-style frames, by pouring out jasper, chrysoprase, aquamarines, marcasite, coral, porphyry, and moonstones, set in lapis lazuli or garnets cut *en cabochon*. That day, I used my gems to copy the most extraordinary, and the most grandiose, of Fouquet's compositions and I lit all the candles. It was his masterpiece: *The Trinity in Its Glory,* the apotheosis of GOD, which, to this day, remains the most marvelous of all the galaxies, a repatriation.[28]

I was lost in contemplation. The candles were slowly burning down, the stones were sparkling, lost and remote like the vibrations of joyfully pealing bells heard through the walls of one's prison cell on a day when they are celebrating a *Te Deum.* I was lost in the unreal, and never have I been so happy, nor so exhausted, as on that day, not even, forty years later, on the day of the Liberation of France, that famous Sunday in September 1944, when I sat in my kitchen-without-a-fire in Aix-en-Provence, where, crushed by the weight of the world, I had been voluntarily confined for four years, listening to the radio and to the *Te Deum* they were celebrating in the Cathedral of Notre Dame, and to the bells of Paris, drunk with freedom...

When I am living through moments of such exaltation, I often imagine the following scene: I put a revolver into my mouth and commit suicide.

That day, with the candles burning right down to the end, the stones dying in the guttering light, and darkness invading the strong room, I could see myself quite clearly, stretching out right along the work table, putting the big boss's Colt into my mouth, shooting in the dark...

All my life I have been haunted by the idea of suicide, and more particularly in moments of joy, of happiness or exaltation rather than in moments of depression or weariness. It is the manifestation of a superabundance of life. I am not afraid to die, I am ready. The idea of death is very familiar to me. Perhaps I acquired a taste for it very early, in my tenderest infancy, as I sucked the black breast of my nurse, who was an Egyptian, a poor, courageous *fellah*, fatalistic and superstitious, as this ancient race in the Land of the Dead has always been, ever since the time of the great Pharaohs, who, immured in their hypogea in the form of pyramids, are still dreaming of their destiny today, and who took their revenge on Lord Carnarvon, who came to disturb them. Perhaps this haunting, which is by no means an obssession, is also atavistic, for my father made a failed attempt at suicide by throwing himself off a bridge at the age of eighty-five, not out of despair but, as he wrote to me, announcing his fateful decision: "Because I am beginning to get a little hard of hearing in my right ear. Nature is badly arranged, dear boy. Man should die like a thousand-year-old oak tree in the forest, in a single crash, crumbling to dust."

That day, I had a choice between the nickel Browning Rogovine had given me and Lyouba's big Colt, and it was the long black gun I inserted into my mouth because it was of higher caliber. More certain. I had often rehearsed this gesture in front of a mirror. I did not want to botch it and blind myself.

Today, I am looking at a page torn out of a little notebook. I wonder why this scrap of writing, rediscovered by chance among my papers, has managed to survive so many upheavals, not to say setbacks and disasters—journey, changes of address, flights, the loss of papers and books, the

245

seizure of all my goods, affluence and poverty, wars, revolutions, and other adventures and misadventures in my career as a journalist, which have been among the most vivid in my eventful life. I remember the notebook this page was torn out of. It was a little notebook with gilt edges, bound in Russia leather. I used it to take notes on my reading, and I also transcribed chemical formulae for the manufacture of bombs into it. Many of the pages had been yellowed and corroded by the acids that splashed out of test tubes. It had been lost at the time when they searched my villa in Terrioki (Finland),[29] that Sunday morning when they came to arrest Lenotchka. I do not remember when or why I tore out that page. Here it is, without further comment. It is all that I have left of a grim epoch:

> *Hostem cum fugeret, se Faunius ipse peremit.*
> *Hic, rogo, non furor est, ne memoriare, mori?*
> > M. Val. Martialis Epigrammata
> > Lib II, Epig. LXXX.
> > (Clarendon Press)

> *Himself he slew, when he the foe would fly,*
> *What madness this, for fear of death to die!*
> > (G. Belland Sons, 1877)

> *To escape death Phaunius killed himself,*
> *Tell me, what madness is that to have no thought or memory of death?*

XI

REALITY

The "coal-sack" in the sky is aiming at me like the close up of a revolver on the cover of an American detective story.

My eye can reach into the depths of its soul and, from the internal void of this mouth of burnished fire, it can retrace, in the opposite direction, the trajectory of the eye that is aiming at me point blank, a hard eye, a fixed eye, a steely eye, an eye that surely does not see me and in which my own is reflected: blue on blue, shading into black.

I tear myself away from this hypnotic star and turn my back on the gun.

I come back to consciousness abruptly, as if someone has dropped a bunch of keys down my back.

I jump and the shot goes off.

But was I really "absent"?

All this has happened in a quarter of a second, in the winking of an eye.

I was standing up before the shot was fired.

Besides, it was not a shot in the true sense of the word. But there *was* the sound of an explosion behind me, down there in the valley, and, as if awakened from a nap and with my head still dazed from dreams and visions, I have suddenly come back to myself to see, at my feet but in the air, flares, vermilion palms, serpents, garlands, gold and platinum lightning, all spurting and sizzling, emptying themselves, emitting their thunder and falling again into the depths of the valley, the small fragments pattering down and some larger, unbearably bright splinters trailing multi-colored smoke, coiling, uncoiling, undulating, wavering, tangling, and knotting, before sowing themselves like poisonous seeds on the marshy banks of the Tiété, in whose waters they are reflected for an instant before they disappear. It is not a vision, these fiery stars literally slough their skins, copulate, tie themselves in knots.

It is exactly midnight. The cinema is turning out. The traditional fireworks. Bombs. Suns. Catherine wheels. Squibs. The crowning set piece. The show is over. I hear the brassy notes of a fanfare. I guess there is a procession in the streets of Glaréola. And suddenly the electricity is cut off. A regimen of economy for these early days. It is one minute past midnight. The fête is over. The fairy Electricity has flown away. The valley is plunged back into the darkness of its natural savagery, made up of the miasmas from the Tiété, the backs of the mountains, which suddenly seem very close, and the foliage of the forest, which now stands out opaquely in the foreground.

The moon is no longer visible. In the blue immensity, the stars are also reptiles which slough off the old and put on a new skin, and are there not gems in the head of the Serpent, gems that are the source of this sidereal glimmer?

I get back into the car. I start the engine. I set off again, slowly, in search of the *fazenda* of the Morro Azul.

The heat is pitiless and the road I am heading along haphazardly is all potholes.

My whining engine and I are but a single body.

I am bumping down a slippery track bordered by tree stumps and cut by ravines. I climb up, run down again, climb up again, zigzag, undulate, weave in and out. The high plateau is deserted, rutted and riddled with bifurcations like rents in the surface of the darkness. I skid on the loose stones. I sink into craters full of soft soil. I hit a bump and fly over it, or founder in a deep, eroded trench as the crust of dried mud covering it collapses. One or other of the wheels spins in a hole filled with sedimentary dust.

With all these acrobatics, the engine is overheating.

Nothing stirs, nothing is alive in this solitude, and when I stop to get my bearings, there is not a whisper, not a breath, not even the bewildered cry of a nocturnal bird or the whirring of an insect, no trace of any creature crawling along the road, no armadillo trotting along, no frog hopping at the side of the road, not a moth, apart from the billions of silent fireflies that flutter around me and fall helplessly into my headlights, fall like the petals of a blossoming almond tree in a breeze, but here there is no spring breeze, no almond tree, only hostile cactus, mimosa, stinging weeds, a hot reflected breath, and the fireflies, who extinguish themselves in droves against my head lights, fall like the spent heads of matches, sizzle, drip, and sweat a kind of greasy jam that caulks up the honeycomb-patterned grille of my radiator, and has a taste and gives off an indefinable smell of rat poison, lead acetate, phosphorus, and garlic (I had to devote the whole of the next day to cleaning out these little crystals of cyanide and the shreds of wings with a nail file, a long hairpin, a toothbrush, a bottle of Scrubb's ammonia and emery paper, and I had to polish my radiator with a chamois leather and a special product called "Mirror").

I light a cigarette. Have a shit under a fig tree. I think about the snakes. When I start the car again, the landscape is so ravaged that I get the feeling I am a parasite lost on the body of someone afflicted with pellagra. Rough, sloping tracks, sunken dirt roads, landslides, paths running down from scree-covered banks debouch in all directions, forest trails end in the newly made clearings and the roughly staked-out land claims. I am lost. There is a stench of bull, getting stronger and stronger.

I keep forging on.

Now the stars have moved up a notch. The coal-sack in the sky has emptied itself. It is nothing more than a skin turned inside out, crumpled, sloughed off. The chthonian Being has grown a new skin and, splitting itself, has disappeared, sunk back into the firmament. The lair of the Devourer of the World is empty. On Earth, it is the time of Renewal, the time of a popular meteorological and agricultural god. The *caboclos* are waiting for him: the sorcerer, the medicine man, the soothsayer, the conjurer, the salesman who goes on his rounds every year peddling his illustrated almanacs in the settlements in the interior, and his remedies against the sickness of love; the storyteller, the joker, the matchmaker, the caster of spells, the bone setter, the astrologer, the vagabond of the woods, the demon of solitude, the murderer, the Old Man, or the *sùrùcùrî,* the great bloated boa.

I hear them winding up the spring of the Universe...

With just a few turns of the wheel one can find oneself far from everything one has ever known and loved!

It is a rout.

Kilometer after kilometer, I am driving along between barbed-wire fences behind which the plantations look like the encamped armies of Babylon. And suddenly, at a turning, on a sharp corner, I enter the valley of the *fazenda* of the Blue Mountain.

The Morro Azul!

I was to have spent just one night there, but I stayed more than a month. After that, I did not penetrate any further into the interior, I turned around, barely two hundred and twenty-five kilometers from São Paulo and went back. That year, the revolution broke out, General Isidoro's positivist revolution.[30] It was only in the following year, and the year after that and another and yet another year, much later, that I pushed on into the interior. Between each trip, I went back to Paris to write, to work, to set up some kind of business venture and make some money, and to prepare the next expedition. My stay at Dr. Oswaldo Padroso's place, like my stay with Lyouba in Saint Petersburg, was an apprenticeship, the apprenticeship for my calling as a novelist, for it was on my return from that first trip in the province of São Paulo that Grasset published *L'Or,* a book I had been thinking about for more than ten years, a manuscript I worked at only intermittently, and which I very nearly abandoned, a marvelous story which I suddenly began to prune and pluck with the aim of making it into a true story, a narrative that I rewrote entirely in the present tense, choosing from among the five modes of the verb the one that expresses the state, the existence, or the action in a definite, positive, and absolute manner, and this struck some of the very few writers among my friends as a novelty, but displeased the great majority of men of letters and literary critics who took note of this little volume, in which its publisher had no faith, and which has nevertheless made the tour of the world (for, today, I know of two dozen editions in at least a dozen languages) and which appeals to all classes of society, for, since its appearance in 1927, this novel has been published in serial form in *l'Humanité,*[31] it has been printed in Braille for the blind in America, and it has been used as a set book for French reading in the schools in Holland. (Jacques Bainville, in *L'Action française,* said that its author was "a Rimbaud out of the school of La Fontaine.") It was a linear form of writing in direct contradiction to the polymeric or polymorphous style, but apparently its appeal was universal and I am going to use it again now to draw the portrait of a somnambulist.

XII

THE SOMNAMBULIST

Senhor Oswaldo Padroso was a human being full of sweetness and man-suetude, he was kindly and shy—and panic-stricken at the flood of his own words when, like many solitaries who rarely get the chance, he suddenly began to talk at random and could no longer master this garrulousness that overcame him; he did not stop talking until he was exhausted, and then, gurgling a few more syllables and smiling into space, he rested his beauti-ful deep-set eyes on me like a man who is not too sure what he has said, having let himself be carried away by his own momentum.

He was a quaint little body, a dumpy, faded little man with soft hands that habitually held a long reed pipe between swollen fingers, his legs were flabby or, at any rate, his trousers were puckered into concertina folds, he wore black at all times, with brightly colored silk socks and patent leather dancing pumps on his feet, cuffs at his wrists, a kind of narrow jabot hem-stitched with gold trembling on his starched shirt front, a black shoelace by way of a tie and a high, stiff collar that sawed at his closely shaven jaw and cheeks. During the day, he wore a flowing dressing gown and, in the evening, a suit, with an enameled decoration in his buttonhole (an emblem of his fidelity to the positivism of Auguste Comte, his adherence to a humanitarian religion, his membership in a lay church!). His sparse hair was brilliantined, his mustaches thin and drooping. This was not at all how I had imagined a *fazendeiro!*

However, Dr. Oswaldo Padroso did not concern himself overmuch with the *fazenda* of the Morro Azul, he had let it go to rack and ruin, the bushes, the hundred-year-old Bourbon palms were being suffocated by a climbing weed, but the plantation was full of birds that took refuge there because firing a rifle was forbidden, and Dr. Oswaldo must have imposed this ban on principle, and for sentimental reasons, for a single rifleshot was enough to stir him out of the idleness that he seemed to enjoy, shut up in his study, rocking to and fro all day long in his rocking chair, smoking behind his venetian blinds, and he would go out on to the verandah, shade his eyes with his hand, inspect the horizon, call for Chavin, his overseer, his facto-tum, a *mamaluco,* half white and half Indian, who was always close at hand and whom he sent galloping like the wind on the one and only horse the estate boasted to seek out the guilty man from among the hundred or so old, broken-down blacks who lived, or rather vegetated, on this domain of ten thousand hectares, at the last gasp, like the plantation itself, exhausted, having served their time but finding themselves comfortably housed and protected from want under the indolent administration of Dr. Oswaldo, who let things drift along in their own sweet way, kept himself to himself, and had no other ambition than to be left in peace, fearing nothing so much as visitors, upheavals, and business affairs, and quite content with a small crop of coffee, which was, however, of a quality unique in the world, highly sought after in Santos, worth its weight in gold and always bespoke in advance, and this assured him an income that was more than adequate, given his way of life, his horror of novelty and change.

Nevertheless, if I understood correctly, as far as the Glaréola region was concerned. Dr. Oswaldo Padroso was the legal representative of the bank that, Caïo had assured me, held almost all the mortgages of the ruined planters in the municipality, but this consultancy must have been a sinecure, if my guess is right, for the doctor rarely went out, and then only to go and telephone to the city, and, on these occasions, with his long reed pipe in his hand, a Panama hat on his head, which was screwed down into his high celluloid collar, and wearing a black morning coat, he would go and sit himself in an old-fashioned Renault coupé, which stood high on its wheels and was upholstered in angel's skin, like a courtesan's car, and so highly polished and gleaming that the great tropical landscape was anachro-nistically reflected in the bodywork as it passed, first, the imperial palms planted in front of the house, then the banana groves, and then the rows of coffee shrubs, stretching into infinity, reflections that alternated, curved, mingled, tangled, and jumped when the car hit the least bump, in the way that, on the cinema screen, the spokes of a wheel set in motion seem to go backwards for a little way, start uncertainly forward again, then jolt as if the brakes have locked, and finally the ancient vehicle would disappear in a cloud of red dust and be swallowed up in a halo of palpitating heat-haze; it always took a different road from the one by which I had arrived, a road suitable for cars that went straight down to Gläreola on the other slope, without having to cross the col of the Blue Mountain, and Dr. Oswaldo had become extraordinarily indignant on the day when he learned from my own lips that it was Caïo himself who had told me to take the old mule track, instead of recommending the new road, the highway that his bank had quite rightly built to improve the viability of the region where, today, the bank has so many interests, which, said Dr. Padroso, were upsetting the time-honored economy of the municipality: building bridges, dams, locks, irrigation canals, and power stations, tearing out the old coffee plantations, clearing away what remained of the virgin forest to plant groves of oranges, for which they had a guaranteed market in Australia, chasing out the old planters to make room for the Italian immigrants who were being settled in colonies in brand new housing developments whose little prefabricated houses were being sold to them on credit, mass-produced homes modeled after Swiss chalets—an absurdity in this climate—but they were neat and had water, gas, electricity, and telephone (amenities that Dr. Padroso had not wished to have installed at the Morro Azul at any price!), each development had a school, social services, a cooperative, as well as a garage, a cinema, and a dance hall, and the men could buy little Fords, also on credit, so that each new arrival found himself up to his neck in debt before he had even settled in, dug up his plot, planted his trees, and enclosed his orchard, and these newcomers led a much more precarious and poverty-stricken existence in their smart little homes with all their modern conveniences than, at one time, the black slaves on the plantations, for the contracts, the commitments, the debts, their freely given consent and signature, the hire-purchase payments for costly agricultural implements, which were difficult for them to meet, plus the false comfort, the superfluity, the risks and disappointments of all kinds that they alone had to suffer in a new country, to which they were not yet acclimatized, chained them to the soil more surely than the shackles around the ankles of the slaves in the *zensala,* the square behind the master's house where the blacks were shut up for the night.

I let Dr. Oswaldo Padroso talk. How old could he have been? He was several years younger than I was and looked ten years older. Such a waking dreamer ruling a little kingdom, what kind of man could that produce?

"Caïo is a filibuster," said the Doctor. "Imagine misleading you like that! A man like you... a poet! That boy has no respect. Do you know, Monsieur Cendrars, you could have been killed on that col, it's a famous death trap! And to encourage you to set out at night on this track that leads nowhere and disappears in the hinterland, why, it's criminal!"

"But perhaps Caïo wanted to give me the chance to admire the new construction sites the bank has opened everywhere, and which augur so well for the future of Brazil, Senhor Padroso?"

"Don't talk to me about the future of Brazil! They are anticipating all this success in the future, but, so far, it's been nothing but bankruptcy! And as for the bank's famous public works, which they keep dinning into my ears, they are making this country uninhabitable at the moment, for God alone knows where they recruit all the riff-raff they send us, a lot of jailbirds and cutthroats. Even the birds in the sky are finding it intolerable with all these stone crushers, cement-mixers, sawmills, locomotives, and steamrollers, all the dynamite reducing everything to rubble, and all these internal-combustion engines farting and backfiring on every corner, at every turning, even in the heart of the jungle! Fortunately, I am here, and the ten thousand hectares of the Morro Azul are a sanctuary for the birds. They cannot encroach upon my land and hunting is forbidden here. They can't just come walking in here."

Dr. Padroso talked to me about birds (and he could talk about them for hours), marveling at the cloud of hummingbirds plundering the banana trees, pointing out that they were aggressive, intolerant, jealous fighters, each one ferociously defending his sector against any incursion by his neighbors, cantankerous, angry, quarreling creatures, always on the alert, full of cheek and fury and, like insects, the whole flock utterly indifferent to the presence of human beings, humming, buzzing, frolicking, squabbling, flitting in all directions at one hundred kilometers an hour like a flight of precious gems. I let him talk, talk... happy as I was to have discovered such a phenomenon, and I smiled at the thought of the good—or dirty?—trick that Caïo thought he had played on me.

On the night of my arrival, as he accompanied me into the Emperor's palace, where he had had a bed made up for me, Dr. Oswaldo Padroso had already declared, in an effusion of honor and homage that left me confused (I was certainly not used to it in France, where, on the contrary, a war veteran was looked at rather askance):

"As Caïo must have told you, this little palace was constructed by my predecessor to receive Dom Pedro, who had announced a forthcoming visit, but he never came and his palace has never been lived in. I am extremely proud of being able to offer you accommodation here, for I consider you worthy of it on two counts, firstly, as a poet and, secondly, as a Frenchman. I adore France, Monsieur Cendrars, and no Frenchman has ever yet visited the Morro Azul, you are the first. How can I ever thank you? The palace is yours. Make yourself at home. Do whatever you wish. But Caïo, who is a secretive devil and an intriguer, did not tell me you had been disabled in the war. Monsieur Cendrars, this is too great an honor for me. I am overcome. I am suffocating. I feel quite ill. Kindly allow me to go outside and take the air. It is the emotion. I am weeping. Excuse me. I will leave you now. I will wait for you in my humble hermit's abode. Come and join me on the verandah, and please hurry, I *must* talk to you. Oh, forgive me... Your presence disturbs me. I no longer know what I'm doing, what I'm saying. It's so unexpected! A Frenchman in my home... A hero of Verdun!... What a memorable day!"

"Dr. Oswaldo is nervous today, and I admit he has good reason to be. Me, too, I adore France, Monsieur. I had my little girl christened Joffrinette, my wife wanted to call her 'Battle-of-the-Marne,' but I preferred to name her after the great general who saved Paris, for a name is as good as a title, and my little girl is a saint," Bueno, the doctor's manservant told me. This gigantic, rubicund black had stayed behind to unpack my cases and, as I was apologizing for the late hour of my arrival and the disturbance I was causing, Bueno replied:

"Don't worry, Monsieur, Dr. Oswaldo never sits down to dinner before two in the morning, so Monsieur is only a little late. It's perfectly all right, Leontine and I are used to it, Dr. Oswaldo is a sublunary."

"Sublunary."

"Yes, a... what's the word, now? He gets up at night and walks. He walks up and down."

"A somnambulist, Bueno?"

"Yes, perhaps that's it, if Monsieur says so. Let's say a somnambulist. But in my opinion, Dr. Oswaldo is more of a sublunary, because I believe it's the moon that makes him walk up and down..."

There was a kerosene lamp with an alabaster shade standing on a marble-topped console table.

So, I was in the Emperor's palace. In effect, everything from floor to ceiling was made of pink marble. It was much more like a Roman-style atrium or even an antique tomb than the great drawing room of the Petit Trianon, designed by Gabriel. This vast room on the ground floor, where Bueno was busy arranging my things on the marble curule benches attached to the walls, formed an enormous cube. A smaller cube had been added to one of the walls to make the vestibule through which we had entered the palace and, on the opposite wall, another little cube of similar dimensions made a pendant to it, and this was a bathroom with a pool, a badly arranged room with no sense of proportion at all. It was ugly, naked, massive, ponderous, and solid, and, although built for eternity, seemed unfinished, something or other was lacking. It was an assemblage of blocks, tiles, and columns, all prefabricated and numbered and set clumsily in place without balance or grace. The whole thing was cumbersome, crushing, the walls were too thick and the windows too mean—there were five on each of the north and south façades, while, to the east and west, the two false, bricked-up windows framed the door of the vestibule on one side and the door of the bathroom on the other. It was boringly symmetrical and devoid of any decoration whatsoever. It was rich and it was bleak. It was very obvious that it had never been inhabited. All that polished marble must have cost a fortune. It was as fine as Carrara marble.

In the middle of this immense room there was a raised dais with four square columns and a balustrade enclosing a low bed, set directly on the tiled floor, which was also made of pink marble but surmounted by a mosquito-net, a billowing pleated muslin like a bridal gown draped on a gibbet, a scaffold made up of three interlocking slabs of marble.

Above this bed, which would have been more suitable as a bier for the lying-in-state of some dignitary, and gave one no more desire to make love in it than if one were lying there in agony, awaiting the end of the consultation, the verdict of the illustrious doctors summoned by telegraph and flown in by special plane—as I tossed and turned in terror on this great dusty bed, I could not help imagining some monarch struck down by lung cancer, longing for a last Havana cigar, but unable to call out because of the operation on his throat, and with the bell-pull out of reach (in any case, I could not imagine hanging a bell on these walls of smoothest marble!)—above this imperial couch, were I knew at once I would never be able to sleep, above this tragically, mortally tedious bed, there hung, by way of a velarium, a thick matting of plaited reeds suspended at its four corners by four long cords, each knotted to one of the four columns; this matting, through whose interstices I could perceive the stars in the sky shining intermittently and around which the blue fringes of the Brazilian night overflowed, was of such proportions that its center was distended and made a kind of pouch, as if some creature was curled up there, a cat, for example, with her bellyful of kittens, and, all the time I was undressing, shaving with my Razvite, giving myself a cat's lick before rejoining Dr. Oswaldo Padroso and sitting down to dinner (instead of being astonished by this ceiling open to the sky, I was impatient to meet the Dulcinea of the Morro Azul, whose existence Caïo had hinted at!), I kept lifting my head and

pricking my ears, thinking I had heard the matting creak and crackle, as if
something had nibbled at the reeds, and under the pressure of imperceptible movements, tiny straws detached themselves, floated in the air, and fell
down on to the mosquito net in an eddying of dust and mildew. I had the
very distinct impression that I was being watched, that my slightest movements were observed, that something up there in the matting was moving,
something living, a being, an extraordinary creature, but at the same time
I thought it was probably nothing more than a nest of mice, mice who
would dance a sarabande in the dark, as soon as the lamp was extinguished.
No, never would I sleep in that bed, not for a single night.

"Bueno," I called, "come and show me how the taps of the bathing pool
work, it looks rather complicated, and I'd like to have a dip and make
myself respectable for your boss before I get dressed and go down to dinner."

(I wanted to make myself seductive by some special little touch to my
appearance, for this is what all women expect of a Frenchman abroad, and
by my conversation, bringing the gossip, the latest tittle-tattle from Paris,
echoes of the current fashions, a little impertinence, or wit, I wanted to
amuse, to shine, even in the eyes of the doctor's old mistress or the mad
servant-woman whom Caïo had laughed at when he told me Padroso's love
had been an open secret for twenty years!)

"Good God! Don't risk it, Monsieur!" cried Bueno, flinging his arms up
to heaven. "It's full of poisonous spiders."

I found this malicious response a bit exaggerated, knowing the traditional phlegm of the blacks but I did not resent it in the least, given the
lateness of the hour—Leontine, Bueno's wife, must have been getting
impatient over her stove, perhaps the food was already burned, and Senhor
Padroso must be tired of waiting on the verandah, so, as Bueno did not
seem inclined to make the slightest allusion to the lady of the house, I said
to him: "Take this flask... no, not that one, the other one, the bottle of
lavender-water, and give me a good rubdown."

"Monsieur does not seem to believe me," said Bueno, as he conscien-
tiously massaged me, "but Monsieur has only to try for himself! There's a
lot of machinery underneath and the pipes are so complicated they make
you lose your wits. I've tried to make out how it all works, but when you
turn on the taps, it's neither hot nor cold water that comes out but infuriated spiders, great black ones, hairy ones, the kind that stink and bite, venomous, devilish things. One day, I had to fire my revolver to save myself,
they were as big as my hand and I was covered with them, they even got
into my hair and into my trousers. They were crawling all over me. I only

just managed to get away, and I was ill for six months with horrible sores on my stomach and hips. Monsieur has only to ask my wife, Leontine, she was sickened and revolted but she put plasters and poultices on me and boiled up a broth of roots and bitter herbs, into which she threw the same venomous spiders, but grilled, pounded, reduced to a spicy powder like red pepper, and she recited prayers and cast the necessary spells, as Chavin, the *capita* had told her to do, for this Creole broth is an Indian medicine and the *capita*, who was born here on the estate, learned all the secrets of nature from his mother, and without my wife's help I would never had had the courage to swallow that disgusting concoction, not even once, just to try it, out of curiosity. It was diabolical, but Leontine is a strong character. She did it all and it was she who cured me. Without his wife, a man is nothing! Now, if Monsieur would like to see for himself, go ahead! But will Monsieur please bear in mind that, up until this very day, *nobody* has yet succeeded in taking a bath in that bewitched pool."

"Certainly I will try, Bueno, and tomorrow morning at the latest! Here, pass me my white suit."

"Well, then, good luck! But Monsieur must not count on me to pull him out, I am much too scared. Ask Chavin, the *capita*, to do it, he has the keys to the basement."

And the giant Negro made the sign of the cross and touched the amulet he was wearing around his neck, a bunch of *balaladenga* comprising the thirteen good-luck charms: the Bahian hand making the sign against the Evil Eye; Momus, the erotic double hunchback, who protects you from spells cast by wizards; the dice of Fortune; Saint Joseph's set-square, to ensure accurate work; the house dog, symbol of fidelity; the gourd, against thirst; a small loaf in a basket, against hunger, but which also has a sexual connotation, the satisfaction of uterine hunger; the traveler's staff or the magician's wand; a pirogue, to prevent you perishing at sea; the bells of madness; the squirrel or the Tumbler, for imagination; the head of the fish, for wisdom; the rabbit's foot, the most magical of the thirteen. Bueno handed me my white suit, helped me to put it on and laced up my shoes.

"Thank you, Bueno. Now, let's go down, I'm ready. But first, tell me frankly, what animal is that couched above our heads?"

"Ah! Monsieur has guessed!"

"Yes, there's something watching us, something that moves. My guess is that it is a ..."

"Sssshhh! O *bicho*[32] is listening. Monsieur, please don't speak her name. Come!"

And Bueno grabbed the lamp and went out quickly.

I followed him.

Outside, I found the black waiting for me at the head of the great marble staircase that led down from the terrace of the Emperor's palace to the house of the *fazenda*.

"I will lead the way, Monsieur," he said, "take care, there are a hundred and one steps."

Holding the lamp aloft to light my way, he went down the staircase, stopping after ten steps, counting very fast and saying:

"1, 2, 3, 4, 5, 6, 7, 8, 9, 10!... Ah, Monsieur is almost as shrewd as she is!"

"But what is it, Bueno?"

"11, 12, 13, 14, 15, 16, 17, 18, 19, 20!... And to think that Monsieur pretended it was nothing!"

(This is the way they must have gone from the top to the bottom of Jacob's Ladder, pausing at certain significant stages or fatidic steps, at the *golden numbers,* even when they were going up, but more especially as they came down, *so as to remember,* in the way that one ties knots in one's handkerchief, or like the large beads on the rosary where you stop saying the *Ave Marias* when telling your beads; the *quipus,* the knotted cords of the Incas, are based on this arithmological principle and so are the knotted strips of bark used in Benin and the Congo and the raised scars of the Senegalese, a type Bueno resembled, with two crescent-shaped gashes on his cheek.)

"...31, 32, 33!... Thank God! On the thirty-third step, we are out of range!"

"But... range of what, Bueno?"

"It's a liana!"

"A liana, Bueno?"

"Ssshhh! It's better not to pronounce her real name. I'm going down to the fiftieth step..."

On the fiftieth step, Bueno was waiting for me, smiling, winking, holding the lamp high:

"Here, we are out of her range, absolutely safe from committing an indiscretion. It's safer not to pronounce her name, but I can say it to Monsieur under the seal of secrecy, and if I whisper it into his ear: it's a rattlesnake!"

"A rattlesnake?"

"Ssshhh! No, no, no, Monsieur knows nothing! I haven't breathed a word. Bueno is an idiot Monsieur is quite right. Bueno has not spoken! But Monsieur played his part so well that I had to laugh, and Monsieur knows about it, anyway—it's not a male snake, it's a female: the Mistress of the Morro Azul... Ah, poor me, it will bring me bad luck! I have spoken..."

And Bueno clattered down the remaining fifty steps of the staircase.

On the penultimate step he was waiting for me, he had blown out the lamp and was standing there, blacker than the night, his eyes dilated.

I came right up close to him: "Bueno," I whispered, "did you want to speak to me about Our Lady of the Morro Azul, about the Senhora?"

"Ah! Monsieur knows her? Thank God, then she does exist! Here, nobody has ever seen her, not even the photographer who came by special train to take her photograph. But, come," he said, "the Master is waiting for us. I believe she is called *Maa-Eiffel*... but, ssshhh!"

We went down the last two steps.

"100, 101!" Bueno counted aloud.

We approached silently from the corner of the verandah.

"You see, Dr. Oswaldo is not here. He is wandering about again like a soul in agony. Monsieur will find him in front of the house, pacing up and down under the palm trees, or else at the end of the avenue, sitting on a bench. I must run to the kitchen to warn Leontine to be ready to serve."

Senhor Padroso was in fact sitting dreaming on the bench, under a magnificent tuft of giant bamboos that formed a quivering arbor at the end of the avenue. This retreat was the the most heavenly, the most romantic spot you could wish for, with its star-shaped clump of imperial palm trees, more than thirty meters high, which swayed and floated against the tropical night. All that was lacking was a trick of the moonlight, or a spotlight, to transform this verdant cabinet into a fairy-like decor for the opera.

As soon as he saw me, Dr. Padroso came to meet me, hugging me emotionally and giving me a few sonorous claps on the back in the Brazilian fashion.

"At last, there you are, dear friend," he exclaimed, "come quickly, let's sit down to table. Bueno's wife must be wondering what's happened to us and you must be hungry."

An open secret, Caïo had said.

At table, there were just the two of us and Dr. Oswaldo Padroso spoke of nothing but HER.

It was the most moving thing imaginable.

Oh, what a passion!

The story of another great love, the lightning-stroke, to add to my first chronicle of *La Femme aimée*.[33]

This woman was famous throughout the world, and it so happened that I had witnessed her end while working as assistant to the American film director, whose name I have forgotten, who directed her last film. She played the part of a fortune-teller at Le Chat Noir in Montmartre, the film was absolutely cretinous, which explains why I have also forgotten the title. This moronic American, who spoke not one word of French and yelled into his megaphone like a deaf man, afraid that the great actress was slipping away from him, for she was dying, and fearing to lose her before the last shot was in the can, had summoned me to give him a hand and hurry things up, thus keeping one jump ahead of the Grim Reaper before he could snatch away the great star whose presence ensured good publicity for the film and who was costing him the eyes out of his head. He wanted his money's worth. Filthy lucre! The famous tragedienne also needed it and she was exhausted. She could barely carry on, she was ill and came down from her bedroom into the large drawing room of her own private house on the Avenue de Villiers, which we had transformed into a studio—the generators farting away on the pavement outside, cables coming in through every window, an army of prop men, movie extras, technicians, and camera crew invading the house, coming in, going out, shouting, yelling, occupying all the rooms, which resounded with the sound of carpenters and set-dressers hammering, driving in and pulling out nails like there was no tomorrow, overturning the furniture, ruining the carpets, ripping the curtains, moving the ornaments, the statues, the pictures, putting their filthy paws on the intimate souvenirs of this most passionate of lives and the golden crowns, the trophies of the career of an outstanding artiste, a woman who had achieved a universal triumph, a glory unequaled in the annals of the theater, setting up the scenery anywhere and everywhere to meet the requirements of the various set-ups, the painters covering the ceilings and doors with that dull gray so beloved of photographers—the great actress, the old, exhausted woman who, to cap it all, was one-legged, this unfortunate creature crippled with debts, hunted and hounded, came down into her drawing room, shivering with fever, to put on her makeup, wrapped in furs, in front of the fireplace where an enormous fire was burning, and, at the age of seventy-nine, she was always professional, always ready for her call, she would get up immediately at the pitiless summons of the megaphone and come to expose herself to the voracious blaze of the blinding arc lights, to the unbearable

261

glare of the reflectors and the mirrors they trained on her, to the dazzle of the aluminium screens and submit herself to the exigencies of the camera, rehearsing the scene as often as necessary so that they could work out the range of the shot and adjust the lighting, and she would take direction and, finally, shoot... "Lights! Roll 'em, boys!"... begin again and uncomplainingly obey, she, the most capricious, the most willful woman in the world, and the most original, the most imaginative, the most independent performer ever to tread the boards, she, whose whole career had been nothing but scandal and recklessness, in her private as well as in her theatrical life, she, who, as a debutante actress, had not hesitated to slam the door of the Comédie Française behind her, once, twice, in order to be free to act and live as she desired, and to make a tour that revolutionized the United States, she, this headstrong woman, obeyed without flinching the orders roared through the megaphone, which the authoritarian American seemed unable to do without (and at that period this was even more offensive, because it was only 1923, the cinema was still silent and the tragedienne had a golden voice, a voice that carried, a voice that could draw forth tears and exalt her audiences, a voice that was on the brink of being silenced forever and alas! could not yet be recorded on film!) and when the woman's nerves were shattered and she was about to faint, a young doctor, specially attached to this crew of assholes, rushed forward to give her an injection.

I can testify to the fact that Sarah Bernhardt died in harness, working flat out, doped, drugged, whipped, and spurred on like a filly who neatly pulls away from the rest of the leading runners, gets into a winning stride, takes another stride and another, and whose heart bursts just as he reaches the finish line, where she collapses and dies... when the race was over, we had only ten or so scenes left to shoot.

It was utterly inhuman. Madness...

Several years earlier, on the day after the premiere of Shakespeare's *Romeo and Juliet,* Jean Cocteau had telephoned me:

"Blaise, how wrong you were not to come to the theater with me—it was a triumph! Sarah was fantastic. Everyone thought she was done for after her leg was amputated, but she's proved to all Paris that she's not dead yet. She's a *sacred monster!*"

That was the first time I heard that phrase from Jean's lips, and I truly believe it was the first time he had ever used it.

And that was already inhuman, too...

Sarah Bernhardt, in drag had played the part of Romeo, and, during the balcony scene, that dialogue between two children who are carried on the wings of love and each seducing the other, instead of approaching the silk ladder that hung down from Juliet's window, putting one foot on the bottom and blithely climbing to the top, like an intoxicated lover, Bernhardt had to cross the entire width of the stage of her large theater like a snake, like a lumbering larva, rolling along jerkily in her rubber tired wheel chair which she propelled with her two hands, and then stand up and lean painfully on her stick, while her solitary, skinny, old woman's leg trembled visibly in its tights and puffed-out pageboy bloomers... and this scene, this sophisticated scene had brought the house down, there were shouts of enthusiasm, hysteria, repeated curtain calls, the inextinguishable applause of *le Tout-Paris,* everybody who was anybody in Paris, an audience of snobs, of dubious nouveaux-riches, of conquering Allied generals, ministers, and diplomats, delegates to the signing of the Treaty of Versailles.

I had not wanted to accompany Jean Cocteau to the theater because a spectacle like that would have been abhorrent to me. It was the aftermath of the First World War. I had seen too many soldiers, the very flower of France's young men, her future, suffering without a word, forgotten on the camp beds in the field hospitals and not daring to go home and show themselves to their fiancées with their disfigured faces, their war blindness, their lungs ruined by gas, their tuberculosis, their amputated arms or legs, their trepanned skulls or their insanity, and I myself had only just come out of hospital...

Sarah?

Picasso?

The Russian Ballet?

The New Spirit?

Before long, I left Paris, this sophisticated Paris, for good.

Departure!

But the whole world is sophisticated, even Russia, in spite of the purges.

And today, in the aftermath of the Second World War, the sequel to this mania, this misunderstanding, this snobbism is Existentialism, both in the theater and in philosophy: Sartre and all those young literature-scribbling men of letters who flutter their wings in the cellars of Saint-Germain-des-Prés, the leaders of the extreme avant-garde of poetic exegesis, men who plunge in backwards and make careers in conformism, who cannot live except in a group, in a gang, trailing behind a Headmaster, for bread and butter comes first... *"À nous la liberté!"*

In this distress and in this boredom,
There is no one's hand to shake...

says the great poet Nekrassov, who committed suicide out of boredom, in the tradition of Russian poets, or who died of consumption, and the vagabond, Maxim the Bitter (Maxim Gorky) added... "and no one's jaw to break!"[34]

XIII

THE ROMANCE OF THE MORRO AZUL

Senhor Padroso told me this story:

"You remember, Monsieur Cendrars, the beginning of Alphonse Daudet's *Sappho,* when the student runs up the six flights of his furnished rooming house, four steps at a time, carrying a woman in his arms, a masked woman he has kidnapped from the Ball at the Opera, and lays his heavy burden on his bed and falls on top of her, panting, breathless, his heart beating painfully, fit to burst, to explode with emotion, eagerness, impatience, and youthful triumph, but also from physical exhaustion after the effort of climbing all those stairs without flagging, and without once setting down the unknown woman who became heavier at each flight of stairs, and without dropping her on the top landing? Well, I was in the same state of agitation, emotion, and nervous anguish, sweating, out of breath, and with my heart hammering in my throat when I set Sarah Bernhardt down, except that I set her down on her feet in the middle of her room with a thousand precautions, for the divine Sarah seemed to me so fragile, and, instead of falling upon the famous actress, like the student on his unknown woman, I was overcome at my own audacity in having carried off the illustrious tragedienne and I fell on my knees, groveling at her feet and kissing the hem of her gown devotedly, while an icicle seemed to pierce my heart.

"In 1909, when Sarah Bernhardt came to do a one-night stand in São Paulo, it was not the noisy, congested capital city you know today, where they build one house an hour amid a deafening uproar and a cloud of dust that never settles and which can only be pierced by the forty-seven stories of the Automobile Club, the skyscraper they're so proud of, no, São Paulo was then a peaceful little provincial town, with 125,000 inhabitants instead of the million they boast of today, the streets weren't even paved and there were more pack mules and laden donkeys trotting along the road than there are pedestrians on the sidewalk nowadays. Fifteen years ago, there weren't even any sidewalks in São Paulo. People didn't spend their time running about the streets. They stayed at home. And they watched each other, from the windows of their houses, which were all one-story buildings. Sarah Bernhardt had been installed at the Rotisserie Française, which was the only building in town to have a second story, it was a grand drawing room with a loggia, a room for meetings or banquets, and the only way to get to it from the bar on the ground floor was up a staircase as straight as a ladder and even more slippery than the marble stairs that lead from here to the Emperor's palace, for it was parquet, made of Brazilian redwood, and they kept it well-polished with beeswax, since it was the only staircase in São Paulo on that scale, as wide as an avenue and with a hundred and one steps, exactly the same number as the Emperor's staircase here at the Morro Azul, and a monumental staircase like that had never before been seen in São Paulo! I don't know how I managed to dash up it at a run, and without getting dizzy. I might have slipped and broken the divine Sarah's bones. Where did I get such self-confidence, such courage, such strength? And the authority! Oh, the nerve of it! I was barely twenty and I had never been one to put myself forward, I was rather timid by nature. And I was an orphan, to boot...

"After the play, which had been performed in the hall of the Law Faculty as São Paulo still did not have a theater in 1909, the enthusiasm for the divine diva was so great that the students unhitched the horses from her carriage and dragged and half-carried the Victoria, with the illustrious French visitor in it, back to her hotel amid an indescribable uproar, the audience were running along beside the carriage, the poor people and even the blacks among them, and several times the vehicle was in danger of being overturned, while bouquets of flowers, thrown from every direction, filled the carriage, the famous actress blew kisses to the crowd, a bunch of students escorted her, closely surrounding the carriage with flaming torches in their hands, and rockets and squibs were going off in all the side streets and alleyways, but even these could not drown the thunder of the applause and the acclamations as she passed. They carried her all around the town, making her do the grand tour. Everyone was delirious. I stood close by the right hand door and my best friend by the left to protect the divine Sarah from the furor of her most ardent admirers. Knowing how passionate my compatriots are, and fearing the extremes they might go to,

I had armed myself with a revolver and my friend had done the same. The beloved Sarah was the object of several wagers, and some sons of rich families, certain planters from the interior, had sworn to kidnap the great Parisian artiste, not to ransom her or steal her jewels, but to marry her by force! It was a crazy gamble, and just shows what savages we really are, for the Tupí lurks under the skin of every Brazilian! And that's why, the moment we arrived at the hotel, I snatched Sarah Bernhardt up in my arms and began to run, rushing up that terrible, dazzling staircase at the Rotisserie Française in one mad gallop, while behind me came a group of my friends, brandishing torches, closely followed by a gang of young maniacs who were fighting on the staircase and who came and banged shamelessly on the door, which I had slammed in their faces and bolted, dying of embarrassment...

"'Stand up, Monsieur,' the divine Sarah said to me.

"There she was, standing in the brilliantly lit drawing room littered with her one hundred trunks (which the newspapers had talked about), her fifty hat-boxes, her furs, her umbrellas, her little boots, all of which exhaled a deliciously feminine odor, her tattered gown, her disheveled hair, her seagreen eyes that smiled at me through the flowers she was holding in her arms, slim, superb, feverishly happy at this unanimous passion she had aroused, while the knocking at the door and the acclamations of the crowd outside, under the windows, redoubled, and they called to her to come out on to the balcony, thousands of voices rhythmically chanting her name: 'Sarah! Sarah!' ... there she was, with her mouth open, full of joy, her mouth that frightened me as if it had been a reptile's, her mouth that was drawing closer, her lips moving, her tongue... and her arms opened to embrace me, to draw me to her, to hug me against her breast, to clasp me, and her tongue penetrated my mouth, while I... I was seized with frigidity and I heard her say: 'Poor little one!'... and I heard myself, absolutely rigid and frozen, murmur:

"'Forgive them, Madame. They don't know what they're doing. But listen to their hearts, and how they beat for you, and also for France, the heart of every young man in my country is beating with love...'

"I could hear her heart beating, beating wildly, my own had stopped...

"'And now, go away, little one,' the divine Sarah said to me.

"And, tucking up her skirt, she tore a piece of lace off her underclothing and pressed it into my hand, explaining, as she nervously pushed me out of the door:

"'As a souvenir...! A souvenir of the woman...'"

"I was paralyzed with emotion. I could not take a step. Everything was spinning around. I sat down on the top step of the staircase with this piece of lace between my fingers. I don't know what my companions must have thought of me. Eventually, I found myself downstairs in the bar. The place was full of gilded youth. Everyone was swigging champagne. The first skirmish broke out and then a general battle royal. Finally, they had to evacuate the Rotisserie Française, and, next morning, the papers were full of this scandal: I had fought a duel with my best friend and, as a man had died, the newspapers published the love poems I had addressed to the divine Sarah! I was the hero of the day, I, who had been touched profoundly, to the very depths of my soul, and wanted to keep my passion a secret! And all this on account of a scrap of lace.

"What more can I tell you? Afterwards, I read Sarah Bernhardt's *Memoirs* and, I truly believe, everything that was ever written about her, right up until her death, for I subscribed to the Argus agency and they sent me all the press cuttings about her. She has become my religion. I know that she had innumerable adventures both in the theater and out off it, and, in particular, I know that, in the United States, she was pursued by a man who exhibited whales, and by a rancher who was mad about her and wanted to make her a present of an immense herd of wild cattle, so he had his cowboys drive them to a forsaken little railroad station in the Far West, where they held up the locomotive, and by a Texan outlaw who stopped her train in the middle of the night to plunder her baggage and carry off some blouses and a dozen pairs of lacy little underpants, and by gold- and diamond-prospectors who offered her their meager fortunes, not to mention the crowned heads of Europe, the Princes and the Grand Dukes who sent her the most beautiful jewels in the world, and the pleasure seekers who made up her court, and the poets who wrote immortal masterpieces for her, such as Jean Lorrain and Edmond Rostand. Today, I am conscious of how ridiculous and juvenile my chivalrous sentiments were. And to think that I fought for her, and that my life has been transformed by that one, unique kiss, for, on the morning of the following day, after the duel, I went to my guardian and told him I could no longer live as I had been doing, that I had been touched by grace and wanted to retreat, to live in solitude, and the old gentleman, who was afraid I might indulge in some new extravagance, and claim the money held in trust for me, so that I could follow the divine Sarah to Paris, hastily agreed and made arrangements with Caïo's father so that I could come and settle here, in the old *fazenda* of the Morro Azul, the *fazenda* of the forgotten Emperor, and that is how I came to be

living here, far from everything, living on this estate that is falling into
rack and ruin, and all this led to the discovery that I have made for her, the
discovery of a new constellation in the sky, the Sidereal Eiffel Tower, which
I wanted to talk to you about, and, since I have such confidence in you,
Monsieur Cendrars, I wanted to beg you to take the necessary steps in Paris
to have my discovery officially registered—it would give me so much joy
before I die!—for, in my thoughts, I am rendering a supreme homage to
my beloved Sarah, and to France, by locating the Eiffel Tower in the sky,
and in our southern hemisphere... It is a symbol... I worried so desperate-
ly about them both during the war. Sarah and the Tower are the two spiritual projections of France today, and they are intimately united in my
mind, as you will see, for I have explained it in the communication I sent
to the Académie des Sciences, and it is not just a passing fancy... but the
Institute never replies to me, in spite of the document I have sent them, an
astronomic photograph that leaves not the slightest doubt about the reality
of my discovery, and in spite of all the detailed messages and the appeals I
have addressed to them from time to time, ever since the Battle of the
Marne, through the intermediary of our Minister of Foreign Affairs and our
Ambassador in Paris. So it will no longer be just a matter of Sarah
Bernhardt. Don't say a word to me about her. Don't say anything. I don't
want to know anything more about her. But listen to me.

"Fifteen years. How can I not speak of her, and how can I tell you about
my life here without pronouncing her name? What appalls me about Sarah
Bernhardt is that, in her *Memoirs,* she allowed them to publish a photograph of her in hunting dress, taken somewhere on tour, in Canada, with a
group of companions who are enjoying the pleasures of the hunt. In the
photo, Sarah is shouldering a rifle and aiming at a bird. No doubt she
fired, and my heart bleeds... I have been living here for fifteen years. Every
time I hear a shot, I feel ill. Another song silenced. A wild song of love.
Feathers floating in the sun. A little crumpled heap. An opera hat in a pool
of blood. The bloodless face of my friend. It was dawn. A *sabiá* was singing
in the heart of a palm tree. Our automatic revolvers had gone off by themselves. Clumsily, I had not moved a finger. I can live only at night. When
you have lived in such profound anguish, whether or not you deserve the
suffering you endure, you come out of the abyss as a condemned man. It is
dreadful. I cannot find words to express myself. I wanted to tell you how
the soul cuts all bonds in an attempt to escape from love... but it is impossible to make anyone understand, unless they themselves have been subjected to the garotte and felt the knot slacken, the strangling cord relax,

the shackles imperceptibly loosen and fall. It is a shattering experience. You come back from so far away! You no longer recognize yourself and you wonder, in agony, to what extent you have been able to play a part in your own progress towards liberation... You make so many involuntary movements, such secret efforts, you suffer from obscure impulses, reflexes that at least allow you to breathe, to defend yourself, to hold a reserve of alien breath in you chest and, suddenly, in a supreme effort, to tense all your muscles aggressively and burst out of the straitjacket that has been oppressing you. But you are not free yet, there are still the walls to be climbed, although the soul is already dreaming of freedom regained, and you are still nailed to the floor of your cell, for you are still hampered by your heavy clothing, which is bound to you with a thousand thongs, and you struggle and writhe, anxious and ill-at-ease, and it will take you a long time to untie all these tangled cords, tapes, and strings and to undo the awkwardly placed laces. There are fastenings on the back you cannot get at. Your fists are permanently clenched. You roll on the ground. You tear at the knots with your teeth. You strain. Arch your back. Stretch out rigid. Jump up. Rub yourself against the hinges of the door in an attempt to saw through them. Callouses form, and they bleed. You scrape your shoulders against the wall. They itch. You break your nails. You do splits and almost dislocate your joints. The seams are strong, they will not give. You become mad with rage and when at last everything bursts in an access of tears and fury, the madman finds that he is still wearing a whole harness of leather thongs and broken, dangling straps and shreds and tatters of ticking which float around his body in the wind, and all this would make him ridiculously conspicuous if he tried to run away. So then he resigns himself to waiting until these rags rot and fall off of their own accord, or else, becoming impatient, he begins shaking himself again, floundering, tangling, and tying himself into such knots that, in the end, he strangles himself. One sudden twist will do it. Secret suicide?... Death?... Death to the world... Time passes... Fifteen years... The slightest thing was enough to plunge me once more into the abyss, often just a press cutting, an echo...

"Every day, up until her death, I wrote her letters, but I never sent them, and even today I still write her loving, adoring poems, and I never sent any of my poems to the divine Sarah, either, but I was weak enough to allow certain people to take copies of them and perhaps you have already heard some of them No?... I am amazed, because people gloat over them at the Automobile Club, reading into them all sorts of indelicate allusions, which they interpret in their own way, and I would never have believed that Caïo, with that wicked tongue of his, would have had the decency to keep quiet about them!... And he didn't tell you anything about my Eiffel Tower, which everybody laughs at just as much?... No? Well, my dear Caïo must have changed, what's happened to him?... I see you are smiling. Ah, then, the fact is, you've made an impression on him, as you have on me, with your calmness, your good nature, and your way of listening and understanding everything one says. What patience you have! I am confused, excuse me. But I must come back to the divine Sarah again in order to tell you about my Eiffel Tower.

"It must seem to you that I am rambling on and on and always falling back into the same rut. It's not that at all. It's a progressive disease, the cancer at the heart of solitude. Without my love for Sarah, and for France, I would never have made my discovery. I was haunted, and when war was declared, I began to suffer terrible anxiety for my beloved, and it was this agony that made me lift up my eyes to the sky and then, just when I was in despair, at the very moment when the Germans were marching on Paris, I discovered the Eiffel Tower in the sky, and this made me believe in the destiny of France, and I prophesied the Victory of the Marne and the deliverance of Paris. The dates bear me out. What a day that was! I spent it in Glaréola, telephoning every newspaper in the country, and every paper in Brazil published my predictions. It was the 7th of September, 1914. France is immortal. The telegrams officially confirming the great victory of the battle of the Marne arrived only in dribs and drabs and kept trickling in right up to the end of the month, and the first ones, which arrived ten days after I had made my prediction, were very dubious and uncertain. But, by then, I had already arranged for a photographer from the observatory in Rio to come here by special train, and I was busy having him photograph my Eiffel Tower in the sky of Brazil and drafting my report to the Institut de France. I was in haste to make my Sidereal Eiffel Tower known to the entire world. The Institute did not deign to reply to me, however, nor have they done so to this day, but, believe me, Monsieur, I am very proud of my discovery.

"So, every day I wrote letters to my beloved, letters that I never sent her, and today they fill my letter file to bursting, and I wrote poems, too, but she never received those, either, and I put them away in an American filing cabinet, a little safe with a rolltop and a lock fitted with an alarm bell, one cubic meter in volume, which is full to overflowing and whose key I always carry on me—look, here it is!—one cubic meter of poetry, probably more than one hundred thousand verses, in round figures... work it out, fifteen

271

years of writing, every night, up till two o'clock in the morning, and letters written all day long. At two in the morning, I go out for a stroll in
front of the house, I pace up and down under the palms, from one end of
the avenue to the other, thinking about her, composing verses as I walk,
and finally I flop down on the bench in front of the tuft of bamboos,
exhausted, overcome, my head spinning beneath the vault of the foliage,
and I evoke her and begin to dream of her, and I raise my eyes to the skies
and see her there, as if in a theater, for I do not sleep, I lost the habit of
sleep long ago, my manservant claims that I am a somnambulist and he
pities me in my lovelorn state and scolds me in a gentle way, and then I
watch the moving constellations, journeying on and changing position
according to the hours and the seasons, I lean to the left, I lean to the right,
to observe them through the fronds of my imperial palm trees, which I
have seen growing during these fifteen years and are now so high that they
obstruct the sky, they are like the wings of my theater, and indeed, isn't
that enough to overwhelm one... the profundity of the night? You, you
poets of France, you are inimitable. It's enough to discourage any would-be
poet. I have read everything by Victor Hugo and Edmond Rostand. I will
never publish anything. Don't worry, I'm not going to bore you with my
poetry. I am ashamed of it. But, just imagine pacing up and down in front
of my house for fifteen years—if I'd walked in a straight line, I could have
reached Paris! And the amount of paper I've wasted in fifteen years!
Perhaps I would have done better to set up a papier-mâché factory. It's discouraging. My life is lost. I am a failure, except for this discovery I still
believe in, although the whole world mocks it, this Eiffel Tower in the sky.

"France. Paris. The Eiffel Tower. Sarah Bernhardt. A unique woman. A
shining monument. A city, the City of Light, the capital of the world. A
country, the homeland of Human Fraternity. Don't forget I'm not a
Christian, I'm a positivist. And my master, Auguste Comte, was also a
Frenchman. I know that one can really know nothing precisely except
those truths one has verified through observation and experience. I sincere-
ly believe that nobody has ever had the opportunity to observe and experience his life in such optimum conditions as I have. I am shut up in the
immense wilderness of Brazil as if in a test tube. And my experiment is
this: I have never left the Morro Azul. I have never crossed the confines of
my native province. I do not even know Rio. I have never been to Europe. I
have never set foot in Paris. I have never stood beneath my beloved's window. I have never trembled with emotion in the wintry rain as I followed
her shadow on the curtains of her illumined dressing room in the vain hope

of glimpsing her silhouette. I have never been to the Théâtre Sarah-Bernhardt on the Place du Châtelet. I have never mingled with the crowd at the exit from the theater, nor have I waited at the Stage Door. The notion, the knowledge I have of all these things is composed of nostalgia and some more or less accurate details gleaned here and there, it is startlingly true and unreal or surreal, like everything that comes to us from the imagination or from reading or through abstraction, deduction, study, contemplation, the poetry of a map of France pinned to the wall of my study, reveries I indulge in front of a plan of Paris, or while leafing through a panorama or a photograph album of postcards of the city and the pinups of famous actresses I have sent to me from a shady agency on the Grands Boulevards. Nevertheless, in my innocence, I was absolutely shattered, utterly prostrate at the news of the declaration of war in 1914, the invasion of Belgium, the lightning advance of the German armies, and their drive toward Paris. I was in despair. I wanted to go and enlist with the Foreign Legion, but there were no more ships leaving for Europe.

"Just imagine—when I began living here, I wanted to install myself in the little palace of the Emperor, so as to live in a setting worthy of her, but the spiders, the creepy-crawlies, and the snakes frightened me, and I have never set foot up there again until this evening, when I had the Emperor's bed made up for you. And the old colonial dwelling house where I live is full of ghosts, of dismal Negro legends, rapping spirits, and the tragic history of my predecessor, Herr Karl Vogt, a stern and cruel master murdered by his own slaves on the day of their liberation and whose ghost still haunts the house. I had the *senzala* demolished to wipe out the memory of those times and those awful events. For fifteen years I have been living with my manservant, who is as devoted as he is superstitious, and the overseer of the plantation, who is nostalgic for the old days, a vindictive and narrow-minded man, but loyal, although he is greedy for money. His father was the right-hand man of the old master here, and it was he who branded the slaves with a redhot iron and punished them with the whip. Slavery was abolished in 1887, and after they had murdered Herr Karl Vogt, the man who had the palace built for the Emperor who never came, the blacks dispersed. Some of them traveled as far as Rio and Pernambuco, others made pilgrimages to Bahia, the superstitious Mecca of Brazilian blacks, then the eldest ones started coming back, having failed to find either work or lodging, the liberty they had just been granted meant nothing to them except the right to die of starvation at the corner of some road, where nobody would take the slightest responsibility for them. When I came to settle in the Morro Azul, which had been abandoned for some twenty years, about fifty Negroes had already drifted back to this plantation where they had sweated and suffered so much in former times. Chavin, the overseer, jeered at them and ruled them with a rod of iron, but they preferred that to their newfound liberty, and when they found out what sort of man I was, and how I was a prey to a perpetual torment, and the rumor got about that the new master was a somnambulist, other blacks came back, not all of whom had belonged to this estate. Today, I have more than a hundred of these old men and they surround me with veneration and solicitude, for the Negro lives in his own kingdom, he dreams, and whether he is awake or sleeping, he believes he can see what has already happened or is happening at this very moment somewhere in the world, or what will happen at some time in the future. You think he's totally engrossed in his work, you supervise him, you assess the task he has accomplished, but in reality he is obeying the dictates of an invisible world—his own. It is in this way that I resemble them, and we are brothers. For them, I am their magic father and they all help me, guessing at my suffering, honoring it, participating in it in one way or another through occult words or ceremonies. The truth is, let me tell you, this is a *fazenda* of madmen, and the only thing that keeps it alive is nostalgia! Come now, let's go outside, I want to show you the Sidereal Eiffel Tower that that imbecile, Bueno, has never been able to see or make out, not even on the photograph, and which he calls *Mâa-Eiffel,* and whose cult he propagates among his fellow blacks as if it were a *Mâa-d'Aguas* or a *Mâa-do-Ceo,* the Fairy of the Waters or the Fairy of the Sky, an evil genie, a spirit, a Mother. I know all this for certain from the reports that my overseer, that brute Chavin, makes to me, begging me to take drastic action. 'You never know what may happen with these blacks, nor what they're getting up to. You must deal with them severely,' he says. 'Perhaps they've cast a spell on you!' Bewitched or not, my life is nothing but a long, slow decaying, and now it seems to me that even my discovery is a fiasco. But come, let's go out, I'll show it to you. This is the time when it shines with incomparable brilliance, with all its fires blazing. Will you tell me whether the Eiffel Tower in Paris is as beautiful?...

"There. There we are. Sit down. Look, it's just as I said. On a bright, moonlit night, you would think you were at the theater, and how many times have I evoked her, the divine Sarah, and heard her recite verses for me alone, long, pathetic tirades, the most impassioned scenes in her repertoire, which I know by heart... and I have answered her, stammering with emotion. Or, she has recited verses I myself wrote for her, recited them in her golden voice. Imagine, furthermore, what the idea of spending the night out of doors must mean to a man born in Brazil, in a city. It took me a long time to pluck up the courage, on account of the nocturnal animals, the insects, the vampire bats, the hissing snakes that you hear moving in the bamboos, the flying foxes, the tree rats, which move heavily and are liable to fall on your head, and there's an enormous ash gray bird of prey that habitually perches on the roof ridge of the little palace of the Emperor, ululating all night long and turning around and around, pecking at things and shaking himself, ruffling his feathers with a sound like a shutter closing. His cry is grotesque and sinister, it frightens me. I am a coward. Even now, it sometimes happens that I run back into the house, unable to bear it anymore, and I shut the door and bolted and, in my terror, biting so hard on the stem of my pipe that it chatters between my clenched teeth. At my age, it is ridiculous to be so sad and so sensitive and to indulge in all these terrors. But, in our country, the solitude is too vast. How slowly the dawn comes! Only the song of the birds consoles me, it is like a lullaby. But I have already confessed that sleep has deserted me. How slowly the dawn comes, when you are in tears behind the door, waiting for it to come and release you from your fears. All this seems, and indeed, *is*, very childish. But knowing it does not temper the soul. Quite the contrary. You may laugh at it, but it is hopeless to believe you will ever be cured, or succeed in curing yourself. You are doomed. The soul of the solitary man is self-condemning. You cannot love a phantom without becoming perverted... your own phantom, for often I am split in two...

"Well then, on the night of the sixth to the seventh of September, 1914, here I was, on this bench, thinking of the awful news that had come from France, absolutely disoriented and in despair. Paris was about to suffer an appalling fate: She would be crushed by shells, enemy troops would invade the ruins, Gallieni would blow up the Eiffel Tower, the Teutonic soldiers would capture the divine Sarah, take her prisoner, hit her with the butts of their rifles to make her keep on marching through the rubble, she would be tied up, shackled, with a gag over her mouth to prevent her calling the people to insurrection in that strong, golden voice of hers that was like a trumpet, the woman, Sarah Bernhardt, defying them with her eyes, symbolizing France, O my love! I wept bitter tears. Out of habit, I raised my eyes to the skies, looking to see if the greatest historical catastrophe of modern times was reflected in the gleaming of the stars when, VICTORY! through my tears, I suddenly discovered a constellation in the sky that I had never seen before during all the fifteen years that I had been spending

275

my nights on this bench.... you see... there, between those intertwined palms... no, there, there... between the second and third palm trees, there, not there... a little higher up... there you are, do you see, at the tip of my finger, among all this restless tangle of palm fronds fanning themselves there is a kind of opening, a triangular skylight, a glass pane giving on to the sky... there, you can count them, there are four large stars that form the base, the legs of the Tower, then, a little higher up, three stars that form the first platform, then, much higher up, two more, not quite so brilliant, that form the second platform and, at the top, a good deal higher up, that beautiful, brilliant but intermittent star, the beacon of the Eiffel Tower. The whole structure seems to be leaning slightly toward us. Now, don't you see that this new constellation is the very image of the Eiffel Tower?... You can't fail to perceive it... Oh, yes, I know perfectly well that these ten stars belong to various other constellations, well-known and already catalogued, but the fronds of the palms screen these from us at the moment, and, in the way that we are seeing them now, from this point, there is no doubt that these ten neatly arranged stars delineate the silhouette of the great tower in Paris. This was also the opinion of the photographer from the Observatory in Rio, whom I had summoned specially, and he immediately located them and managed to obtain a very beautiful astronomical photograph without too much difficulty. You will allow me to give you a copy as a souvenir of your stay at the Morro Azul. But don't you agree that I have a right to borrow these stars from other constellations to make up a new one, the Sidereal Eiffel Tower, in memory of the sudden joy this discovery gave me, and of the illumination I received, which enabled me to predict the victory on the Marne and announce next day, *urbi et orbi,* that France was saved? The photographer from Rio was doubtful about it and told me I would never get astronomers to recognize my new constellation officially. And perhaps that's why the Institut de France does not answer my letter!... However, the sky does not belong to anyone, they don't have exclusive ownership of the heavens, and all the vulgar, senseless names the astronomers have written all over the sky to fill up their maps, which are still so defective and incomplete, signify nothing, whereas this Tower set in the sky of my homeland, Brazil, signifies something worthy of being immortalized for all Mankind, when you take into account the circumstances surrounding my discovery, the Shakespearean drama that took place in France—"to be or not to be"—the unexpected deliverance of the City of Light, and even without insisting on the symbolic role I attribute to Sarah Bernhardt, it was a remarkable case of second sight, of prophecy in a state of genuine trance. Can I count on you to make one last attempt to have my discovery ratified?... Thank you, my dear friend, thank you with all my heart..."

XIV
BANZO!

The month slipped by. I was anxious to be off because I could feel depression stealing up on me. I was restless. Every day, I announced that I would be leaving on the next day and, next day, I put it off till later so as not to disappoint Dr. Oswaldo Padroso, whose confession had been an act of courage and a gesture of fraternal and limitless confidence in me. But this confession somehow poisoned our relationship, and, without actually avoiding each other, we met as rarely as possible other than at the after-midnight dinner table. The doctor must have been embarrassed at having said too much, and, out of discretion, I did not dare to question him further and make him go over the ground again to give me more facts and greater detail, or go right back to his childhood as an orphan, to his very earliest infancy, as if I were a psychoanalyst, and make him analyze his abortive dreams. At about two o'clock in the morning, we would meet at table and discuss vague, impersonal topics, he was always a little aloof but ate with a good appetite (something which, he admitted with a sad smile, had not happened to him for a long time), and I drank a lot, told jokes and, without appearing to do so, observed this poor man for whom I felt the warmest sympathy and whose history had touched me deeply, wondering to what extent he had managed to free himself from his haunting by exposing his secret burden to me.

During the day, I was always tinkering with my car or wandering around the plantation in search of Chavin, with whom I had made friends. At the beginning, his cynicism and his alcohol cheered me up, but, in the end, I found them both equally depressing. Sometimes, I would take a trip into the surrounding country, taking the car as far as Glaréola, the little town that was busy modernizing itself, so that every time I went there

there was an inauguration—a urinal, a public wash-house, a new square, a health center, a municipal anti-mosquito service—and every one was the pretext for a fiesta, so I would stay late at the Pinhão, an inn and the town's first dance hall, and, on my way back, I would stop at all the work sites that were revitalizing the area, chatting to the workmen, mostly Italians, although there were also plenty of Germans and Poles, victims of the war in Europe, who had been able to find work as soon as they disembarked but who, for the most part, were disillusioned and bitterly regretting having emigrated. "It's the same thing everywhere," they said to me, "we're always the ones who break our backs. They exploit us." They all complained of being bossed about by Negro foremen! As for the doctor, he remained shut up in his study all day long, following his usual habit, and only once did he open the door to me, on the afternoon when he handed me the photograph of the Sidereal Eiffel Tower, rolled up like a diplomatic dispatch in a cardboard tube sealed with red wax. This gave me the chance to see the famous piece of furniture stuffed with letters addressed to Sarah Bernhardt and the curious little rolltop American safe, made of corrugated iron and fitted with an alarm bell, which contained one cubic meter of poetry, that is, 100,000 verses which, unlike certain people, I had no desire to copy, and so much the worse for him if Senhor Padroso should take offense! On the other hand, I stopped dead in my tracks in front of a glass showcase hanging on the wall between the map of France and the plan of Paris. It contained a little scrap of yellowed lace.

"Is that it?" I asked Dr. Padroso.

"That is indeed it," he replied, turning his back on me to hide his embarrassment.

Chastity is far more wearing to the nerves than debauchery.

He had flopped down into his rocking chair and was filling his pipe. I sat on the corner of a table, accidentally knocking off some files belonging to the bank. I lit a cigarette.

"I'm sorry," I said.

"It doesn't matter. Leave them there, they're of no importance."

"I'm leaving tomorrow," I said.

"Don't go yet," he replied, puffing on his pipe, "I've sent for the photographer, I wanted to have a portrait of you."

The study was very large, dusty, and badly furnished, the ceiling was high and there were three huge windows giving on to the verandah, but the shutters were closed. A cloud of flies was buzzing around and around in an oblique shaft of sunlight. Heaps of papers were lying in every corner

279

and a rickety bookcase contained the whole collection of *La Revue des Deux Mondes*, from the first issue to the last, still in wrappers. I did not see a single book anywhere. There was an enlarged photograph of Auguste Comte on the walls, another of Victor Hugo, and a third of Edmond Rostand, all three in ebony frames. The one of Victor Hugo was hanging slightly crooked.

"Don't leave yet," the Doctor said again. "I would like to have your portrait to hang with the others. The photographer is coming from São Paulo this week, by special train. I've sent for him."

For a long time, we smoked in silence, not knowing what to say.

I should have shaken him, but how could I pull him out of his trance?

"See you this evening," I said as I made for the door.

"Till this evening, my friend."

At dinner, it was the same. We did not know what to say to each other. The conversation languished. He stammered, embarrassed. I drank... and that, too, was due to embarrassment. I laughingly told him jokes... no response. Then I asked him about the redevelopment of the area, people, things, his neighbors, life in the other *fazendas* on the mountain... that brought a response, but a sour one. In the end, I got him to talk about birds, his other hobby-horse, and on this subject he was inexhaustible. I was delighted and felt our friendship revive. The atmosphere warmed up. Perorating, he filled his pipe. I was all ears, often amazed. I smoked a fag. Emptied a flagon. We lingered. What he said about birds made me think of Delamain's book: *Pourquoi les oiseaux chantent* (Why the Birds Sing), the most beautiful title in the world.[35] What a pity Senhor Padroso did not write a book about the birds of Brazil, instead of delivering himself of 100,000 verses in his solitude! But when the meal was over, or he had come to the end of his harangue, the doctor went to pace up and down in front of the house and, finally, to sink down exhausted on his bench. It was enough to make one despair. I did not accompany him. I took my leave, knowing quite well that he had nothing more to say to me about Sarah Bernhardt, the woman of his life. I regretted not having left on the day after his confession. I told myself I had been an idiot to have scruples. I slunk off like a coward, for not everybody can be a somnambulist, only a night prowler at most. I went and stretched out in my car, as on the first night I had spent at the *fazenda*. I did not sleep. I waited impatiently until Senhor Padroso went back into the house, double-locking the door behind him, shooting all the bolts... Then I slipped furtively out of the car, climbed the marble staircase, installed myself on the terrace of the

Emperor's palace, listened to the nocturnal bird of prey ululating above my head, ill-at-ease, jumping at the slightest sound, feeling a black depression overwhelming me, thinking of the rattlesnake, the serpent-mistress of the place, looking at the stars, lost, absorbed in the great nocturnal landscape, waiting for the dawn, shivering in my pajamas.

In the tropics, the birds perform their symphony a quarter of an hour before dawn. The doctor must have been at his window. I should have gone and spoken to him, openly, without beating about the bush. But I lacked the courage. It bored me to have to plough through all that again, although I was extremely interested in his case and all my compassion, my friendship, my brotherly feelings were committed to him. But a case is a case. Being neither priest nor psychiatrist, what could I do for him, other than take his place at the Morro Azul and send him to Paris in mine? I could see no other solution. I thought seriously about it, but Senhor Padroso would never have consented. There are cases in which nobody can do anything for the person concerned. God helps those who help them-selves! Each man must untangle his own knots. Each one of us is all alone in the world with his complexes. But one can dominate and master them. I am not thinking of politics but of the prisms of contemplation...

So, at dawn after the pure, ultra-lucid symphony of the birds, I slipped into the basement beneath the bathing pool, as I had done on the first morning of my stay at the *fazenda,* thinking I would drive the spiders out of the plumbing pipes. Instead, I had surprised Chavin, who was in ambush there, watching a copper retort attached to the furnace for the cen-tral heating and drawing off bottles of the *aqua vita* he was distilling there. As for the poisonous spiders, I'd had it! We drank together, a fine pair of boozers.

Like all *caboclos,* that bastard Chavin was taciturn. You never knew what he was thinking about, whether he was contemplating some bloody revenge or plotting a shady deal to make himself some dough. He was cun-ning, he was dictatorial. He knew that he was indispensable yet he was obsequious. His craftiness gave him the upper hand with the blacks and he rejoiced in it. His face was pitted with smallpox and his grim eyes, with their yellow corneas, were frightening. He had the teeth of a cannibal and almost no neck, he was so muscular that the nape of his neck and his shoul-ders were one solid block. He was of medium height, almost as broad as he was high, with a slight tendency to fat, due to his age. He could have been seventy years old, he was unmarried, lived alone, but got all the black women within a ten-league radius pregnant, he knew the area like the back of his hand, traveled over the mountain at night, came back at dawn, sneaking under cover, using the most hidden paths and tracks, like a jaguar, avoiding rifle-shots, traps, knives, fighting with a short stick which he handled like a virtuoso, always getting out of scrapes, a survivor, alert, ready for anything, provocative and cynical. When I teased him about his exploits as a billy-goat of the woods, he said nothing, but swaggered, flattered and pleased with himself, and winked his eyes, his sexual appetite aroused, but if I asked him about the conditions the blacks lived in, he had a whole string of arguments ready for me:

"They are a people of the dust. Beat the Negro and he turns, not white, but gray. He's a coward. Make him work, and he gets fat. He's lazy. Moreover, he's a weird animal. If you feed him, he falls asleep. Fuck his wife and you'll find out he has set her up as bait. You've been trapped. They are hogs and sows. Good meat for the butcher. Their god is the *jacare,* the crocodile: 'Come here so's I can eat you, otherwise I'll get eaten myself!' That's their morality, a nightmare of digestion. And if one of them has a full belly, the whole household dreams of a full belly. The black man is a sorcerer. Don't ever trust him. He likes to be beaten, it helps him to become more proficient in magic, and it's incredible how much punishment they can take without uttering a word or even mumbling a swear word between their teeth. It's their way of defying everybody. Like their dances. They belong to a race that is not of this world."

In spite of having to be on the alert all the time, because of his illegal distilling racket, Chavin's mind dwelt on the past. It was he who first told me about the "flogging tree" from which, in former times, they used to cut the sticks for beating the blacks, and he showed me the last specimen, which he had jealously preserved in a coppice in a hidden corner of the plantation, for he was convinced the time of slavery would soon return.

"Things can't go on like this. It's a mess. The world turned upside down. Just imagine, blacks are giving whites the orders and making them work on these new work-sites all around the Morro Azul! The old master would have died of indignation! You've seen them, these black foremen with their high collars and their fancy ties, their fuzzy hair smarmed down with brilliantine and with notebooks and pencils in their hands. They never do a day's work, but by God! I swear they don't miss a trick—they write down all the fines and penalties, take note of all the laggards who turn up late to work, the sick, the absentees, while these poor white buggers are breaking their backs and sweating in their old rags, half-naked under this sun of ours. Now, doesn't a sight like that tell you something?

This whole workforce that's arriving from Europe nowadays will achieve nothing at all, in spite of all their machines, and these fellows don't know how to do a thing. The blacks will fuck their women, I'm telling you! This is no way to live. To get good work out of men, you must make them respect you. And nothing but the big stick will do the job. It's been tried and tested."

The big stick or the whip. I questioned him one day about the cruelties inflicted on the slaves in the plantations of former times, thinking that the idle talk I had heard must be exaggerated and doubting this regime of atrocities, which seemed to me contrary to the interests of the master himself, who must surely have valued his flock and looked after them, just as one values and looks after a flock of pedigree sheep, but Chavin burst out laughing:

"Oh, yes, sure! Herr Karl Vogt valued his blacks, he paid enough for them, after all, they were hand-picked at the slave auctions! Herr Karl Vogt was a just and stern master who knew his business and knew how to wield the whip. His blacks worshiped him for that very reason. He had an iron fist and was inflexible. The Negroes came begging for more, and even today the oldest ones still talk about the famous collective whippings that used to be administered here at the Morro Azul, they were epoch-making events, like the *batucadas,* those wonderful nights of dancing. But, since that time, there aren't any *men* anymore! The fact that they killed him on the day they were freed is no accident, nor was it an act of vengeance, it was the culmination of a long magic ritual, the last syllable of a formula for casting spells, the last act of their collective madness. A bad dream. What amazes me is that they didn't eat him. Freedom scared them. The proof is that plenty of them came back to the old plantation of their own accord. Come on, I'm going to show you what my father was capable of, and you'll see whether I'm lying when I tell you the black man loves blows. For the supply meets the demand, you know, and if the Negro hadn't begged for punishment, they would never have invented whips, shackles, the thumb-screw, and all the other instruments of torture which were perfected at a time when the primitive hoe was still the only tool they possessed for clearing the land. Come and see. It seems to me you've got some pretty queer notions about the matter, my young master. You can't start up a first-rate plantation, and set out the coffee bushes in nice straight lines, and the rows in orderly rectangles, without bending your back, the ground is low down and only the whip has proved its worth. Come."

Chavin led me to an isolated shed where, after rummaging in a dark

corner and knocking over a pile of old things, he brought out some knotted whips to show me, whips with nail-studded lashes, an iron mask they
used to padlock on to the heads of certain depraved blacks who ate the red
earth, the famous fertile diabase of Brazil which they loved to eat kneaded
with white soil (probably barite), chains, shackles, iron neck-halters, a
whole arsenal of thumbscrews, manacles, and fetters, rings for the ankles, a
double iron choker for the neck, back-braces with sharp points, combs for
flaying the skin off the stomach, a kind of clog for crushing the foot, and a
Chinese cangue.

"What do you say, huh? And if Doctor Oswaldo knew I'd kept all this
stuff, I think he'd turn me out, in spite of all the services I've rendered
him, because, when it comes right down to it, I'm the one who's saved this
fazenda! But I know for sure that the old times will come back again.
You've only got to look at the mess they're making of everything all
around the Morro Azul. It can't last. It's a joke. You know—and I'm
telling you this under the seal of secrecy, and presently we'll go and have a
drink together, at the pool—it's the people from the bank who gave me
permission and who secretly delivered all my distilling equipment. They
recommended me to sell as much *caninha* as possible, and at the highest
price I could get, to the workers in the surrounding work-sites, and they
warned me not to get caught. What do you say to that, huh? Cunning devils! If you pass this way ten years from now, you'll see the result. I'm
telling you, it's all bunkum, what's going on now."

And Chavin started showing me how they used to tie the slaves up with
cords, dexterously tying a series of knots, each of which had its own particular name and its particular use, like in the navy, the most complicated
being used to garotte the recidivist runaways with their necks tightly
bound to their heels, and he undertook to enlighten me on the training of
the dogs they used to set on the tracks of runaway slaves, mastiffs, hunting
dogs, man-eaters who were trained to give the "stab in the back," ham-
stringing a man with a single bite or tearing out his throat. But, that day, I
had heard enough and I did not feel like drinking one more drop of his
lousy alcohol, so I went off on my own, wandering among the infinite rows
of coffee shrubs, which, laid out like a checkerboard or in a uniform quin-
cunx, stretched as far as the eye could see. The imprint of civilization.

God, I was pissed off!

It was enough to drive you crazy, *banzo!* as they used to say at one time
in Brazil of the black slaves who committed suicide in a sudden fit of
despair, which was attributed to nostalgia for their lost Africa. The planters

were scared stiff of *banzo!* for it spread like an epidemic, provoking isolated cases of insane fury or mania and decimating the plantations; it was as contagious as the running *amok* of native workers today on the East Indian and Malayan plantations where these men, on coming into contact with whites and their morality, their discipline and methods of work, find themselves cut off from their tutelary gods of the jungle and are driven to violate all the taboos for a handful of rice, or to commit suicide *en masse,* a phenomenon not known anywhere else on the planet of Man. Chavin was right, the Negroes are not of this world.

Listen to their music. It is the indigenous voice of their Ancestors. Their magic tom-tom. The voice of God in the wilderness. The heart of black Africa. The last pulsations. Nobody pays any attention. North American jazz announces the end of the world and the Brazilian *batutas* the end of the reign of Man. Collective suicide.

Banzo!

Syncope. Voodoo.

XV

THE CEILING OPEN TO THE SKY

Nobody paid any attention. The records alternated, one minute jazz, the next sambas, the troubled passages on the trumpet or the menacing growl of the *batuta*. These oh-so-nostalgic sequences were reaching me in waves, floating up from the bar on the sun deck to the spot where I lay stretched out beside the open-air swimming pool, sunbathing with a towel over my eyes. We had just lost sight of the coast of Brazil and her last little egg-shaped islands, and the *Andes,* a magnificent liner of the Royal Mail Line, was making for Cherbourg. At last, I was on board. Next day we passed Fernando Noronha, whose pyramid and rocky terraces are the last vestiges of Atlantis. The sea looked like a parquet floor, smooth, sparkling, composed of polished woodblocks as far as the eye could see, and the passengers were dancing day and night, like mad things.

Whether I was swimming, drinking, smoking, or just basking in the Equatorial sun, these rags and tatters of Negro music that reached me on the quarter-deck made me think of Dr. Oswaldo Padroso, of his solitude, his sadness, and of the imaginary theatrical performance he attended every night under the imperial palms of the Morro Azul, like Ludwig II of Bavaria, shut up in the grilled box of his royal residence, occupying the theater all on his own, and Senhor Padroso's somnambulism also made me think of Marcel Proust and his remembrance of things past, Proust, who let himself die of hunger, revolted at the thought of going on living after he had put the last full stop to his masterpiece, Proust who, in effect, committed suicide elegantly by ceasing to feed himself... and I wondered whether Dr. Oswaldo would end up, like the illustrious writer, with the illusion of having recaptured time past... where?... when?... how?... unknown... forgotten... lost in this immense Brazil without a past, with-

286

out a future, with an enigmatic present... between his manservant and his overseer... Bueno and his snake... Chavin and his still... and Isodoro's revolution, which had delayed me a full month in São Paulo, for the old positivist general had occupied the capital of modernism in Brazil and was fighting in the streets out of respect for the pure principles of Auguste Comte, hoping to achieve a return to those principles with the aim of saving the Republic from all the political wheeling and dealing, and his partisans, especially the *gauchos* of the Rio-Grande-do-Sud, were leaving locomotives stuffed with explosives on the lines used by the legalist troops, and enjoying themselves like overgrown kids, and I had not wanted to miss that, I had wanted to stay to the end... the revolution, a pretext that had given me the chance to take my leave of the doctor, who was in tears and who had stuffed a sack of coffee into my car, the famous coffee of the Morro Azul, Sarah Bernhardt's favorite. "I used to send a sack to the divine Sarah every year, and I'll do the same for you!" Padroso said to me, reminding me for the last time not to forget his Eiffel Tower...

The Sidereal Eiffel Tower. I contemplated it every night, as well as the "coal-sack," until the ship crossed the line and the Southern Cross was lost to sight behind us, far behind us, in that ceiling open to the sky which is the night as seen by a man lying on his back on the deck of a ship on the high seas...

Everything is afloat. The mainmast is swaying, its trunk is describing circles in the sky and pointing to each of the stars in turn, one after the other. I am dreaming.

I am nowhere.

One should never arrive...

"It was Herr Karl Vogt who had the Emperor's palace built," Caïo had told me when I spoke to him about the bedroom with the ceiling open to the sky, Dr. Oswaldo's eccentricities and the rattlesnake that was lolling on the mat suspended above the Emperor's bed, a vile creature I had hauled down, standing on top of a ladder, and whose photograph I now showed to Caïo. Meanwhile, the guns of the legalist troops had been bombarding São Paulo for the last twenty days and the locomotives blown up by Isodoro's gauchos were shattering the windows of the bank, where I had taken refuge since my hotel room, facing the station of La Luz, had become untenable due to the crossfire of the machine guns. "It was Herr Karl Vogt, a stubborn old man, who had the Emperor's palace built. Moreover, he ruined himself in the process. At that time, there were no stonecutters in Brazil, and certainly not out in the country. Nor were there any working quarries, although, since then, the bank has been extracting the most beautiful marble in the world, at Itu, on the Sorocaba, barely fifty kilometers from the capital. So Herr Karl Vogt had marble sent from Italy, already cut into blocks that were carefully numbered so that the whole lot could be assembled on site. They came by sailing ship from Carrara to Santos, and were then carried on wagons drawn by twelve pairs of oxen, along those terrible roads you know, as far as the Morro Azul, but they arrived months and months behind schedule, the roof tiles arrived before the columns, the door frames and the windows often got there before the blocks for the walls, the balustrades arrived before the treads for the staircases, it was all a frightful jumble. The amazing thing is that Herr Karl Vogt nevertheless succeeded in building his palace. The ceiling open to the sky, which you told me about, is not due to some outlandish whim of the would be architect, nor to his incompetence as an amateur builder, but simply to the loss of a sailing ship that went down, with all hands, in the Atlantic. I have read a report concerning this affair. The marble was loaded on board between Viareggio and La Spezia. It is always cut up and rough-hewn on the spot to reduce transport costs, for the waste material remains at the work site. Like all extremely heavy merchandise, marble puts a great strain on a ship if she takes on a full cargo. In those days, the average block measured from 4.5 to 6 *palmes,* the *palme* being 0.249 meters. A great many sailing ships were never heard of again after taking on a heavy cargo of marble. The brig schooner *Thérèse et Nelly,* which transported what was to have been the vault of the ceiling of the Emperor's bedroom, but which, of course, is missing, set sail from Viareggio. Her arrival at Gibraltar was reported, when she put in there, but, after that, nothing more was ever heard of her. As for the rattlesnake, it would be absurd to suppose Dr. Oswaldo knew anything about it. That Negro played a filthy trick on you, that's all. So don't talk about it anymore, Cendrars, it makes you look ridiculous."

"You think so, Caïo? Don't you think it was more likely a plot on Bueno's part to drive me out of the place, like his story of the poisonous spiders?"

"But why?"

"Because of Chavin's still, of course!"

"You think so? But that's not of the slightest importance, either. Look, don't talk about it anymore…"

Postscript in memory of an old, wise, smiling, and skeptical Frenchman.
Naturally, in Paris, everybody laughed at me and none of the newspapers wanted to publish my report on the Sidereal Eiffel Tower, they would not even print the astronomical photograph, and the negative finally went astray in the archives of a great daily newspaper and they never managed to lay hands on it again. As for the venerable old man, he was the doyen, in years and in date of election, of both the Institut and the Académie des Sciences, to whose Astronomical Department he belonged, for he was ninety-three years old and had been elected in 1902. He was much too polite to laugh in my face. He listened to my plea benevolently and concluded the interview by saying:

"What you tell me about your Brazilian friend is very touching, but allow me to tell you, he is a crank. Our archives are full of reports from madmen. We receive them every day, especially in the spring. It would be amusing to draw up the statistics and study the influence of springtime on the irrational activities of pseudo-scientific lunatics who bombard the Institute with astounding projects—squaring the circle, perpetual motion, etc., etc. The curve of the graph would be very odd and most interesting and it would enable us to confirm that this feverish increase of activity coincides with the thrust of the obscure forces of nature that influence all living creatures in spring."

Postscript for the pessimist that I am. Twenty years later, on the 21st of August, 1944, the day when Aix-en-Provence was liberated by the invading American army, an international group of my colleagues, attached to this army and all wearing war correspondents' uniforms, invaded my kitchen and brought me the wonderful news of the landings and the certainty of victory. I uncorked all the bottles. We drank endless toasts, laughing and shouting jubilantly. They produced cigarettes from every pocket. I wanted to ask them a million things, but it was they who questioned me, busily plying their pens, interviewing me and taking photos. Such frankness and cordiality, after so many years of stagnation, doubt, silence, dejection, and disgust, ever since I had transformed this same kitchen into a listening post, with its radio and its map of the front riddled with red and blue strokes of the pen, a map which so often gave me cause to despair and lean my head against the wall, a kitchen whose tiled walls had been my self-imposed prison ever since June 1940! Interrupting a Brazilian colleague, I asked him, through all the uproar, if he knew Senhor Oswaldo

Padroso, since he represented a São Paulo newspaper, and if he could give me any news of him?

"What's become of him?" I asked.

"Dr. Oswaldo of the Morro Azul? Who *doesn't* know him in São Paulo!" exclaimed my Brazilian colleague with a laugh. "Just imagine, he's left the *fazenda* and gone to live in the capital! You didn't know? And, what's more, he's married! Yes, Dr. Oswaldo, the poet devoted to Sarah Bernhardt, the man who made a vow to remain faithful to her, and the members of the Automobile Club gave him a fine send-off on his wedding night! Well, what can you expect ... after the defeat of France in June 1940, and Pétain's Armistice, Dr. Padroso lost faith, he no longer believed in anything."

I was delighted with this prosaic end, which, for my friend, marked the end of a long hypnotic trance, broke the enchantment of a spell, and brought him liberation, yet I could not help thinking, and feeling, that it was like an abdication—a humiliation for Poetry.

Well, that's life...

Aix-en-Provence,
11th August 1946
Villefranche-sur-Mer,
1st September 1948
Saint-Segond,
9th March–1st May 1949

Notes

1. J. Berlioz: *La Vie des Colibris,* Paris, 1944.

2. April 1948: a young Brazilian physicist has just photographed, at both the University of Manchester and the University of California, this nuclear bombardment, which originates neither on earth nor on the sun nor in the Milky Way nor in the nebulae, nor, it seems, from any point in the universe where matter exists in a condensed state, hence the name: cosmic rays (from newspaper reports).

3. In honor of the memory of Jacques Decour, I would like to quote three sentences from *Philisterburg* (Paris, 1932), which are still relevant today: "The writer who is a real traitor, or so it seems to me, is the one who carries a party card in his pocket. Injustices in defense of party solidarity, falsifications imposed by propaganda, compromises forced on him by doctrine—the writer has no business with any of these things. They belong to a world that is not his."

4. A word from Valéry (the curator of Charles X's libraries, not the author of "Cimetière marin": "There are unhappy times when solitude and silence become a means to liberty" (quoted by Guy Lavaud in a newspaper article concerning the "tyrannies" which came out of the Liberation).

5. Paris, 1947.

6. Blaise Cendrars: *Dan Yack,* Paris, 1946, p. 84 (trans. Nina Rootes, New York, 1987, p. 66).

7. Blaise Cendrars: *Bourlinguer,* Paris, 1948, p. 238 *(Planus,* trans. Nina Rootes, London, 1972).

8. Blaise Cendrars: *Anthologie nègre,* Paris, 1946, p. 14 (African Saga, trans. Margery Bianco, New York, 1972).

9. Blaise Cendrars: *L'Eubage,* Paris, 1926, p. 17.

10. Blaise Cendrars: *L'Homme foudroyé,* Paris, 1945, pp. 173 and 230 *(The Astonished Man,* trans. Nina Rootes, London, 1970).

11. This historic refrain sung by the Foreign Legion, which reflects the absurdity of war so well, is also the most perfect illustration of the law of intellectual constancy, at least in terms of *the permanence of language,* a factor that historians do not take sufficiently into account when considering the vicissitudes of the formation of Europe. Fighting wars to alter frontiers that correspond to profound differences between populations—of which the language and, therefore, the mentality and the national idiosyncrasies are manifestations—has never yet been successful! For example, in the West: The Saxon emperors wanted to push the frontier of Germany as far as the Rhône-Saône line by occupying Lotharingia, and this led to five centuries of wars. France wanted to push this frontier back to the Rhine, and this again led to another five centuries of particularly bloody wars, and yet, after a thousand years of struggle, the linguistic frontier is still there, exactly where it was originally, and it has never changed!

12. Blaise Cendrars: *La Main coupée,* pp. 76 and 21, Paris, 1946 (*Lice,* trans. Nina Rootes, London, 1973).

13. Blaise Cendrars: *Aujourd'hui,* Paris, 1931, p. 141.

14. In the Polynesian language, *Papaoutemari* means *"the glances of a virgin."* Cf. Émile Chautard: *La Vie étrange de l'argot,* Paris, 1931, p. 374.

15. In 1936, on a day when I was down on my luck and had to pay the rent for my lodgings on the Avenue Montaigne, I sold everything of Arthur Cravan's that I possessed to Matarasso, the literary dealer on the Rue Bonaparte: papers, letters, watercolors, the rough draft of a major poem, which is still unpublished, and the extremely rare complete run of his magazine *Maintenant,* one issue of which included the original of the famous report of his duel with Apollinaire, with his signature followed by the thirty-two titles the poet awarded himself, from "nephew of Oscar Wilde" to "taxi-driver and burglar in Berlin" (a quarter of a century before Jean Genet). Well, that's the way of the world.

16. See the Appendix for the Unknown Reader, at the end of this volume,

which proves that I did not lose sight of mathematics, any more than Lautréamont did.

17. Pasadena (California), 15th of June, 1949 (A.P.)—The first celestial atlas will be put on sale in four years' time and it will cost $2,000.

This work, produced by the California Institute of Technology and the National Geographic Society, will show all the stars visible from the northern hemisphere, that is to say, three-quarters of the sky, up to a distance of 300 million lightyears.

This publication has been made possible thanks to the 48-inch Schmidt photo-telescope, installed on Mount Palomar together with the famous 200-inch telescope.

The Schmidt telescope is comparable to the photographer's wide-angle lens. It allows the observer to cover, in four years, an extent of space whose exploration with the aid of the 200-inch telescope would require from one to five thousand years (from newspaper reports).

18. "It is certain that, many centuries before our era, the natives of the Pacific knew how to build the beautiful double pirogues they use today, which are twice as long as the caravelles used by Columbus, da Gama, and Magellan at the time of their celebrated voyages. It is also known that, well before the Europeans, they knew how to exploit the force of the wind for their large boats, which are as swift as our fine modern schooners and sail into the wind like racing yachts.... The Arab *boutres* in the Red Sea and the *dahabiahs* used on the Nile today are still analogous to those which were built in the time of the last Pharaohs. Similarly, the Polynesian pirogues are the same as those that existed in the first centuries of our era, and even earlier. Their manufacture, with the means then available to the islanders, required remarkable ingenuity and a well-tried patience. They hollowed out some parts of the hull with fire, finished them with jade hatchets, knives, and scissors made of stone, or the shells of giant clams, and built them up with planks taken from the trees of the forests and trimmed with hatchets. These planks were sewn together with coir, the joints were sealed with gum resin supplied by the breadfruit tree, which, mixed with wood ash, makes a high quality mastic; the spines of the sea urchin and the tooth of the sawfish served as drills for the primitive braces and bits made of ironwood.... Mats plaited from the leaves of the pandanus, and arranged like the wing of a bird, still make graceful sails on the giant bamboo masts and are held in place by rot-proof coconut ropes.... On the platforms, which were raised several feet above the water level, the crew could rest at

their leisure and cook their food, for, ever since the most distant times, the Polynesian pirogues have been crossing the Pacific in all directions, and so their builders were obliged to make the necessary provisions for long voyages.... Like the Asian shepherds of Biblical times, the South Sea Islanders had a practical knowledge of astronomy, and this no doubt enabled them to navigate at sea long before any of the peoples of Europe... Ever since the time of Cook and Bougainville, there have been reports of the means by which the hardy Maori sailors managed to find their routes, i.e., the primitive and yet fairly accurate maps of the islands they frequented. On these maps, drawn on finely woven mats, the particular signs—shells, bones, mother-of-pearl, or little sticks—represented the winds, currents, reefs, and havens.... A kind of sextant, an example of which, brought back by Captain Darmandaritz, still existed in Nantes less than half a century ago, gave them an approximate latitude.... They also carried leeches, preserved in clay, and it seems that their movements indicated the approach of very bad weather.... Finally, caged birds, released at the opportune moment, told them the direction of the nearest land.

"While the food on European ships, up until the 19th century, consisted of nothing but salt provisions and chick-peas, they already knew how to prepare food for the long crossings. Yams and taros, either fresh or in the form of flour, dried cakes of manioc and breadfruit, coconut milk and flesh, dried or smoked fish permitted them to spend many days at sea. In the same way that the first inhabitants of Peru made use of cola to appease their hunger, they also had a certain nut that calmed the gnawing of the stomach and nourished them at the same time. In the case of an absolute lack of water, certain herbs they chewed allowed them to drink sea water with impunity for several days. And they navigated their sailing ships all over the Pacific." (Louis Lacroix: *Les Derniers baleiniers français,* Nantes, 1947, pp. 73–74).

19. Cf. Blaise Cendrars: *Le Panama ou les Aventures de mes sept oncles,* Paris, 1918; a slim volume reprinted in my *Poésies complètes,* Paris, 1944, vide p. 89. ("Panama or the Adventures of my seven Uncles," trans. John Dos Passos, in Blaise Cendrars, *Selected Writings,* New Directions, 1962).

20. Several of these books had, in fact, been published in Neuchâtel: Cust's *Les Langues modernes de l'Afrique,* Neuchâtel, 1884; Junod's *Nouveaux contes Rongas,* Neuchâtel, 1898; Trilles's *Contes et legends Fân,* Neuchâtel, 1898, etc. Encouraged by their pastors, the devout of Neuchâtel willingly gave up one sou per franc of their Sunday expenses for the upkeep of evangelic

missions to the savages and the printing of propaganda destined for the pagans, so the local publishers had specialized and did not refuse to publish these pseudoscientific works!

21. Paris, 1921. New edition: Paris, 1927. Definitive edition, revised and corrected, Paris, 1947.

22. On rereading this, there suddenly sprang to my mind that old engraving that shows Restif de la Bretonne in the guise of a night watchman. It is a standing portrait and he appears in his greatcoat, with his iron-tipped truncheon and dark lantern, a cap in the shape of an owl with its wings spread pulled low over his eyes and a hood shaped like a pannier on his head. He looks like a villain who prowls by night, or a kidnapper of little children, and his alarming appearance is more like the profile of an escaped lunatic than that of a Nosey Parker writer taking notes in the infamous back alleys. The truth is that this picker of locks was also a police spy, an informer, and a journalist whose pen cut both ways. I wonder why the leaders of the Surrealist movement have never had this portrait printed as a postcard and distributed by the million, for this effigy could easily be Lautréamont's! The 18th century... I will never cease to be astonished by its strangeness...

23. A certain young man devoted himself to inquiring of writers what their second profession was. I told him that writing was, in fact, my second profession. Well then, he wanted to know, what is your first profession? And I replied that my first profession was dreaming, doing nothing. Naturally, this journalist, who prided himself on being literary, did not publish my answers to his questions.

24. Cf. Blaise Cendrars: *Moravagine,* Paris, 1926, p. 283 (trans. Alan Brown, New York, 1990).

25.　　　Here the League of Silence is unknown
　　　　As in all new countries
　　　　The joy of living and of earning money is expressed
　　　　　　by the voice of the klaxons and the farting
　　　　　　of open exhausts

　　　　Like the Negro fetishes in the bush
　　　　The gas pumps are naked

(Blaise Cendrars: *Poésies complètes,* pp. 235 and 271.)

26. Cf. *Bourlinguer,* pp. 230, 94, 318.

27. Cf. *Bourlinguer,* p. 94.

28. In 1936, in Los Angeles, I visited the jeweler who supplied all the Hollywood stars. You have to make an appointment. You must arrive punctually at the appointed hour. You get out of your car and are met at the door of what looks like a small private house by a group of private detectives. A photoelectric cell, a magic eye. The door opens automatically. You go in. The door shuts behind you with a dry little click, then lets out a deep sigh. You find yourself in a hall, which is artistically imprisoned in a grille, a wrought-iron grille, but a cage nevertheless. An impressive black major-domo, sitting at a mahogany table, asks you to write your name in a register, then he ceremoniously takes your hand, blackens the tips of your fingers with an indelible-ink roller and takes your fingerprints, pressing your fingertips down, one after the other, into this same register, below your signature, and grinning from ear to ear. A signal sounds, a gong. The grille slides back silently. You take three steps forward. The grille closes behind your back with the sharp click of a latch and again lets out a profound sigh. You find yourself at the bottom of a perpendicular well and have trouble getting used to the fluorescent lighting and the ozonized air. The detectives push you forward, toward a huge staircase whose double spiral, ascending and descending, winds all around the chromium-plated steel walls of this well of anguish. The whole interior of the house, from attic to cellar, is armor-plated. You reach the first landing. The fluorescent lighting goes out and now the plates slide apart, the shutters open and on each story crystal globes light up, like so many goldfish bowls in an aquarium, and in each of these is displayed, behind bulletproof and shatterproof glass, a precious gem or a piece of jewelry that sparkles gently under indirect lighting or glows in a flash of lightning. Shutters close, others slide open to reveal new niches on each floor, luminous cavities like the ones in a dovecote where the birds come to lay their golden eggs, and all the time you are climbing or descending the length of the wall, following its curves and the convolutions of a noble staircase, conducted from one landing to the next by the voice emerging from a loudspeaker to act as your Cicerone and command (while the detectives stand close to you): "Look to your right!" "Look to your left!" "Do not stand in front of this one hundred and twenty-three-carat diamond for more than three seconds, otherwise its dazzling brilliance will damage your eyes!" and all this skillfully graduated: the effect of surprise, the layout of the display, the arrangement of the jew-

els, the way they appear and disappear automatically, the showman's spiel of the invisible speaker, the lights that go on and off, the shutters, the clicking steel plates, the mystery of this well with walls so smooth that you cannot detect the slightest groove or join, even when you run your fingers over them; the whole place is full of gadgets and every movement, even those of the visitors, which, as they are shepherded from place to place are recorded on film, is controlled by a radio-electric machine hidden behind the sliding shutters. On each floor there is a niche, a kind of booth or telephone kiosk from which the client can get in touch by telephone with an invisible expert-salesman; after suitable negotiations, and if the presiding God of the machine deems her worthy and agrees to her desires, he presses a button and the client is lifted into the air and vanishes through a trap door into the topmost story, where the salesrooms and workshops are installed. If, having climbed to the top of the stairs and reached the upper landing, you lean over the banisters before going down once more to the bottom of the well, you get the impression that you are about to float down as if you were on board a bathysphere in the depths of the ocean, the goldfish bowls that light up and extinguish themselves like luminous fish in the very abysses of the sea, make you feel giddy and oppressed. I do not know how I got out into the street again, but I found myself outside, with the private detectives standing around me, laughing. The tour had lasted exactly seventeen minutes. Just before the final plunge, the loudspeaker had announced in stentorian tones: "You have twenty-five million dollars' worth of jewels before your eyes!"

"Have a drink, man!" the chief of the detectives said, pushing me toward the door of a nearby bar. "You're knocked out, aren't you?" And he offered me a good cigar. I let myself be led away, I stood drinks all around, the first, and two or three others later. I felt groggy.

29. Cf. *Bourlinguer,* p. 194.

30. Blaise Cendrars: *Histoires vraies,* 1937, pp. 207–15.

31. "A book that made an impact—*According to statements made by Serebrovski, the People's Commissar for Mines, it was reading* L'Or, *by Blaise Cendrars, that decided Stalin to industrialize the Urals.*"

Le XXe Siècle (14th of March, 1946).

"*One day, in 1932, I was visiting Sergo Ordzhonikidze when Serebrovski, the chief of the Central Administration of Gold Mines, called at his office. In the course of their conversation, Ordzhonikidze thanked Serebrovski for the book he had given*

*him and which he, in turn, had passed on to Stalin. When Serebrovski had gone, I
asked Ordzhonikidze about the book. He told me it was by Blaise Cendrars, its title
was Sutter's Gold. Ordzhonikidze had given the book to Stalin, he said, because of
the boss's interest in the references to gold mining in the works of Jack London."*

(V. A. Kravchenko, *Saturday Evening Post,* Nov. 30, 1946.)

I believe the above two items of information have come from one common source: the report *Gold-mining in Soviet Russia* by Littleteach, the American specialist who, for ten years, collaborated on the industrial equipping of the gold mines in Siberia, a report that if my memory is correct, must have appeared in one of the Payot collections, Paris, 1936 (?) and which contains this item about Stalin reading my novel, *L'Or.* Stalin is known to be a great reader of novels and probably, like Churchill with his painting, it is a way of relaxing from affairs of state.

The translation of *L'Or* into Russian was done without my knowledge by Victor Serge and published under the title of *Zoloto,* still without my knowledge, by the State (?) publishers, Leningrad (?) in 1929 (?).

The first American edition of *L'Or,* entitled *Sutter's Gold,* was published by Harper of New York in 1926. Universal made a film of it in Hollywood in 1936. (Recent edition: *Gold,* trans. Nina Rootes, New York, 1970.)

L'Or was first published by Grasset, in Paris, in 1925.

I am struck by the fact that the principle center exploited by Serebrovski's super-trust, Souiz-Zoloto, for the extraction of native gold in the territories of Yakuty is called Kolyma, and I cannot help making a mental association between this name, Kolyma, and Coloma, the name of General Sutter's mill where the fateful blow of Marshal the carpenter's pickaxe brought to light the first Californian nugget, which was to unleash the Gold Rush of 1848. It is a known fact that there were numerous Russian settlements along the west coast of America, on the northern Pacific, reaching right down to Mexico, and that General Sutter bought the most beautiful farms on the littoral from the Russians, before the arrival of the Americans in California. According to my information, the discovery of gold deposits in the Golden Valley, the Zolotaya Dolina in Yakuty, and their first exploitation in Kolyma, date from 1863.

Gold is damned.

The Golden Fleece. The Pacific is the internal sea of modern Argonauts. What can the personal politics of Jason have been? Jason, who veils himself in his legend, the plot of which gives birth to a whole mythology and to some poetic traditions from Plato to Atlantis, from Christopher Columbus to the New World, from Cortes to the palace of Montezuma *(Thalassa!*

"The sea, the sea!" Vasco Nuñez de Balboa must have cried in 1513 when he discovered the waters of the Pacific and urged his sweating horse into the sea...), from Morgan the Pirate to the sack of Lima and the burying of an inestimable treasure in the Cocos Islands (again, you find the same epic of damned gold in the traditions of India, of ancient China, and of the Bantus in the heart of black Africa). Was Jason's voyage really a question of pure politics, and not of blood, sensual pleasure and adventure, in short, of Life, Death, and the passions of Mankind?

Politics and its motives, the names of heroes, conquerors and victims, cultures, civilizations all melt away, they are effaced, the monuments crumble, countries and their peoples are forgotten, only Poetry endures as the intermittent and almost unconscious memory of a childhood dream: the deification of humanity, the REAL man.

32. *O bicho:* "the beast," but always with a nuance of respect since, in Brazil, there are all kinds of superstitions in which animals are seen as beneficent or maleficent *spirits,* and they are alleged to have great influence in a thousand and one different circumstances of daily life, for example, a prime role in the lottery called Os Bichos, the most popular one of all, in which everybody secretly has a stake, in the capital cities as well as in the country, betting on *the animals,* which are the occult doubles of the numbers in the official lotteries run by the state or the federal governments, etc.

33. *La Vie dangereuse,* Paris, 1938, pp. 221–72.

34. Cf. Victor Serge: *L'Affaire Toulaév,* Paris, 1948.

35. Jacques Delamain: *Pourquoi les oiseaux chantent.* Coll. Livres de la Nature, Paris, 1929.

APPENDIX
For the Unknown Reader

Appendix

Just as the present work is going to press, I read a magnificent article by Pierre Lepine in *Le Figaro Littéraire*. It is dated December 11, 1948 and entitled "The Electronic Telescope Teaches Us Something New about the Universe." I send a telegram to my publisher asking him to be so kind as to contact the *Figaro* and our colleague there and ask permission for me to reproduce this splendid article of current news, and, therefore, of POETRY, in full, so as to give my *Unknown Reader* a chance to read it. I would like to express to both *Figaro* and M. Pierre Lepine my warmest gratitude for their cordial and fraternal cooperation.

B.C.

"The passing of a comet, which is visible at the moment in the limpid night skies of California, is distracting men for an instant from their ephemeral problems, and reminding those of them who are still capable of thought that here, on this terrestrial shore, they are on the borders of the infinite.

"In the course of the last fifty years, our knowledge of the universe has progressed by giant strides. Now we must wait a little, as astrophysics develops, as new instruments, like the telescope on Mount Palomar, in California, are put into commission, and as electronic telescopes become practicable, to see the horizons of our discoveries broaden still further.

"To what infinitesimal scale will these reduce the planet where we spend our precarious days? It is noteworthy that, ever since the dawn of astronomy, the relative importance of Earth has steadily diminished at the same rate as our conception of the universe becomes more and more accurate.

"It was perfectly natural for the first astronomers—who certainly seem to have been the Sumerians, several thousand years ago—to place the earth at the center of the cosmos and surround it with concentric spheres in which the sun, the moon, and the planets moved beneath a vault in which the fixed stars were suspended.

"Aristarchus of Samos, who died in Alexandria in 230 B.C., conceived of a helio-centric system, which was remarkably precise for that epoch, but even he failed to impose this concept on others. It took eighteen centuries and Copernicus's book, *De Revolutionibus orbium celestis,* which appeared in 1543, to initiate the Galilean reform which relegated the earth to the rank of a minor satellite of the sun.

"But the sun, the heavenly body of our days, was itself dethroned by the progress of the sciences, and we must now be content to recognize it as a dwarf yellow star, hardly bigger than the fifth size, an infinitesimal supernumerary amid the billions of stars that make up the scintillating spiral of the Milky Way.

"Our galaxy, seen in section, presents the aspect of a lenticular disc rotating slowly on itself at the rate of one turn every two hundred million years; its diameter is about 78,000 lightyears (a lightyear is the distance covered in one year by light traveling at the speed of 300,000 kilometers per second, that is, about 8,500 billion kilometers). The sun is some 30,000 lightyears from the center, toward the thin edge of the spiral, with a mass of barely one 165-billionth of the whole.

"But is the galactic system, to whose destiny we are thus linked, the center of the universe? No. Like those toys from Nuremburg in which each element is enclosed in a larger envelope, so each time man believes he has touched the confines of his universe, he has only pushed the limits of that enigma further out.

"There exist other galaxies, other nebulae besides our own. Many of the stars visible to the naked eye resolve themselves, when seen through the telescope, into spiral constellations of dense or gaseous structure. But our chief weapon for hunting the extra-galactic nebulae is photography. Each improvement to the telescope increases the number—and therefore the distance—of these. The least astral snap reveals dozens of them. Their estimated number is well over a million. Which is as good as to say that the number of stars in existence grows in fantastic proportions when you realize that one of the nearest nebulae, Andromeda, which is 800,000 lightyears distant from us and whose size—a diameter of 65,000 lightyears—comes near to the modest proportions of the Milky Way, containing about 200 billion stars, which are as many suns.

"Is that all? Far from it! The use of the spectroscope to examine the light emitted by these nebulae has revealed one of the most astonishing discoveries of astrophysics. If one considers the characteristic rays that give the spectral analysis of the elements in the composition of the luminous source, for example, those of calcium, which are easily registered on the spectrograms, one affirms that these rays, whose position is constant in solar light, are displaced toward the red extremity of the spectrum, and the further away from us the nebulae which emit them are, the more this is the case. Theoretically, this phenomenon is explained by a Doppler effect, due to the very rapid speed at which the source recedes into the distance, a speed that attains 5,500 kilometers a second for the nebulae situated at 23 lightyears, and 23,000 kilometers a second for the nebulae of the constellation of the Gemini, situated at 133 million lightyears.

"The result of this is that, since the speed of recession increases with distance, we have to conceive that, beyond the limits so far attained by our telescopes (about 500 million lightyears), and those which will be attained by telescopes of the future, there will still be other nebulae, millions of lightyears away, which are receding from us so fast that their light will never succeed in reaching us.

"On the other hand, everything happens as if sidereal space was expanding at a uniform rate, which means that the facts observed do not imply a real movement, in the ordinary sense of the word, but a function of Space-Time, like a sort of drawing-out of the universe, which would give to any observer, placed in any one of the galaxies, the impression that all the nebulae were moving away from him.

"This is analogous to the way in which our own conception of the universe is evolving at a surprising speed. If, around 1915, the application of Einstein's theory of relativity (a theory of genius which has advanced our concepts of physics as much as the discovery of inertia by Galileo and of gravity by Newton) enabled us to arrive at the static construction of a universe, stable but finite, with a diameter of about 70 billion lightyears, today we are led to envisage, along with Sir Arthur Eddington, an infinite universe in continuous expansion, a dynamic concept which completes rather than contradicts the static conception by throwing us outside spatial limits.

"The idea of a non-static universe brings, moreover, different interpretations at different epochs, according to whether you start or end with an empty universe, as the Dutch astronomer Willem de Sitter would have it, or again, whether it is a matter of an oscillating system without beginning and without end.

"To give an appropriate image, instead of comparing the universe to a number of ping-pong balls, representing the galaxies, moving within an empty sphere larger than the earth, let us compare it to grains of lead-shot projected into space by an initial explosion and diverging along infinite trajectories.

"This last image corresponds to the theory, propounded in Belgium by the Abbé Lemaître, according to which the entire universe, from the infinitely small to the infinitely large, derives from the dispersal of a single atom, a theory that at the same time takes into account the analogies of structure in the two fields, the unity of the composition of matter and the transmutations of elements as data accumulated regarding the age of the universe.

"It is a striking fact, and one of the most curious recent discoveries, that the different methods by which we are enabled to evaluate both the age of the earth and that of the solar system, the stars and the galaxies—that is to say, the different stages of the universal system—methods which rely on the most diverse techniques, such as the proportion of lead isotopes resulting from the disintegration of uranium, the percentage of helium in the sun, the distance/speed ratio of the nebulae starting from a common origin, the mass/luminosity ratio of the stars or the evolution of double stars, all lead to figures of a very comparable size, from three to five billion years, but, in any case, less than ten.

"It is therefore deduced that, contrary to what was imagined in former times, the entire universe must be palpably of the same age, that it is a question of extinct worlds or gaseous nebulae, and that it has scarcely begun its evolution.

"It even appears that it is continuing to create itself in front of our eyes, through the condensation into matter of the energy spread throughout interstellar space.

"Here again, the established facts come into slight collision with the notions of common sense, by affirming the predominance of the void over concrete matter, on the astronomic scale as well as on the atomic scale.

"The nebulae, those 'islets in the universe,' are distributed through space at the rate of about one galaxy to every three billion billion cubic lightyears, and interstellar space is 100,000 times more perfect than that which our best machines can give. Nevertheless, condensed matter only represents a fraction of the matter dispersed throughout space.

"To give an idea, let us say that the atoms of hydrogen scattered throughout sidereal space (atoms so minute that it takes more than six billion billion to make a thousandth of a milligram, and whose nucleus, formed by a proton, apparently plays a role in the genesis of cosmic rays on striking the earth) are one or two centimeters distant from one another. Nevertheless, a cone of the diameter of the earth stretching as far as the very near sun (only 150 million kilometers away) would enclose 150,000 tons.

"It is currently thought that this interstellar material has a tendency to draw together slowly in the equatorial plane of the galaxies, which are themselves composed of gas and stellar dust as much as the stars, and to form there the obscure matter from which future stars will be born.

"At the other end of the chain, we know today that the supernovas, stars which have been especially studied at the observatory on Mount Wilson, and whose sudden increase in luminosity may reach a billion times the brilliance of the sun, correspond to a flaming radiation of energy affecting the total mass of the heavenly body to result in the extreme contraction of the dwarf white stars whose density reaches the stupefying figures of several million times that which we attribute to the heaviest metals. Thus, astrophysics makes us observe all the terms of the energy-light cycle on a sidereal scale.

"At the beginning of the 18th century, Fontenelle and the Abbé Pluche lectured to cultivated minds on the plurality of worlds, an entertainment that was as good as playing bridge or listening to the radio. Today, astronomy is the crown of the physical sciences, to which she lends the most delicate techniques and the most daring mathematical theories. It is becoming difficult for untrained minds to follow its progress. But one cannot be churlish and refuse to admire those who, in the monastic silence of the observatories, pursue the secular and disinterested task through which man attempts to pierce the mystery of the universe."

Pierre Lepine